Financial Valuation Workbook

Fifth Edition with Website

Financial Valuation Workbook

Step-by-Step Exercises and Tests to Help You Master Financial Valuation

Fifth Edition with Website

JAMES R. HITCHNER

WILEY

Published by John Wiley & Sons, Inc., Hoboken, New Jersey.
Published simultaneously in Canada.

For general information on our other products and services or for technical support, please contact our Customer Care Department within the United States at (800) 762-2974, outside the United States at (317) 572-3993 or fax (317) 572-4002.

Wiley also publishes its books in a variety of electronic formats. Some content that appears in print may not be available in electronic formats. For more information about Wiley products, visit our web site at www.wiley.com.

Library of Congress Cataloging-in-Publication Data

Names: Hitchner, James R., author.
Title: Financial valuation workbook : step-by-step exercises and tests to
   help you master financial valuation / James R. Hitchner.
Description: Fifth edition. | Hoboken, New Jersey : Wiley, [2025] | Revised
   edition of the author's Financial valuation workbook, 2011.
Identifiers: LCCN 2024011133 (print) | LCCN 2024011134 (ebook) | ISBN
   9781119880974 (paperback) | ISBN 9781119880998 (adobe pdf) | ISBN
   9781119880981 (epub)
Subjects: LCSH: Corporations—Valuation. |
   Corporations—Valuation—Handbooks, manuals, etc. | Business
   enterprises—Valuation. | Business enterprises—Valuation—Handbooks,
   manuals, etc.
Classification: LCC HG4028.V3 H585 2025 (print) | LCC HG4028.V3 (ebook) |
   DDC 658.15/5—dc23/eng/20240308
LC record available at https://lccn.loc.gov/2024011133
LC ebook record available at https://lccn.loc.gov/2024011134

Cover Design: Wiley
Cover Image: © Blake Callahan/Getty Images
SKY10087496_101024

To my son, Jason Earle Hitchner, and my godmother, Aunt Thelma Reid
Also to my seven grandchildren: Sienna, Brooke, Eliana, Grace, Nick,
Vivienne, and Lucy

Contents

The *Financial Valuation Workbook* (FVW) contains both educational exercises that guide the reader through a complete business valuation and valuation tools that professionals can use in preparing business valuations. It also contains detailed information on how to run a successful valuation practice. It is structured to be used on a stand-alone basis. It is also a companion text to *Financial Valuation Applications and Models*, 5th edition (FVAM) (John Wiley & Sons), in which the subject matter contained in the workbook is expanded on. This workbook contains basic, intermediate, and advanced topics on valuing businesses conveyed in a series of easily understandable exercises with comprehensive answers.

FVW is targeted to the following professionals and groups that are typically exposed to financial valuation issues:

Appraisers
Appraisal associations and societies
Actuaries
Attorneys
Bankers
Business brokers
Business executives, including CEOs, CFOs, and tax directors
Business owners
CPAs
Estate and gift planners
Financial analysts
Government agencies including the IRS, SEC, and DOL
Insurance agents
Investment advisors
Investment bankers
Judges
Pension administrators
Stockbrokers

FVW contains eight chapters, each with a different purpose.

Chapter 1 contains about 80 exercises that have been placed throughout excerpts of an actual business valuation report presenting numerous valuation topics, including rates of return, the capitalized cash flow and discounted cash flow methods of the income approach, and the guideline company transaction and guideline public company methods of the market approach.

Chapter 2 contains comprehensive answers to the exercises in Chapter 1.

Chapter 3 includes more than 300 exercises that comprise a companion piece and correlate to the relevant chapters of *FVAM*, 5th edition. These exercises/tests can be used to prepare for business valuation certification exams or for university professors in the academic field or as reinforcement to learn the material.

Chapter 4 includes more than 450 ValTips that are extracted from the companion book, *FVAM*. This summary of ValTips can serve professionals as a quick reference source of important concepts, application issues, and pitfalls to avoid.

Chapter 5 presents a Valuation Process Flowchart to allow professionals to follow a more structured process in applying and documenting the income approach.

Chapter 6 highlights strategies for marketing, managing, and making money in a valuation services practice. It discusses risk management in regard to reports and engagement letters, and gives examples of each. This chapter also includes information on how to keep up technically; find, train, and retain staff; and delegate authority.

Chapter 7 includes guidelines for practice management workflow procedures, which starts with the initial prospective client call, highlights checking points through the valuation analysis, then moves on to draft and final record, then to file retention and engagement closure.

Chapter 8 includes more than 40 checklists that can be used by professionals in documenting their valuations. It can also be used by less-experienced professionals as a guide in applying valuation concepts.

This book also includes a companion website, which can be found at www .wiley.com/go/fvamwb5e. The website includes the exhibits and forms found in Chapter 7, and the checklists found in Chapter 8.

Financial valuations are very much affected by specific facts and circumstances. As such, the views expressed in these written materials do not necessarily reflect the professional opinions or positions that the author would take in every business valuation assignment, or in providing business valuation services in connection with an actual litigation matter. Every situation is unique and differing facts and circumstances may result in variations of the applied methodologies. Furthermore, valuation theory, applications, and methods are continually evolving and, at a later date, may be different from what is presented here.

Nothing contained in these written materials shall be construed to constitute the rendering of valuation advice, the rendering of a valuation opinion, the rendering of an opinion as to the propriety of taking a particular valuation position, or the rendering of any other professional opinion or service.

Business valuation services are necessarily fact-sensitive, particularly in a litigation context. Therefore, the author urges readers to apply their expertise to particular valuation fact patterns that they encounter, or to seek competent professional assistance as warranted in the circumstances.

Disclaimer Excluding Any Warranties: This book is designed to provide guidance to analysts, auditors, management, and other professionals, but it is not to be used as a substitute for professional judgment. Procedures must be altered to fit each assignment. The reader takes sole responsibility for implementation of material from this book. The implied warranties of merchantability and fitness of purpose and all other warranties, whether expressed or implied, are excluded from this transaction, and shall not apply to this book. None of the authors, editors, reviewers, or publisher shall be liable for any indirect, special, or consequential damages.

Acknowledgments

Several people were instrumental in preparing this book. Thank you, Kate Morris, ASA, ABV, MBA, and Karen Warner and Janet Kern of Valuation Products and Services, LLC, in Ventnor City, New Jersey. You were all great.

I would also like to thank Mike Mard, CPA/ABV, of The Financial Valuation Group of Florida, Inc., for his important contributions to the first three editions of this book.

I would also like to thank all the coauthors of *Financial Valuation Applications and Models*, 5th edition:

R. James Alerding, CPA/ABV
Rosanne J. Aumiller, CPA/ABV/CFF, ASA
G. Don Barbo, CPA/ABV
Neil J. Beaton, CPA/ABV/CFF, CFA, ASA
Mark Bello, CPA/ABV/CFF, CVA, MAFF, MST
Erica Bramer, CFA, CVA, CIRA
James T. Budyak, CPA/ABV, CFA, ASA
Karolina Calhoun, CPA/ABV/CFF
Carol Carden, CPA/ABV, ASA, CFE
Larry R. Cook, CPA/ABV/CFF, CBA, CVA
Don M. Drysdale, CPA/ABV, ASA
Edward J. Dupke, CPA/ABV/CFF/CGMA, ASA
Jay E. Fishman, FASA
Michelle Gallagher, CPA/ABV/CFF
Chris Hamilton, CPA, CFE, CVA
Bethany Hearn, CPA/ABV/CFF
Ted Israel, CPA/ABV/CFF
Harold G. Martin Jr., CPA/ABV/CFF, ASA, CFE
Lari Masten, CPA/ABV/CFF, CPVA, CVA, MAFF, ABAR
Raymond E. Moran, ASA, MRICS
Katherine E. Morris, ASA, ABV, MBA
Alina Niculita, ASA, CFA, ARM-BV
Maureen Rutecki, CPA/ABV/CFF, ASA
Greg Saunders, CPA/ABV, ASA
Ronald L. Seigneur, CPA/ABV/CFF, ASA, CVA
Mark Smith, CPA

Stacey D. Udell, CPA/ABV/CFF, CVA
Samuel Y. Wessinger, ABV
Laurie-Leigh White, CPA/ABV, ASA, CEIV
Richard M. Wise, CPA, FCA, FCBV, FASA, MCBA, CFF, CVA, C.Arb., EJC, FRICS
Kevin R. Yeanoplos, CPA/ABV/CFF, ASA

About the Author

James R. Hitchner, CPA/ABV/CFF, is the managing director of Financial Valuation Advisors, Inc., in Ventnor City, New Jersey. He is also president of the Financial Consulting Group, LLC, a national association of professional services firms dedicated to excellence in valuation, financial, and litigation/forensic consulting. He is CEO of Valuation Products and Services, LLC, a company that develops educational resources for valuation analysts and fraud/forensics practitioners. He holds the American Institute of Certified Public Accountants (AICPA) specialty designations of Accredited in Business Valuation (ABV) and Certified in Financial Forensics (CFF). Mr. Hitchner has more than 44 years of experience in valuation services. He has often testified as a qualified expert witness on valuations in federal and state courts in numerous states.

He has coauthored more than 20 courses, taught more than 60 courses, published more than 150 articles, and made more than 400 conference presentations and webinars. Mr. Hitchner is editor/coauthor of the book *Financial Valuation Applications and Models (FVAM)*, 5th edition (2025); coauthor of the book *Financial Valuation Workbook (FVW)*, 5th edition (2025); and coauthor of the book *Valuation for Financial Reporting: Fair Value, Business Combinations, Intangible Assets, Goodwill, and Impairment Analysis,* 3rd edition (2011)—all published by John Wiley & Sons. He is coauthor of *PPC's Guide to Business Valuations*, 18th through 31st editions, published by Thomson Reuters, and coauthor of *A Consensus View, Q&A Guide to Financial Valuation* (2016), and the *Discount for Lack of Marketability Guide and Toolkit,* (2017), published by Valuation Products and Services, LLC. He is editor in chief of *Hardball with Hitchner*, a monthly journal that presents views and tools from some of the leading experts in valuation, forensics/fraud, and litigation services.

Mr. Hitchner is an inductee in the AICPA Business Valuation Hall of Fame and was twice a recipient of the AICPA's Business Valuation Volunteer of the Year award. He was also one of the only four members of the original AICPA Business Valuation Standards Writing Task Force and served the entire six years up to the June 2007 official release of the standards. Mr. Hitchner is past chairman of the Business Valuation Committee of the Georgia Society of CPAs, past member of the AICPA Business Valuation Subcommittee, past member of the AICPA ABV Exam Committee, and past chairman of the ABV Exam Review Course Committee. He has a Bachelor of Science degree in engineering from the University of Pittsburgh and Master of Business Administration degree from Rider University.

CHAPTER 1

Valuation Case Study Exercises

1.1 INTRODUCTION

The purpose of this chapter is to highlight and discuss important concepts in valuation through a series of exercises. These exercises have been intermittently placed in excerpts of a valuation report. You should attempt to complete these exercises as you read the report with reasoning and emphasis on an explanation of your conclusion. The authors' solutions to these exercises can be found in Chapter 2.

The following case presents selected excerpts from a business valuation report that, in its entirety, was in full compliance with the AICPA's Statements on Standards for Valuation Services VS Section 100 and the Uniform Standards of Professional Appraisal Practice. For more information on reports and standards compliance, see Chapters 11 and 12 of *Financial Valuation Applications and Models*, 5th edition. This report format is one of many that analysts can use in presenting business valuations. The schedules have been included and are referenced throughout. Some of the terms, numbers, sources, and other data have been changed for ease of presentation.

1.2 THE VALUATION REPORT

February 15, 2023

Sherman E. Hitchner, Esq.
Hitchner & Wessinger
4747 Washington Street, Suite 1740
St. Louis, Missouri 12345

Re: Fair Market Value of a 100 Percent Equity Interest in Nova Fastener & Tool, Inc. as of December 1, 2022

Dear Mr. Hitchner:

At your request XYZ Appraisal Associates LLC (XYZ) was retained to prepare a valuation analysis and appraisal (valuation engagement and conclusion of value) and detailed/comprehensive appraisal report (the report) to assist you and your client, Ms. Louise Atkins, in the determination of the fair market value of a 100 percent equity interest in Nova Fastener & Tool, Inc. (Nova or the Company).

This interest is a controlling interest and is therefore marketable. The value conclusion is considered as a cash or cash-equivalent value. The valuation date is December 1, 2022 (the valuation date). This valuation and report are to be used only as of this date and are not valid as of any other date.

EXERCISE 1 Which of the following is the as of date for valuation?

a. Any time within one year
b. As of a single point in time
c. As of a single point in time or six months later
d. Date that the report is signed

We have prepared a valuation engagement and present our detailed report in conformity with the Statements on Standards for Valuation Services VS Section 100 (SSVS) of the American Institute of Certified Public Accountants (AICPA). SSVS defines a valuation engagement as

> an engagement to estimate value in which a valuation analyst determines an estimate of the value of a subject interest by performing appropriate procedures, as outlined in the AICPA Statements on Standards for Valuation Services, and is free to apply the valuation approaches and methods he or she deems appropriate in the circumstances. The valuation analyst expresses the results of the valuation engagement as a conclusion of value, which may be either a single amount or a range.[1]

SSVS addresses a detailed report as follows:

> The *detailed report* is structured to provide sufficient information to permit intended users to understand the data, reasoning, and analyses underlying the valuation analyst's conclusion of value.[2]

EXERCISE 2 This is a detailed report per SSVS. What other types of reports are allowed under SSVS?

_____

_____

_____

---

[1] Statements on Standards for Valuation Services VS Section 100, American Institute of Certified Public Accountants, Appendix C, Glossary of Additional Terms, Section .82.

Note: The American Society of Appraisers uses the term *estimate* as part of a limited appraisal. The AICPA use of the term is equivalent to the result of the highest scope of work specified by the ASA, which is for an appraisal.

[2] AICPA SSVS Section .51.

This valuation was prepared to assist in the determination of the value solely for purposes of internal operational and tax planning, and the resulting estimate of value should not be used for any other purpose, or by any other party for any purpose, without our express written consent.

EXERCISE 3 The purpose of the valuation of Nova is to assist management in internal operational and tax planning. What other purposes are there?

_____

_____

_____

_____

Our analysis and report are in conformance with the 2020–2021 (extended to 2022 and 2023) Uniform Standards of Professional Appraisal Practice (USPAP) promulgated by the Appraisal Standards Board of the Appraisal Foundation,[3] the ethics and standards of the American Society of Appraisers (ASA), IRS business valuation development and reporting guidelines, and the National Association of Certified Valuators and Analysts (NACVA).

EXERCISE 4 If the analyst belongs to more than one valuation organization with standards, that analyst must comply with the standards of each organization they belong to.

a. True
b. False

Our analysis is also in conformance with Revenue Ruling 59-60, which outlines the approaches, methods, and factors to be considered in valuing shares of capital stock in closely held corporations for federal tax purposes. Revenue Ruling 59-60 is often also considered as useful guidance in valuations performed for nontax purposes.

---

[3] The Appraisal Standards Board (ASB) of the Appraisal Foundation develops, interprets, and amends the Uniform Standards of Professional Appraisal Practice (USPAP) on behalf of appraisers and users of appraisal services. The Appraisal Foundation is authorized by Congress as the source of Appraisal Standards and Appraiser Qualifications. USPAP uses the terms *appraisal* and *appraisal report*, which are defined in pages 3 and 54–55, respectively. SSVS uses the terms *valuation engagement* and *detailed report*, which are defined in Sections .21, .48, .51, and .82, respectively. USPAP also uses the term *appraiser* while SSVS uses the term *valuation analyst*. We use these terms interchangeably in this report.

EXERCISE 5 Revenue Ruling 59-60 is only applicable to estate, gift, and income tax valuations.

a. True
b. False

The standard of value is fair market value, defined in Revenue Ruling 59-60 as

> the price at which the property would change hands between a willing buyer and a willing seller when the former is not under any compulsion to buy and the latter is not under any compulsion to sell, both parties having reasonable knowledge of relevant facts.[4]

Revenue Ruling 59-60 also defines the willing buyer and seller as hypothetical as follows:

> Court decisions frequently state in addition that the hypothetical buyer and seller are assumed to be able, as well as willing, to trade and to be well informed about the property and concerning the market for such property.[5]

Furthermore, fair market value assumes that the price is transacted in cash or cash equivalents. Revenue Ruling 59-60, although used in tax valuations, is also used in many nontax valuations.

Fair market value is also defined in a similar way in the SSVS[6] as

> the price, expressed in terms of cash equivalents, at which property would change hands between a hypothetical willing and able buyer and a hypothetical willing and able seller, acting at arm's length in an open and unrestricted market, when neither is under compulsion to buy or sell and when both have reasonable knowledge of the relevant facts.

EXERCISE 6 Which of these are standards of value?

a. Fair market value, fair value financial reporting, investment value
b. Fair value investment reporting, fair value state actions, intrinsic value
c. Investment value, intrinsic value, equal value
d. Fair market value, equal value, investment value

---

[4] Revenue Ruling 59-60, 1959-1 CB 237–IRC Sec. 2031 Reg § 20.2031-2, Section 2.02.
[5] Ibid.
[6] AICPA Statements on Standards for Valuation Services VS Section 100, page 44, Appendix B, 2001 *International Glossary of Business Valuation Terms*, which has been jointly adopted by the AICPA, American Society of Appraisers (ASA), Canadian Institute of Chartered Business Valuators (CICBV), National Association of Certified Valuators and Analysts (NACVA), and the Institute of Business Appraisers (IBA). Note: The 2022 *International Valuation Glossary–Business Valuation*, defines fair market value in a very similar manner.

The premise of value is going concern. The 2001 *International Glossary of Business Valuation Terms* defines going concern as "an ongoing operating business enterprise," and going concern value as

> the value of a business enterprise that is expected to continue to operate into the future. The intangible elements of going concern value result from factors such as having a trained work force, an operational plant, and the necessary licenses, systems, and procedures in place.[7]

The 2022 *International Valuation Glossary–Business Valuation* defines going concern the same way and defines going concern value as

> a **Premise of Value** that assumes the business is an ongoing commercial enterprise with a reasonable expectation of future earning power.[8]

The liquidation premise of value was considered and rejected as not applicable, as the going-concern value results in a higher value for the interest than the liquidation value, whether orderly or forced.

In our conclusion of value, we considered the following relevant factors, which are specified in Revenue Ruling 59-60:[9]

- The history and nature of the business
- The economic outlook of the United States and that of the specific industry in particular
- The book value of the subject company's stock and the financial condition of the business
- The earning capacity of the company
- The dividend-paying capacity of the company
- Whether or not the firm has goodwill or other intangible value
- Sales of the stock and size of the block of stock to be valued
- The market price of publicly traded stocks or corporations engaged in similar industries or lines of business

Our analysis included, but was not limited to, the previously mentioned factors.

EXERCISE 7   These are the only eight tenets of value in Revenue Ruling 59-60 that need to be considered.

   a. True
   b. False

---

[7] *International Glossary of Business Valuation Terms*, Statements on Standards for Valuation Services, VS Section 100, Valuation of a Business, Business Ownership Interest, Security, or Intangible Asset, American Institute of Certified Public Accountants, June 2007, Appendix B, *International Glossary of Business Valuation Terms*, Section .81.

[8] *International Valuation Glossary–Business Valuation*, November 2021, updated February 24, 2022, jointly published by the ASA, CBV Institute, RICS, and TAQEEM.

[9] Revenue Ruling 59-60, 1959-1 CB 237–IRC Sec. 2031 Reg § 20.2031-2, Section 2.02.

EXERCISE 8   Valuation conclusions can be presented as:

a. A range of values
b. A single value
c. An estimate of value
d. All of the above

1.2.1 Understanding with the Client and Scope of Work

Per AICPA VS Section 100 (SSVS), the valuation analyst should establish an understanding with the client.

> The understanding with the client reduces the possibility that either the valuation analyst or the client may misinterpret the needs or expectations of the other party. The understanding should include, at a minimum, the nature, purpose, and objective of the valuation engagement, the client's responsibilities, the valuation analyst's responsibilities, the applicable assumptions and limiting conditions, the type of report to be issued, and the standard of value to be used.[10]

> Furthermore,

> a restriction or limitation on the scope of the valuation analyst's work, or the data available for analysis, may be present and known to the valuation analyst at the outset of the valuation engagement or may arise during the course of a valuation engagement. Such a restriction or limitation should be disclosed in the valuation report (paragraphs .52(*m*), .68(*e*), and .71(*n*)).[11]

We have established an understanding with the client to perform a valuation engagement and have complied with the requirements of AICPA VS Section 100 (SSVS) as stated previously. There were no scope restrictions or limitations on the work or the data available for analysis.

In accordance with the business valuation standards promulgated by the American Society of Appraisers and the Appraisal Foundation (USPAP), we have prepared an appraisal.

> The objective of an appraisal is to express an unambiguous opinion as to the value of a business, business ownership interest, or security, which opinion is supported by all procedures that the appraiser deems to be relevant to the valuation.[12]

---

[10] AICPA VS Section 100 (SSVS), Section .17.

[11] AICPA VS Section 100 (SSVS), Section .19.

[12] ASA Business Valuation Standards, BVS-1 General Requirements for Developing a Business Valuation, copyright 2022 American Society of Appraisers.

It is based on all relevant information available to the appraiser as of the valuation date; the appraiser conducts appropriate procedures to collect and analyze all information expected to be relevant to the valuation, and the appraiser "considers all conceptual approaches deemed to be relevant."[13]

In accordance with the Scope of Work Rule in USPAP, we must do the following:

1. Identify the problem to be solved.
2. Determine and perform the scope of work necessary to develop credible assignment results.
3. Disclose the scope of work in the report.[14]

To gain an understanding of the operations of Nova, we reviewed Company financial information as provided by management and interviewed Company management. To understand the environment in which Nova operates, we researched the status of and trends in the various industries that have an impact on it. We also studied economic conditions as of the valuation date and their impact on Nova and the industry. To understand the Company's financial condition, we analyzed its financial statements as available.

We considered all three valuation approaches and relevant methods and applied the most appropriate methods from the income, asset, and market approaches to value to derive an opinion of value of the subject equity interest (100 percent controlling, marketable interest). Our conclusion of value reflects these findings, our judgment and knowledge of the marketplace, and our expertise in valuation.

Our valuation is set out in the attached report, which contains the following sections:

- History and Nature of the Business
- General Economic and Industry Outlook
- Book Value and Financial Position
- Approaches to Value
- Income Approach
- Market Approach
- Reconciliation of Valuation Methods
- Conclusion of Value
- Appendixes
  - Appendix A—Assumptions and Limiting Conditions
  - Appendix B—Valuation Representation/Certification
  - Appendix C—Professional Qualifications of the Appraiser
  - Appendix D—Other Sources Consulted
  - Appendix E—Exhibits
  - Appendix F—Additional Information from Mercer Capital's National Economic Review

---

[13] Ibid.

[14] USPAP 2020–2021 (extended to 2022 and 2023), p. 13.

In performing our work, we were provided with and/or relied on various sources of information, including (but not limited to):

- Audited financial statements for Nova for the fiscal years ended December 31, 2017, through December 31, 2021
- Internal interim financial statements for Nova for the 11 months ending December 1, 2022, and December 1, 2021
- One-month December financials for all years 2017 to 2021.
- Tax returns for the Company for the fiscal years ended December 31, 2017, through 2021.
- Information regarding the management and shareholders of Nova
- Information regarding the Company's history and current operations
- Nova's Articles of Incorporation and Bylaws
- Data from the Kroll *Cost of Capital Navigator*
- Federal Reserve statistical releases
- Current and future economic conditions as forecast by various sources, listed in the Appendix
- Miscellaneous other information

The procedures employed in valuing the subject interest in Nova included such steps as we considered necessary, including (but not limited to) the following:

- An analysis of Nova's financial statements
- An analysis of Nova management's future expectations as of late 2022 and other information supplied by management
- Discussions with management
- An analysis of the fastener industry, as well as the domestic automotive industry
- An analysis of the general economic environment as of the valuation date, including investors' equity and debt-return expectations
- An analysis of other pertinent facts and data resulting in our conclusion of value

There were no restrictions or limitations in the scope of our work or data available for analysis.

Based on our analysis as described in this valuation report, and the facts and circumstances as of the valuation date, the estimate of value as of December 1, 2022, of a 100 percent equity interest in Nova Fastener & Tool, Inc. on a control, marketable basis is $33,000,000.

This conclusion is subject to the Statement of Assumptions and Limiting Conditions and to the Valuation Analyst's Representation/Certification found in Appendixes A and B of this report. We have no obligation to update this report or our conclusion of value for information that comes to our attention after the date of this report.

EXERCISE 9 This valuation is being done on a marketable, control interest basis. It is also on a control stand-alone basis. Name six levels of value that are considered in a valuation.

1. _____
2. _____
3. _____
4. _____
5. _____
6. _____

Distribution of this letter and report and associated results, which are to be distributed only in their entirety, is intended and restricted to you and your client, solely to assist you and your client in the determination of the fair market value of the subject interest for internal operational and tax planning purposes, and is valid only as of December 1, 2022. This letter and accompanying report are not to be used, circulated, quoted, or otherwise referred to in whole or in part for any other purpose, nor to be provided to any other party for any purpose, without our express written consent.

As is usual in appraisal practice, the approaches and methodologies used in our work did not comprise an examination or any attest service in accordance with generally accepted auditing standards (GAAS), the objective of which is an expression of an opinion regarding the fair presentation of financial statements or other financial information, whether historical or prospective, presented in accordance with generally accepted accounting principles (GAAP). We express no opinion and accept no responsibility for the accuracy and completeness of the financial information (audited, reviewed, compiled, internal, prospective, or tax returns), or other data provided to us by others, and we have not verified such information unless specifically stated in this report. We assume that the financial and other information provided to us is accurate and complete, and we have relied upon this information in performing our valuation.

If you have any questions concerning this valuation, please contact Ms. Margaret E. Smith, CPA/ABV/CFF, ASA, CVA, at (800) 000-1234.

Very truly yours,
XYZ Appraisal Associates LLC

1.2.2 Executive Summary

Purpose of Valuation	To assist you in the determination of the fair market value for internal operational and tax planning purposes of a 100 percent equity interest in Nova Fastener & Tool, Inc. as of December 1, 2022
Standard of Value	Fair market value
Premise of Value	Going concern
Conclusion	Based on our analysis as described in this valuation report, and the facts and circumstances as of the valuation date, the estimate of value as of December 1, 2022, of a 100 percent equity interest in Nova Fastener & Tool, Inc. on a control, marketable basis is $33,000,000.

1.3 HISTORY AND NATURE OF BUSINESS[15]

1.3.1 Overview

Nova Fastener & Tool, Inc. began its history as a manufacturer of brake lining and harness rivets in 1920, under the name Nova Specialty Co. By 1925, the Company built its first rivet-setting machine and in 1927, incorporated under the laws of the State of Missouri and changed its name to its current form. Nova's influence in the industry continued to grow, and during World War II it received formal recognition from the United States government for its efforts as a vital governmental supplier for fasteners used in aircraft wings and other various munitions of the U.S. military.

By 1964, Nova expanded its operations to manufacturing fasteners, screw parts, and metal assembly equipment. Three years later, A&B Tool Company was acquired by Nova. A&B Tool Company is based in Monroe, Illinois, and manufactures rivets, gears, spring studs, tube nuts, splines, and knurls through cold-forming technology and precision turning, as well as hand and machine tools. Nova later expanded its manufacture of gears to include other power transmission parts. In 2010 Nova purchased a small manufacturer of metal returnable packaging products, primarily racks and tote bins.

As of the valuation date, Nova operates in three segments: fasteners and parts, tools and assembly equipment, and returnable packaging. The fastener and parts segment consists of the manufacture and sale of rivets, cold-formed fasteners and parts, screw machine products, gears, and other power transmission parts. The assembly equipment segment consists of the manufacture of automatic rivet-setting machines, automatic assembly equipment, parts and tools for such machines, and various other hand and machine tools, such as measuring and cutting tools. The returnable packaging segment consists of the manufacture of metal racks and tote bins. Almost all of the revenues for the fiscal year ended December 31, 2021 (over 80 percent of consolidated revenues) was generated by the fasteners segment. The Company is structured as a C corporation for tax reporting.

EXERCISE 10   The subject of this exercise is a C corporation, but analysts will frequently be required to value noncontrolling interests in S corporations. Valuation of S corporations is one of the most controversial issues in business valuations today. The main issue is how to tax-affect S corporation income and, if appropriate, compute an S corporation adjustment. What are three models that have been used in valuing S corporations?

1. _____

2. _____

3. _____

---

[15] The text of this section is largely drawn from interviews with management, the Company's website (www.nova.com), and other available information. Language has, in places, been extracted wholly or largely verbatim and/or substantially paraphrased.

1.3.2 Market Area and Customers

The principal market for the Company's products is the North American automotive industry. Sales are solicited by employees of the Company and by independent sales representatives.

Revenues are primarily derived from sales to customers involved, directly or indirectly, in the manufacture of automobiles and automotive components. Although Nova sells primarily to automotive markets, it also sells in smaller quantities to truck, off-road, aerospace, marine, and rail applications. The level of business activity for the Company is closely related to the overall level of industrial activity in the United States.

Nova serves a variety of customers; however, sales to three major companies accounted for approximately 36 percent (13 percent, 12 percent, and 11 percent) of revenues during 2021. Recently, the Company signed a manufacturing contract with a new customer, which is expected to generate significant revenue growth in the near future.

The Company has no foreign operations. Sales to foreign customers represent approximately 16 percent of the Company's total sales in 2021, and the proportion of sales to foreign customers is expected to grow.

1.3.3 Competition

The fastener, tools and assembly equipment, and returnable packaging markets are characterized by active and significant competition. No single company in particular dominates. The Company's competitors include both larger and smaller manufacturers, and segments or divisions of large, diversified companies with substantial financial resources. The primary competitive factors for the Company's products in the market are price, quality, and service. Based on discussions with management, Nova's primary competitors in various segments include Midwest Fasteners Corp.; National Fastening Systems; Haven Fastener, Inc.; The Eastern Co.; Twin Disc, Inc.; and The L.S. Starrett Co.

The competitive environment has changed considerably in recent years as the Company's customers have experienced intense international competition and pressure to reduce costs. As a result, these customers have expanded their sourcing of components beyond domestic boundaries. Nova's competition now includes suppliers in other parts of the world that enjoy economic advantages, such as lower labor costs, lower healthcare costs, and fewer regulatory burdens. However, the recent COVID pandemic has shown the risks of global supply chains, which management believes may benefit Nova with U.S. customers.

1.3.4 Suppliers

The Company maintains alternative sources for raw materials. The market is served by multiple suppliers, so prices for raw materials are generally competitive. The Company is not under any long-term contracts for raw materials. Orders are made through purchase orders based on pricing sheets negotiated biannually.

1.3.5 Employees

As of December 2021, the Company had 201 full- and part-time employees. The employees are party to a collective bargaining agreement. The Company is on good terms with the union representing its employees and has recently renegotiated the union contract that now has an X-year term. There are no employment or noncompete agreements.

1.3.6 Management and Key Persons

As of the valuation date, management and key personnel of Nova include the following individuals, with their titles shown in Exhibit 1.1.

EXHIBIT 1.1   Executive Management

Name	Title	Years with Company
Tony Atkins	Chief Executive Officer	34
Michael Johanson	Chief Operating Officer	16
Kimberly A. Kirhofer	Chief Financial Officer and Treasurer	13

A key person situation exists at the Company in that the business relies heavily on Mr. Atkins, with no formal succession plan in place.

1.3.7 Facilities

The corporate headquarters of Nova is located in St. Louis, Missouri. There is also warehouse space at this location. The Company operates manufacturing facilities in Reading, Ohio, which is used for both fasteners and tools and assembly equipment operations, and in Ames, Iowa, which is also used for the tools and assembly equipment segment, as well as for returnable packaging. Nova also owns the warehouse and manufacturing facility used by A&B Tool Company, Inc. in Monroe, Illinois. The Company also maintains a small sales and engineering office in Boston, Massachusetts, in a leased office. Management indicates that the Company's facilities are adequate but not excessive for its needs. On August 12, 2022, the Company entered into a Purchase and Sale Agreement (the PSA) with Big Arch Properties LLC (the Purchaser) pursuant to which the Company agreed, subject to the terms and conditions of the PSA, to sell its facility in St. Louis, in which the Company headquarters and warehouse space are located, to the Purchaser. On September 27, 2022, the Company's sale of the facility to the Purchaser was completed. The net gain on the transaction was $4,738,394. A portion of the net proceeds was invested in U.S. Treasury bills and included in cash and cash equivalents on the Company's balance sheet.

Concurrently with the completion of the sale of the St. Louis facility, the Company and the Purchaser entered into a lease agreement pursuant to which the Company will lease much of the facility from the Purchaser.

1.3.8 Intangibles

The Company has intangible assets such as relationships with customers, its proprietary trademark, and assembled workforce.

1.3.9 Stock and Stockholders

Nova is a privately held company owned by the same family that founded the Company many years ago. The Company has a single class of common stock with

10,000 shares issued and outstanding. Exhibit 1.2 presents the ownership of the shares of the Company as of the valuation date.

EXHIBIT 1.2　Ownership

Stockholder	Number of Shares	Percentage
Tony Atkins	5,500	55.00%
Louise Atkins	1,500	15.00%
Veronica Atkins	1,500	15.00%
Anthony Atkins	1,500	15.00%
		100.00%

EXERCISE 11　We are valuing a 100 percent controlling interest in Nova. The percentage of ownership of individual shareholders is not an issue here. However, assume we are valuing the 55 percent interest of Tony Atkins as opposed to the 100 percent in Nova. The value of a 55 percent interest in Nova would be calculated as 55 percent of the 100 percent control value in Nova.

  a. True
  b. False

No independent valuations or appraisals of Nova have been performed recently. Based on discussions with management, there have been no serious offers or expressions of interest in purchasing the Company, and there have been no transactions in the Company's stock within the past five years. Prior transactions included minority common share gifts from Mr. Atkins to his son, Anthony, and daughters, Louise and Veronica, as detailed previously.

The Company has strong dividend-paying capacity. However, the Company has generally retained earnings to support capital investment requirements and internal growth, while minimizing debt.

1.3.10 Outlook

In the upcoming year, management plans to continue making significant investments in its equipment and facilities. A modest expansion of the Monroe plant is planned for the fourth quarter of 2023 to increase capacity and improve production efficiency. Investments aimed at supplying parts for electric vehicles (EVs) are also planned. Continuing efforts to foster new customer relationships and build on existing ones in all markets served are also a primary focus.

1.4 GENERAL ECONOMIC AND INDUSTRY OUTLOOK

The financial success of investments in Nova as of the valuation date is dependent on conditions within the economy and financial/capital markets. A prospective investor tempers the use of historical financial statistics on the basis of anticipated general economic conditions. An analysis of these factors as of the valuation date is therefore incorporated into this valuation analysis. Certain items in the following discussion have been extracted from the cited sources and/or substantially paraphrased based on them.

1.4.1 General Economic Overview[16]

1.4.1.1 TagniFi[17]

1.4.1.1.1 Summary   In the 3rd quarter of 2022, inflation continued to be the focal point of the U.S. economic picture. The Federal Reserve's hawkish interest rate hikes and quantitative tightening plans have thus far underperformed expectations to temper blazing inflation. Further, volatile energy costs are no longer at the forefront of price increases; while inflation among all items fades slightly, "core" inflation, which sets aside traditionally volatile categories, is accelerating. Meanwhile, elevated interest rates have taken a heavy toll on capital markets and slowed the housing industry's seemingly unstoppable momentum.

The Federal Reserve has repeatedly declared their intent to continue aggressive counterinflationary policies, particularly interest rate raises, despite the constraints such policies are placing on the U.S. economy. In the view of the Fed, the need to contain inflation exceeds the need to keep the economy from the grips of recession.

EXERCISE 12   What types of industries would most likely be affected by anticipated changes in interest rates?

_____

_____

_____

_____

Concerns of recession abated slightly with the first positive real GDP reading of 2022; however, the major factor behind the boosted production numbers, a narrowing trade deficit, is expected to be short-lived. The labor market continued to be a bright spot in the 3rd quarter of 2022, with the unemployment rate finally reaching its pre-pandemic level and the labor force participation rate continuing to slowly recover as well.

Recorded COVID-19 cases waned throughout the 3rd quarter of 2022. With widely available at-home tests and relaxed testing policies in public and private spaces across the U.S., official COVID case rates likely no longer give an accurate picture of the virus's reach.

Vaccines have been established as a reliable way to limit serious illness and death from COVID-19; 4.29 million people were newly vaccinated in the U.S. during the 3rd quarter. Additionally, 1.1 million booster doses were distributed,

---

[16] We have reviewed two sources for economic data: TagniFi's *Quarterly Economic Update* and Mercer Capital's *National Economic Review*.

[17] All the contents of this section of this valuation report are quoted largely or wholly verbatim from the *Quarterly Economic Update* third quarter of 2022, published by TagniFi, reprinted with permission, https://about.tagnifi.com/q3-2022-quarterly-economic-update/.

including bivalent vaccines authorized for use as booster doses on August 31, 2022. While speculation continues as to when COVID-19 will reach an endemic phase in the U.S., a combination of vaccination and prior infection has allowed many aspects of life and commerce to return closer to normal, a situation reflected by increased spending on travel-related services in the 3rd quarter.

A multifactor indicator of economic strength, the Philadelphia Fed's coincident index[18] of economic activity in the U.S. rose 0.4% in September 2022 and 1.0% during the 3rd quarter. For the quarter, coincident indexes increased in 44 states, decreased in 3 states, and were unchanged in 3 states. Coincident indexes reflect unemployment, payroll employment, manufacturing hours, and wages and salaries.

1.4.1.1.2 Q3 Economic Highlights

- The Philadelphia Fed's coincident index of economic activity in the U.S. rose 0.4 percent in September 2022 and 1.0 percent during the third quarter.
- Real GDP for the third quarter of 2022 grew at an annualized rate of 2.6 percent, following a 0.6 percent decrease in the second quarter of 2022.
- The U.S. dollar index rose 5.44 percent during the third quarter of 2022 and 11.3 percent since September 2021.
- The effective federal funds rate rose 1.35 percentage points to 2.56 percent during the third quarter, continuing the climb from near-zero levels in March.
- The 1-year and 2-year annual Treasury yields ended the third quarter at 4.05 percent and 4.22 percent, respectively. The benchmark 10-year Treasury yielded 3.83 percent at the end of the quarter, and the 30-year treasury yielded 3.79 percent.
- Unemployment inched down to 3.5 percent during the third quarter of 2022. Nonfarm payrolls grew by 1.1 million jobs in the third quarter.
- The Consumer Price Index rose 8.2 percent year-over-year in September, down from its 40-year high of 9.0 percent in June. Excluding volatile energy prices, the annual increase was 7.3 percent.
- Crude oil prices ended the quarter at $79.91 per barrel, 25.8 percent lower than one quarter earlier.
- New home starts fell to 1.44 million in September, down 8.6 percent for the quarter and 7.7 percent for the year.
- The Dow Jones Transportation Average dropped 8.4 percent during the third quarter of 2022, the Dow Jones Composite fell 7.4 percent, and the Dow Jones Industrial decreased 6.7 percent. The S&P 500 was down 5.3 percent.

1.4.1.1.3 Outlook
In June 2022, the Federal Open Market Committee (FOMC) revised its near-term inflation and unemployment rate projections slightly upward and real GDP projections sharply downward. Adjustments to longer-run projections for all three indicators were mild yet followed a similar pattern, with inflation and unemployment rising and real GDP declining.

The FOMC revised its projection for real GDP[19] to 0.20 percent growth in 2022, rising to 1.00 percent in 2023, then to 1.70 percent by 2024. They expected Personal

---

[18] Federal Reserve Bank of Philadelphia, Coincident Economic Activity Index for the United States [USPHCI], retrieved from FRED, Federal Reserve Bank of St. Louis; https://fred.stlouisfed.org/series/USPHCI, Oct. 31, 2022.

[19] Federal Reserve Bank of St. Louis, FOMC Summary of Economic Projections for the Growth Rate of Real Gross Domestic Product [GDPC1CTM], retrieved from FRED, Federal Reserve Bank of St. Louis; https://fred.stlouisfed.org/series/GDPC1CTM , Oct. 31, 2022.

Consumption Expenditures (PCE) inflation[20] to grow to 5.50 percent in 2022 but moderate to 3.05 percent by 2023 and 2.35 percent by 2024. They forecast that the unemployment rate[21] would be 3.85 percent in 2022, rising to 4.30 percent in 2023 and 2024. The board again increased projections of future target rates and maintained their resolve to continue tightening monetary policy against blazing inflation despite expected consequences, including a potential recession (see Table 1.1).

TABLE 1.1   FOMC Summary of Economic Projections

Year	Real GDP (%)	PCE (%)	Unemployment (%)
2022	0.20	5.50	3.85
2023	1.00	3.05	4.30
2024	1.70	2.35	4.30
2025	1.80	2.10	4.25

EXERCISE 13   What two economic indicators are probably the most important in valuation?

  a. Unemployment levels and gross domestic product (GDP)
  b. Dow Jones Industrial Average and Producer Price Index
  c. GDP and inflation
  d. Inflation and unemployment levels

EXERCISE 14   In valuing a small geographically concentrated business, which of these types of economic data should be considered?

  a. International, national, regional, local
  b. National, regional, local
  c. Regional, local
  d. Local only

1.4.1.2 Mercer Capital[22]

1.4.1.2.1 Summary and Outlook   After declining at an annualized rate of 1.6% in the first quarter of 2022 and 0.6% in the second quarter, U.S. GDP increased in the third quarter at an annualized rate of 2.6%. Inflation continued to weigh on economic growth and activity in the third quarter, as the unadjusted CPI increased

---

[20] Federal Reserve Bank of St. Louis, FOMC Summary of Economic Projections for the Personal Consumption Expenditures Inflation Rate, Central Tendency, Midpoint [PCECT-PICTM], retrieved from FRED, Federal Reserve Bank of St. Louis; https://fred.stlouisfed.org/series/PCECTPICTM , Oct. 31, 2022.

[21] Federal Reserve Bank of St. Louis, FOMC Summary of Economic Projections for the Civilian Unemployment Rate, Central Tendency, Midpoint [UNRATECTM], retrieved from FRED, Federal Reserve Bank of St. Louis; https://fred.stlouisfed.org/series/UNRATECTM, Oct. 31, 2022.

[22] All the contents of this section of this valuation report are quoted largely or wholly verbatim from *The National Economic Review*, third quarter of 2022, published by Mercer Capital, reprinted with permission, www.nationaleconomicreview.net.

0.4% in September 2022 and 8.2% in the twelve months ended September 2022. Core CPI increased 0.6 percent in September 2022 and 6.6% in the twelve months ended September 2022.

The Dow Jones Industrial Average (DJIA), NASDAQ, S&P 500, and broad market Wilshire 5000 all posted quarter-over-quarter losses in the third quarter of 2022, compounding U.S. equity markets' dismal performance through the first nine months of 2022. The Dow dropped 6.7% from its second quarter close, while the S&P shed 5.2%, the NASDAQ fell 4.1%, and the Wilshire 500 was down 4.6% in the third quarter of 2022.

Prior to the disruption caused by the pandemic, the unemployment rate had remained stable for several months in the range of 3.5% to 4.0%, continually nearing all-time lows. The unemployment rate held steady at 3.6% during the second quarter of 2022 and fell to 3.5% in September 2022. Labor force participation has improved but remains low relative to historic levels at 62.3%.

Following the increase in GDP in the third quarter, economists expect GDP growth to stagnate in the next two quarters. A survey of economists conducted by The *Wall Street Journal* reflects an average GDP forecast of 0.4% annualized growth in the fourth quarter of 2022, followed by an annualized decline of 0.2% in the first quarter of 2023. Economists anticipate annualized growth in GDP of 0.2% in 2022, 0.4% in 2023, 1.8% in 2024, and 2.1% in 2025.

For additional detail from Mercer Capital's *National Economic Review*.

1.4.2 Industry Overview

We employed Porter's[23] model of analysis to examine more closely the fastener industry defined by SIC 34, Fabricated Metal Products, Except Machinery and Transportation Equipment, and SIC 37, Transportation Equipment, specifically focusing on subcategory SIC 3714, Motor Vehicle Parts and Accessories.

1.4.2.1 Fabricated Metal Products Industry In the fasteners industry, globalization remained a fact even as the COVID-19 pandemic illustrated the risks of global supply chains and reduced demand for industrial fasteners.

According to one report,

> the global industrial fasteners market size was valued at USD 88.43 billion in 2021 and is expected to expand at a compound annual growth rate (CAGR) of 4.5% from 2022 to 2030. The market is expected to be driven by the growing population, high investments in the construction sector, and rising demand for industrial fasteners in the automotive and aerospace sectors. The COVID-19 outburst in early 2020 negatively impacted the supply channels across the globe as international and domestic trade was interrupted to curb the spread of the virus.[24]

---

[23] Michael E. Porter, *Competitive Strategy: Techniques for Analyzing Industries and Competitors* (New York: The Free Press, 1998).

[24] "Industrial Fasteners Market Size, Share & Trends Analysis Report by Raw Material (Metal, Plastic), by Product (Externally Threaded, Internally Threaded, Non-threaded), by Application (Aerospace), By Distribution Channel (Direct, Indirect), by Region, and Segment Forecasts, 2022–2030," https://www.grandviewresearch.com/industry-analysis/industrial-fasteners-market.

The report notes that the U.S. is "one of the largest fasteners importing countries," and that due "to the growing demand for lightweight vehicles and aircraft, companies are shifting from standard to customized fasteners, which, in turn, is expected to drive the demand."[25]

Metal fasteners accounted for the largest share of fasteners—over 90.0 percent in 2021. However, increasing demand for lightweight products favors the growth of nonmetal alternatives such as plastic fasteners, tapes and adhesives, and so on, as well as innovation in metal fasteners.

The report notes that

> the automotive segment accounted for the largest revenue share of over 30.0% in 2021. Automotive OEM is one of the key markets for industrial fasteners. High production volumes of automotive vehicles across Asia Pacific have been driving the industry over the past few years.[26]

1.4.2.2 Auto Parts Industry   According to RSM Global,

> automotive suppliers and manufacturers—like most other industries—are watching inflation and the Federal Reserve's rate actions closely as the industry's production environments continue to experience labor shortages, supply chain unpredictability and high consumer demand. While inflation is now at its highest level in over 40 years and interest rates are rising, opportunities will continue to abound for many automotive manufacturers and suppliers that align themselves to the electrified future of the industry.[27]

RSM notes that raw materials, labor, and other costs have made auto parts production more expensive and constrained margin growth, but also that "original equipment manufacturers have benefited from incredible market demand after the earlier phases of the pandemic."[28]

Acknowledging that automotive is "one of the most rate-sensitive sectors in the economy," increased borrowing costs are expected to make R&D and capital expenditures more costly, putting continued pressure on margins. However, the report also notes that on "the demand side, while many might expect increased vehicle financing costs would immediately affect car buyers and slow down demand, the industry is adept in responding to such changes and will likely reinstate incentives when necessary or promote longer financing terms," and it also notes the material ($2.5 trillion) excess savings accumulated by Americans during the pandemic, and the strong labor market.[29]

RSM predicted that North American automotive production would increase from approximately 13 million units in 2021 to over 17 million units in 2026.

> This means strong sales demand should continue into the foreseeable future, allowing suppliers' and manufacturers' operating cash flows to fund legacy

---

[25] Ibid.

[26] Ibid.

[27] James Ward, "Automotive Industry Outlook: Fall 2022, Economic Headlines Not Cause for Deceleration Among Automotive Suppliers, Manufacturers," Aug. 29, 2022, https://rsmus .com/insights/industries/automotive/automotive-outlook.html.

[28] Ibid.

[29] Ibid.

technologies while at the same time allowing for the investment in future-facing EV technology strategies.[30]

As of the valuation date, the business press had grown somewhat more optimistic about the short-term outlook for automotive. For example, *Forbes* wrote that

> supply chain woes will ease a bit, and rising vehicle supply will mean less pressure on the prices of older used cars. New-vehicle markups and used-vehicle wholesale prices have both eased since their peaks this past spring. Falling prices are only just reaching the retail level, but inflation-stretched used car shoppers may find some relief in 2023.[31]

On a related note, *Insider* wrote that "experts from AutoForecast Solutions say that by the end of 2022, the semiconductor shortage won't be nearly as bad as it was last year. Better yet, 2023 could look even rosier," noting that although in 2021 "automakers built 3.23 million fewer vehicles than expected in North America because of the chip shortage," that shortage was expected to be only 1.5 million for 2022, with further improvement expected in 2023.[32]

1.4.2.3 Industry Competition   The domestic automotive parts industry is highly competitive with many independent domestic and international suppliers competing on price, quality, and service.

1.4.2.4 Threat of Substitute Products   The threat of substitute products is moderate and includes both import substitution and competition from innovation in lightweight alternatives such as plastic parts and tapes and adhesives. Though internal combustion engines still account for the vast majority of vehicles on the road, the trend toward EVs also has implications for substitute products among parts manufacturers. To a material degree, however, existing products still compete primarily on price.

1.4.2.5 Threat of New Entrants   Foreign companies have been competing significantly in the U.S. market, increasing competition for existing market share. At the same time, some U.S. companies have increased exports. Just-in-time manufacturing, preferring supplier facilities with close proximity to manufacturing facilities, is a check on international competition.

1.4.2.6 Bargaining Power of Suppliers   Bargaining power of suppliers is low because of the competitive alternatives available to buyers.

1.4.2.7 Bargaining Power of Buyers   Bargaining power of buyers is very high because the smaller parts manufacturing companies are part of a chain serving very large auto manufacturers with multiple alternative sourcing options.

---

[30] Ibid.

[31] Alex Kwanten and Sasha Lekach, "Car Market Outlook: What to Expect In 2023," *Forbes*, December 12, 2022, https://www.forbes.com/wheels/features/car-market-outlook-2023/. *Note:* Although this article is a few days post-valuation date, this information is presumed knowable as of December 1, 2022.

[32] Alexa St. John, "The Chip Shortage Could Be Just About Done Pummeling the Auto Industry, Experts Say—So Cars May Get a Whole Lot Cheaper in 2023," *Business Insider*, December 5, 2022, https://www.businessinsider.com/chip-shortage-auto-industry-car-buying-dealerships-consumers-inventory-2022-12?op=1. *Note:* Although this article is a few days post-valuation date, this information is presumed knowable as of December 1, 2022.

1.4.3 Summary

Based on analysis of the industry and economic outlook, as chip shortages ease, and despite recent higher inflation and interest rates, pent-up demand and the requirement for aging vehicles to be replaced and repaired should eventually support a return to stable growth for the Company, with continuing price pressures from off-shore competition. The Company's recent sales and margins as of the valuation date have been constrained by supply chain issues, labor shortages, and high inflation, but management believes underlying demand remains positive in the near term and closely tied to the overall performance of the economy in the long-term. The median 10-year forecast CPI and real GDP estimates from the *Livingston Survey* imply a combined forecast 10-year nominal GDP of 4.65 percent.[33] Based on the industry and economic data, a long-term perpetuity growth rate of 4.5 percent was assumed for the Company. Additional Company-specific risk was identified in the reliance of the Company on a key executive, Mr. Atkins. The analysis of competitors and suppliers indicated that for the most part, the Company had similar risks to the rest of its industry. However, the Company does generate over a third of its revenue from just three customers. Such heavy customer reliance poses additional Company-specific risk as compared to what was observed about the other participants in the industry.

EXERCISE 15 Which industry outlook factors are generally the most important in supporting valuation assumptions?

a. Growth rates, profit margins, and risk
b. Regulatory and legal issues
c. Unemployment figures
d. Minority discounts and/or control premiums

1.5 BOOK VALUE AND FINANCIAL POSITION

Nova's historical comparative income statements are presented in Exhibit 1.3, and comparative balance sheets are presented in Exhibit 1.4. Income statements adjusted to reflect elimination of unusual and/or nonrecurring items are shown in Exhibit 1.5. Certain financial ratios of Nova are computed and presented in Exhibit 1.6. Five years of financial data are presented for the fiscal years from 2017 through 2021 and the trailing 12 months (TTM) ended December 1, 2022.

EXERCISE 16 What is the most important use of historical financial data?

a. To determine how the company has performed
b. To assist in supporting anticipated performance
c. To highlight profitability
d. To determine average profits

---

[33] Combined nominal GDP calculated as $(1 + CPI)^* (1 + real GDP) - 1$. Based on the information from the *Livingston Survey* $(1 + 2.10\%)^* (1 + 2.50\%) - 1 = 4.65\%$.

EXHIBIT 1.3 Comparative Income Statement

Nova Fastener & Tool, Inc.
Comparative Income Statement
Valuation Date: December 1, 2022 $

	Trailing 12 Months November 30, 2022 $	%	2021 $	%	2020 $	%	2019 $	%	2018 $	%	2017 $	%	Three-Year Average 2019 to 2021 $	%	Growth Rates '19-'21 %
							Years Ended December 31,								
Net Revenues	34,538,367	100.0	33,974,558	100.0	27,590,653	100.0	32,873,002	100.0	37,174,249	100.0	35,764,714	100.0	31,479,404	100.0	1.7
Total Costs of Goods Sold	28,848,313	83.5	27,509,466	81.0	22,675,451	82.2	27,128,472	82.5	29,268,490	78.7	27,850,992	77.9	25,771,130	81.9	0.7
Gross Profit	5,690,054	16.5	6,465,092	19.0	4,915,202	17.8	5,744,530	17.5	7,905,759	21.3	7,913,722	22.1	5,708,275	18.1	6.1
Total Selling, General, and Administrative Expenses	4,979,152	14.4	5,106,177	15.0	4,998,216	18.1	5,252,946	16.0	5,503,111	14.8	5,548,541	15.5	5,119,113	16.3	-1.4
Net Operating Profit (Loss)	710,902	2.1	1,358,915	4.0	(83,014)	-0.3	491,584	1.5	2,402,648	6.5	2,365,181	6.6	589,162	1.9	66.3
Other Expense (Income)															
Interest (income)	(11,059)	0.0	(19,797)	-0.1	(94,956)	-0.3	(144,730)	-0.4	(120,141)	-0.3	(75,926)	-0.2	(86,494)	-0.3	-63.0
Interest expense	0	0.0	0	0.0	0	0.0	0	0.0	0	0.0	0	0.0	0	0.0	N/M
(Gain) / loss on asset sale or disposal	(4,738,394)	-13.7	21,564	0.1	0	0.0	228	0.0	13,086	0.0	(1,700)	0.0	7,264	0.0	872.5
Other (income) / expense	(36,100)	-0.1	(57,324)	-0.2	(53,508)	-0.2	(47,228)	-0.1	(46,482)	-0.1	(23,275)	-0.1	(52,687)	-0.2	10.2
Total Other Expense (Income)	(4,785,553)	-13.9	(55,557)	-0.2	(148,464)	-0.5	(191,730)	-0.6	(153,537)	-0.4	(100,901)	-0.3	(131,917)	-0.4	-46.2
Income (Loss) Before Income Taxes	5,496,455	15.9	1,414,472	4.2	65,450	0.2	683,314	2.1	2,556,185	6.9	2,466,082	6.9	721,079	2.3	43.9
Income Tax Provision (Benefit)	1,235,000	3.6	301,000	0.9	15,000	0.1	145,000	0.4	555,000	1.5	387,000	1.1	153,667	0.5	44.1
Net Income (Loss)	4,261,455	12.3	1,113,472	3.3	50,450	0.2	538,314	1.6	2,001,185	5.4	2,079,082	5.8	567,412	1.8	43.8
Net Income to Invested Capital	4,261,455	12.3	1,113,472	3.3	50,450	0.2	538,314	1.6	2,001,185	5.4	2,079,082	5.8	567,412	1.8	43.8
Earnings Before Interest & Taxes (EBIT)	5,496,455	15.9	1,414,472	4.2	65,450	0.2	683,314	2.1	2,556,185	6.9	2,466,082	6.9	721,079	2.3	43.9
Earnings Before Int., Taxes, Depr. & Amort. (EBITDA)	6,784,165	19.6	2,733,026	8.0	1,412,755	5.1	2,065,549	6.3	3,864,633	10.4	3,697,628	10.3	2,070,443	6.6	15.0
Depreciation & Amortization	1,287,710	3.7	1,318,554	3.9	1,347,305	4.9	1,382,235	4.2	1,308,448	3.5	1,231,546	3.4	1,349,365	4.3	-2.3
Capital Expenditures	779,356	2.3	670,898	2.0	824,136	3.0	1,802,914	5.5	1,998,347	5.4	1,333,988	3.7	1,099,316	3.5	-39.0
Effective Tax Rate	22.5%		21.3%		22.9%		21.2%		21.7%		15.7%		21.3%		
Dividends	850,196	2.5	850,196	2.5	502,388	1.8	1,140,036	3.5	1,101,391	3.0	1,111,052	3.1	830,873	2.6	-13.6

Note:
(1) Source: Audited financial statements for the years ended December 31, 2017 through 2021, internal financial statements for the eleven months ended November 30, 2022 and 2021.

EXHIBIT 1.4 Comparative Balance Sheet

Nova Fastener & Tool, Inc.
Comparative Balance Sheet
Valuation Date: December 1, 2022 $

	At November 30, 2022		2021		2020		At December 31, 2019		2018		2017		Three-Year Average 2019 to 2021		Growth Rates '19–'21
ASSETS	$	%	$	%	$	%	$	%	$	%	$	%	$	%	%
Current Assets															
Cash and cash equivalents	5,328,732	14.7	2,036,954	6.4	2,567,731	8.2	1,429,454	4.5	706,873	2.1	1,152,569	3.6	2,011,380	6.4	19.4
Certificates of deposit	2,741,000	7.6	2,741,000	8.6	4,733,000	15.2	6,574,000	20.7	7,063,000	21.2	7,810,000	24.5	4,682,667	14.8	-35.4
Accounts receivable, net	6,578,114	18.1	5,647,984	17.8	5,163,450	16.5	4,609,314	14.5	5,529,307	16.6	5,326,650	16.7	5,140,249	16.3	10.7
Inventories	9,921,472	27.3	8,519,780	26.8	5,153,294	16.5	4,951,177	15.6	6,100,391	18.3	4,528,100	14.2	6,208,084	19.7	31.2
Prepaid income taxes	0	0.0	440	0.0	85,940	0.3	58,186	0.2	150,686	0.5	84,112	0.3	48,189	0.2	-91.3
Other current assets	422,002	1.2	346,236	1.1	383,772	1.2	427,192	1.3	438,222	1.3	357,918	1.1	385,733	1.2	-10.0
Total Current Assets	24,991,320	68.8	19,292,394	60.7	18,087,187	57.9	18,049,323	56.9	19,988,479	60.1	19,259,349	60.5	18,476,301	58.5	3.4
Fixed Assets															
Land and improvements	1,310,513	3.6	1,778,819	5.6	1,636,749	5.2	1,636,749	5.2	1,632,299	4.9	1,571,552	4.9	1,684,106	5.3	4.2
Buildings and improvements	6,545,058	18.0	8,456,983	26.6	8,534,317	27.3	8,331,804	26.3	8,292,749	24.9	8,039,831	25.3	8,441,035	26.7	0.7
Production equipment and other	36,933,750	101.7	36,679,114	115.5	36,239,971	116.0	36,408,746	114.8	35,568,876	107.0	34,571,389	108.7	36,442,610	115.4	0.4
Gross Fixed Assets	44,789,321	123.4	46,914,916	147.7	46,411,037	148.6	46,377,299	146.2	45,493,924	136.8	44,182,772	138.9	46,567,751	147.5	0.6
Accumulated depreciation and amortization	(33,481,667)	-92.2	(34,441,052)	-108.4	(33,260,153)	-106.5	(32,703,246)	-103.1	(32,235,778)	-97.0	(31,625,819)	-99.4	(33,468,150)	-106.0	2.6
Net Fixed Assets	11,307,654	31.2	12,473,864	39.3	13,150,884	42.1	13,674,053	43.1	13,258,146	39.9	12,556,953	39.5	13,099,600	41.5	-4.5
Total Assets	36,298,974	100.0	31,766,258	100.0	31,238,071	100.0	31,723,376	100.0	33,246,625	100.0	31,816,302	100.0	31,575,902	100.0	0.1
LIABILITIES & STOCKHOLDERS' EQUITY															
Current Liabilities															
Accounts payable	897,430	2.5	692,635	2.2	466,424	1.5	490,580	1.5	1,060,231	3.2	737,040	2.3	549,880	1.7	18.8
Accrued wages and salaries	838,030	2.3	509,332	1.6	482,008	1.5	629,972	2.0	701,434	2.1	674,316	2.1	540,437	1.7	-10.1
Other accrued expenses	411,519	1.1	366,418	1.2	322,968	1.0	349,069	1.1	475,973	1.4	495,132	1.6	346,152	1.1	2.5
Unearned revenue and customer deposits	175,330	0.5	302,424	1.0	249,498	0.8	152,644	0.5	328,154	1.0	312,775	1.0	234,855	0.7	40.8
Current interest-bearing debt	0	0.0	0	0.0	0	0.0	0	0.0	0	0.0	0	0.0	0	0.0	N/M
Federal and state income taxes	1,164,586	3.2	0	0.0	0	0.0	0	0.0	0	0.0	0	0.0	0	0.0	N/M
Total Current Liabilities	3,486,895	9.6	1,870,809	5.9	1,520,898	4.9	1,622,265	5.1	2,565,792	7.7	2,219,263	7.0	1,671,324	5.3	7.4
Interest-bearing debt, less current maturities	0	0.0	0	0.0	0	0.0	0	0.0	0	0.0	0	0.0	0	0.0	N/M
Deferred income taxes, net	900,084	2.5	926,084	2.9	1,011,084	3.2	943,084	3.0	921,084	2.8	737,084	2.3	960,084	3.0	-0.9
Total Liabilities	4,386,979	12.1	2,796,893	8.8	2,531,982	8.1	2,565,349	8.1	3,486,876	10.5	2,956,347	9.3	2,631,408	8.3	4.4

Stockholders' Equity

	$	%	$	%	$	%	$	%	$	%	$	%	$	%	%
Common stock	1,138,096	3.1	1,138,096	3.6	1,138,096	3.6	1,138,096	3.4	1,138,096	3.6	1,138,096	3.6	1,138,096	3.6	0.0
Additional paid-in capital	447,134	1.2	447,134	1.4	447,134	1.4	447,134	1.3	447,134	1.4	447,134	1.4	447,134	1.4	0.0
Retained earnings	34,248,863	94.4	31,306,233	98.6	31,042,957	99.4	31,494,895	99.3	32,096,617	96.5	31,196,823	98.1	31,281,362	99.1	-0.3
Less: Treasury stock, 171,964 shares at cost	(3,922,098)	-10.8	(3,922,098)	-12.3	(3,922,098)	-12.6	(3,922,098)	-12.4	(3,922,098)	-11.8	(3,922,098)	-12.3	(3,922,098)	-12.4	0.0
Total Stockholders' Equity	31,911,995	87.9	28,969,365	91.2	28,706,089	91.9	29,158,027	91.9	29,759,749	89.5	28,859,955	90.7	28,944,494	91.7	-0.3
Total Liabilities & Stockholders' Equity	36,298,974	100.0	31,766,258	100.0	31,238,071	100.0	31,723,376	100.0	33,246,625	100.0	31,816,302	100.0	31,575,902	100.0	0.1
Net Working Capital	21,504,425	59.2	17,421,585	54.8	16,566,289	53.0	16,427,058	51.8	17,422,687	52.4	17,040,086	53.6	16,804,977	53.2	3.0
Net Working Capital excluding Cash & CDs	13,434,693	37.0	12,643,631	39.8	9,265,558	29.7	8,423,604	26.6	9,652,814	29.0	8,077,517	25.4	10,110,931	32.0	22.5
Debt-Free Net Working Capital	21,504,425	59.2	17,421,585	54.8	16,566,289	53.0	16,427,058	51.8	17,422,687	52.4	17,040,086	53.6	16,804,977	53.2	3.0
Debt-Free Cash-Free Net Working Capital excluding Cash & CDs	13,434,693	37.0	12,643,631	39.8	9,265,558	29.7	8,423,604	26.6	9,652,814	29.0	8,077,517	25.4	10,110,931	32.0	22.5
Total Interest-Bearing Debt	0	0.0	0	0.0	0	0.0	0	0.0	0	0.0	0	0.0	0	0.0	N/M

Note:
(1) Source: Audited financial statements for the years ended December 31, 2017 through 2021, internal financial statements for the eleven months ended November 30, 2022 and 2021.

EXHIBIT 1.5 Adjusted Comparative Income Statement

Nova Fastener & Tool, Inc.
Adjusted Comparative Income Statement
Valuation Date: December 1, 2022

	Note	Trailing 12 Months November 30, 2022 $	%	2021 $	%	2020 $	%	Years Ended December 31, 2019 $	%	2018 $	%	2017 $	%	Three-Year Average 2019 to 2021 $	%	Growth Rates '19-'21 %
Net Revenues		34,538,367	100.0	33,974,558	100.0	27,590,653	100.0	32,873,002	100.0	37,174,249	100.0	35,764,714	100.0	31,479,404	100.0	1.7
Total Cost of Goods Sold (except D&A)	(1)	27,560,603	79.8	26,190,912	77.1	21,328,146	77.3	25,746,237	78.3	27,960,042	75.2	26,619,446	74.4	24,421,765	77.6	0.9
Depreciation & Amortization		1,287,710	3.7	1,318,554	3.9	1,347,305	4.9	1,382,235	4.2	1,308,448	3.5	1,231,546	3.4	1,349,365	4.3	-2.3
Total Operating Expenses		4,979,152	14.4	5,106,177	15.0	4,998,216	18.1	5,252,946	16.0	5,503,111	14.8	5,548,541	15.5	5,119,113	16.3	-1.4
Net Operating Profit (Loss)		710,902	2.1	1,358,915	4.0	(83,014)	-0.3	491,584	1.5	2,402,648	6.5	2,365,181	6.6	589,162	1.9	66.3
Total Other Expense (Income)		(4,785,553)	-13.9	(55,557)	-0.2	(148,464)	-0.5	(191,730)	-0.6	(153,537)	-0.4	(100,901)	-0.3	(131,917)	-0.4	-46.2
Income (Loss) Before Income Taxes		5,496,455	15.9	1,414,472	4.2	65,450	0.2	683,314	2.1	2,556,185	6.9	2,466,082	6.9	721,079	2.3	43.9
Adjustments:																
(Gain) / Loss on sale of equipment, facilities	(2)	(4,738,394)	-13.7	21,564	0.1	0	0.0	228	0.0	13,086	0.0	(1,700)	0.0	7,264	0.0	872.5
Interest income	(3)	(10,537)	0.0	(15,877)	0.0	(71,926)	-0.3	(59,275)	-0.2	(39,475)	-0.1	(23,163)	-0.1	(49,026)	-0.2	-48.2
Total Adjustments		(4,748,931)	-13.7	5,687	0.0	(71,926)	-0.3	(59,047)	-0.2	(26,389)	-0.1	(24,863)	-0.1	(41,762)	-0.1	N/M
Adjusted Income Before Taxes		747,524	2.2	1,420,159	4.2	(6,476)	-0.3	624,267	1.9	2,529,796	6.8	2,441,219	6.8	679,317	2.2	50.8
Estimated Income Tax	(4)	167,961	0.5	302,210	0.9	(1,484)	0.0	132,470	0.4	549,270	1.5	537,068	1.5	144,399	0.5	51.0
Adjusted Net Income		579,562	1.7	1,117,949	3.3	(4,991)	0.0	491,797	1.5	1,980,525	5.3	1,904,151	5.3	534,918	1.7	50.8
Adjusted Debt-Free Net Income		579,562	1.7	1,117,949	3.3	(4,991)	0.0	491,797	1.5	1,980,525	5.3	1,904,151	5.3	534,918	1.7	50.8
Adj Earnings Before Interest & Taxes (Adj. EBIT)		747,524	2.2	1,420,159	4.2	(6,476)	0.0	624,267	1.9	2,529,796	6.8	2,441,219	6.8	679,317	2.2	50.8
Adj Earn Bef Int, Taxes, Depr & Amort (Adj. EBITDA)		2,035,234	5.9	2,738,713	8.1	1,340,829	4.9	2,006,502	6.1	3,838,244	10.3	3,672,765	10.3	2,028,682	6.4	16.8
Interest expense		0	0.0	0	0.0	0	0.0	0	0.0	0	0.0	0	0.0	0	0.0	N/M
Depreciation & Amortization		1,287,710	3.7	1,318,554	3.9	1,347,305	4.9	1,382,235	4.2	1,308,448	3.5	1,231,546	3.4	1,349,365	4.3	-2.3
Estimated Tax Rate	(4)	22.5%		21.3%		22.9%		21.2%		21.7%		22.0%		21.3%		

Notes:

(1) Excludes depreciation and amortization expense.

(2) Sales of equipment used in the fastener segment and, in the trailing twelve months, of a company warehouse.

(3) Interest income has been adjusted downward due to the presence of excess debt-free working capital, which is added back as a non-operating asset. As shown on Exhibit 1.9, the estimated normal level of debt-free working capital is 40.0% of revenue. This figure is used to estimate the normal amount of debt-free working capital each year, which is then subtracted from actual to estimate the excess. To calculate the interest income adjustments, these excess working capital amounts are multiplied by each year's implicit effective rate of interest income earned on the Company's combined balance of cash and certificates of deposit.

Effective rate of interest income earned	0.14%	0.41%	1.30%	1.81%	1.55%	0.85%
Ending actual debt-free working capital	21,504,425	17,421,585	16,566,289	16,427,058	17,422,687	17,040,086
Normalized debt-free working capital	13,815,347	13,589,823	11,036,261	13,149,201	14,869,700	14,305,886
Excess debt-free working capital estimate	7,689,078	3,831,762	5,530,028	3,277,857	2,552,987	2,734,200
Estimated interest adjustment	10,537	15,877	71,926	59,275	39,475	23,163

(4) The Company's actual historical tax rates have been imputed to adjusted income before tax as long as they fall between 20.0% and 30.0%. Outside this range, an effective combined tax rate of 22.0% is used, per management's estimate.

EXHIBIT 1.6 Adjusted Ratio Analysis

Nova Fastener & Tool, Inc.
Adjusted Ratio Analysis Valuation
Date: December 1, 2022

	AT November 30, 2022	2021	2020	2019	2018	2017	Average 2019 to 2021
				Years Ended December 31,			
Liquidity Ratios (3)							
Current Ratio	7.17	10.31	11.89	11.13	7.79	8.68	11.11
Debt-Free Current Ratio	7.17	10.31	11.89	11.13	7.79	8.68	11.11
Quick Ratio	3.41	4.11	5.08	3.72	2.43	2.92	4.30
Debt-Free Quick Ratio	3.41	4.11	5.08	3.72	2.43	2.92	4.30
Leverage Ratios							
Debt (1) to Assets	0.00	0.00	0.00	0.00	0.00	0.00	0.00
Debt (1) to Equity	0.00	0.00	0.00	0.00	0.00	0.00	0.00
Debt (1) to Total Capital (2)	0.0%	0.0%	0.0%	0.0%	0.0%	0.0%	0.0%
Preferred Stock to Total Capital	0.0%	0.0%	0.0%	0.0%	0.0%	0.0%	0.0%
Stockholders' Equity to Total Capital (2)	100.0%	100.0%	100.0%	100.0%	100.0%	100.0%	100.0%
Interest Coverage	N/M	N/M	N/M	N/M	N/M	N/M	N/M
Asset Management Ratios							
Average Collection Period	65.94	57.28	63.76	55.52	52.57	53.60	58.85
Working Capital Turnover	1.61	1.95	1.67	2.00	2.13	2.10	1.87
Debt-Free Working Capital Turnover	1.61	1.95	1.67	2.00	2.13	2.10	1.87
Inventory Turnover	3.27	4.02	4.49	4.91	5.51	6.14	4.47
Fixed Asset Turnover	2.88	2.65	2.06	2.44	2.88	2.86	2.38
Total Asset Turnover	1.00	1.08	0.88	1.01	1.14	1.14	0.99
Accum Depr to Gross Fixed Assets	74.8%	73.4%	71.7%	70.5%	70.9%	71.6%	71.9%

Notes:
(1) Debt defined as Total Interest-Bearing Debt
(2) Capital defined as Total Interest-Bearing Debt + Total Stockholders' Equity + Total Preferred Stock

Profitability Ratios

Gross Profit Margin	16.5%	19.0%	17.8%	17.5%	21.3%	22.1%	18.1%
EBITDA Profit Margin	5.9%	8.1%	4.9%	6.1%	10.3%	10.3%	6.3%
EBIT Profit Margin	2.2%	4.2%	0.0%	1.9%	6.8%	6.8%	2.0%
Net Profit Margin	1.7%	3.3%	0.0%	1.5%	5.3%	5.3%	1.6%
Return on Equity	1.9%	3.9%	0.0%	1.7%	6.8%	6.7%	1.8%
Return on Assets	1.7%	3.5%	0.0%	1.5%	6.1%	6.0%	1.7%

Growth Rates (Year-to-Year and Compound Annual)

					CAGR 2019 to 2021
Revenues	23.1%	-16.1%	-11.6%	3.9%	1.7%
Gross Profit	31.5%	-14.4%	-27.3%	-0.1%	6.1%
Earnings Before Int., Taxes, Depr & Amort	104.3%	-33.2%	-47.7%	4.5%	16.8%
Earnings Before Interest & Taxes	N/M	-101.0%	-75.3%	3.6%	50.8%
Net Income	N/M	-101.0%	-75.2%	4.0%	50.8%
Total Assets	1.7%	-1.5%	-4.6%	4.5%	0.1%
Debt-Free Net Working Capital	5.2%	0.8%	-5.7%	2.2%	3.0%
Total Interest-Bearing Debt	N/M	N/M	N/M	N/M	N/M
Total Stockholders' Equity	0.9%	-1.5%	-2.0%	3.1%	-0.3%

> **EXERCISE 17**   Analysts typically spread five years of financial statements because:
>
> a. Revenue Ruling 59-60 requires five years.
> b. USPAP and SSVS require five years.
> c. An economic cycle is often captured in five years.
> d. Most business plans are based on five years of projections.

1.5.1 Summary

- Revenues and margins were highest in the first two years shown on Exhibit 1.3: 2017 and 2018.
- Management notes that in earlier years (not shown) margins were higher still.
- The Company's results for 2019 reflect the beginning of a cyclical downturn for the Company's products. Declining North American light vehicle production lowered 2019 demand by automotive customers, and the Company also saw sales to nonautomotive customers decline. Management indicates that the sales decline was the primary reason the Company's gross margin declined in 2019.
- In early 2020 the worldwide pandemic caused a further sharp reduction in revenue and held margins down.
- In late 2020 and early 2021 underlying demand drove some recovery in vehicle and other sales, and therefore in the Company's performance, but supply chain issues (e.g., computer chip shortages) and rising inflation limited unit growth in the second half of 2021 and into 2022. Gross margin thus recovered only partially in 2021, before declining again in the trailing 12 months due to these factors, and also to staffing shortages, resulting in less efficient production. There is thus no recent period that reflects only "normal," cyclical business conditions.
- Because management indicates that more recent data is most pertinent for Nova's business as of the valuation date, averages and rates of compound annual growth (CAGR) are presented for the latest three fiscal years, from December 31, 2019 to 2021.
- However, management also believes that a return to higher revenue and margin levels over time is expected and has projected such a return, as discussed later in this report.

1.5.2 Income Statement Analysis[34]

1.5.2.1 Net Revenues   Net revenues for the fiscal year ended December 31, 2021, were $34.0 million, 23.1 percent higher than the prior year. Revenue increased at a CAGR of only 1.7 percent, however, from fiscal 2019 to 2021. Revenue decreased at a CAGR of 1.3 percent from 2017 to 2021, reflecting the cyclical downturn and decline in auto production underway at the time the pandemic began. For the TTM ended December 1, 2022, net revenues increased to $34.5 million.

1.5.2.2 Gross Profit   The Company's gross profit margin declined from 22.1 percent of revenues in 2017 to 17.5 percent in 2019, before rebounding partially to 19.0

---

[34] This discussion is based on unadjusted income statement data. Adjustments are discussed later in this section of the report.

percent in 2021. The initial decline and partial recovery in gross margin were primarily the result of sales volume, but as the country began to emerge from the pandemic in 2021, supply chain disruptions, labor market shortages, and historically high inflation resulted in much higher costs. Pricing of raw material remains volatile and difficult to forecast.

Gross margin averaged 18.1 percent during the most recent three fiscal years and decreased to 16.5 percent for the TTM ended December 1, 2022. This compares to 22.1 percent and 21.3 percent in the first two years of the period studied. Gross profit increased at a CAGR of 6.1 percent from fiscal 2019 to 2021, to $6.5 million, though over the five-year period gross profit declined, and was $5.7 million for the TTM preceding December 1, 2022.

1.5.2.3 Selling, General, and Administrative Expenses   Selling, general, and administrative (SG&A) expenses increased as a percentage of revenues in 2019 and 2020, when they were 18.1 percent on depressed revenues, from a 2017 and 2018 level of about 15 percent. In 2021 operating expenses decreased to 15.0 percent of revenues, and for the TTM ended December 1, 2022, they were 15.1 percent. SG&A expenses averaged 16.3 percent of revenues in the most recent three fiscal years and declined at a −1.4 percent compound annual growth rate from fiscal 2019 to 2021.

1.5.2.4 Other Income and Expense   Other income and expense fluctuated between −0.2 percent of revenue and −0.6 percent of revenue during 2017 to 2021, and in most years included primarily interest income on certificates of deposit and gains on the sales of equipment. In the trailing 12 months, however, other income was 13.9 percent of revenue, due to the September 2022 sale of the office and warehouse facility in St. Louis, which produced a one-time gain on sale of $4.7 million.

1.5.2.5 Adjustments   As shown in Exhibit 1.5, adjustments were made to eliminate nonrecurring income and expense items from Nova's reported income before tax.
Adjustments included the following:

- The gains and losses on the sale of tooling equipment and for the sale of the Company's St. Louis facilities.
- Excess working capital was identified at Nova as of the valuation date. The value of excess working capital is added separately to the operating value of the equity of the Company. To avoid double-counting the value of this working capital, we have reduced interest income in each year by an amount equal to each year's effective interest rate earned times the amount of working capital in excess of the estimated normal working capital requirement.

1.5.2.6 Adjusted Income Before Taxes   Adjusted income before taxes for the year ended December 31, 2021, was $1.4 million or 4.2 percent of revenue, up considerably from the loss before tax of $6 thousand (0.0 percent of revenue) in the prior fiscal year. For the TTM ended December 1, 2022, adjusted income before taxes was $748 thousand or 2.2 percent of revenue.

1.5.2.7 Adjusted Net Income   Adjusted net income decreased from $1.9 million in 2017 to $1.1 million in 2021. However, over the most recent three years it increased at a 50.8 percent compound rate of growth, from $492 thousand in 2019. For the TTM ended December 1, 2022, adjusted net income decreased to $580 thousand. The

Company's effective tax rate remained relatively flat over most periods analyzed, except for 2017, when it was 15.7 percent. In all other periods it ranged from 21.2 percent (in 2019) to 22.9 percent (in 2020). It was 22.5 percent for the trailing 12 months ending December 1, 2022.

1.5.3 Balance Sheet Analysis

1.5.3.1 Working Capital Nova held current assets of $25.0 million as of December 1, 2022, composed primarily of inventory, accounts receivable, cash, and certificates of deposit. The increase from the December 31, 2021, level was primarily attributable to cash realized from the gain on sale of the Company's St. Louis facility.

Current assets grew from $18.0 million at December 31, 2019, to $19.3 million at December 31, 2021, increasing at a CAGR of 3.4 percent. This increase was due primarily to a decline in the Company's combined cash and certificate of deposit balances, from $8.0 million to $4.8 million, that was more than offset by increases in inventories and accounts receivable. Going back to 2017, there has been no growth in current assets through 2021, but during the fiscal years 2017 to 2021, the percent of total assets accounted for by certificates of deposit decreased from almost 25 percent to less than 9 percent, and that accounted for by inventory rose from just over 14 percent to almost 27 percent.

The Company's historically conservative position with respect to cash and investments helped it weather the pandemic. The Company did not require or obtain a PPP loan.

To meet customer requirements, the Company retains a significant level of inventory on hand. The amount of inventory has increased substantially over the last few years, from $5.0 million at December 31, 2019, to $8.5 million at December 31, 2021, a 31.2 percent CAGR. As of December 1, 2022, inventory stood at $9.9 million. Management indicates that the increase in inventory is due to higher prices for raw materials, accelerated purchases in anticipation of yet more price increases, and efforts to mitigate continuing shortages and difficulties caused by supply chain disruptions.

Accounts receivable terms are fairly long. Payments for raw materials are generally due on receipt of goods. As such, the Company maintains cash and the certificates of deposit to support working capital requirements.

Current liabilities (in most periods composed primarily of accounts payable and accrued wages and salaries) increased from December 31, 2019, to December 31, 2021, from $1.6 million to $1.9 million, a CAGR of 7.4 percent. As of December 1, 2022, current liabilities were $3.5 million, with the bulk of the increase attributable to accrued federal and state income taxes of $1.2 million.

EXERCISE 18 The main drawbacks of publicly available benchmark financial ratios are:

a. There are very few SIC codes.
b. They calculate the ratios incorrectly.
c. The companies that make up the data cannot be used to determine pricing ratios or capitalization rates.
d. The information is from public companies.

1.5.3.2 Total Assets   Total assets were flat during the fiscal years studied, standing at $31.8 million at December 31, 2017, and $31.8 million at December 31, 2021. Total assets were $36.3 million at December 1, 2022. The increase was primarily due to the cash arising from the gain on sale of the Company's St. Louis facility.

1.5.3.3 Interest-Bearing Debt   During the periods analyzed, Nova maintained no interest-bearing debt on its balance sheet, instead relying on working capital and internal cash to fund operations.

1.5.3.4 Total Liabilities   Total liabilities as of December 31, 2021, were $2.8 million, consisting of $1.9 million of current liabilities and $0.9 million of deferred income taxes. The level of total liabilities had increased slightly from the prior year, but decreased over the prior five years from $3.0 million at December 31, 2017. Total liabilities were $4.4 million as of December 1, 2022, with the bulk of the increase again attributable to accrued federal and state income taxes of $1.2 million.

1.5.3.5 Stockholders' Equity   The book value of stockholders' equity at December 31, 2021, was $29.0 million, or 91.2 percent of total assets, and was down slightly from $29.2 million as of December 31, 2019. On December 1, 2022, stockholders' equity was $31.9 million, and represented 87.9 percent of total assets.

1.6 PROJECTIONS

Management provided projections for the Company for the month ending December 31, 2022, and the years ending December 31, 2023, 2024, 2025, and 2026, which are presented in Exhibit 1.7.

- Management expects labor market shortages and supply chain disruptions, including the shortage of computer chips that limited auto production in 2021 and 2022, to ease in late 2023 but to limit growth in December 2022 and the first two or three quarters of 2023.
- Management's projections reflect higher revenue growth beginning in late 2023 and continuing into 2026, due to the expected easing of supply chain and labor issues and to the recent execution of a manufacturing agreement with a new customer.
- Cost of sales is difficult for management to project because of volatility in raw material pricing, but management assumed that cost of sales before depreciation and amortization expense will trend downward over the next several years as a percent of sales, from its record high of almost 80 percent as of the TTM ended December 1, 2022.
- Management assumed that operating expenses would grow to support future operations, but that due to the projected increase in sales volume operating expenses will decline slightly as a percentage of revenues throughout the projected period.
- Future capital expenditures to maintain the operating facilities were assumed to be approximately 3.5 percent of revenues.
- Management provided projected tax depreciation associated with existing assets and future purchases.

EXHIBIT 1.7 Management's Projections

Nova Fastener & Tool, Inc.
Comparative Income Statement
Valuation Date: December 1, 2022

Management's Assumptions for Projections

Year	Revenue Growth, Annual	% of Revenue		
		Cost of Goods (Excluding Depr. & Amort.)	SG&A*	EBITDA Margin
2022	2.0%	79.8%	14.3%	5.9%
2023	3.5%	78.4%	14.2%	7.4%
2024	12.0%	77.0%	14.1%	8.9%
2025	10.0%	75.6%	14.0%	10.4%
2026	8.0%	74.2%	13.9%	11.9%
2027	4.5%	72.8%	13.7%	13.5%

* SG&A is net of interest income and other income and expense

Capital expenditures as % of revenue: 3.5%

	December 2022 One-Month Budget		2023		2024		2025		2026	
Revenue	2,887,837	100.0	35,866,941	100.0	40,170,974	100.0	44,188,071	100.0	47,723,117	100.0
Growth			3.5%		12.0%		10.0%		8.0%	
Cost of Goods (excluding D&A)	2,304,494	79.8	28,119,682	78.4	30,931,650	77.0	33,406,182	75.6	35,410,553	74.2
Gross Profit	583,343	20.2	7,747,259	21.6	9,239,324	23.0	10,781,889	24.4	12,312,564	25.8
Operating Expenses	412,961	14.3	5,093,106	14.2	5,664,107	14.1	6,186,330	14.0	6,633,513	13.9
EBITDA	170,382	5.9	2,654,154	7.4	3,575,217	8.9	4,595,559	10.4	5,679,051	11.9
Adjustments:										
(Gain) loss on sale of assets	-	-	-	-	-	-	-	-	-	-
Interest income adjustment	-	-	-	-	-	-	-	-	-	-
EBITDA	170,382	5.9	2,654,154	7.4	3,575,217	8.9	4,595,559	10.4	5,679,051	11.9
Capital Expenditures	101,074	3.5	1,255,343	3.5	1,405,984	3.5	1,546,582	3.5	1,670,309	3.5
Depreciation, Tax	78,733	2.7	1,653,837	4.6	1,599,911	4.0	1,547,308	3.5	1,185,438	2.5

1.7 APPROACHES TO VALUE

Three approaches can be used to value an interest in an operating business such as Nova: the income approach, the market approach, and the cost or asset approach.[35]

1.7.1 Income Approach

Income (Income-Based) Approach—a general way of determining a value indication of a business, business ownership interest, security, or intangible asset using one or more methods that convert anticipated economic benefits into a present single amount. (2001)

Income Approach—a general manner of estimating the value of an asset, business, or investment using one or more methods that convert expected Economic Income into a present amount. (2022)

The application of the income approach establishes value by methods that discount or capitalize earnings and/or cash flow by a discount or capitalization rate that reflects market rate of return expectations, market conditions, and the relative risk of the investment. Generally, this can be accomplished by the capitalization of earnings or cash flow method and/or the discounted cash flow method.

1.7.2 Market Approach

Market (Market-Based) Approach—a general way of determining a value indication of a business, business ownership interest, security, or intangible asset by using one or more methods that compare the subject to similar businesses, business ownership interests, securities, or intangible assets that have been sold. (2001)

Market Approach—a general manner of estimating a value of an asset, business, or investment by using one or more Valuation Methods that compare the valuation subject to other assets, businesses, or investments that have been sold or for which price and other information is available. (2022)

Generally, this can be accomplished by a comparison to publicly traded guideline companies or by an analysis of actual transactions of similar businesses sold. It may also include an analysis of prior transactions in the company's stock, if any.

1.7.3 Asset or Cost Approach

Asset (Asset-Based) Approach—a general way of determining a value indication of a business, business ownership interest, or security using one or more methods based on the value of the assets net of liabilities. (2001)

Asset Approach—a general manner of estimating the value of a business using one or more methods based on a summation of the value of the assets, net of liabilities, where each has been valued using either the market,

---

[35] Definitions for the income, market, and asset/cost approaches are taken from the 2001 *International Glossary of Business Valuation Terms* and the 2022 *International Valuation Glossary–Business Valuation.*

income, or cost approach. Also known as asset-based approach. See also Cost Approach. (2022)

Cost Approach—a general way of determining a value indication of an individual asset by quantifying the amount of money required to replace the future service capability of that asset. (2001)

Cost Approach—a general manner of estimating the value of an asset, investment, or (in limited circumstances) a business using one or more methods that reflect the economic principle that a buyer will generally pay no more for an asset than the cost to obtain another asset of equal utility, whether by purchase or by construction. The approach considers the current replacement or reproduction cost and the physical deterioration and all other relevant forms of obsolescence. See also Asset Approach. (2022)

This approach can include the value of both tangible and intangible assets. However, this approach is often unnecessary in the valuation of a profitable operating company as a going concern, as the tangible and intangible assets are inherently included, in aggregate, in the market and income approaches to value.

EXERCISE 19   In what type of valuation setting is the excess cash flow method most often used?

a. ESOPs (employee stock ownership plans)
b. Estate tax
c. Dissenting rights
d. Marital dissolution

EXERCISE 20   On which Revenue Ruling is the excess cash flow method based?

a. Revenue Ruling 59-60
b. Revenue Ruling 83-120
c. Revenue Ruling 68-609
d. Revenue Ruling 77-287

1.7.4 Summary of the Valuation Approaches and Methods

In our valuation of Nova, we considered all three approaches to value. Under the income approach, we used the discounted cash flow method. We also considered, but rejected, the capitalized cash flow method (which is still presented herein for learning illustration only). Under the market approach, we prepared an analysis using the guideline public company method and the guideline company transactions method. We did not rely on the underlying asset approach for the valuation of Nova, as the business enterprise value exceeds the value of the underlying tangible and financial assets and captures the value of all intangible assets and goodwill. Nova is worth more as a going concern than in liquidation, whether orderly or forced. It is important to note that the expected cash flows of the business do not fully support all intangible assets and goodwill. We believe this is due to economic obsolescence, that is, the Company barely supports the value of the net tangible assets.

EXERCISE 21   All three approaches to value must be applied in all valuations.

  a. True
  b. False

1.8 INCOME APPROACH

The income approach estimates the fair market value of the Company based on the earnings, cash flow, and dividend-paying capacity of the Company. The approach evaluates the present worth of the future economic benefits that accrue to the investors in a business. These benefits are discounted to present value at a rate of return that is commensurate with the Company's risk. This present value determines the fair market value of a business.

We first analyzed the fair market value of the common equity of Nova as of December 1, 2022, and attempted to apply the capitalized cash flow method on an invested capital basis (i.e., by capitalizing after-tax cash flows prior to principal payments and interest expense). In the case of Nova, the resulting value is both an invested capital and equity value because there is no interest-bearing debt on its balance sheet as of the valuation date. We applied this method using data provided by management, economic and industry data, analysis of historical and anticipated trends, and discussion of the Company's future expectations with management. Because of the anticipated intermediate-term, higher growth rate of the Company, the application of this method undervalued the Company and was rejected (and is presented for learning illustration only).

We also prepared a discounted cash flow analysis relying on management's projections. A discussion of each of these methods is included in this report.

1.8.1 Capitalized Cash Flow Method (Learning Illustration Only)

The capitalized cash flow method values a business based on its ability to generate future cash flows. The method considers measures of normalized historical cash flow as indicators of expected future normal cash flow, along with future growth expectations. The capitalized cash flow to invested capital method as applied to Nova is summarized in Exhibit 1.8.

EXERCISE 22   Which method(s) is(are) considered valid under the income approach?

  a. Guideline public company method
  b. Discounted cash flow method
  c. Capitalized cash flow method
  d. Excess cash flow method

EXERCISE 23   In which situation(s) would a capitalized cash flow method be more applicable?

    a. When a company's future performance is anticipated to change from its prior performance
    b. In litigation settings
    c. When a single historical or pro forma amount of cash flow is anticipated to be earned with a constant growth in the future
    d. When valuing very small businesses

EXERCISE 24   List the two main bases when using the capitalized cash flow (CCF) or discounted cash flow (DCF) methods of the income approach.

    1. _____

    2. _____

1.8.1.1 Cash Flow to Invested Capital Adjustments   We considered whether adjustments were necessary to arrive at the normalized cash flow to invested capital of the Company. These adjustments fell into the following categories.

EXERCISE 25   Under the direct equity basis, what are the components of net cash flow?

_____

_____

_____

_____

EXERCISE 26 For the invested capital basis of the income approach, list the components of net cash flow.

_____

_____

_____

_____

EXHIBIT 1.8 Capitalized Cash Flow to Invested Capital Method (Illustration Only)

Nova Fastener & Tool, Inc.
Capitalized Cash Flow to Invested Capital Method
Valuation Date: December 1, 2022 $

Assumptions:

(1) WACC	13.0%
(2) Debt-Free Working Capital as a % of Revenues	40.0%
(3) Perpetuity Growth Rate	4.5%
(4) Capital Expenditures as % Revenue	3.5%
(4) Normal Tax Depreciation % of Capital Expenditures	100.0%

		Trailing Twelve Months	Most Recent Fiscal Year	Three-Year Average
Net Revenues		34,538,367	33,974,558	31,479,404
Growth Rate		1.045	1.045	1.045
Following Year's Net Revenues		36,092,594	35,503,413	32,895,978
Incremental Net Revenues		1,554,227	1,528,855	1,416,573
(2) Debt-Free Working Capital as a % of Revenues		40.00%	40.00%	40.00%
(2) Estimated Incremental Working Capital		621,691	611,542	566,629
Adjusted Income before Taxes		747,524	1,420,159	679,317
Add: Actual Book Depreciation		1,287,710	1,318,554	1,349,365
(4) Less: Normal Tax Depreciation		(1,208,843)	(1,189,110)	(1,101,779)
Adjusted Income before Taxes, w/Normal Tax Depreciation		826,391	1,549,604	926,902
Add: Interest Expense		-	-	-
Adjusted Income to Invested Capital Before Taxes		826,391	1,549,604	926,902
Less: Taxes @	22.0%	(181,806)	(340,913)	(203,919)
Adjusted Net Income to Invested Capital		644,585	1,208,691	722,984
Growth @	4.5%	1.045	1.045	1.045
Following Year's Net Income to Invested Capital		673,591	1,263,082	755,518
(4) Plus: Following Year's Normal Tax Depreciation		1,263,241	1,242,619	1,151,359
(4) Less: Following Year's Capital Expenditures		(1,263,241)	(1,242,619)	(1,151,359)
Less: Incremental Working Capital		(621,691)	(611,542)	(566,629)
Following Year's Normalized Cash Flow to Invested Capital		51,901	651,540	188,889
Capitalization Rate		8.50%	8.50%	8.50%
Indicated Value of 100% of the Business Enterprise		610,595	7,665,178	2,222,223
Adjustment for Mid-Year Convention		1.063	1.063	1.063
Indicated Value of 100% of the Business Enterprise		649,071	8,148,196	2,362,255
Less: Interest-Bearing Debt		-	-	-
Indicated Value of 100% of the Equity		649,071	8,148,196	2,362,255
Indicated Value of 100% of the Equity, Rounded		600,000	8,100,000	2,400,000
Preliminary Value of the Operating Equity			8,100,000	
(5) Working Capital Excess / (Deficit)			7,689,078	
Indicated Value of 100% of the Equity, Rounded			$ 15,800,000	

Notes:
(1) See Exhibit 1.18 for details.
(2) DFWC as % of revenues based on analysis of historical requirements of the Company and data for the industry. See Exhibit 1.9 for details.
(3) Long-term growth assumption based on analysis of industry and other factors, including inflation and GDP growth.
(4) Normal tax depreciation is assumed to be 100.0% of normal capital expenditures into perpetuity. This is a simplifying assumption, since depreciation is in historical dollars and capital expenditures are in current dollars. The actual relationship will be influenced by the level of in fixed assets' tax depreciation categories, and other factors. Normal capital expenditures were estimated by management at 3.5% of revenue.
(5) Based on the working capital assumption, the Company had excess working capital as of the valuation date:

Ending Debt-Free Working Capital at November 30, 2022	21,504,425
Normalized DFWC Based on Analysis (40.0% of Revenue)	(13,815,347)
Excess DFWC	7,689,078

EXHIBIT 1.9 Debt-Free Working Capital (DFWC)—Benchmark Data Analysis

Nova Fastener & Tool, Inc.
Debt-Free Working Capital (DFWC) Statistics
Benchmark Data Analysis (1)

| | | NAICS # 332722 | | |
| | | Bolt, Nut, Screw, Rivet, and Washer Manufacturing | | |
As a % of Total Assets	4/1/19 - 3/31/20 All	4/1/20 - 3/31/21 All	4/1/21 - 3/31/22 All	4/1/21 - 3/31/22 Sales > 25 MM
Current Assets	65.3%	64.4%	69.1%	64.9%
Less: Current Liabilities	27.7%	27.5%	26.2%	18.1%
Working Capital	37.6%	36.9%	42.9%	46.8%
Working Capital	37.6%	36.9%	42.9%	46.8%
Plus: Notes Payable - Short-Term	9.5%	8.0%	6.1%	5.1%
Plus: Current Mat. - Long-Term Debt	2.3%	2.3%	2.6%	0.7%
Debt-Free Working Capital (DFWC)	49.4%	47.2%	51.6%	52.6%
Debt-Free Working Capital	49.4%	47.2%	51.6%	52.6%
Times: Total Assets - $000	$ 1,599,109	$ 1,580,760	$ 1,189,956	$ 970,689
Debt-Free Working Capital - $000	$ 789,960	$ 746,119	$ 614,017	$ 510,582
Debt-Free Working Capital - $000	$ 789,960	$ 746,119	$ 614,017	$ 510,582
Divided by: Total Sales - $000	$ 2,394,832	$ 1,979,537	$ 1,553,946	$ 1,246,587
DFWC As a % of Sales	33.0%	37.7%	39.5%	41.0%

NAICS # 336390
Other Motor Vehicle Parts Manufacturing

As a % of Total Assets	4/1/19 - 3/31/20 All	4/1/20 - 3/31/21 All	4/1/21 - 3/31/22 All	4/1/21 - 3/31/22 Sales > 25 MM
Current Assets	59.7%	59.8%	65.7%	61.7%
Less: Current Liabilities	39.4%	39.3%	38.3%	42.9%
Working Capital	20.3%	20.5%	27.4%	18.8%
Working Capital	20.3%	20.5%	27.4%	18.8%
Plus: Notes Payable - Short-Term	8.5%	8.8%	7.2%	7.2%
Plus: Current Mat. - Long-Term Debt	4.0%	2.9%	3.1%	4.1%
Debt-Free Working Capital (DFWC)	32.8%	32.2%	37.7%	30.1%
Debt-Free Working Capital	32.8%	32.2%	37.7%	30.1%
Times: Total Assets - $000	$ 7,901,996	$ 5,529,225	$ 4,968,960	$ 4,656,823
Debt-Free Working Capital - $000	$ 2,591,855	$ 1,780,410	$ 1,873,298	$ 1,401,704
Debt-Free Working Capital - $000	$ 2,591,855	$ 1,780,410	$ 1,873,298	$ 1,401,704
Divided by: Total Sales - $000	$ 13,735,300	$ 8,687,157	$ 7,206,974	$ 6,696,087
DFWC As a % of Sales	18.9%	20.5%	26.0%	20.9%

Nova Fastener & Tool, Inc.
Debt-Free Working Capital (DFWC) Statistics
Benchmark Data Analysis

	Subject Company DFWC Turns	DFWC as a % of Revenues	Guideline Public Company DFWC Turns Median	Guideline Public Company DFWC as a % of Revenues (1)
Three-Year Average	1.87	53.4%	2.57	39.0%
Most Recent Fiscal Year	1.95	51.3%	2.58	38.8%
Trailing Twelve Months	1.61	62.3%	2.60	38.4%
Concluded Debt-Free Working Capital Requirements		40.0%		

Notes:
(1) Source: Benchmark data publication.
(2) See Exhibit 1.10 for more information.

EXERCISE 27 What is the difference between minority cash flows and control cash flows?

_____

_____

_____

_____

EXERCISE 28 Which adjustment(s) are made when valuing both minority and control cash flows?

a. Nonrecurring items
b. Nonoperating assets
c. Excess compensation
d. Perquisites
e. Taxes

EXERCISE 29 Assume the company does not have any control adjustments and the company is run to the benefit of all shareholders without any shareholders taking out cash flow over or above what they are entitled. Is this value control or minority?

_____

_____

_____

_____

1.8.1.2 Adjustments for Nonoperating Assets

EXERCISE 30 List some of the nonoperating/excess assets that are sometimes encountered in a business valuation.

_____

_____

_____

_____

EXERCISE 31 In valuing a controlling interest in a corporation, most analysts agree that the nonoperating and/or excess assets of the business must be removed from the cash flows and valuation of the operating business and then be added back at fair market value.

  a. True
  b. False

EXERCISE 32 In valuing a minority interest of a company, most analysts agree that the nonoperating and/or excess assets of the business must be removed from the cash flows and valuation of the operating business and then be added back at fair market value.

  a. True
  b. False

If any cash flows related to nonoperating assets are included in projected cash flows, they may need to be removed. This adjustment is necessary when the value of nonoperating assets (such as nonoperating real property or securities) is calculated separately in the determination of business enterprise value. In these instances, the potential for double counting exists if an adjustment is not made to projected operating cash flows. Based on an analysis of the industry, guideline companies, and discussions with management, Nova has excess working capital as of the valuation date. This excess working capital is considered a nonoperating asset.

Industry data indicates that normal debt-free working capital requirements for Nova are 40.0 percent of revenue. See Exhibits 1.9 and 1.10 for an analysis of working capital requirements. This assumption was corroborated by management of the Company, which has traditionally maintained excess liquidity and avoided the use of debt. Based on this requirement, as of December 1, 2022, the Company held $7,689,078 in excess working capital as calculated on Exhibit 1.12.

Excess working capital was added to the operating value of Nova when computing the value of the equity under the capitalized cash flow method (Exhibit 1.8) and the discounted cash flow method (Exhibit 1.11).

For consistency, historical income was adjusted to exclude interest income in excess of (i) each year's effective interest rate times (ii) excess debt-free working capital in order to avoid double counting the value of the excess working capital (Exhibit 1.5).

EXHIBIT 1.10 Debt-Free Working Capital (DFWC) Statistics

Nova Fastener & Tool, Inc.
Debt-Free Working Capital (DFWC) Statistics
Guideline Public Company Analysis (1)
(As % of Revenue)

							Guideline Companies	
	Nova	EML	PFIN	SCX	TWIN	VC	Average	Median
TTM								
Working Capital	62.3%	33.6%	37.3%	36.3%	47.8%	17.7%	34.5%	36.3%
Debt-Free Working Capital	62.3%	36.6%	50.9%	38.4%	48.8%	17.9%	38.5%	38.4%
Most Recent Fiscal Year (MRFY)								
Working Capital	51.3%	30.1%	45.9%	36.2%	50.8%	20.6%	36.7%	36.2%
Debt-Free Working Capital	51.3%	33.1%	56.7%	38.8%	51.8%	20.8%	40.2%	38.8%
MRFY - 1 Year								
Working Capital	60.0%	36.0%	43.3%	30.7%	51.9%	20.3%	36.4%	36.0%
Debt-Free Working Capital	60.0%	39.2%	50.1%	38.0%	53.0%	20.3%	40.1%	39.2%
MRFY - 2 Year								
Working Capital	50.0%	32.2%	37.7%	37.9%	43.4%	18.6%	34.0%	37.7%
Debt-Free Working Capital	50.0%	34.3%	47.3%	40.1%	45.4%	19.8%	37.4%	40.1%

Note:
(1) Underlying financial data for computing working capital and debt-free working capital as percentages of revenue can be found in Exhibit 1.21.
Source: Guideline Public Company Analysis

EXHIBIT 1.11 Discounted Cash Flow to Invested Capital Method

Nova Fastener & Tool, Inc.
Discounted Cash Flow to Invested Capital Method (1)
Valuation Date: December 1, 2022

Assumptions

WACC (2)	13.0%	Perpetuity Growth Rate (3)	4.5%	Capitalization Rate (5)	8.5%
		DFWC as a % of Revenue (4)	40.0%	Tax Rate (6)	22.0%

($ in thousands)

Years Ended December 31,

	2021		2022		2023		2024		2025		2026		Terminal Year	
						Projected								
	$	%	$	%	$	%	$	%	$	%	$	%	$	%
Revenues														
Net Revenues	33,974,558	100.0	2,887,837	100.0	35,866,941	100.0	40,170,974	100.0	44,188,071	100.0	47,723,117	100.0	49,870,657	100.0
Growth Rate (Year Over Year)						3.5%		12.0%		10.0%		8.0%		4.5%
Earnings Before Interest and Tax, Depreciation and Amortization	2,738,713	8.1	170,382	5.9	2,654,154	7.4	3,575,217	8.9	4,595,559	10.4	5,679,051	11.9	6,732,539	13.5
Less: Tax Depreciation and Amortization			(78,733)	(2.7)	(1,653,837)	(4.6)	(1,599,911)	(4.0)	(1,547,308)	(3.5)	(1,185,438)	(2.5)	(1,745,473)	(3.5)
Earnings to Invested Capital Before Tax / EBIT			91,649	3.2	1,000,316	2.8	1,975,305	4.9	3,048,251	6.9	4,493,613	9.4	4,987,066	10.0
(6) Estimated Income Tax			20,163	0.7	220,070	0.6	434,567	0.6	670,615	1.5	988,595	2.1	1,097,154	2.2
Adjusted Net Income to Invested Capital			71,486	2.5	780,247	2.2	1,540,738	3.8	2,377,636	5.4	3,505,018	7.3	3,889,911	7.8
(4) Less: Incremental Debt-Free Working Capital			(46,273)	(1.6)	(485,157)	(1.4)	(1,721,613)	(4.3)	(1,606,839)	(3.6)	(1,414,018)	(3.0)	(859,016)	(1.7)
(7) Plus: Tax Depreciation and Amortization			78,733	2.7	1,653,837	4.6	1,599,911	4.0	1,547,308	3.5	1,185,438	2.5	1,745,473	3.5
(7) Less: Capital Expenditures			(101,074)	(3.5)	(1,255,343)	(3.5)	(1,405,984)	(3.5)	(1,546,582)	(3.5)	(1,670,309)	(3.5)	(1,745,473)	(3.5)
Cash Flow to Invested Capital			2,872	0.1	693,584	1.9	13,052	1.9	771,523	1.7	1,606,129	3.4	3,030,895	6.1
(8) Terminal Value													35,657,590	
Cash Flow to Invested Capital			2,872.5		693,584.4		13,052.2		771,522.7		1,606,128.7			
Period			0.04		0.58		1.58		2.58		3.58		3.58	

(continued)

EXHIBIT 1.11 (continued)

($ in thousands)

		Years Ended December 31,				Terminal Year
		Projected				
Discount Factors	0.9950	0.9313	0.8242	0.7294	0.6455	0.6455
Present Value of Cash Flows to Invested Capital	2,858.1	645,947.9	10,757.3	562,717.0	1,036,676.3	23,015,203.7

Present Value Through 2026	2,258,957
Terminal Value	23,015,204
Present Value of Invested Capital	25,274,160
(9) Plus: Excess Debt-Free Working Capital	7,689,078
(10) Plus: Present Value of Depreciation Overhang	(362,052)
Less: Interest-Bearing Debt	-
Indicated Value of 100% of the Equity	32,601,187
SAY	32,600,000

Notes:

(1) Projections provided by management. Projection for 2022 is for month of December only. See Exhibit 1.7 for additional detail.

(2) See Exhibit 1.18 for calculation of the weighted average cost of capital.

(3) The long-term growth rate reflects industry and other factors, including expected inflation and GDP growth.

(4) Debt-free working capital (DFWC) requirements are based on analysis of historical requirements and analysis of the industry. See Exhibit 1.9 for normalized DFWC requirements, and Exhibit 1.12 for calculation of the incremental DFWC amounts used in this discounted cash flow analysis.

(5) The capitalization rate equals the discount rate less the long-term growth rate.

(6) Based on projected combined state and federal tax rate per management.

(7) Depreciation expense and capital expenditures are per client projections. See Exhibit 1.7 for detail. Depreciation is set equal to capital expenditures in the long term as a simplifying assumption. The actual long-term relationship between deprecation and capital expenditures will be influenced by the level of inflation and the mix of the class lives of the Company's fixed assets for tax purposes.

(8) To compute the terminal value, the terminal year cash flow is divided by the capitalization rate.

(9) See Exhibit 1.12 for calculation of excess DFWC.

(10) In the terminal year tax depreciation is set equal to an estimated long-term level of 100% of capital expenditures. The overhang adjustement represents the tax benefit or cost anticipated from projected differences in this long-term level of depreciation, which must be used in the terminal value calculation, and the actual projected tax depreciation from the terminal year forward over the next few years following it. The occurrence of a negative depreciation "overhang" is due in part to the sunset of 100% bonus depreciation. See Exhibit 1.13 for calculation and additional information.

EXHIBIT 1.12 Discounted Cash Flow Method: Calculation of Incremental Debt-Free Working Capital

Nova Fastener & Tool, Inc.
Discounted Cash Flow Method
Calculation of Incremental Debt-Free Working Capital (DFWC)
Valuation Date: December 1, 2022

	12 Months Ended 11/30/2022	Running Rate December 2022	2023	2024	2025	2026	Terminal Year
				Years Ended December 31,			
Revenue	34,538,367	34,654,049	35,866,941	40,170,974	44,188,071	47,723,117	49,870,657
Growth			3.5%	12.0%	10.0%	8.0%	4.5%
Normal DFWC as % of Net Revenues	40.0%	40.0%	40.0%	40.0%	40.0%	40.0%	40.0%
Normal DFWC	13,815,347	13,861,620	14,346,776	16,068,390	17,675,228	19,089,247	19,948,263
Incremental DFWC		46,273	485,157	1,721,613	1,606,839	1,414,018	859,016
Actual DFWC at 11/30/2022	21,504,425						
Less: Normal DFWC at 11/30/2022	13,815,347						
Excess (Deficient) DFWC at 11/30/2022	7,689,078						

EXHIBIT 1.13 Discounted Cash Flow Method: Calculation of Depreciation Overhang

Nova Fastener & Tool, Inc.
Discounted Cash Flow Method
Calculation of Depreciation Overhang
Valuation Date: December 1, 2022
000s $

	Years Ending December 31,					
	2027	2028	2029	2030	2031	2032
Projected Depreciation, Tax (1)	823,872	1,090,931	1,305,704	1,485,998	1,639,967	1,771,346
Depreciation Embedded in Terminal Year Calculation	1,745,473	1,824,019	1,906,100	1,991,875	2,081,509	2,175,177
Projected Depreciation Less Embedded Depreciation	(921,601)	(733,089)	(600,396)	(505,877)	(441,542)	(403,831)
Tax Benefit (Cost) @ Tax Rate of 22.0%	(202,752)	(161,280)	(132,087)	(111,293)	(97,139)	(88,843)
PV Period	4.58	5.58	6.58	7.58	8.58	9.58
PV Factor	0.5712	0.5055	0.4473	0.3959	0.3503	0.3100
Present Value of Tax Benefit (Cost)	(115,811)	(81,524)	(59,086)	(44,057)	(34,030)	(27,543)
Sum of PV of Depreciation Overhang	(362,052)					

Notes:
(1) From management's projections.
(2) The occurrence of a negative depreciation overhang is due in part to the sunset of 100% bonus depreciation. The existence and sunset of bonus depreciation will create a period during which capital expenditures must be capitalized but there are few existing assets with tax basis to depreciate.

1.8.1.3 Adjustments for Financial (Invested Capital) Cash Flow Financial cash flows include the sources and uses of cash related to interest-bearing debt. To accurately calculate the value of operating cash flows (or the business independent of its financing policies), financial cash flows must be removed from the projections. Because there is no interest-bearing debt on the balance sheet as of the valuation date, there was no need to exclude interest expense from each year's projected results.

1.8.1.4 Adjustments for Incremental Investment in Working Capital As the revenues of a business increase, its working capital typically grows. Because the increase in working capital represents additional investment that is not incorporated into the income statement, an adjustment is necessary to reflect its impact on cash flow. Likewise, if sales are projected to decline, an adjustment is necessary to reflect the decreased investment in working capital. Based on an analysis of the historical working capital requirements of the Company, discussions with management, and an analysis of industry benchmark data, we calculated incremental debt-free working capital requirements assuming a working capital requirement of 40.0 percent of revenues (incremental working capital requirements were calculated on a debt-free basis).

This estimate of normal required working capital was also used to estimate the amount of excess working capital present on the Company's balance sheet as of December 1, 2022.

1.8.1.5 Adjustments for Growth A long-term perpetuity growth rate of 4.5 percent was applied to Nova. This reflects the Company's anticipated long-term growth considering the nominal (inflation and real GDP) growth of the United States economy, industry data, the Company's performance and outlook, and discussions with management.

1.8.1.6 Adjustments for Capital Expenditures and Depreciation To accurately reflect investment in operations, the effect of future expansion and upkeep of the facility should be included in expected cash flows. Also, any noncash reduction in cash flows such as depreciation and/or amortization should be added back to operating cash flows. In order to determine operating cash flows, we have subtracted capital expenditures from net income (before interest and after tax) and added back total depreciation. We have assumed that expectations regarding these items are offsetting at their historical levels, as they have been relatively stable historically. This is a simplifying assumption because there may be some difference between capital expenditures, which are purchased in current dollars, and depreciation, which is in historical dollars. Again, the Company's historical performance supports this assumption of offsetting capital expenditures and depreciation.

1.8.1.7 The Gordon Growth Model We used the widely accepted Gordon Growth Model to determine the value of the continuing operations of Nova into perpetuity.

The Gordon growth or perpetuity model can be defined as follows:[36]

$$\text{Terminal Value} = \frac{\text{Free Cash Flow}}{(\text{Cost of Capital} - \text{Growth Rate})}$$

Free Cash Flow = The normalized level of free cash flow in the
first year after the explicit projected period

We applied the Gordon Growth Model on an invested capital basis. Issues that were addressed in this calculation included the proper growth rate in light of economic, industry, and company expectations and the reserve for replacement and depreciation.

1.8.1.8 Conclusion We considered indications of value based on Nova's trailing 12 months, most recent, and three-year average cash flow to invested capital, capitalized at an 8.5 percent capitalization rate. This capitalization rate is equal to the cost of capital of 13.0 percent (discussed in Section 1.9) less the long-term growth rate of 4.5 percent.

EXERCISE 33 In the valuation of Nova, one of the periods that the analyst decided to use was a straight average of the adjusted income before income taxes for three historical years. Besides a straight average, what other method(s) can be used to determine the appropriate cash flow to be capitalized into perpetuity?

a. Weighted average
b. Most recent fiscal year
c. Most recent trailing 12 months
d. Trend line analysis/next year's budget
e. DCF average of next three years

---

[36] In the DCF method it is referred to as the terminal year value. In the CCF method it is the expected value as of the valuation date.

EXERCISE 34 Analysts will generally use a straight historical average where the earnings and cash flows are more volatile.

  a. True
  b. False

We adjusted the resulting preliminary indications of the value of the Company's invested capital for estimated excess debt-free working capital. See Exhibit 1.8.

Based on the capitalized cash flow method, the indicated value of 100 percent of the equity of Nova as of December 1, 2022, was $15,800,000. See Exhibit 1.8.

EXERCISE 35 Which situation is most appropriate when adjusting cash flows for depreciation and capital expenditures?

  a. Capital expenditures should be similar to or exceed depreciation.
  b. Depreciation should exceed capital expenditures.
  c. The actual unadjusted amounts should be capitalized.

EXERCISE 36 Assuming taxes are to be deducted, what two choices may be made in making the tax adjustments?

  a. Tax each year historically, then calculate an average.
  b. Taxes should never be deducted in the value of an S corporation.
  c. Make all adjustments in the historical period pre-tax, determine the average, then deduct for taxes.

EXERCISE 37 Which economic benefit stream(s) can be used for cash flow in a capitalized cash flow method?

  a. After-tax income
  b. Pre-tax income
  c. Net cash flow
  d. EBITDA (earnings before interest, taxes, depreciation, and amortization)
  e. Revenues
  f. Debt-free net income
  g. Debt-free cash flow

1.8.2 Discounted Cash Flow Method

EXERCISE 38 When is it more appropriate to use a discounted cash flow method instead of a capitalized cash flow method?

_____

_____

_____

_____

Management provided projections for the Company for the month ending December 31, 2022, and the years ending December 31, 2023, through 2026, as presented in Exhibit 1.7. These projections reflect expected revenue growth and margin improvement associated with the anticipated easing of supply chain issues and labor shortages, new investments, and a recently executed manufacturing contract with a new customer. With planned capital investments, production capacity and efficiency are such that the facilities can support such growth in production.

The discounted cash flow analysis relying on management's projections is presented in Exhibit 1.11. The analysis relied on a WACC of 13 percent and perpetuity growth rate of 4.5 percent. Incremental and excess debt-free working capital were calculated based on a requirement of debt-free working capital as a percent of revenues of 40 percent. Management estimated their tax rate to be 22 percent. Nova uses a variety of strategies to minimize its tax burden and expects to be able to continue to do so in the future.

Adjusted cash flow to invested capital was calculated for each year of the projections and for the terminal year based on subtracting the incremental debt-free working capital requirements (see Exhibit 1.12 for calculation) and capital expenditures and adding back depreciation and amortization. We used a mid-year convention to reflect the fact that earnings and cash flow come in throughout the year. In the terminal year, depreciation and amortization were set equal to capital expenditures. Based on management's projected tax depreciation, tax depreciation will be below capital expenditures for several years beyond the discrete projection period. The deficiency of actual projected depreciation expense as compared to the level of normalized depreciation expense embedded in the terminal year will result in extra tax costs for a few years beyond the discrete projection period, which are not captured in the terminal value. Instead of a depreciation "overhang," there is a depreciation "underhang." This previously unusual situation is a result of the pending sunset of the 100 percent bonus depreciation provided for in the Tax Cuts and Jobs Act. This sunset will create a period during which capital expenditures must be capitalized, but there are few existing assets with tax basis to depreciate.

The value of the negative depreciation overhang was captured by calculating the present value of the additional tax costs for the years beyond the discrete projection, as illustrated in Exhibit 1.13. The calculation relies on the same WACC used in the discounted cash flow analysis. Based on the calculation, the present value is ($362,052), which is adjusted from the operating value of the Company in the discounted cash flow analysis.

EXERCISE 39 In the terminal year of a discounted cash flow analysis, analysts often use the simplifying assumption that depreciation equals capital expenditures.

a. True
b. False

The excess debt-free working capital of $7,689,078 is also added to the operating value of the Company.

The concluded value of the Company based on the discounted cash flow method is $32,600,000. See Exhibit 1.11 for the discounted cash flow analysis.

1.9 COST OF CAPITAL

The formula for determining the weighted average cost of capital (WACC) is

$$WACC = \left(k_e \times W_e\right) + \left(k_p \times W_p\right) + \left(k_{d/(pt)}[1-t] \times W_d\right)$$

where
  WACC = Weighted average cost of capital
   k_e = Cost of common equity capital
   W_e = Percentage of common equity in the capital structure, at market value
   k_p = Cost of preferred equity
   W_p = Percentage of preferred equity in the capital structure, at market value
   $k_{d/(pt)}$ = Cost of debt (pre-tax)
   t = Tax rate
   W_d = Percentage of debt in the capital structure, at market value

EXERCISE 40 When using the direct equity basis instead of the invested capital basis, assumptions of capital structure can be avoided.

a. True
b. False

EXERCISE 41 When using the invested capital basis to determine a control value, the analyst should always use an optimal capital structure in the weighted average cost of capital.

a. True
b. False

1.9.1 Cost of Equity

As shown in Exhibit 1.14, we used two widely accepted methods to estimate the cost of equity applicable to Nova: the build-up model and the modified capital asset pricing model (modified CAPM or MCAPM). The concluded cost of equity is 18.00 percent as of December 1, 2022.[37]

1.9.1.1 Modified CAPM   The modified CAPM can be summarized as follows:

$$E(R_i) = R_f + \beta \times (RP_m) + RP_s \pm RP_c$$

where

$E(R_i)$ = Expected rate of return on the security i
R_f = Rate of return available on a risk-free security as of the valuation date
β = Beta
RP_m = Equity risk premium (market risk)
RP_s = Risk premium for small size
RP_c = Risk premium attributable to other company risk factors (company-specific risk)

1.9.1.2 Build-Up Model   The build-up method can be summarized as follows:

$$E(R_i) = R_f + RP_m + RP_s \pm RP_i \pm RP_c$$

where

$E(R_i)$ = Expected rate of return on security i
R_f = Rate of return available on a risk-free security as of the valuation date
RP_m = Equity risk premium (market risk)
RP_s = Risk premium for small size
RP_i = Industry risk premium
RP_c = Risk premium attributable to other company risk factors (company-specific risk)

EXERCISE 42   Name the two methods most often used to derive a cost of equity in the income approach.

1. _____

2. _____

EXERCISE 43 Should the build-up method and MCAPM rates of return be applied to income or cash flow?

_____

_____

_____

_____

---

[37] Notation system based on Shannon P. Pratt and Roger J. Grabowski, *Cost of Capital Applications and Examples*, 5th ed. (John Wiley & Sons, 2014).

EXHIBIT 1.14   Cost of Equity

Nova Fastener & Tool, Inc.
Cost of Equity
Valuation Date: December 1, 2022

Build-Up Method, Cost of Equity: $K_e = R_f + RP_m + RP_s + RP_i + RP_c$

	Historical	Supply Side
(1) Risk-Free Rate (R_f)	3.85%	3.85%
(2) Market Premium (RP_m)	7.46%	6.22%
(3) Size Premium (RP_s)	4.80%	4.80%
(4) Industry Risk Premium (RP_i)	0.00%	0.00%
(5) Company-Specific Risk Premium (RP_c)	2.00%	2.00%
$K_e =$	18.11%	16.87%

MCAPM Method, Cost of Equity: $K_e = R_f + (\beta \times RP_m) + RP_s + RP_c$

	Historical	Supply Side
(1) Risk-Free Rate (R_f)	3.85%	3.85%
(6) Beta (β)	1.14	1.14
(2) Equity Risk Premium (RP_m)	7.46%	6.22%
(3) Size Premium (RP_s)	4.80%	4.80%
(5) Company-Specific Risk Premium (RP_c)	2.00%	2.00%
$K_e =$	19.15%	17.74%

Build-Up Method, Based on Kroll, LLC *Cost of Capital Navigator* Data, Size-Specific Equity Risk Premium

(1) Risk-Free Rate (R_f)	3.85%
Equity Risk Premium (RP_m)	N/A
(7) Size-Specific Equity Risk Premium ($RP_m + RP_s$)	14.00%
(4) Industry Risk Premium (RP_i)	0.00%
(5) Company-Specific Risk Premium (RP_c)	2.00%
$K_e =$	19.85%

MCAPM Method, Based on Kroll, LLC *Cost of Capital Navigator* Data

(1) Risk-Free Rate (R_f)	3.85%
(6) Beta (β)	1.14
(8) Equity Risk Premium (RP_m)	6.03%
(9) Size-Specific Equity Risk Premium over CAPM	5.00%
(5) Company-Specific Risk Premium (RP_c)	2.00%
$K_e =$	17.72%

Build-Up Method, Based on Kroll, LLC *Cost of Capital Navigator* Data, Based on Risk Characteristics

(1) Risk-Free Rate (R_f)	3.85%
(10) Risk-Specific Equity Risk Premium	13.00%
(4) Industry Risk Premium (RP_i)	0.00%
(5) Company-Specific Risk Premium (RP_c)	2.00%
$K_e =$	18.85%
Range of $K_e =$	16.87% to 19.85%
Concluded Cost of Equity =	18.00%

(continued)

EXHIBIT 1.14 (continued)

Notes:

(1) 20-Year Treasury Bond as of December 1, 2022.
(2) Kroll, LLC, *Cost of Capital Navigator*, 2021 Data.
(3) Kroll, LLC, *Cost of Capital Navigator*, 2021 Data. Size premium for the 10th decile (market capitalization between $10.588 million and $289.007 million).
(4) No usable data. The Kroll IRP for GICS 201060, Machinery (which includes related parts) was 1.64%, which includes three of the selected guideline public companies but also includes dozens of additional companies not used in our analysis.
(5) Based on analysis of company and industry and on the financial and economic environment as of the valuation date.
(6) See Exhibit 1.17 for the calculation of beta. Note that the Kroll Vasicek-adjusted beta for GICS 201060, Machinery (which includes related parts) was 1.22, which includes the three of the selected guideline public companies but also includes dozens of additional companies not used in our analysis.
(7) Size-specific equity risk premiums are based on comparison of the Company to risk premium groups presented in the Kroll, LLC, *Cost of Capital Navigator*, 2021 Data.
(8) Market premium embedded in Kroll, LLC, *Cost of Capital Navigator*, 2021 Data.
(9) Size-specific equity risk premiums over CAPM are based on comparison of the Company to risk premium groups presented in the Kroll, LLC, *Cost of Capital Navigator*, 2021 Data.
(10) Risk-specific equity risk premiums are based on comparison of the Company to risk premium groups presented in the Kroll, LLC, *Cost of Capital Navigator*, 2021 Data.

Certain parameters used in one or both cost of equity methods are discussed next.

1.9.1.3 Risk-Free Return (R_f) The rate of return on a risk-free security was found by looking at the yields of United States Treasury securities. Ideally, the duration of the security used as an indication of the risk-free rate should match the horizon of the projected cash flows that are being discounted (which is assumed to be into perpetuity). We used a 20-year Treasury rate that was equal to 3.85 percent as of December 1, 2022.

> **EXERCISE 44** Why are long-term 20-year U.S. Treasury coupon bonds most often used for the risk-free rate of return in both the build-up method and the MCAPM?
>
> _____
>
> _____
>
> _____
>
> _____

1.9.1.4 Equity Risk Premium (RP_m) The risk premiums, which are widely used, for the equity market are drawn from the *Cost of Capital Navigator* online database application published by Kroll, LLC.[38] The risk premium for the market can be calculated by subtracting the mean income return for long-term government bonds from the mean return for large-company stocks. According to the *Cost of Capital Navigator*, the unconditional (raw data) equity risk premium based on analysis of the historical period from 1926 to 2021 was 7.46 percent and the unconditional equity risk

---

[38] https://www.kroll.com/en/cost-of-capital. This application and/or the data it provides were formerly published by others, including Kroll, Morningstar, and Ibbotson Associates.

premium based on the long-term supply-side market equity premium was 6.22 percent. These data are referred to as the CRSP[39] equity risk premiums.

1.9.1.5 Size Premium (*RP_s*)   Various studies and analyses have shown an inverse relationship between company size and rates of returns, that is, the smaller the size of a company, the higher the rate of return. See the following chart for the past four years:

Cost of Capital Benchmark Data–December 31, 2019, 2020, 2021, and 2022

	2019	2020	2021	2022
U.S. 30-day Treasury bill[1]	1.52%	0.08%	0.04%	3.72%
U.S. 5-year Treasury note[2]	1.69%	0.36%	1.26%	3.99%
U.S. 20-year Treasury bond[3]	2.25%	1.45%	1.94%	4.14%
Aaa corporate bond[5]	3.04%	2.23%	2.71%	4.70%
30-year conventional mortgage[6]	3.74%	2.67%	3.11%	6.42%
Baa corporate bond[7]	3.90%	3.11%	3.37%	5.87%
Prime Rate[4]	4.75%	3.25%	3.25%	7.50%
Large-cap stock ($29 billion–$2 trillion)[8]	11.04%	11.25%	11.39%	11.54%
Micro-cap stock ($2.2 million–$452 million)[8]	17.67%	17.73%	17.92%	17.93%
Small-cap stock ($2.2 million–$190 million)[8]	19.80%	19.90%	20.04%	20.04%
Subdecile category 10b ($2.2 million–$95 million)[8]	22.67%	22.73%	22.98%	22.95%
D&P size category 25 ($9 million–$385 million)[9]	23.35%	22.98%	23.09%	23.37%
Subdecile category 10z ($2.2 million–$47 million)[8]	24.97%	25.02%	25.55%	25.62%
VS Bridge/IPO[10]		20%–35%		
VC second stage/expansion[10]		30%–50%		
VC first stage/early development[10]		40%–60%		

Notes:
[1] https://fred.stlouisfed.org/series/TB4WK
[2] https://fred.stlouisfed.org/series/DGS5
[3] https://fred.stlouisfed.org/series/DGS20
[4] https://fred.stlouisfed.org/series/DPRIME
[5] https://fred.stlouisfed.org/series/DAAA
[6] https://fred.stlouisfed.org/series/MORTGAGE30US
[7] https://fred.stlouisfed.org/series/DBAA
[8] Kroll 2023 *Cost of Capital Navigator,* CRSP Deciles Size Study- Supplementary Data Exhibits, all data from 1926 to 2022, large-cap is decile 1, micro-cap is deciles 9 and 10, small cap is decile 10.
[9] Kroll 2023 *Cost of Capital Navigator,* CRSP Deciles Size Study and Risk Premium Report Study- Supplementary Data Exhibits, Resource Library, all data from 1963 to 2022.
[10] *Valuation of Privately-Held-Company Equity Securities Issued as Compensation, Accounting & Valuation Guide,* 2013, American Institute of Certified Public Accountants, p. 148. (2019, 2020, 2021, 2022, 2023)

The size premium (over the risk premium for the market) can be calculated by subtracting the estimated (i.e., CAPM predicted) return in excess of the riskless rate from the realized return in excess of the riskless rate. In the case of Nova, we applied the size-premium return in excess of CAPM of companies in the 10th decile (i.e., in the smallest decile) from Kroll.

---

[39] Because they are prepared using securities prices provided by the Center for Research in Securities Prices (CRSP).

The source of these data was the Center for Research in Security Prices at the University of Chicago. For 2021, this decile includes companies with less than approximately $289.0 million in market value of equity. The indicated size premium (RP_s) was 4.80 percent.

Note: Although there have been some criticisms of the size premium, the vast majority of professional valuation analysts consider the size premium and its application when preparing a business valuation.

1.9.1.6 Combined Market and Size Premium (RP_{m+s}) In addition to the CRSP data, which is based on the market value of equity, Kroll publishes a separately computed set of equity risk premium data in the *Cost of Capital Navigator* called the "Risk Premium Report" data. These data provide two different types of premia: combined market and size risk premia (risk premium over the risk-free rate) and beta-adjusted size premia (risk premia over CAPM). The data allows for comparative analysis between the subject company and market data for various portfolios of public companies that are grouped using several different provided measures of size to capture the impact of size differences on risk based on these various measures of size. The Risk Premium Report data go back to 1963 (as opposed to the CRSP data, which go back to 1926), and exclude speculative start-ups, distressed companies, high-financial-risk companies, and financial services companies. The Risk Premium Report data presents eight measures of size in 25 different size portfolios, with Portfolio 1 including the largest companies and Portfolio 25 including the smallest companies. The size characteristics include market value of invested capital, book and market value of equity, historical revenue and earnings, and number of employees.

We compared the parameters of the Company to the criteria presented in the *Cost of Capital Navigator*'s Risk Premium Report data to identify into which portfolios the Company would fall. The assumption of category for the factors of market value of equity and market value of invested capital is based preliminarily on an estimate of the likely category and is refined based on an iterative process. Based on this analysis, we concluded to the combined market and size premium of 14.00 percent and the smoothed premium over CAPM of 5.00 percent. The historical market equity risk premium embedded in the *Cost of Capital Navigator's* Risk Premium Report data over the 1963 to 2021 time period, which is used in calculating all of the Risk Premium Report risk premia for that period, is 6.03 percent. See Exhibit 1.15 for comparison of the subject company to the portfolios in the Risk Premium Report data.

We also compared the parameters of the Company to additional combined market and size risk premiums provided in the *Cost of Capital Navigator*, which are based on the Company's operating margin, coefficient of variation in operating margin, and coefficient of variation in return on equity. The combined risk premium based on this data was 13.00 percent. See Exhibit 1.16.

EXERCISE 45 What benchmark is the Kroll common stock equity risk premium return most often based on?

a. S&P 500
b. New York Stock Exchange
c. Dow Jones Industrial Average
d. Russell 5000

EXHIBIT 1.15 Comparison to Historical Equity Risk Premiums by Characteristic

Nova Fastener & Tool, Inc.
Comparison to Historical Equity Risk Premiums by Characteristic
Based on Kroll, LLC, *Cost of Capital Navigator*, 2021 Data
Valuation Date: December 1, 2022
$

Characteristic	Subject Co.	Implied Category	Smoothed Average Premium Over the Risk-Free (RP_{m+s})	Smoothed Premium over CAPM (RP_s)
(1) Market Value of Equity	$ 33,000,000	25	13.96%	5.84%
(2) Book Value of Equity	$ 31,911,995	25	12.62%	4.52%
(3) 3-Year Avg. Adj. Net Income	$ 534,918	25	13.78%	5.47%
(4) Market Value of Invested Capital	$ 33,000,000	25	13.94%	5.63%
(2) Total Assets	$ 36,298,974	25	13.55%	5.22%
(3) 3-Year Avg. Adj. EBITDA	$ 2,028,682	25	13.60%	5.33%
(5) Sales	$ 34,538,367	25	13.28%	5.35%
(6) Number of Employees	207	25	13.43%	5.88%
		Minimum	12.62%	4.52%
		Maximum	13.96%	5.88%
		Mean	13.52%	5.41%
		Median	13.58%	5.41%
		Selected	14.00%	5.00%

Notes:
(1) See Exhibit 1.25. Implied category assumption is based on an iterative process.
(2) As of November 30, 2022.
(3) Three-Year Average, 2019 to 2021.
(4) Market value of equity, plus interest-bearing debt as of November 30, 2022. Implied category assumption is based on an iterative process.
(5) Twelve months ended November 30, 2022.
(6) As of November 15, 2022, per company management.

1.8.1.7 Beta Beta is a measure of the systematic risk of a particular investment relative to the market for all investment assets. Betas for each of the guideline companies were computed using 60 monthly returns based on the companies' split and dividend adjusted prices, and on 60 monthly market returns based on the S&P 500 Total Return index. Based on these data we concluded to an unlevered beta of 0.81 (see Exhibit 1.17). The identified unlevered beta was then levered at the estimated long-term capital structure of Nova. Management is in the process of obtaining financing for the Company's operations at an estimated level of approximately one-third of the invested capital of the business. This level of financing is within the range of the debt to invested capital of the guideline companies and approximates the level of debt employed by three of the five guideline companies. It is reasonable considering analysis of industry levels of debt financing.

EXHIBIT 1.16 Comparison to Historical Equity Risk Premiums Ranked by Risk Measures

Nova Fastener & Tool, Inc.
Comparison to Historical Equity Risk Premiums Ranked by Risk Measures
Based on the Kroll, LLC, *Cost of Capital Navigator*, 2021 Data
Valuation Date: December 1, 2022
$

Coefficient of Variation of Operating Margin

		2021	2020	2019	2018	2017
(1) Net Sales		33,974,558	27,590,653	32,873,002	37,174,249	35,764,714
(1) Adjusted Operating Income		1,358,915	(83,014)	491,584	2,402,648	2,365,181
Adjusted Operating Margin		4.0%	-0.3%	1.5%	6.5%	6.6%
Standard Deviation of Operating Margin	3.0%					
Average Operating Margin	3.7%					
Coefficient of Variation	83.3%					

Coefficient of Variation of Return on Book Value of Equity

		2021	2020	2019	2018	2017
(1) Book Value		28,969,365	28,706,089	29,158,027	29,759,749	28,859,955
(1) Adjusted Net Income		1,117,949	(4,991)	491,797	1,980,525	1,904,151
Return on Book Equity		3.9%	0.0%	1.7%	6.7%	6.6%
Standard Deviation of ROE	3.0%					
Average ROE	3.8%					
Coefficient of Variation	78.8%					

Characteristic	Subject Co.	Implied Category	Smoothed Ave. Premium
Operating Margin	3.7%	24	13.97%
CV of Operating Margin	83.3%	2	12.99%
CV of Return on Book Equity	78.8%	7	11.41%
		Mean	12.79%
		Median	12.99%
		Selected	13.00%

Note:
(1) See Exhibits 1.14 and 1.15.

EXHIBIT 1.17 Industry Beta Analysis

Nova Fastener & Tool, Inc.
Industry Beta Analysis
Valuation Date: December 1, 2022

Ticker	Guideline Companies	Levered Beta (1)	Interest-Bearing Debt 000s	%	Market Value of Equity 000s	%	Total Invested Capital 000s	Tax Rate	Unlevered Beta
EML	The Eastern Company	0.96	74,744	34.3%	142,948	65.7%	217,692	26.0%	0.69
PFIN	P&F Industries, Inc.	0.44	8,087	32.7%	16,612	67.3%	24,699	26.0%	0.33
SCX	The L.S. Starrett Company	0.55	29,391	33.7%	57,804	66.3%	87,195	26.0%	0.40
TWIN	Twin Disc, Incorporated	1.11	41,955	21.5%	153,589	78.5%	195,544	26.0%	0.93
VC	Visteon Corporation	1.79	34,900	7.7%	416,907	92.3%	451,807	21.2%	1.68
	Median			32.7%		67.3%			0.69
	Mean			26.0%		74.0%			0.81
							Selected Unlevered Beta:		0.81
							Estimated Company Levered Beta:		1.14

Assumptions:

(2)   Estimated Company Capital Structure
% of Debt to Invested Capital	34.0%
% of Equity to Invested Capital	66.0%

(3)   Estimated Effective Tax Rate   22.0%

Subject Company Levered Beta = Unlevered Beta × [1 + [(Debt/Equity) × (1 – Tax Rate)]]

Notes:
(1) Calculated using 60 month-end returns, using the companies' split and dividend adjusted prices and the S&P 500 Total Return index.
(2) Based on analysis of the industry and discussions with management regarding plans to finance the Company's operations.
(3) Based on projected combined state and federal tax rate per management.

Based on an assumption of 34.0 percent debt and 66.0 percent equity as percentages of invested capital, the calculated levered beta was 1.14.

EXERCISE 46   When using the MCAPM to derive an equity cost of capital for a control interest, it is sometimes necessary to adjust beta for differences between the capital structure of the public companies and the capital structure of the subject company being valued. This is not necessary if the capital structure is assumed to be the same. Given the following information, calculate the unlevered and releveled beta using the Hamada formula.

a. Average beta of guideline public companies = .66

Tax rate = 33 percent

Market value capital structure = 10 percent debt, 90 percent equity

The formula for unlevered beta is:

$$Bu = Bl / (1 + (1 - t)(Wd / We))$$

Where:

Bu = Beta unlevered

Bl = Beta levered

 t = Tax rate for the company

Wd = Percentage of debt in the capital structure (at market value)

We = Percentage of equity in the capital structure (at market value)

b. Assuming that Nova has a capital structure of 20 percent debt and 80 percent equity, what would be the beta?

The formula to relever the beta is:

$$Bl = Bu(1 + (1 - t)(Wd/We))$$

1.9.1.8 Industry Risk Premium (*RP*)   A risk premium for the industry is also provided in the Kroll *Cost of Capital Navigator*. Kroll estimates a risk index for each industry, which compares the risk level of the industry with the market as a whole. The industry risk premium is calculated by multiplying the risk index (beta) for the specific industry by the long-horizon expected equity risk premium, and then subtracting from this product the long-horizon expected equity risk premium.

For Nova, we considered Kroll's industry risk premium for Global Industry Classification Standard (GICS) 201060, Machinery (which includes related parts). We did not rely on the data because this broad category is not representative of the risk of the subject company.[40] We determined that the Kroll industry risk premium for GICS 201060 included three of our selected guideline public companies,

---

[40] In 2020 Duff & Phelps, which provided the *Cost of Capital Navigator* prior to its acquisition by Kroll, replaced the previously used SIC code system for the computation of industry risk premia with GICS. GICS is more modern but much less granular than the SIC system.

but they also included dozens of additional companies that we did not deem sufficiently comparable to Nova.

1.9.1.9 Risk Premium Attributable to the Specific Company (RP_c) The risk premium for unsystematic risk attributable to the specific company is designed to account for additional risk factors specific to the Company. In the case of Nova, an additional risk premium of 2.00 percent was applied to reflect risk associated with meeting projected levels of revenue growth and margin improvement, customer concentration, and reliance on key executive leadership without a formal succession plan.

EXERCISE 47 A list of risk factors was previously presented for Nova to calculate the specific risk premium. Discuss the different methods for determining what the actual company-specific risk premium should be.

_____

_____

_____

_____

_____

EXERCISE 48 Company-specific risk premiums can be determined from Kroll data.

 a. True
 b. False

EXERCISE 49 Which of these rates of return are derived using Kroll data?

 a. Minority rates of return
 b. Control rates of return
 c. Majority rates of return
 d. Neutral

1.9.1.10 Cost of Equity Conclusion The cost of equity implied by the build-up method, using CRSP data, was 18.11 percent using the historical market equity premium and 16.87 percent using the supply-side premium. The cost of equity implied by the MCAPM method was 19.15 percent using the historical market equity premium, and 17.74 percent using the supply-side premium. The indicated cost of equity using the Kroll combined equity risk premium and size premium was 19.85 percent. The MCAPM cost of equity with Kroll's risk premiums based on size characteristics was 17.72 percent.

We also calculated the equity risk premium using Kroll data through 2021 based on certain risk characteristics of the Company, including operating margin, coefficient of variation of operating margin, and coefficient of variation of return on equity. Based on these data, the indicated cost of equity was 18.85 percent. Further, we also calculated the cost of equity capital using the historical embedded Risk Premium Report equity risk premium of 6.03 percent and the previously concluded smoothed premium over CAPM of 5.00 percent in a build-up model along with Kroll's normalized risk-free rate of 2.50 percent and Kroll's recommended equity risk premium of 5.50 percent. This resulted in a cost of equity within a reasonable range of our other calculations.

EXERCISE 50   Assume that the Kroll historical CRSP equity risk premium is 7.46 percent and the 10th-decile size premium is 4.8 percent. Assume that the relevered beta of the guideline companies is 1.14 under MCAPM and that the industry risk premium is not relied on in the build-up model (BUM). Calculate the cost of equity for Nova under the MCAPM and BUM methods.

EXERCISE 51   Assume that the Kroll supply-side CRSP equity risk premium is 6.22 percent and the 10th-decile size premium is 4.8 percent. Assume that the relevered beta of the guideline companies is 1.14 under MCAPM and that the industry risk premium is not relied on in the BUM. Calculate the cost of equity for Nova under the MCAPM and BUM methods.

EXERCISE 52   Assume that the Kroll historical market risk premium for use with the smoothed premium over CAPM is 5.05 percent and the 25th-size category premium is 6.10 percent. Calculate the cost of equity for Nova.

EXERCISE 53   Assume that the Kroll combined equity risk premium and size premium for the 25th-size category is 14.0 percent. Calculate the cost of equity for Nova.

EXERCISE 54   In addition to equity risk premium based on eight alternative measures of size, Kroll presents risk premium data based on three measures of risk that are not based initially on size. Name those three measures of risk.

1. _____

2. _____

3. _____

EXERCISE 55   Assume that the analysis using the three alternative measures of risk from Kroll results in a cost of equity of 18.85 percent. What is the range of the seven costs of equity for Nova and what is the conclusion for the cost of equity? Explain your reasons and support.

Range of costs of equity: _____ percent to _____ percent

Concluded cost of equity _____ percent

Supporting reasons:

_____

_____

_____

_____

_____

We concluded to a cost of equity of 18.00 percent for the Company. See Exhibit 1.14.

1.8.2 Cost of Debt

The discount rate for debt in the capital structure is usually defined as the marginal borrowing rate of the subject company net of tax benefit associated with the deductibility of interest expense. The marginal borrowing rate of Nova was estimated by analyzing its financial statements and discussions with management and was estimated to be approximately 6.00 percent before tax. After reflecting the tax deductibility of interest expense, the after-tax cost of debt for Nova, using a 22.0 percent tax rate, was estimated to be 4.68 percent. See Exhibit 1.18.

EXERCISE 56   Which of these factors causes the cost of debt to be tax-affected?

a. Debt principal is tax deductible.
b. Interest expense is tax deductible.
c. It should not be tax-affected because equity is not tax-affected.
d. Debt and interest are tax deductible.

EXERCISE 57   Using the information in the text, calculate the weighted average cost of capital for Nova.

_____

_____

_____

_____

_____

EXHIBIT 1.18 Weighted Average Cost of Capital

Nova Fastener & Tool, Inc.
Weighted Average Cost of Capital
Valuation Date: December 1, 2022

(1)	Cost of Equity	$k_e = 18.00\%$

After Tax Cost of Debt: $k_d = K_b(1 - t)$	
(2) Borrowing Rate (K_b)	6.00%
(3) Estimated Tax Rate (t)	22.0%
Cost of Debt	$k_d = 4.68\%$

Weighted Average Cost of Capital (WACC)

		Capital Structure	Cost	Weighted Cost
(4)	Debt	34.0%	4.68%	1.59%
(4)	Common Equity	66.0%	18.00%	11.88%
			WACC =	13.47%
			Rounded =	13.00%

Notes:
(1) See Exhibit 1.14.
(2) Based on analysis of the Company, the prime rate as of December 1, 2022 (7.00%), Moody's Aaa and Baa bond rates as of December 1, 2022 (4.43% and 5.62%, respectively), and other data.
(3) Based on projected combined state and federal tax rate per management.
(4) Based on analysis of industry and discussions with management regarding plans to finance the operations.

EXERCISE 58 Which methods can be used to determine the weights in the weighted average cost of capital?

a. Iterative process
b. Guideline public companies
c. Aggregated public industry data
d. Risk Management Associates
e. Book values
f. Anticipated capital structure

EXERCISE 59 Explain the iterative process for determining the weights in the weighted average cost of capital.

_____

_____

_____

_____

_____

EXERCISE 60 Changing the amount of debt in the capital structure of the company has no effect on the return on equity.

a. True
b. False

EXERCISE 61 When valuing a controlling interest in a company, should you use the optimal capital structure based on public data or the capital structure anticipated to be employed by the owner of the company?

_____

_____

_____

_____

_____

1.9.3 Capital Structure

Based on analysis of Nova's financial statements, the guideline companies, and statements by Nova's management that they would be adding financing (already bank approved) in the future, a normalized capital structure of 34.0 percent debt and 66.0 percent equity was assumed for Nova as of December 1, 2022.

1.9.4 Weighted Average Cost of Capital Conclusion

The indicated weighted average cost of capital for Nova as of December 1, 2022, was as follows:

$$\text{WACC} = (4.68 \text{ percent} \times 34.0 \text{ percent}) + (18.00 \text{ percent} \times 66.0 \text{ percent})$$
$$= 1.59 \text{ percent} + 11.88 \text{ percent}$$
$$= 13.47 \text{ percent}$$

or 13.00 percent, rounded. Refer to Exhibit 1.18 for the calculation of the weighted average cost of capital.

EXERCISE 62 Calculate the capitalization rate from the information in the text and calculate the value based on the trailing 12 months cash flow.

_____

_____

_____

_____

_____

EXERCISE 63   Items used to support growth rates in the capitalized cash flow method of the income approach include:

   a. Inflation
   b. Nominal gross domestic product
   c. Industry growth rate
   d. Actual historical company growth rate
   e. All of the above

1.10 MARKET APPROACH

Under the market approach, the guideline public company method and guideline company transactions method were considered. As discussed elsewhere in this report, we did not rely on the guideline company transactions method as a primary method but considered it as a general check on our primary valuation methods due to the relative quantity and quality of available data.

1.11 GUIDELINE PUBLIC COMPANY METHOD

The valuation of a business merits a comparative analysis of the subject company with guideline publicly traded companies in the same or similar industries or lines of business. Although no two companies are completely alike, it is possible to find publicly traded companies that are engaged in the same or similar lines of business. In theory, investors could view investments in appropriately selected guideline companies as alternative investments to an investment in Nova. The guideline companies and the subject company should be similarly affected by similar economic and industry factors.

1.11.1 Selection of Guideline Companies

We performed an independent search for guideline companies using a database of public companies. Some of the criteria were as follows:

- Companies listed under SIC codes 3452 (Bolts, Nuts, Screws, Rivets, and Washers), and 3714 (Motor Vehicle Parts and Accessories), and the broader classifications 3540x (Metalworking Machinery and Equipment) and 342x (Cutlery, Handtools & General Hardware)
- A search for "fastener" in company descriptions, and also for "rivet"
- Confirmation that adequate financial data were available for the company
- Confirmation that the company's stock was actively traded on an exchange or in the over-the-counter market with price data available on a daily basis

We also considered a list of competitors and other companies provided by management. After discussing the prospective guideline companies with management, we concluded that five guideline public companies were similar enough to include in our analysis.

These companies are discussed briefly next.[41]

The Eastern Co. (NASDAQ: EML)—The Eastern Company manages industrial businesses that design, manufacture, and sell unique engineered solutions to industrial markets. Eastern pursues organic growth strategies as well as attractive external growth and acquisition opportunities. Eastern's businesses design, manufacture, and market a diverse product line of custom and standard vehicular and industrial hardware, including turnkey returnable packaging solutions, access and security hardware, mirrors, and mirror-cameras. Eastern's TTM revenues as of October 1, 2022, were $269.8 million.

P&F Industries, Inc. (NASDAQ: PFIN)—Imports, manufactures, and markets pneumatic hand tools of its own design, primarily to the retail, industrial, automotive, and aerospace markets. P&F also designs, manufactures, and markets industrial tools, systems, gearing, accessories, and a wide variety of replacement parts under various brands, including products sold directly to original equipment manufacturers (OEMs) and industrial branded products sold through a broad network of specialized industrial distributors. P&F's TTM revenues as of September 30, 2022, were $59.4 million.

The L.S. Starrett Co. (NYSE: SCX)—Manufactures various measuring and cutting products throughout the world, including North America, Brazil, and China. Some of its products include precision tools, electronic gauges, optical, vision and laser measuring equipment, custom-engineered granite solutions, tape measures, levels, and various types of saw blades. TTM revenues as of September 30, 2022, were $252.6 million.

Twin Disc, Inc. (NASDAQ: TWIN)—Designs, manufactures, and sells marine and heavy-duty off-highway power transmission equipment. Products offered include marine transmissions, azimuth drives, surface drives, propellers, and boat management systems as well as power-shift transmissions, hydraulic torque converters, power take-offs, industrial clutches, and controls systems. Its TTM revenues as of September 30, 2022, were $251.1 million.

Visteon Corp. (NYSE: VC)—A global automotive technology company that designs and manufactures innovative automotive electronics and connected car products for various original equipment vehicle manufacturers, including Ford, BMW, Mazda, Volkswagen, Renault, Nissan, Daimler, General Motors, Stellantis, and Jaguar/Land Rover. Visteon's products include digital instrument clusters, information displays, audio and infotainment systems, various domain controllers, advanced driver assistance systems, and battery management systems.

Visteon also has a rivet division. Its TTM revenues as of September 30, 2022, were $347.8 million.

---

[41] Descriptions of the guideline companies are largely drawn from SEC filings. Language has, in places, been extracted wholly or largely verbatim and/or substantially paraphrased.

EXERCISE 64 Size is often a consideration in selecting guideline public companies. The general criterion for using size as a selection parameter is:

a. 2 times
b. 5 times
c. 10 times
d. None of the above

EXERCISE 65 In the valuation of Nova, only one company, P&F Industries, Inc. was comparable in size, but all the guideline companies operate in the same industry and were not considered too big to provide growth, margin, and multiple data for Nova. Given that fact, which option would probably result in the best presentation of the GPCM in the valuation of Nova?

a. Only use P&F Industries.
b. Use all guideline public companies.
c. Reject the guideline public company method.
d. Use the guideline public company method but only as a reasonableness test for the other approaches.

EXERCISE 66 Guideline public company methods are not applicable to smaller businesses such as Nova.

a. True
b. False

EXERCISE 67 Which initial selection criteria are generally used by analysts in choosing guideline public companies?

a. Size
b. Return on equity
c. Profit margin
d. Industry similarity
e. Similar products and services
f. Growth rates
g. Investors' similarities

1.11.2 Analysis of Guideline Companies

Using the most recently filed 10-Ks and 10-Qs of the guideline companies, we calculated their historical financial ratios. A summary of guideline company multiples is presented in Exhibit 1.19. A comparative financial analysis of guideline companies is presented in Exhibit 1.20. A summary of historical financial data, margins, and ratios for each of the guideline companies is presented in Exhibits 1.21 a through f.

EXHIBIT 1.19 Guideline Public Company Method: Ranking of Market Multiples

Nova Fastener & Tool, Inc.
Guideline Public Company Method
Ranking of Market Multiples

	Most Recent 12 Months			
	Price to Earnings	Invested Capital to		
		Net Revenues	EBIT	EBITDA
The Eastern Company	11.1	0.8	11.2	8.1
P&F Industries, Inc.		0.4		24.5
The L.S. Starrett Company	3.8	0.3	3.9	3.0
Twin Disc, Incorporated	31.7	0.8	22.4	11.0
Visteon Corporation	27.4	1.3	22.0	14.6
Mean	18.5	0.7	14.9	12.2
Median	19.2	0.8	16.6	11.0
Coefficient of Variation	71.7%	52.2%	60.2%	65.8%

	Most Recent Fiscal Year			
	Price to Earnings	Invested Capital to		
		Net Revenues	EBIT	EBITDA
The Eastern Company	10.8	0.9	11.1	8.1
P&F Industries, Inc.		0.5		132.1
The L.S. Starrett Company	3.6	0.3	3.8	2.9
Twin Disc, Incorporated	31.1	0.8	22.2	10.7
Visteon Corporation	59.3	1.6	43.0	21.2
Mean	26.2	0.8	20.0	35.0
Median	21.0	0.8	16.7	10.7
Coefficient of Variation	95.3%	61.1%	85.4%	156.2%

	Three-Year Average			
	Price to Earnings	Invested Capital to		
		Net Revenues	EBIT	EBITDA
The Eastern Company	10.7	0.9	10.9	8.1
P&F Industries, Inc.		0.5		
The L.S. Starrett Company	5.2	0.4	5.5	3.8
Twin Disc, Incorporated		0.8		27.1
Visteon Corporation	63.5	1.6	45.2	22.1
Mean	26.5	0.9	20.5	15.3
Median	10.7	0.8	10.9	15.1
Coefficient of Variation	121.6%	58.7%	105.0%	72.4%

Note:
(1) Multiples are summarized from Exhibit 1.21. Multiples which are not meaningful are shown as blanks above.

EXHIBIT 1.20 Guideline Public Company Method: Comparative Financial Analysis

Nova Fastener & Tool, Inc.
Guideline Public Company Method
Comparative Financial Analysis
(000s $, all companies)

	Subject	Mean	Median	EML	PFIN	SCX	TWIN	VC
Comparative Size								
Total Revenues	34,538	236,142	252,648	269,816	59,381	252,648	251,065	347,800
Total Assets	36,299	206,520	232,600	275,946	60,074	194,429	269,551	232,600
Total Market Capitalization	NA	195,388	195,544	217,692	24,699	87,195	195,544	451,807
Asset Management Ratios								
Debt-Free Working Cap Turnover	1.6	3.0	2.6	2.7	2.0	2.6	2.0	5.6
Asset Turnover	1.0	1.2	1.0	1.0	1.0	1.3	0.9	1.6
Liquidity Ratios								
Debt-Free Current Ratio	7.2	3.4	3.5	3.5	5.3	3.9	2.5	1.6
Debt-Free Quick Ratio	3.4	1.2	1.4	1.4	1.4	1.5	0.7	1.1
Leverage Ratios								
Debt to Equity (Book)	0.0%	39.1%	33.6%	60.3%	19.0%	28.9%	33.6%	53.8%
Debt to Capital (Book)	0.0%	27.2%	25.2%	37.6%	16.0%	22.4%	25.2%	35.0%
Times Interest Earned	N/M	8.2	10.0	10.0	-6.0	15.7	4.0	17.1
Profitability								
Net Profit Margin	1.7%	3.0%	4.4%	4.8%	-2.3%	6.1%	1.9%	4.4%
EBIT Margin	2.2%	4.5%	5.9%	7.2%	-2.7%	8.8%	3.5%	5.9%
EBITDA Margin	5.9%	7.8%	8.9%	10.0%	1.7%	11.4%	7.1%	8.9%
Return on Assets	1.7%	4.3%	5.1%	5.1%	-2.1%	8.6%	2.4%	7.4%
Return on Common Equity (Book)	1.9%	11.0%	10.9%	10.9%	-3.3%	16.6%	3.8%	26.6%
Profitability (3-Year Averages)								
Net Profit Margin	1.6%	1.3%	2.4%	5.8%	-4.2%	4.7%	-1.9%	2.4%
EBIT Margin	2.0%	2.4%	3.6%	8.6%	-5.5%	6.9%	-1.7%	3.6%
EBITDA Margin	6.3%	6.3%	7.4%	11.6%	-0.5%	9.9%	3.0%	7.4%
3-Year Historical Annual Growth								
Net Revenues	1.7%	0.6%	-1.0%	-1.0%	-4.5%	12.2%	-0.8%	-3.0%
Net Income	50.8%	41.3%	30.5%	-6.9%	68.0%	113.1%	N/M	-9.1%
Earnings Before Interest & Taxes	50.8%	43.2%	40.3%	-6.6%	87.1%	99.9%	N/M	-7.6%
Earnings Bef Int., Taxes, Depr & Amort.	16.8%	26.9%	-2.3%	-3.6%	-67.8%	51.5%	156.6%	-2.3%

EXHIBIT 1.21   Guideline Public Company Method: Detail by Company

THE EASTERN COMPANY
EML

FINANCIAL STATEMENT DATA ($)	TTM Ended (10/1/2022) 2022/09	Fiscal Year Ended (1/1/2022) 2021/12	(1/2/2021) 2020/12	(12/28/2019) 2019/12	'19–'21 Growth Rate
Net Revenues	269,816,341	246,522,823	197,614,590	251,742,619	–1.0%
Depreciation & Amortization	7,441,604	7,241,073	6,815,783	6,454,881	5.9%
Interest Expense	1,943,105	1,747,723	2,058,600	1,857,961	–3.0%
Earnings Before Taxes (1)	17,609,516	19,070,560	13,216,810	16,205,971	8.5%
Net Income (1)	14,796,242	16,182,343	11,034,919	13,266,142	10.4%
Net Profit Margin	5.5%	6.6%	5.6%	5.3%	
Effective Tax Rate	16.0%	15.1%	16.5%	18.1%	
Cash, Equiv., Mkt. Sec. & Accts Rec.	56,129,995	49,319,804	47,124,983	55,972,710	–6.1%
Total Current Assets	137,821,314	123,674,861	111,735,772	115,938,483	3.3%
Total Current Liabilities	47,254,828	49,563,726	40,665,962	34,896,915	19.2%
Net Working Capital	90,566,486	74,111,135	71,069,810	81,041,568	–4.4%
Short-Term Interest-Bearing Debt	8,125,000	7,500,000	6,437,689	5,187,689	20.2%
Debt-Free Net Working Capital	98,691,486	81,611,135	77,507,499	86,229,257	–2.7%
Total Assets	275,946,214	266,328,935	275,528,354	280,662,976	–2.6%
Average Total Assets	281,624,513	270,928,645	278,095,665		
Long-Term Interest-Bearing Debt	66,619,231	63,813,522	82,255,803	93,577,544	–17.4%
Common Equity	123,988,410	114,602,264	104,306,458	105,437,257	4.3%
Average Common Equity	118,189,171	109,454,361	104,871,858		
Interest-Bearing Debt to Invested Capital	37.6%	38.4%	46.0%	48.4%	
ADJUSTED EARNINGS ($)					
Earnings Before Taxes (as reported)	17,609,516	19,070,560	13,216,810	16,205,971	8.5%
Goodwill impairment	0	0	(972,823)	0	
Gain on sale of assets	355,000	1,841,000	0	0	
Factory relocation and start-up costs	(215,000)	(604,000)	(679,000)	0	
Restructuring costs	0	0	(665,861)	(2,664,651)	
Transaction expenses	0	0	(300,000)	(1,699,862)	
Total Adjustments	(140,000)	(1,237,000)	2,617,684	4,364,513	
Adjusted Earnings Before Taxes	17,469,516	17,833,560	15,834,494	20,570,484	–6.9%
Estimated Income Tax Rate	26.0%	26.0%	26.0%	26.0%	
Adjusted Net Income	12,927,442	13,196,834	11,717,526	15,222,158	–6.9%
Adjusted Net Profit Margin	4.8%	5.4%	5.9%	6.0%	
Adjusted Debt-Free Net Income	14,365,340	14,490,149	13,240,890	16,597,049	–6.6%
Adj. Earnings Before Interest & Taxes	19,412,621	19,581,283	17,893,094	22,428,445	–6.6%
Adjusted EBIT Margin	7.2%	7.9%	9.1%	8.9%	
Adj. Earnings Before Int., Taxes, Depr. & Amort.	26,854,225	26,822,356	24,708,877	28,883,326	–3.6%
Adjusted EBITDA Margin	10.0%	10.9%	12.5%	11.5%	

Note:
(1) From continuing operations, in the trailing twelve months and fiscal 2021 and 2020.

THE EASTERN COMPANY
EML

MARKET CAPITALIZATION ($)	At 2022/09	
Short-Term Interest-Bearing Debt	8,125,000	
Long-Term Interest-Bearing Debt	66,619,231	
Total Interest-Bearing Debt	74,744,231	
Preferred Equity (Book)	0	
Common Equity	142,947,829	
Total Equity	142,947,829	
Total Invested Capital	217,692,060	
Shares Outstanding at Valuation Date	6,215,123	*Shares Outstanding as of October 1, 2022, per 10-Q for period ending 10/1/22*
Price at 12/1/2022	$23.00	

FINANCIAL RATIOS	Most Recent	3-Year Average
Debt-Free Working Capital Turnover	2.7	2.8
Asset Turnover	1.0	
Debt-Free Current Ratio	3.5	3.4
Debt-Free Quick Ratio	1.4	1.5
Debt to Equity (Book)	60.3%	80.3%
Debt to Capital (Book)	37.6%	44.2%
Times Interest Earned	10.0	10.7
Net Profit Margin	4.8%	5.8%
EBIT Margin	7.2%	8.6%
EBITDA Margin	10.0%	11.6%
Return on Average Assets	5.1%	
Return on Average Common Equity (Book)	10.9%	

MARKET MULTIPLES	Most Recent 12 Months		Most Recent Fiscal Year		3-Year Average	
	Parameter	Multiple	Parameter	Multiple	Parameter	Multiple
Price/Earnings	12,927,442	11.1	13,196,834	10.8	13,378,839	10.7
Price/Book (Common Equity)	123,988,410	1.2	114,602,264	1.2	N/M	N/M
Invested Capital/Revenues	269,816,341	0.8	246,522,823	0.9	231,960,011	0.9
Invested Capital/EBIT	19,412,621	11.2	19,581,283	11.1	19,967,607	10.9
Invested Capital/EBITDA	26,854,225	8.1	26,822,356	8.1	26,804,853	8.1

(continued)

P&F INDUSTRIES, INC.
PFIN

FINANCIAL STATEMENT DATA ($)	12 Months Ended 2022/09	Fiscal Year Ended 2021/12	2020/12	2019/12	'19–'21 Growth Rate
Net Revenues	59,381,000	53,554,000	49,136,000	58,674,000	−4.5%
Depreciation & Amortization	2,619,000	2,696,000	2,740,000	2,524,000	3.4%
Interest Expense	268,000	45,000	140,000	198,000	−52.3%
Earnings Before Taxes	167,000	2,288,000	(6,855,000)	6,708,000	−41.6%
Net Income	31,000	2,290,000	(4,954,000)	4,911,000	−31.7%
Net Profit Margin	0.1%	4.3%	−10.1%	8.4%	
Effective Tax Rate	81.4%	0.0%	0.0%	26.8%	
Cash, Equiv., Mkt. Sec. & Accts Rec.	9,868,000	8,089,000	8,372,000	9,693,000	−8.6%
Total Current Assets	37,199,000	36,676,000	29,540,000	34,072,000	3.8%
Total Current Liabilities	15,074,000	12,078,000	8,282,000	11,957,000	0.5%
Net Working Capital	22,125,000	24,598,000	21,258,000	22,115,000	5.5%
Short-Term Interest-Bearing Debt	8,087,000	5,765,000	3,357,000	5,648,000	1.0%
Debt-Free Net Working Capital	30,212,000	30,363,000	24,615,000	27,763,000	4.6%
Total Assets	60,074,000	58,190,000	53,367,000	61,743,000	−2.9%
Average Total Assets	57,811,500	55,778,500	57,555,000		
Long-Term Interest-Bearing Debt	0	0	946,000	0	N/M
Common Equity	42,525,000	43,840,000	41,538,000	46,506,000	−2.9%
Average Common Equity	42,721,500	42,689,000	44,022,000		
Interest-Bearing Debt to Invested Capital	16.0%	11.6%	9.4%	10.8%	
ADJUSTED EARNINGS ($)					
Earnings Before Taxes (as reported)	167,000	2,288,000	(6,855,000)	6,708,000	−41.6%
Gain (loss) on sale of fixed assets	45,000	(27,000)	(35,000)	7,817,000	
Impairments of goodwill, and of other assets	(48,000)	(88,000)	(1,612,000)	(194,000)	
PPP forgivness, other gains on settlement of obligations	19,000	2,929,000	136,000	0	
Employee retention credit	2,028,000	2,028,000	0	0	
Total Adjustments	(2,044,000)	(4,842,000)	1,511,000	(7,623,000)	
Adjusted Earnings Before Taxes	(1,877,000)	(2,554,000)	(5,344,000)	(915,000)	67.1%
Estimated Income Tax Rate	26.0%	26.0%	26.0%	26.8%	
Adjusted Net Income	(1,388,980)	(1,889,960)	(3,954,560)	(669,881)	68.0%
Adjusted Net Profit Margin	−2.3%	−3.5%	−8.0%	−1.1%	
Adjusted Debt-Free Net Income	(1,190,660)	(1,856,660)	(3,850,960)	(524,924)	88.1%
Adj. Earnings Before Interest & Taxes	(1,609,000)	(2,509,000)	(5,204,000)	(717,000)	87.1%
Adjusted EBIT Margin	−2.7%	−4.7%	−10.6%	−1.2%	
Adj. Earnings Before Int., Taxes, Depr. & Amort.	1,010,000	187,000	(2,464,000)	1,807,000	−67.8%
Adjusted EBITDA Margin	1.7%	0.3%	−5.0%	3.1%	

P&F INDUSTRIES, INC.
PFIN

MARKET CAPITALIZATION ($)	At 2022/09
Short-Term Interest-Bearing Debt	8,087,000
Long-Term Interest-Bearing Debt	0
Total Interest-Bearing Debt	8,087,000
Preferred Equity (Book)	0
Common Equity	16,612,435
Total Equity	16,612,435
Total Invested Capital	24,699,435
Shares Outstanding at Valuation Date	3,194,699
Price at 12/1/2022	$5.20

Shares Outstanding as of November 7, 2022, per 10-Q for period ending 9/30/22

FINANCIAL RATIOS	Most Recent	3-Year @ Average
Debt-Free Working Capital Turnover	2.0	2.0
Asset Turnover	1.0	
Debt-Free Current Ratio	5.3	5.7
Debt-Free Quick Ratio	1.4	1.5
Debt to Equity (Book)	19.0%	11.9%
Debt to Capital (Book)	16.0%	10.6%
Times Interest Earned	−6.0	−32.2
Net Profit Margin	−2.3%	−4.2%
EBIT Margin	−2.7%	−5.5%
EBITDA Margin	1.7%	−0.5%
Return on Average Assets	−2.1%	
Return on Average Common Equity (Book)	−3.3%	

MARKET MULTIPLES	Most Recent 12 Months		Most Recent Fiscal Year		3-Year Average	
	Parameter	Multiple	Parameter	Multiple	Parameter	Multiple
Price/Earnings	(1,388,980)	N/M	(1,889,960)	N/M	(2,171,467)	N/M
Price/Book (Common Equity)	42,525,000	0.4	43,840,000	0.4	N/M	N/M
Invested Capital/Revenues	59,381,000	0.4	53,554,000	0.5	53,788,000	0.5
Invested Capital/EBIT	(1,609,000)	N/M	(2,509,000)	N/M	(2,810,000)	N/M
Invested Capital/EBITDA	1,010,000	24.5	187,000	132.1	(156,667)	N/M

(continued)

THE L.S. STARRETT COMPANY
SCX

FINANCIAL STATEMENT DATA (Tho. $)	12 Months Ended 2022/09	Fiscal Year Ended			'20–'22 Growth Rate
		2022/6	2021/6	2020/6	
Net Revenues	252,648	253,701	219,644	201,451	12.2%
Depreciation & Amortization	6,684	6,630	6,292	7,196	–4.0%
Interest Expense	1,415	1,265	999	975	13.9%
Earnings Before Taxes	20,200	21,519	17,426	(19,997)	N/M
Net Income	13,702	14,878	15,533	(21,839)	N/M
Net Profit Margin	5.4%	5.9%	7.1%	–10.8%	
Effective Tax Rate	32.2%	30.9%	10.9%	–9.2%	
Cash, Equiv., Mkt. Sec. & Accts Rec.	49,964	57,484	44,181	42,470	16.3%
Total Current Assets	130,191	133,053	119,220	104,098	13.1%
Total Current Liabilities	38,514	41,180	51,689	27,834	21.6%
Net Working Capital	91,677	91,873	67,531	76,264	9.8%
Short-Term Interest-Bearing Debt	5,384	6,547	15,959	4,532	20.2%
Debt-Free Net Working Capital	97,061	98,420	83,490	80,796	10.4%
Total Assets	194,429	199,554	184,486	172,683	7.5%
Average Total Assets	192,013	192,020	178,585		
Long-Term Interest-Bearing Debt	24,007	24,905	6,010	26,341	–2.8%
Common Equity	101,833	102,429	83,535	45,983	49.2%
Average Common Equity	92,541	92,982	64,759		
Interest-Bearing Debt to Invested Capital	22.4%	23.5%	20.8%	40.2%	
ADJUSTED EARNINGS (Tho. $)					
Earnings Before Taxes (as reported)	20,200	21,519	17,426	(19,997)	N/M
Restructuring charges	(621)	(431)	(3,664)	(1,580)	
Goodwill and intangible asset impairments	0	0	0	(6,496)	
Gain on sale of real estate	0	0	3,204	0	
Pension liability charge, marked to market methodology	0	0	0	(16,753)	
Total Adjustments	621	431	460	24,829	
Adjusted Earnings Before Taxes	20,821	21,950	17,886	4,832	113.1%
Estimated Income Tax Rate	26.0%	26.0%	26.0%	26.0%	
Adjusted Net Income	15,408	16,243	13,236	3,576	113.1%
Adjusted Net Profit Margin	6.1%	6.4%	6.0%	1.8%	
Adjusted Debt-Free Net Income	16,455	17,179	13,975	4,297	99.9%
Adj. Earnings Before Interest & Taxes	22,236	23,215	18,885	5,807	99.9%
Adjusted EBIT Margin	8.8%	9.2%	8.6%	2.9%	
Adj. Earnings Before Int., Taxes, Depr. & Amort.	28,920	29,845	25,177	13,003	51.5%
Adjusted EBITDA Margin	11.4%	11.8%	11.5%	6.5%	

THE L.S. STARRETT COMPANY
SCX

MARKET CAPITALIZATION (Tho. $)	At 2022/09	
Short-Term Interest-Bearing Debt	5,384	
Long-Term Interest-Bearing Debt	24,007	
Total Interest-Bearing Debt	29,391	
Preferred Equity (Book)	0	
Common Equity	57,804	
Total Equity	57,804	
Total Invested Capital	87,195	
Shares Outstanding at Valuation Date (000s)	7,382	*Shares Outstanding as of October 26, 2022, per 10-Q for period ending 9/30/22*
Price at 12/1/2022	$7.83	

FINANCIAL RATIOS	Most Recent	3-Year Average
Debt-Free Working Capital Turnover	2.6	2.6
Asset Turnover	1.3	
Debt-Free Current Ratio	3.9	3.9
Debt-Free Quick Ratio	1.5	1.6
Debt to Equity (Book)	28.9%	41.4%
Debt to Capital (Book)	22.4%	28.2%
Times Interest Earned	15.7	14.4
Net Profit Margin	6.1%	4.7%
EBIT Margin	8.8%	6.9%
EBITDA Margin	11.4%	9.9%
Return on Average Assets	8.6%	
Return on Average Common Equity (Book)	16.6%	

MARKET MULTIPLES	Most Recent 12 Months		Most Recent Fiscal Year		3-Year Average	
	Parameter	Multiple	Parameter	Multiple	Parameter	Multiple
Price/Earnings	15,408	3.8	16,243	3.6	11,018	5.2
Price/Book (Common Equity)	101,833	0.6	102,429	0.6	N/M	N/M
Invested Capital/Revenues	252,648	0.3	253,701	0.3	224,932	0.4
Invested Capital/EBIT	22,236	3.9	23,215	3.8	15,969	5.5
Invested Capital/EBITDA	28,920	3.0	29,845	2.9	22,675	3.8

(continued)

TWIN DISC, INCORPORATED
TWIN

FINANCIAL STATEMENT DATA (Tho. $)	12 Months Ended 2022/09	Fiscal Year Ended			'19–'21 Growth Rate
		2022/06	2021/06	2020/06	
Net Revenues	251,065	242,913	218,581	246,838	–0.8%
Depreciation & Amortization	9,137	9,547	11,243	11,925	–10.5%
Interest Expense	2,164	2,128	2,358	1,860	7.0%
Earnings Before Taxes (1)	5,248	10,229	(9,839)	(43,740)	N/M
Net Income (1)	4,495	8,406	(29,519)	(39,571)	N/M
Net Profit Margin	1.8%	3.5%	–13.5%	–16.0%	
Effective Tax Rate	14.3%	17.8%	–200.0%	0.0%	
Cash, Equiv., Mkt. Sec. & Accts Rec.	53,221	57,973	51,831	41,370	18.4%
Total Current Assets	201,818	204,452	191,967	173,985	8.4%
Total Current Liabilities	81,864	81,078	78,560	66,734	10.2%
Net Working Capital	119,954	123,374	113,407	107,251	7.3%
Short-Term Interest-Bearing Debt (1)	2,607	2,576	2,541	4,924	–27.7%
Debt-Free Net Working Capital	122,561	125,950	115,948	112,175	6.0%
Total Assets	269,551	276,523	275,413	294,127	–3.0%
Average Total Assets	272,899	275,968	284,770		
Long-Term Interest-Bearing Debt (1)	39,348	38,983	34,921	38,653	0.4%
Common Equity	124,768	131,188	130,660	139,958	–3.2%
Average Common Equity	128,196	130,924	135,309		
Interest-Bearing Debt to Invested Capital	25.2%	24.1%	22.3%	23.7%	
ADJUSTED EARNINGS (Tho. $)					
Earnings Before Taxes (as reported)	5,248	10,229	(9,839)	(43,740)	N/M
Restructuring expenses	(936)	(973)	(7,377)	(5,138)	
PPP loan forgivness	0	0	8,200	0	
Covid relief (U.S. and Netherlands programs)	(600)	1,400	2,400	0	
Impairments of goodwill and other assets	0	0	0	(27,603)	
Gain on sale of assets	229	3,126	0	0	
Total Adjustments	1,307	(3,553)	(3,223)	32,741	
Adjusted Earnings Before Taxes	6,555	6,676	(13,062)	(10,999)	N/M
Estimated Income Tax Rate	26.0%	26.0%	26.0%	26.0%	
Adjusted Net Income	4,851	4,940	(9,666)	(8,139)	N/M
Adjusted Net Profit Margin	1.9%	2.0%	–4.4%	–3.3%	
Adjusted Debt-Free Net Income	6,452	6,515	(7,921)	(6,763)	N/M
Adj. Earnings Before Interest & Taxes	8,719	8,804	(10,704)	(9,139)	N/M
Adjusted EBIT Margin	3.5%	3.6%	–4.9%	–3.7%	
Adj. Earnings Before Int., Taxes, Depr. & Amort.	17,856	18,351	539	2,786	156.6%
Adjusted EBITDA Margin	7.1%	7.6%	0.2%	1.1%	

Note:
(1) Income before tax and net income include non-controlling interest. Interest-bearing debt amounts include finance leases.

TWIN DISC, INCORPORATED
TWIN

MARKET CAPITALIZATION (Tho. $)	At 2022/09	
Short-Term Interest-Bearing Debt	2,607	
Long-Term Interest-Bearing Debt	39,348	
Total Interest-Bearing Debt	41,955	
Preferred Equity (Book)	0	
Common Equity	153,589	
Total Equity	153,589	
Total Invested Capital	195,544	
Shares Outstanding at Valuation Date (000s)	13,787	*Shares Outstanding as of October 24, 2022, per 10-Q for period ending 9/30/22*
Price at 12/1/2022	$11.14	

FINANCIAL RATIOS	Most Recent Year	3-Year Average
Debt-Free Working Capital Turnover	2.0	2.0
Asset Turnover	0.9	
Debt-Free Current Ratio	2.5	2.6
Debt-Free Quick Ratio	0.7	0.7
Debt to Equity (Book)	33.6%	30.5%
Debt to Capital (Book)	25.2%	23.4%
Times Interest Earned	4.0	−1.8
Net Profit Margin	1.9%	−1.9%
EBIT Margin	3.5%	−1.7%
EBITDA Margin	7.1%	3.0%
Return on Average Assets	2.4%	
Return on Average Common Equity (Book)	3.8%	

MARKET MULTIPLES	Most Recent 12 Months		Most Recent Fiscal Year		3-Year Average	
	Parameter	Multiple	Parameter	Multiple	Parameter	Multiple
Price/Earnings	4,851	31.7	4,940	31.1	(4,288)	N/M
Price/Book (Common Equity)	124,768	1.2	131,188	1.2	N/M	N/M
Invested Capital/Revenues	251,065	0.8	242,913	0.8	236,111	0.8
Invested Capital/EBIT	8,719	22.4	8,804	22.2	(3,680)	N/M
Invested Capital/EBITDA	17,856	11.0	18,351	10.7	7,225	27.1

(continued)

VISTEON CORPORATION
VC

FINANCIAL STATEMENT DATA (Tho. $)	12 Months Ended 2022/09	Fiscal Year Ended			'19–'21 Growth Rate
		2021/12	2020/12	2019/12	
Net Revenues	347,800	277,300	254,800	294,500	–3.0%
Depreciation & Amortization	10,500	10,800	10,400	10,000	3.9%
Interest Expense	1,200	1,000	1,600	1,300	–12.3%
Earnings Before Taxes (1)	16,500	8,100	(2,000)	10,600	–12.6%
Net Income (1)	13,000	5,000	(4,800)	8,200	–21.9%
Net Profit Margin	3.7%	1.8%	–1.9%	2.8%	
Effective Tax Rate	21.2%	38.3%	–140.0%	22.6%	
Cash, Equiv., Mkt. Sec. & Accts Rec.	109,800	100,400	98,400	98,300	1.1%
Total Current Assets	159,400	142,400	134,100	134,500	2.9%
Total Current Liabilities	98,000	85,200	82,400	79,800	3.3%
Net Working Capital	61,400	57,200	51,700	54,700	2.3%
Short-Term Interest-Bearing Debt	900	400	0	3,700	–67.1%
Debt-Free Net Working Capital	62,300	57,600	51,700	58,400	–0.7%
Total Assets	232,600	223,400	227,100	227,100	–0.8%
Average Total Assets	219,300	225,250	227,100		
Long-Term Interest-Bearing Debt	34,000	34,900	34,900	34,800	0.1%
Common Equity	64,900	61,600	51,000	59,500	1.7%
Average Common Equity	57,100	56,300	55,250		
Interest-Bearing Debt to Invested Capital	35.0%	36.4%	40.6%	39.3%	
ADJUSTED EARNINGS (Tho. $)					
Earnings Before Taxes (as reported)	16,500	8,100	(2,000)	10,600	–12.6%
Restructuring and impairment expense	(2,800)	(1,400)	(7,600)	(400)	
Total Adjustments	2,800	1,400	7,600	400	
Adjusted Earnings Before Taxes	19,300	9,500	5,600	11,000	–7.1%
Estimated Income Tax Rate	21.2%	26.0%	26.0%	22.6%	
Adjusted Net Income	15,206	7,030	4,144	8,509	–9.1%
Adjusted Net Profit Margin	4.4%	2.5%	1.6%	2.9%	
Adjusted Debt-Free Net Income	16,152	7,770	5,328	9,515	–9.6%
Adj. Earnings Before Interest & Taxes	20,500	10,500	7,200	12,300	–7.6%
Adjusted EBIT Margin	5.9%	3.8%	2.8%	4.2%	
Adj. Earnings Before Int., Taxes, Depr. & Amort.	31,000	21,300	17,600	22,300	–2.3%
Adjusted EBITDA Margin	8.9%	7.7%	6.9%	7.6%	

Note:
(1) From continuing operations; includes non-controlling interest.

VISTEON CORPORATION
VC

MARKET	At
CAPITALIZATION (Tho. $)	2022/09
Short-Term Interest-Bearing Debt	900
Long-Term Interest-Bearing Debt	34,000
Total Interest-Bearing Debt	34,900
Preferred Equity (Book)	0
Common Equity	416,907
Total Equity	416,907
Total Invested Capital	451,807
Shares Outstanding at Valuation Date (000s)	2,814
Price at 12/1/2022	$148.14

Shares Outstanding as of October 21, 2022, per 10-Q for period ending 9/30/22

FINANCIAL RATIOS	Most Recent Year	3-Year Average
Debt-Free Working Capital Turnover	5.6	4.9
Asset Turnover	1.6	
Debt-Free Current Ratio	1.6	1.7
Debt-Free Quick Ratio	1.1	1.2
Debt to Equity (Book)	53.8%	63.5%
Debt to Capital (Book)	35.0%	38.8%
Times Interest Earned	17.1	8.2
Net Profit Margin	4.4%	2.4%
EBIT Margin	5.9%	3.6%
EBITDA Margin	8.9%	7.4%
Return on Average Assets	7.4%	
Return on Average Common Equity (Book)	26.6%	

MARKET MULTIPLES	Most Recent 12 Months		Most Recent Fiscal Year		3-Year Average	
	Parameter	Multiple	Parameter	Multiple	Parameter	Multiple
Price/Earnings	15,206	27.4	7,030	59.3	6,561	63.5
Price/Book (Common Equity)	64,900	6.4	61,600	6.8	N/M	N/M
Invested Capital/Revenues	347,800	1.3	277,300	1.6	275,533	1.6
Invested Capital/EBIT	20,500	22.0	10,500	43.0	10,000	45.2
Invested Capital/EBITDA	31,000	14.6	21,300	21.2	20,400	22.1

EXERCISE 68   Which of these are commonly used guideline public company valuation multiples?

a. Price/earnings
b. Invested capital/revenues
c. Price/gross profits
d. Invested capital/book value of equity
e. Invested capital/EBITDA
f. Invested capital/EBIT
g. Price/assets
h. Invested capital/debt-free net income
i. Invested capital/debt-free cash flow

EXERCISE 69   When using the guideline public company method, at what point in time are the prices of the public companies' stock valued?

a. 30-day average
b. As of valuation date
c. 6-month average
d. 3-year average

EXERCISE 70   What type of value is the result of the application of the guideline public company method?

a. Control
b. Minority
c. Neutral

Based on this analysis, we established a relative basis for comparison between the guideline public companies and the Company. We calculated selected market multiples based on stock prices for each of the guideline companies as of the valuation date. Using the relative basis for comparison developed via financial ratios, growth rates, company outlook, and so on, appropriate multiples were selected to estimate the value of Nova.

1.11.3 Guideline Company Ratio Analysis

We performed a quantitative analysis of the guideline companies' financial performance in relation to Nova. The comparison was based primarily on size, leverage, profitability, and growth. The following is a summary of this comparative analysis of the Company and the guideline companies.

Based on its net revenues of $34.5 million for the TTM ended November 30, 2022, and its total assets of $36.3 million at November 30, 2022, Nova was smaller in size than all the guideline companies. The TTM revenues of the guideline companies ranged from $59.4 million to $347.8 million, and total assets of the guideline companies ranged from $60.1 million to $275.9 million.

Nova had a book debt-to-equity ratio of 0.0 percent at November 30, 2022, which was lower than the mean and median of the guideline companies. The mean and median debt-to-equity ratio of the six guideline companies was 39.1 percent and 33.6 percent, respectively.

Nova's debt-free working capital turnover ratio was 1.6 at November 30, 2022, which was lower than the mean and the median of the guideline companies, which were 3.0 and 2.6, respectively. These statistics do not reflect adjustments for excess cash.

The mean and median net profit margins of the guideline companies were 3.0 percent and 4.4 percent, respectively, in a range of –2.3 to 6.1 percent. Nova's net profit margin was 1.7 percent for the TTM ended November 30, 2022. Nova's EBITDA margin of 5.9 percent more closely approached the mean and median EBITDA margins of the guidelines in the most recent TTM, which were 7.8 percent and 8.9 percent, respectively. On a three-year average basis, Nova's EBITDA margin of 6.3 percent was close to the 6.3 percent mean and 7.4 percent median of the guidelines.

Analyzing the prior three fiscal years, the mean and median compound annual revenue growth rates for the guideline companies were 0.6 percent and negative 1.0 percent, respectively. Nova's compound annual revenue growth during this time was 1.7 percent, which was higher than the performance of the guideline companies as a group. Four of the five guideline companies saw a revenue decline during the prior three years and only Starrett had a revenue growth rate higher than Nova.

Nova's net income, EBIT, and EBITDA growth were greater than its revenue growth, reflecting improved profitability over the prior three years. These growth rates were generally higher than the rates of the guideline public companies, except for The L.S. Starrett Co.[42]

1.11.4 Selection of Multiples

Nova is smaller in size and less leveraged than the public guideline set and generally less profitable than the guidelines in the most recent period and similarly profitable on a three-year average basis. The three-year revenue growth rate of Nova has been higher than the guideline companies. Considering these and other factors outlined previously, we applied the median guideline company market multiples less a 5 percent fundamental discount for the periods analyzed to the parameters of the Company. See Exhibits 1.19 and 1.22.

The following multiples were applied to the subject company parameters: equity to net earnings and of invested capital to revenue, EBIT, and EBITDA. In concluding to the value of the Company, we relied primarily on the indications of value derived from the EBITDA multiples. We note that the result is consonant with the values indicated by the revenue multiples. We added the estimated excess debt-free working capital to the indicated operating value of the Company.

---

[42] Note that the positive number for P&F's EBIT growth reflects the deepening of losses at the EBIT line, and the apparently strong EBITDA growth for Twin Disc is off of a relatively low initial base level of profitability.

EXHIBIT 11.22 Guideline Public Company Method: Summary

Nova Fastener & Tool, Inc.
Guideline Public Company Method
Summary

$	Earnings Parameter	Selected Multiple (1)	Invested Capital	Less: Interest-Bearing Debt	Equity Value
Most Recent Twelve Months					
Equity Multiples					
Price/Earnings	$579,562	18.2			$10,548,035
Business Enterprise Multiples					
Invested Capital/Net Revenues	34,538,367	0.8	27,630,694	0	27,630,694
Invested Capital/Earnings Bef Int & Taxes	747,524	15.8	11,810,874	0	11,810,874
Invested Capital/EBITDA	$2,035,234	10.5	21,369,953	0	21,369,953
Most Recent Fiscal Year					
Equity Multiples					
Price/Earnings	$1,117,949	20.0			$22,358,983
Business Enterprise Multiples					
Invested Capital/Net Revenues	33,974,558	0.8	27,179,646	0	27,179,646
Invested Capital/Earnings Bef Int & Taxes	1,420,159	15.9	22,580,535	0	22,580,535
Invested Capital/EBITDA	2,738,713	10.2	27,934,877	0	27,934,877
Three-Year Averages					
Equity Multiples					
Price/Earnings	$534,918	10.2			$5,456,166
Business Enterprise Multiples					
Invested Capital/Net Revenues	31,479,404	0.8	25,183,523	0	25,183,523
Invested Capital/Earnings Bef Int & Taxes	679,317	10.4	7,064,897	0	7,064,897
Invested Capital/EBITDA	$2,028,682	14.3	29,010,148	0	29,010,148

Selected Value of 100% of Equity	$26,100,000
Plus: Excess Debt-Free Working Capital (2)	7,689,078
Indicated Value of 100% of Equity, Rounded	$33,800,000

Notes:

(1) Selected multiples equal the median multiples less a 5% fundamental discount for various factors including size, rounded. Calculations may not reconcile exactly due to rounding in presentation.

(2) See Exhibit 11.12 for calculation of excess DFWC.

Based on the application of the guideline public company method, the indicated value of 100 percent of the equity of Nova as of December 1, 2022, was $33,800,000 million (operating value of $26,100,000 million plus $7,689,078 in excess working capital, rounded). See Exhibit 1.22.

EXERCISE 71 In selecting multiples from guideline public companies for application to a subject company such as Nova, what options do analysts typically have?

a. Mean or harmonic mean average of the multiples
b. Median average of the multiples
c. Individual guideline company multiples
d. Average multiples with a fundamental discount
e. All of the above

EXERCISE 72 Which of these time periods can be used to derive valuation multiples from publicly traded companies?

a. Most recent four quarters
b. Most recent fiscal year-end
c. Three-year average
d. Five-year average
e. One-year projected
f. Three-year future average

1.12 GUIDELINE COMPANY TRANSACTIONS METHOD

It is possible to develop an indication of value of a company based on the price multiples indicated by merger and acquisition (M&A) transactions of companies in the same or a similar industry in recent years. In order to use M&A information in a valuation engagement, the following two conditions must be met:

- The target company must be similar to the company being valued in at least some respects.
- One must be able to obtain details of the merger or acquisition transaction. If at least one of the parties in the M&A transaction (either the purchaser or the seller) is a public company, relevant information is often available.

EXERCISE 73 Which of these are general transaction databases considered by analysts in valuing companies?

a. *DealStats*
b. RMA
c. Bizcomps
d. *Mergerstat Review*

> **EXERCISE 74**   What is one of the most significant problems when attempting to use transaction data?
>
> _____
>
> _____
>
> _____
>
> _____
>
> _____

We searched the *DealStats* transaction database for transactions that occurred between November 30, 2017, and November 30, 2022, in SIC codes 3452 (Bolts, Nuts, Screws, Rivets, and Washers), and 3714 (Motor Vehicle Parts and Accessories).[43] We also searched NAICS codes 332722 (Bolt, Nut, Screw, Rivet, and Washer Manufacturing) and 336390 (Other Motor Vehicle Parts Manufacturing), and for companies that included "fastener" or "rivet" in their company descriptions.

We excluded transactions in which the target company's operations were not similar to Nova and/or in which the target company's revenues were not between $3.0 million and $350.0 million. Three transactions in *DealStats* involved targets within these search criteria, and these transactions are included in our analysis. One of those three transactions had a public acquirer, and therefore additional financial and other information was available through a form 8-K filed with the SEC in connection with this transaction. We also searched for and reviewed the forms 8-K filed by the guideline public companies included in our analysis for the five years preceding the December 1, 2022, valuation date. This produced usable information regarding one additional transaction, which is also included in our analysis.

Exhibit 1.23 provides a summary of the valuation multiples considered.

We considered multiples of invested capital (IC) to revenue; IC to earnings before interest and taxes (EBIT); and IC to earnings before interest, taxes, depreciation, and amortization (EBITDA). The implied multiples of revenue, EBITDA, and EBIT for the Company based on the conclusion of value under the guideline public company method and the discounted cash flow method were close to the range of the transaction multiples. We did not rely on the guideline company transactions method as a primary method (discounted cash flow and guideline public company methods) but did use it as a check for reasonableness of the conclusions of the other valuation methods. See Exhibit 1.24 for application of the adjusted transaction multiples to Nova.

1.13 RECONCILIATION OF VALUATION METHODS

The selected guideline public companies are somewhat comparable to Nova and provide valuable market data for purposes of valuation analysis. However, none are

[43] We also searched *DealStats* for transactions in the broader classifications 3540x (Metalworking Machinery and Equipment) and 342x (Cutlery, Handtools, & General Hardware), but found the business descriptions inadequate to determine whether the resulting transactions were comparable to the tools produced by Nova in its relatively small tools segment.

EXHIBIT 1.23 Guideline Company Transactions Method: Detail

Nova Fastener & Tool, Inc.
Market Approach: Guideline Company Transactions Method (1)
Valuation Date: December 1, 2022

Date	Primary SIC	Primary NAICS	Acquirer	Target	Description	TIC $	Revenues $	EBITDA $	Deprec. $	EBIT $	TIC/ Rev.	TIC/ EBITDA	TIC/ EBIT
04/01/2022	003452	332722	Simpson Manufacturing Co., Inc. (2)	ETANCO Group	Designer, Manufacturer and Distributor of Fixing and Fastening Solutions for the Building Construction Market	$824,405,000	$305,115,000	$71,098,874	$16,544,874	$54,554,000	2.70	11.60	15.11
12/09/2021	003452	332722	NA (7)	NA	Manufacturer of Threaded Metal Screw Products Primarily for Aerospace, Military Applications and Commercial Applications	$52,000,000	$15,908,965	$5,132,726	$69,466	$4,988,581	3.27	10.13	10.42
08/30/2019			The Eastern Co. (3)	Big 3 Precision	Manufacturer of Custom Returnable Packaging and Blow Mold Tools for truck, automotive and other markets	$81,531,000	$69,351,742	$11,586,814	$2,052,335	$9,534,479	1.18	7.04	8.55
05/23/2022	003429	332722	NA (6)	Bay Standard	Fastener Manufacturing and Distribution	$15,000,000	$32,164,559	$3,501,191	$0	$11,623,620	0.47	4.28	1.29
					Mean						1.90	8.26	8.84
					Median						1.94	8.58	9.49
					Minimum						0.47	4.28	1.29
					Maximum						3.27	11.60	15.11
					Coefficient of Variation						0.68	0.39	0.65
					Implied Subject Company Multiples						TTM	TTM	TTM
					Guideline Public Company Method–Conclusion (Multiples Calculated Excluding Excess DFWC)						0.76	12.82	34.92
					Discounted Cash Flow Method–Conclusion (Multiples Calculated Excluding Excess DFWC)						0.73	12.33	33.58

(continued)

EXHIBIT 1.23 (continued)

Notes:

(1) Data from *DealStats* and from SEC filings.

(2) *DealStats* does not consider trailing twelve-month income statement data, and the three transactions from it (all but Big 3) closed between 235 and 366 days after the dates of the income statement data *DealStats* used. Therefore TTM multiples could be different. For two of the three transactions there is no further infromation. For ETANCO, because Simpson Manufacturing Co., Inc. is public, additional target financial information is available in a 6/17/2022 8-K/A. TTM figures reported there are used above (most are from the 8-K's Ex. 99.3; depreciation and amortization is computed from information given in euros in Exs. 99.1 and 99.2, and translated to dollars at the 1.1938 rate given in Ex. 99.3; figures are before transaction accounting adjustments). As reported by *DealStats*, the ETANCO transaction data was:

| 04/01/2022 | 003452 | 332722 | Simpson Manufacturing Co., Inc. | ETANCO Group | Designer, Manufacturer and Distributor of Fixing and Fastening Solutions for the Building Construction Market | $824,405,000 | $257,168,000 | $56,767,000 | $12,145,000 | $44,622,000 | 3.21 | 14.52 | 18.48 |

(3) One of the guideline public companies, The Eastern Company, acquired Big 3 Precision during 2019. Big 3's audited financials and pro forma combined information, with adjustments, were published as attachments (99.5 and 99.6, respectively) to The Eastern Company's 10-Q for the quarter ended 9/30/2019. Unaudited information through 6/30/2019 was also provided (as attachment 99.7) but did not include income statement information for the six months ended 6/30/2018. Therefore, we used income statement information through 12/31/2018. EBITDA reflects adjustments for management fees, acquisition costs, and non-recurring tax consulting fees and insurance proceeds. Eastern also sold certain divisions and subsidiaries in 2020 and 2021, and acquired the assets of Hallink, RSB in August 2020. Insufficient information was available to use these transactions in the transaction method.

(4) Another guideline public company, P&F Industries, acquired small gear manufacturers in late 2019 and early 2022. Very limited information was provided. A P&F 8-K dated 10/25/2019 and P&F's 10-K for the year ended 12/31/2019 together indicate that P&F paid a multiple of approximately 1.0× revenue for its acquisitions of Blaz-Man Gear, Inc. and Gear Products & Manufacturing, Inc., combined. An 8-K dated 1/14/2022 and P&F's 10-Q for the quarter ending 9/30/2022 together indicate that P&F paid approximately 0.80× revenue, annualized, for its acquisition of Jackson Gear Company. Insufficient information to calculate EBITDA or EBIT multiples.

(5) Certain other acquisitions by the guideline public companies, such as Twin Disc's 2018 acquisition of Veth Propulsion, were not considered because the target's product lines were not closely related to products produced by Nova.

(6) There are apparent irregularities in the financial information reported in *DealStats* for this transaction (EBITDA is reported as much smaller than EBIT; depreciation and amortization are reported as zero).

(7) EBITDA as indicated by *DealStats'* reported income statement figures is slightly different from EBITDA as reported directly by *DealStats* ($5,058,047 instead of $5,137,726).

EXHIBIT 1.24 Guideline Company Transactions Method: Summary

Nova Fastener & Tool, Inc.
Market Approach: Guideline Company Transactions Method Summary

	Earnings Parameter	Selected Multiple (1)	Invested Capital	Less: Interest-Bearing Debt	Equity Value
Trailing Twelve Months					
Business Enterprise Multiples					
Invested Capital/Net Revenues	34,538,367	2.4	82,892,081	0	82,892,081
Invested Capital/Earnings Bef Int & Taxes	747,524	9.4	7,026,722	0	7,026,722
Invested Capital/EBITDA	2,035,234	9.1	18,520,626	0	18,520,626
Most Recent Fiscal Year					
Business Enterprise Multiples					
Invested Capital/Net Revenues	33,974,558	2.4	81,538,939	0	81,538,939
Invested Capital/Earnings Bef Int & Taxes	1,420,159	9.4	13,349,499	0	13,349,499
Invested Capital/EBITDA	2,738,713	9.1	24,922,292	0	24,922,292
Three-Year Average					
Business Enterprise Multiples					
Invested Capital/Net Revenues	31,479,404	2.4	75,550,570	0	75,550,570
Invested Capital/Earnings Bef Int & Taxes	679,317	9.4	6,385,580	0	6,385,580
Invested Capital/EBITDA	2,028,682	9.1	18,461,003	0	18,461,003

Selected Value of 100% of the Equity	20,600,000
Plus: Excess Debt-Free Net Working Capital (2)	7,689,078
Indicated Value of 100% of the Equity (Rounded)	28,300,000

Notes:
(1) Selected multiples equal the median multiples calculated excluding the Bay Standard acquisition, less a 10% fundamental discount for various factors including potential deal synergies. Calculations may not reconcile exactly due to rounding in presentation.
(2) See notes to Exhibit 1.12 and text for additional information.

primarily manufacturers of rivets for automotive markets, which is Nova's primary business. The discounted cash flow method represents an analysis of management's expectations for the growth and profitability of the business in the future. In concluding to a value for Nova, we relied on the value indications under both of these methods, with greater consideration to the discounted cash flow method.

The guideline company transactions provide market data for the purpose of valuation analysis of Nova. However, as is often the case with this method, we lack full details on the transactions, and we therefore rely on the transaction method as a corroborating method to check the reasonableness of the multiples implied from the guideline public company method and discounted cash flow method.

As shown in Exhibit 1.25, the indicated value of 100 percent of the equity of Nova based on the market approach is $33,800,000 and based on the income approach it is $32,600,000. Giving somewhat greater consideration to the income approach, the concluded fair market value of the Company as of December 1, 2022, was therefore $33,000,000.

EXHIBIT 1.25   Summary of Findings

Nova Fastener & Tool, Inc. Summary of Findings
Valuation Date: December 1, 2022
$

	Value Indication
Income Approach	
Capitalized Cash Flow to Invested Capital	$ 15,800,000
Discounted Cash Flow to Invested Capital	$ 32,600,000
Market Approach	
Guideline Public Company Method	$ 33,800,000
Guideline Company Transactions Method	$ 28,300,000
Asset Approach	
Net Tangible Book Value (Rounded)	$ 31,900,000
Selected Value of 100% of the Equity	**$ 33,000,000**

Based on our analysis as described in this valuation report, and the facts and circumstances as of the valuation date, the estimate of value as of December 1, 2022, of a 100 percent equity interest in Nova Fastener & Tool, Inc. on a control, marketable basis is $33,000,000.

1.14 CONCLUSION OF VALUE

We have performed a valuation engagement, as that term is defined in the Statement of Standards for Valuation Services VS Section 100 (SSVS) of the American Institute of Certified Public Accountants, of a 100 percent equity interest in Nova Fastener & Tool, Inc. as of December 1, 2022, on a control, marketable basis.

EXERCISE 75 Is a 100 percent controlling interest marketable or non-marketable?

_____

_____

_____

_____

EXERCISE 76 Discounts for lack of marketability/liquidity can be applied to 100 percent control interests in a company such as Nova.

  a. True
  b. False

EXERCISE 77 Which discounts for lack of marketability studies and/or data are available in determining discounts?

  a. *Mergerstat Review*
  b. Restricted stock studies
  c. IPO studies
  d. Court cases
  e. Flotation costs
  f. CAPM
  g. Kroll
  h. Quantitative marketability discount model (QMDM)
  i. Option pricing models

EXERCISE 78 Although a 100 percent control interest is valued in Nova, numerous other levels of ownership interests can exist in a closely held company. Provide some examples of other levels of ownership.

_____

_____

_____

_____

_____

A marketability/liquidity discount is intended, among other things, to account for the issues a controlling owner must face as they begin to liquidate their control interest in the company. A number of studies and cases over the years have attempted to identify this discount.

EXERCISE 79 A discount for lack of marketability/liquidity should be applied to all of the valuation methods used in the valuation of Nova.

a. True
b. False

EXERCISE 80 Which method can be used to correlate and reconcile value?

a. Straight average of the indications of value
b. Numerical weights assigned to each of the value indications
c. Qualitative judgment in selection of value
d. All of the above

This valuation was performed solely to assist in the determination of the value solely for internal operational and tax planning purposes and the resulting estimate of value should not be used for any other purpose, or by any other party for any purpose. The estimate of value that results from a valuation engagement is expressed as a conclusion of value.

There were no restrictions or limitations in the scope of our work or data available for analysis.

Based on our analysis as described in this valuation report, and the facts and circumstances as of the valuation date, the estimate of value as of December 1, 2022, of a 100 percent equity interest in Nova Fastener & Tool, Inc. on a control, marketable basis is $33,000,000. See Exhibit 1.25.

This conclusion is subject to the Statement of Assumptions and Limiting Conditions and to the Valuation Analyst's Representation/Certification found in Appendix A and Appendix B. We have no obligation to update this report or our conclusion of value for information that comes to our attention after the date of this report.

1.14 ADDENDUM: DISCOUNT CASE STUDY EXERCISES

1.14.1 Exercise A

Assume that we are determining the fair market value of a minority nonmarketable interest in a company for gift tax purposes. The minority marketable value derived by various methods is $100 per share. We are in a state where you need over 50 percent for full control. What is the relative discount for lack of marketability in these situations?

a. Value of a 10 percent interest with one 90 percent owner

_____

_____

_____

_____

b. Value of a 10 percent interest with nine other 10 percent owners

_____

_____

_____

_____

c. Value of a 50 percent interest with one other 50 percent owner

_____

_____

_____

_____

d. Value of a 33.33 percent interest with two other 33.33 percent owners

_____

_____

_____

_____

e. Value of a 2 percent interest with two 49 percent owners

_____

_____

_____

_____

1.14.2 Exercise B

Again, assume we are determining the fair market value of a company for gift tax pur-poses. In this case study, we are valuing a 100 percent controlling interest on a stand-alone basis in a closely held company. What is the discount for lack of marketability/liquidity in these situations where the prediscount value is determined by using:

a. P/E ratios from control transactions information (i.e., *DealStats*)

_____

_____

_____

_____

b. P/E ratios from guideline public companies

_____

_____

_____

_____

c. Discounted cash flow (DCF) with a discount rate determined using Kroll information

_____

_____

_____

_____

d. Capitalized cash flow method

_____

_____

_____

_____

e. Asset approach

_____

_____

_____

_____

CHAPTER 2

Valuation Case Study Exercises: Solutions and Explanations

EXERCISE 1   Which of the following is the as of date for valuation?

a. Any time within one year
b. As of a single point in time
c. As of a single point in time or six months later
d. Date that the report is signed

ANSWER: b. As of a single point in time

The valuation date is always as of a single point in time, typically a day. Valuation of a business is a dynamic, not static, exercise. Values can change constantly, such that a value today may be very different from the value a year from now or even just a few months from now. In the estate tax area, valuations are as of the date of death or six months later. However, this is only for estate tax. The date that the analyst signs the report usually does not coincide with the as of date. The signature date is most often after the valuation date.

EXERCISE 2   This is a detailed report per SSVS. What other types of reports are allowed under SSVS?

ANSWER: a. Summary report
b. Calculation report
c. Oral report

EXERCISE 3   The purpose of the valuation of Nova is to assist management in internal operational and tax planning. What other purposes are there?

ANSWER: Valuations are used for a variety of purposes, including estate tax, income tax, gift tax, ESOPs (employee stock ownership plans), marital dissolution, buying companies, selling companies, shareholder oppression cases, dissenting rights cases, financial reporting, reorganization and bankruptcy, minority stockholder disputes, various types of litigation, and internal planning.

EXERCISE 4 If the analyst belongs to more than one valuation organization with standards, that analyst must comply with the standards of each organization to which they belong.

a. True
b. False

ANSWER: a. True

A valuation analyst is responsible only for adherence to the standards of the associations and organizations to which they belong. For example, a CPA has to comply only with the AICPA standards. That CPA may elect to follow other standards, say, USPAP, but is not required to do so.

EXERCISE 5 Revenue Ruling 59-60 is only applicable to estate, gift, and income tax valuations.

a. True
b. False

ANSWER: b. False

Technically, Revenue Ruling 59-60 should be followed when valuing interests for estate, gift, and income taxes. However, Revenue Ruling 59-60 is often relied on and quoted for other valuations as well. It has withstood the test of time.

EXERCISE 6 Which of these are standards of value?

a. Fair market value, fair value financial reporting, investment value
b. Fair value investment reporting, fair value state actions, intrinsic value
c. Investment value, intrinsic value, equal value
d. Fair market value, equal value, investment value

ANSWER: a. Fair market value, fair value financial reporting, investment value

There are five standards of value: fair market value, investment value, intrinsic value, fair value financial reporting, and fair value state actions.

EXERCISE 7 There are the only eight tenets of value in Revenue Ruling 59-60 that need to be considered.

a. True
b. False

ANSWER: b. False

Although there are eight main tenets of value contained in Revenue Ruling 59-60, there are a multitude of other important factors contained in the Revenue Ruling that must also be considered. Other factors include key person discounts, operating versus holding companies, acceptable approaches and methods, and types of historical information.

EXERCISE 8 Valuation conclusions can be presented as:

a. A range of values
b. A single value
c. An estimate of value
d. All of the above

ANSWER: d. All of the above

Value conclusions can be presented in a variety of formats. It is most often either a single value or a range of values. Values are always estimates because judgment is applied.

EXERCISE 9 This valuation is being done on a marketable, control interest basis. It is also on a control stand-alone basis. Name the six levels of value that are considered in a valuation.

ANSWER: a. Control strategic
b. Minority/Control stand-alone liquid
c. Minority liquid
d. Minority nonmarketable
e. Control liquid
f. Control standalone

Control strategic can refer to level of value in a public or a private company. An example of minority/control stand-alone liquid is the value resulting from the application of the guideline public company method. Some analysts consider the result a minority value. In more recent years, more analysts consider the level of value from the guideline public company method as both minority and control. An example of control liquid is the value derived from the application of the income approach (with control cash flows) where the discount or cap rate is based on returns from the public marketplace. Control standalone is the value of a private company after application of the income approach with a discount to reflect the lesser liquidity of a control interest in a private company versus public stock. An income approach using a rate of return derived from public company data and adjusted for a size risk premium likely reflects a liquid value, but not as liquid as a large company stock. Many small public companies are highly illiquid with large bid/ask spreads (that may contribute to the small size premia).

Publicly traded guideline company data used to calculate a subject value would indicate a marketable liquid value, but the degree of liquidity depends on the liquidity of the guideline companies used. The guideline company transactions method presumably provides a control, illiquid but marketable conclusion of value. The asset approach would likely indicate a control marketable value, depending on the type of assets and the methods used to value the assets of the subject company. Minority nonmarketable is the value after the consideration of and/or application of all discounts for lack of control and lack of marketability.

Some of these "levels" of value may be higher or lower than the others depending on the circumstances. The (DLOM) is considered primarily with the bottom three levels for a private company.

This valuation is prepared on a marketable, controlling interest basis.

The valuation profession lacks consensus on the application of discounts for lack of marketability/liquidity in the valuation of controlling interests. Opponents of marketability discounts generally contend that the lack of marketability is reflected in the pricing of the controlling interest. Proponents believe some discount for lack of marketability/liquidity should be made over and above the applied discount rate or price multiple based on public markets. They argue that when comparisons are made to liquid public stocks in the application of a valuation method, liquidity may be embedded in the private company value. In this case, a discount may be appropriate.

EXERCISE 10   The subject of this exercise is a C corporation, but analysts will frequently be required to value noncontrolling interests in S corporations. Valuation of S corporations is one of the most controversial issues in business valuations today. The main issue is how to tax-affect S corporation income and, if appropriate, compute an S corporation adjustment. What three models have been considered or used in valuing S corporations?

ANSWER: 1. Treharne
               2. Van Vleet
               3. Delaware MRI

EXERCISE 11 We are valuing a 100 percent controlling interest in Nova. The percentage of ownership of individual shareholders is not an issue here. However, assume we are valuing the 55 percent of Tony Atkins as opposed to the 100 percent in Nova. The value of a 55 percent interest in Nova would be calculated as 55 percent of the 100 percent control value in Nova.

a. True
b. False

ANSWER: b. False

A 55 percent interest in the Company may not be equal to 55 percent of the 100 percent controlling interest value. The sum of the parts may not equal the whole. Although Tony still controls the corporation with his 55 percent interest, a nuisance value may possibly be attributable to the other three 15 percent interests. Tony does not have complete control and could be exposed at some time in the future to a dissenting rights action or shareholder oppression action. As such, a 55 percent interest would probably be worth somewhat less than a proportional amount of the 100 percent controlling interest value in Nova.

EXERCISE 12 What types of industries would most likely be affected by anticipated changes in interest rates?

ANSWER: a. Residential housing
b. Banking
c. Auto
d. Manufacturing

Although all industries are ultimately affected by changes in interest rates, these industries would be affected more because changes in interest rates change both supply and demand as well as profit margins.

EXERCISE 13 What two economic indicators are probably the most important in valuation?

a. Unemployment levels and gross domestic product (GDP)
b. Dow Jones Industrial Average and Producer Price Index
c. GDP and inflation
d. Inflation and unemployment levels

ANSWER: c. GDP and inflation

Although all economic indicators can be important, typically the two most important ones are historical and anticipated changes in GDP, which measures the real growth of the U.S. economy, and inflation, typically measured through changes in the Consumer Price Index. These two factors affect all industries and can be important in choosing growth rates in both the discounted cash flow and capitalized cash flow methods of the income approach.

EXERCISE 14   In valuing a small, geographically concentrated business, which of these types of economic data should be considered?

   a. International, national, regional, local
   b. National, regional, local
   c. Regional, local
   d. Local only

ANSWER: b. National, regional, local

Although a small, geographically concentrated business would most likely be affected by local and regional data, the national outlook should also be analyzed in preparing the business valuation. It is true that there are often differences in both the local and regional economy versus the national economy. However, in many industries, what is happening at the national level will eventually trickle down to the regional and local levels. There are exceptions to this rule and each valuation can be different. Although the international economic situation could affect the national economic data, it is unlikely that the international economic situation would directly affect a small local business.

EXERCISE 15   Which industry outlook factors are generally the most important in supporting valuation assumptions?

   a. Growth rates, profit margins, and risk
   b. Regulatory and legal issues
   c. Unemployment figures
   d. Minority discounts and/or control premiums

ANSWER: a. Growth rates, profit margins, and risk

When applicable and available, the industry data should tie to the assumptions used in the valuation for growth rates, profit margins, and risk factors. Regulatory and legal issues and unemployment figures are also important but only to the extent that they affect growth, profits, and risks. Discounts and premiums are separate issues.

EXERCISE 16   What is the most important use of historical financial data?

   a. To determine how the company has performed
   b. To assist in supporting anticipated performance

c. To highlight profitability
d. To determine average profits

ANSWER: b. To assist in supporting anticipated performance

All of the items listed here are important components of a historical review of financial data. However, when applicable, the main purpose of the histori-cal review is to support anticipated performance and the assumptions in the valuation models. The analysis of the historical operating performance of a company also indicates how well the management team is performing overall and can lead to information concerning trends. Alternatively, history may not repeat itself and/or history may not be indicative of future performance. For example, the company may not have performed well in the past because of such factors as loss of a key person or litigation. The absence of those items going forward would indicate better performance. The analysis of the histori-cal information should also be made in light of the local, regional, and national economy, as well as the industry outlook. All these items can be used to sup-port assumptions in the valuation models.

EXERCISE 17   Analysts typically spread five years of financial statements because:

a. Revenue Ruling 59-60 requires five years.
b. USPAP and SSVS require five years.
c. An economic cycle is often captured in five years.
d. Most business plans are based on five years of projections.

ANSWER: c. An economic cycle is often captured in five years.

There is no magic to looking at five years of data. In some industries, only the most recent year or just a few years are relevant. In other industries, five to ten years may be more appropriate. The underlying theme is that it captures enough financial information to indicate trends, the performance of the com-pany, and a reasonable economic cycle. Although Revenue Ruling 59-60 sug-gests that five years of data be reviewed, it is not required. USPAP and SSVS do not have any requirements concerning the number of years of financial infor-mation. Although it may be true that many projections include five years of data, this has no real relevance in terms of a historical review of information.

EXERCISE 18   The main drawbacks of publicly available benchmark finan-cial ratios are:

a. There are very few SIC codes.
b. They calculate the ratios incorrectly.

c. The companies that make up the data cannot be used to determine pricing ratios or capitalization rates.
d. The information is from public companies.

ANSWER: c. The companies that make up the data cannot be used to determine pricing ratios or capitalization rates.

Most of the national databases do have fairly extensive amounts of information by SIC code, and the ratios are typically calculated properly. Most of the information is from closely held companies.

The main drawback of the data is that none of databases are tied to pricing ratios or valuation multiples such as price to earnings or invested capital to EBITDA. There is also no tie to any type of discount or capitalization rate. Therefore, some analysts believe that these types of comparisons are less meaningful. Alternatively, when using the guideline public company method of the market approach, ratios can be tied to valuation multiples. Analysts may observe how the subject company compares to the various ratios of the public companies, then make adjustments to the public company multiples to reflect those differences. Such analysis cannot be performed when using public benchmark data without references or ties to valuation multiples or capitalization rates. However, they can help in a general risk assessment.

It is also important to recognize that many of the ratios are calculated differently and that consistency is important when comparing the subject company being valued to the ratios in the benchmark data.

EXERCISE 19   In what type of valuation setting is the excess cash flow method most often used?

a. ESOPs (employee stock ownership plans)
b. Estate tax
c. Dissenting rights
d. Marital dissolution

ANSWER: d. Marital dissolution

Although the excess cash flow method can be used in any valuation, it is most often used in marital dissolutions. Analysts may use this method because the court in a jurisdiction is familiar with it. In some situations, exclusion of the excess cash flow method could be perceived as an omission.

EXERCISE 20   On which Revenue Ruling is the excess cash flow method based?

a. Revenue Ruling 59-60
b. Revenue Ruling 83-120
c. Revenue Ruling 68-609
d. Revenue Ruling 77-287

ANSWER: c. Revenue Ruling 68-609. The excess cash flow method, sometimes referred to as the formula method or the excess earnings method, was first discussed in ARM 34, which was used to determine goodwill in breweries due to Prohibition. This eventually led to Revenue Ruling 68-609. Revenue Ruling 59-60 contains the basic tenets and procedures for valuing closely held businesses. Revenue Ruling 83-120 deals with valuation of preferred stock. Revenue Ruling 77-287 deals with the valuation of restricted securities.

EXERCISE 21 All three approaches to value must be applied in all valuations.

a. True
b. False

ANSWER: b. False

Although it is true that all three approaches to value should be considered in each valuation, they need not all be applied in every valuation. Most analysts do not use the asset approach (tangible and intangible assets) in valuing an operating company because increases in the accuracy of the appraisal, if any, are not worth the time and expense of having all the assets valued. The value of the aggregated assets, including intangible assets, is reflected in the value derived from the income and market approaches. The asset approach is often the primary approach in valuing investment or holding companies and may be relevant when the net asset values are more than the values from the income and market approaches, which could indicate economic obsolescence of the assets.

EXERCISE 22 Which method(s) is(are) considered valid under the income approach?

a. Guideline public company method
b. Discounted cash flow method
c. Capitalized cash flow method
d. Excess cash flow method

ANSWER: b. Discounted cash flow method, and
c. Capitalized cash flow method

Discounted cash flow and capitalized cash flow are the two main methods under the income approach. There are variations of these two methods. The guideline public company method is a market approach, and the excess cash flow method is a hybrid of the income and asset approaches.

EXERCISE 23   In which situation(s) would a capitalized cash flow method be more applicable?

a. When a company's future performance is anticipated to change from its prior performance
b. In litigation settings
c. When a steady historical or pro forma level of cash flow is anticipated to be earned with a constant growth in the future
d. When valuing very small businesses

ANSWER: c. When a steady historical or pro forma level of cash flow is antic-
                 ipated to be earned with a constant growth in the future, and
              d. When valuing very small businesses

Capitalized cash flow methods are most often used when future performance is anticipated to be at a steady rate, based on either a historical figure, such as an average or recent year, or a pro forma single figure. Discounted cash flow is most often used when future performance is anticipated to be different from the past. Both discounted cash flow and capitalized cash flow methods can be and are used in litigation, although some analysts believe that the capitalized cash flow method is easier to support because it is easier to explain. Capitalized cash flow methods are most often performed in valuations of small businesses, because that is frequently the basis on which they are bought and sold. However, capitalized cash flow can be used for larger companies depending on the historical and expected growth rates.

EXERCISE 24   List the two main bases when using the capitalized cash flow (CCF) or discounted cash flow (DCF) methods of the income approach.

ANSWER: 1. Direct equity
              2. Invested capital

The two primary bases are direct equity methods of valuation, in which interest expense and debt principal are included, or to use invested capital methods, in which interest expense and debt principal are excluded. Theoretically, the use of both models should give you a similar result. Both methods can be used in most valuations, but depending on circumstances one method may be better than the other. For example, the invested capital method may be used in control valuations where the capital structure of the company is anticipated to change. Alternatively, in a minority valuation, some analysts believe that the direct equity method is more appropriate, because the minority shareholder cannot change the capital structure of the company. It is often a matter of preference.

EXERCISE 25   Under the direct equity basis, what are the components of net cash flow?

ANSWER:

> Net income after tax
>> Plus: depreciation/amortization and noncash charges
>> Minus: capital expenditure requirements
>> Plus/minus: working capital requirements
>> Plus: new debt principal paid in
>> Minus: debt principal paid out

EXERCISE 26   For the invested capital basis of the income approach, list the components of net cash flow.

ANSWER:

> Net income after tax
>> Plus: interest expense times 1 minus the tax rate
>> Plus: depreciation/amortization and noncash charges
>> Minus: capital expenditure requirements
>> Plus/minus: working capital requirements (debt-free)

EXERCISE 27   What is the difference between minority cash flows and control cash flows?

ANSWER: The difference between minority cash flows and control cash flows is normalization adjustments. Normalization adjustments for control include excess compensation and perquisites. When such amounts are added back, it is considered a control value. When such amounts exist and are left in as expenses, it is considered a minority value, because the minority shareholder cannot change the policies of the control owner.

EXERCISE 28   Which adjustment(s) are made when valuing both minority and control cash flows?

a. Nonrecurring items
b. Nonoperating assets
c. Excess compensation
d. Perquisites
e. Taxes

ANSWER: a. Nonrecurring items,
b. Nonoperating assets, and
e. Taxes

Adjustments are made to cash flows to calculate a normalized amount of cash flows into perpetuity. Nonrecurring items are typically removed from the cash flows. Most analysts will also adjust the P&L for the effect of removing nonoperating assets from the balance sheet. For example, there may be an adjustment for interest income associated with excess working capital, as is the situation here with Nova. Excess compensation and perquisites are adjusted only in control cash flows. When using after-tax rates of return, taxes are typically an expense in minority and control cash flows.

EXERCISE 29   Assume the company does not have any control adjustments and the company is run to the benefit of all shareholders without any shareholders taking out cash flow over or above what they are entitled. Is this value control or minority?

ANSWER: The value would clearly be control standalone, because the capitalized cash flow is the cash flow of the entire company reflecting the benefits to all shareholders. Because the current owner of the company is operating to the benefit of all shareholders, it becomes a minority value as well. However, it is also a minority value only to the extent that the current owners continue their policies. Policies can change and/or new owners can come in, which increases the risk such that a discount for a lack of control or minority interest may still be appropriate. A possible adjustment for lack of control may be appropriate to reflect the risk of potential future detrimental changes to the minority interest(s) from either the owner or the policies or both.

EXERCISE 30   List some of the nonoperating/excess assets that are sometimes encountered in a business valuation.

ANSWER: Marketable securities
Cash
Inventory
Working capital
Land
Buildings
Condominiums
Boats

EXERCISE 31   In valuing a controlling interest in a corporation, most analysts agree that the nonoperating and/or excess assets of the business must be removed from the cash flows and valuation of the operating business, and then be added back at fair market value.

a. True
b. False

ANSWER: a. True

The rate of return requirements for excess assets and/or nonoperating assets are often less than the cost of capital of the company. As such, including the income and expenses of the nonoperating/excess assets in the P&L, and capitalizing such amounts at a higher rate of return, will undervalue the company. In some situations, nonoperating assets generate no income. The capitalization of cash flow without adjustment for such assets would result in a zero value for those assets. This is why these types of assets are typically removed from the balance sheet with appropriate P&L adjustments, and then added back to the operating value of the business.

EXERCISE 32 In valuing a minority interest of a company, most analysts agree that the nonoperating and/or excess assets of the business must be removed from the cash flows and valuation of the operating business, and then be added back at fair market value.

a. True
b. False

ANSWER: a. True

Most analysts believe that the same methodology should be employed as in valuing a controlling interest; that is, value the nonoperating or excess assets separately and make the related P&L adjustments. They would then apply a discount for lack of control and a discount for lack of marketability to the nonoperating asset value before adding it to the company's discounted operating value. Other analysts believe that a minority stockholder has no access to these types of assets and the P&L should be as it is, reflecting the way the company operates. The assets are not separately valued and added back. This can create a situation where the value of nonoperating/excess assets may be zero, which is difficult to defend.

EXERCISE 33 In the valuation of Nova, one of the periods that the analyst decided to use was a straight average of the adjusted income before income taxes for three historical years. Besides a straight average, what other method(s) can be used to determine the appropriate cash flow to be capitalized into perpetuity?

a. Weighted average
b. Most recent fiscal year
c. Most recent trailing 12 months

    d. Trend line analysis/next year's budget
    e. DCF average of next three years

    ANSWER: a. Weighted average,
                    b. Most recent fiscal year,
                    c. Most recent trailing 12 months, and
                    d. Trend line analysis/next year's budget

The first four items can be considered in valuing and determining how cash flow should be capitalized. An example of a weighted average is (3, 2, 1), which would be used for a three-year average, with the most recent year given the weight of 3, the second year 2, and the most distant year 1. Some analysts will use (5, 4, 3, 2, 1) for five years of data. The weighted average is typically used when the analyst believes there may be an increasing trend but wants to reflect the possibility of potential underperforming years. Fiscal year-end and trailing 12 months are typically used when there is anticipation that the most recent information is indicative of the future. Next year's budget may be used if the analyst believes it is more indicative of the potential performance of the company. DCF is typically used when historical cash flows are not anticipated to continue to grow at a steady level. DCF and capitalized cash flow methods do not average future years.

EXERCISE 34   Analysts will generally use a straight historical average where the earnings and cash flows are more volatile.

  a. True
  b. False

ANSWER: a. True

In the case of Nova, the automotive industry is fairly cyclical such that it is reasonable to consider a straight historical average. The analyst also recognized that the Company has improved margins reflected in the trailing 12 months cash flow and that the financial performance of the company would improve with the addition of an important customer near term, which is reflected better in the DCF method. The other methods are often more appropriate where there is more of a trend in the historical results.

EXERCISE 35   Which situation is most appropriate when adjusting cash flows for depreciation and capital expenditures?

  a. Capital expenditures should be similar to or exceed depreciation.
  b. Depreciation should exceed capital expenditures.
  c. The actual unadjusted amounts should be capitalized.

ANSWER: a. Capital expenditures should be similar to or exceed depreciation.

A common mistake made in business valuation is to capitalize cash flow into perpetuity where the depreciation greatly exceeds the future capital expenditure requirements. This is obviously an impossible situation, because future capital expenditures have to be made in order to generate future depreciation. Many analysts will normalize depreciation and capital expenditures by making them equal or similar. This equalization process is a simplifying assumption, because capital expenditures would exceed depreciation due to the inflationary pressure in a stable business. However, this can have an effect on value. There are situations in which depreciation/amortization can exceed capital expenditures within a definite period of time. This occurs when there is a previous purchase of a long-life asset such as a building, or where goodwill or other intangible assets are amortized over a longer period of time. In those situations, it may be appropriate to calculate separately the value of the tax benefit for the finite period during which depreciation exceeds capital expenditures. See Chapter 5 of *Financial Valuation Applications and Models*, 5th edition, for additional information.

EXERCISE 36   Assuming taxes are to be deducted, what two choices may be made in making the tax adjustments?

a. Tax each year historically, then calculate an average.
b. Taxes should never be deducted in the value of an S corporation.
c. Make all adjustments in the historical period pre-tax, determine the average, and then deduct for taxes.

ANSWER: a. Tax each year historically, then calculate an average, and
         b. Make all adjustments in the historical period pre-tax, determine the average, and then deduct for taxes.

Some analysts will compute taxes in each of the historical years used in the calculation of average income as opposed to making all the adjustments pre-tax, calculating the average, and then adjusting for taxes. When the annual tax rates are the same, this will not have an impact. However, in C corporations, where taxes may differ for each year due to certain types of planning, an average of five years after-tax income may be different from the average of five years pre-tax, which is aggregated with one tax amount applied to it. In some years, the actual taxes might have been lower than the marginal rate. As such, some analysts believe that an average tax-affected rate is more appropriate. Other analysts believe that the company will eventually end up paying close to the marginal rate into perpetuity, and that would be the more appropriate rate.

EXERCISE 37   Which economic benefit stream(s) can be used for cash flow in a capitalized cash flow method?

a. After-tax income
b. Pre-tax income

c. Net cash flow
d. EBITDA (earnings before interest, taxes, depreciation, and amortization)
e. Revenues
f. Debt-free net income
g. Debt-free cash flow

ANSWER: a. After-tax income
          b. Pre-tax income
          c. Net cash flow
          d. Debt-free net income
          e. Debt-free cash flow

Cash flow is used in many business valuations. In certain circumstances, particularly with small businesses, income may be capitalized on both an after-tax and a pre-tax basis. However, income in these cases approximates cash flow (see next paragraph). Also, a pre-tax capitalization rate should be applied to pre-tax income/cash flow. Debt-free net income, after-tax income with interest expense added back, is used in the invested capital basis. Debt-free cash flow is debt-free net income with depreciation added back. Although theoretically EBITDA could be a capitalizable amount, it is more often used in the market approach than the income approach. Revenues are seldom capitalized in the income approach, although they can be capitalized through the market approach.

Some debate occurs in the valuation industry concerning the use of either cash flow or income when performing the income approach, but the point is frequently moot because analysts often make depreciation and capital expenditures similar or somewhat different (capital expenditures exceed depreciation). The only other real adjustment would be incremental working capital. Not all businesses require incremental working capital, particularly cash businesses or businesses whose receivables are turned quickly. As such, and particularly in small businesses, cash flow and income may be similar. However, many businesses require working capital to fund growth. In those situations, working capital should be considered as a cash outflow. Cash flow in a growing business would typically be less than income in those businesses with working capital needs. Debt would also have to be normalized with regard to debt principal in and debt principal out. If they are normalized, they may net out to net income.

EXERCISE 38   When is it more appropriate to use a discounted cash flow method instead of a capitalized cash flow method?

ANSWER: If a company anticipates growing at a steady rate in the future, it is unnecessary to prepare a discounted cash flow method. In such cases, a capitalized cash flow method is sufficient. Discounted cash flow methods are typically used when short-term growth is anticipated to be different from long-term growth and/or the company's cash flow has not reached a stabilized or normalized period that can be capitalized into perpetuity.

For illustrative purposes, a capitalization of cash flows was prepared for Nova, as well as a discounted cash flow analysis. In practice, only one method would generally be prepared, relied on, and presented if the income approach was applicable. In the near term, Nova is expected to grow at rates above the long-term perpetuity growth rate. As such, a discounted cash flow approach can better capture expectations for the future cash flows of the Company.

EXERCISE 39   In the terminal year of a discounted cash flow analysis, analysts often use the simplifying assumption that depreciation equals capital expenditures.

  a. True
  b. False

ANSWER: a. True

In order to determine operating cash flows, we have subtracted capital expenditures from net income (pre-interest and after-tax) and added back total depreciation. We have assumed that expectations regarding these items are offsetting at their historical levels, as they have been relatively stable historically. This is a simplifying assumption because there may be some difference between capital expenditures, which are purchased in current dollars, and depreciation, which is in historical dollars.

EXERCISE 40   When using the direct equity basis instead of the invested capital basis, assumptions of capital structure can be avoided.

  a. True
  b. False

ANSWER: b. False

One of the reasons often given for using the direct equity basis is that the analyst can avoid making assumptions of capital structure with regard to the percent debt and equity a company will use. However, a direct equity model requires assumptions of normalized debt principal in and debt principal out. An assumption to normalize the amount of debt that is used in a company inherently requires an assumption of a capital structure. As such, debt is a consideration in using the direct-equity basis.

EXERCISE 41   When using the invested capital basis to determine a control value, the analyst should always use an optimal capital structure in the weighted average cost of capital.

a. True
b. False

ANSWER: b. False

Although many analysts will use an optimal capital structure, frequently based on a review of public company capital structures, it is not always the basis to use for control value. If the management of a company decides to operate with a different capital structure than the industry, application of management's capital structure assumptions would result in a control value on a stand-alone basis reflecting the current policies of management.

EXERCISE 42   Name the two methods most often used to derive a cost of equity in the income approach.

ANSWER: 1. Modified capital asset pricing model (MCAPM), and
             2. Build-Up method

Controversy exists in the valuation industry regarding whether the MCAPM should be used to value small businesses. Some analysts believe that MCAPM should not be used to value even large businesses. The only difference between the MCAPM and the build-up method is the use of beta. It is often difficult to find betas for small publicly traded companies that could be applicable to small private companies. Betas may be derived from many sources and calculated in many different ways. As such, betas on the same date can differ for the same public company. Sometimes betas are available to be used in a MCAPM for small companies. Some industries include large numbers of public small companies from which betas may be derived. However, if there are no reasonably similar companies whose betas could be used as a proxy for the small closely held company, then the build-up method may be the best method to use. However, if the betas are reasonable and can be used, then the MCAPM may be considered as well. Each of these situations is fact- and circumstance-specific and could differ, depending on the type of company, the industry of the subject company, and the size of the company.

EXERCISE 43   Should build-up method and MCAPM rates of return be applied to income or cash flow?

ANSWER: The general consensus is that these are cash flow rates of return. They are also rates of return after corporate tax but before personal investor tax. The rates of return are based on dividends and capital appreciation. Dividends are paid after-tax by public corporations, and capital appreciation is also after-tax due to retained earnings used to grow the business. However, these returns are pre-tax to an individual investor. According to Kroll, traditional rates of return derived using their data, whether MCAPM or build-up method, should be applied to after-tax cash flows.

EXERCISE 44 Why are long-term 20-year U.S. Treasury coupon bonds most often used for the risk-free rate of return in both the build-up method and the MCAPM?

ANSWER: Most analysts use a 20-year risk-free rate of return from a U.S. Treasury bond because the data used to derive the equity risk premium have been calculated based on this 20-year Treasury bond benchmark for all periods analyzed by the studies (the equity risk premium will be explained in depth later). The rate reflects a long-term investment, an assumption used in most closely held business valuations. Twenty years is the bond that has been in existence over a long period of time.

EXERCISE 45 What benchmark is the Kroll common stock equity risk premium return most often based on?

  a. S&P 500
  b. New York Stock Exchange
  c. Dow Jones Industrial Average
  d. Russell 5000

ANSWER: The risk premium used in this report is from the S&P 500. This is the most commonly used benchmark for determining equity premiums for the marketplace.

EXERCISE 46 When using the MCAPM to derive an equity cost of capital for a controlling interest, it is sometimes necessary to adjust beta for differences between the capital structure of the public companies and the capital structure of the subject company being valued. This is not necessary if the capital structure is assumed to be the same. Given the following information, calculate the unlevered and re-levered beta using the Hamada formula.

  a. Average beta of guideline public companies = .66
     Tax rate = 33 percent

     Market value capital structure = 10 percent debt, 90 percent equity
     The formula for unlevered beta is:

$$Bu = Bl / (1 + (1 - t)(Wd / We))$$

  Where:
                 Bu = Beta unlevered
                 Bl = Beta levered
                  t = Tax rate for the company
                 Wd = Percentage of debt in the capital structure (at market value)
                 We = Percentage of equity in the capital structure (at market value)

b. Assuming that Nova has a capital structure of 20 percent debt and 80 percent equity, what would be the beta?

The formula to relever the beta is:

$$Bl = Bu(1+(1-t)(Wd/We))$$

ANSWER: a. $Bu = .66 / (1+(1-.33)(.10/.90))$

$Bu = .66 / 1+.67(.11)$

$Bu = .66 / 1.074$

$Bu = .61$

b. $Bl = .61(1+(1-.33)(.20/.80))$

$Bl = .61(1+(.67)(.25))$

$Bl = .61(1.1675)$

$Bl = .71$

EXERCISE 47   A list of risk factors was previously presented for Nova to calculate the company-specific risk premium. Discuss the different methods for determining what the actual company-specific risk premium should be.

ANSWER: In this valuation, the analyst made a selection of an aggregate 2 percent risk premium. This was based on the analyst's judgment concerning the additional risk of the previously described items. This is a common method of selecting company-specific risk premiums. Other methods that can be used are some type of numerical system placed on the categories (i.e., –3, –2, –1, 0, 1, 2, 3). However, this sometimes implies accuracy that may not exist and may be difficult to defend in a litigation setting. Other analysts use a plus and minus system to determine the potential amount of company-specific risk.

EXERCISE 48   Company-specific risk premiums can be determined from Kroll data.

a. True
b. False

ANSWER: b. False

Company-specific risk premium data are not included in the Kroll *Cost of Capital Navigator*. In fact, there are no empirical studies indicating company-specific risk premiums. This is a judgment area for the analyst.

EXERCISE 49   Which of these rates of return are derived using Kroll data?

a. Minority rates of return
b. Control rates of return
c. Majority rates of return
d. Neutral

ANSWER: d. Neutral

Another issue is whether the resultant rate represents a minority or controlling interest return. Given that the underlying data used by Kroll (and formerly Ibbotson) in its empirical studies represent minority interest returns in publicly traded companies, many analysts have concluded that the resulting rates derived from the use of this method already incorporate the attributes of minority ownership. Kroll, however, argues that the rates derived from its data are neutral and incorporate neither control nor minority characteristics. The rationale is that most publicly traded companies optimize shareholder returns as a key corporate strategy and that the arrival of a new controlling owner would not be able to improve such returns unless that owner were a strategic buyer (which then may shift the standard of value away from FMV). There is no proof that such a control position could improve the shareholder returns. This issue was further discussed in an article by Eric Vander Linden in the December 1998 *Business Valuation Review* quarterly newsletter, titled "Cost of Capital Derived from Ibbotson Data Equals Minority Value?" Vander Linden concludes, after reference to several other recognized sources, that adjustments for control versus minority attributes are done through the numerator (cash flow) and not the denominator (rate of return). This view is also presented by the American Institute of Certified Public Accountants, the American Society of Appraisers, and the National Association of Certified Valuators and Analysts in their business valuation courses.

EXERCISE 50   Assume that the Kroll historical CRSP equity risk premium is 7.46 percent and the 10th-decile size premium is 4.8 percent. Assume that the relevered beta of the guideline companies is 1.14 under MCAPM and that the industry risk premium is not relied on in the build-up model (BUM). Calculate the cost of equity for Nova under the MCAPM and BUM methods.

ANSWER:

MCAPM Method

R_f = Risk-free rate of return = 3.85%

Beta = 1.14

RP_m = Equity risk premium   = 7.46%

RP_s = Size premium   = 4.8%

RP_c = Company-specific risk = 2.00%

K_e = Cost of equity   = 19.15%

BUM Method

R_f = Risk-free rate of return = 3.85%
RP_m = Equity risk premium = 7.46%
RP_s = Size premium = 4.8%
RP_c = Company-specific risk = 2.00%
K_e = Cost of equity = 18.10%

EXERCISE 51 Assume that the Kroll supply-side CRSP equity risk premium is 6.22 percent and the 10th-decile size premium is 4.8 percent. Assume that the relevered beta of the guideline companies is 1.14 under MCAPM and that the industry risk premium is not relied on in the BUM. Calculate the cost of equity for Nova under the MCAPM and BUM methods.

ANSWER:

MCAPM Method

R_f = Risk-free rate of return = 3.85%
Beta = 1.14
RP_m = Equity risk premium = 6.22%
RP_s = Size premium = 4.8%
RP_c = Company-specific risk = 2.00%
K_e = Cost of equity = 17.74%

BUM Method

Rf = Risk-free rate of return = 3.85%
RP_m = Equity risk premium = 6.22%
RP_s = Size premium = 4.8%
RP_c = Company-specific risk = 2.00%
K_e = Cost of equity = 16.87%

EXERCISE 52 Assume that the Kroll historical market equity risk premium is 5.05 percent and the 25th-size portfolio premium is 6.10 percent. Calculate the cost of equity for Nova.

ANSWER:

R_f = Risk-free rate of return = 3.85%
Beta = 1.14
RP_m = Equity risk premium = 6.03%
RP_s = Size premium = 5.00%
RP_c = Company-specific risk = 2.00%
K_e = Cost of equity = 17.72%

EXERCISE 53 Assume that the Kroll combined equity risk premium and size premium for the 25th-size portfolio is 14.00 percent. Calculate the cost of equity for Nova.

ANSWER:

R_f	= Risk-free rate of return	= 3.85%
$(RP_m \text{ \& } RP_s)$	= Risk premium	= 14.00%
RP_c	= Company-specific risk	= 2.00%
K_e	= Cost of equity	= 19.85%

EXERCISE 54 In addition to equity risk size premiums based on eight alternative measures of size, Kroll presents risk premium data based on three measures of risk that are not based initially on size. Name those three measures of risk.

ANSWER:

1. Five-year average operating margin
2. Coefficient of variation of the operating margin
3. Coefficient of variation of the return on equity over five years

---

EXERCISE 55 Assume that the analysis using the three alternative measures of risk from Kroll results in a cost of equity of 18.85 percent. What is the range of the seven costs of equity for Nova and what is the conclusion for the cost of equity? Explain your reasons and support.

ANSWER:

Range of costs of equity: 16.87% to 19.85%

Concluded cost of equity: 18%

Supporting reasons: The mean average and median average are 18.33 percent and 18.11 percent, respectively. The range is fairly narrow at 3.4 percent. A cost of equity somewhere inside the range is reasonable. See *Financial Valuation Applications and Models*, 5th edition, for further information, particularly Chapter 6 addendums and the report that is part of Chapter 11.

EXERCISE 56 Which of these factors causes the cost of debt to be tax-affected?

a. Debt principal is tax deductible.
b. Interest expense is tax deductible.

c. It should not be tax-affected because equity is not tax-affected.
d. Debt and interest are tax deductible.

ANSWER: b. Interest expense is tax deductible. Principal is never tax deductible for a corporation (ESOP exception). Because interest expense is a cost of debt and is tax deductible, an adjustment for taxes is appropriate. Equity returns derived by using Kroll data are already on an after-tax basis, so no adjustments need to be made to equity returns.

EXERCISE 57   Using the information in the text, calculate the weighted average cost of capital for Nova.

ANSWER: 66% (18%) + 34% (4.68%) = 13.47%

EXERCISE 58   Which methods can be used to determine the weights in the weighted average cost of capital?

a. Iterative process
b. Guideline public companies
c. Aggregated public industry data
d. Risk Management Associates
e. Book values
f. Anticipated capital structure

ANSWER: a. Iterative process
b. Guideline public companies
c. Aggregated public industry data, and
f. Anticipated capital structure

Both guideline public company information and aggregated public industry data are often viewed as optimal capital structures with the idea that public companies use an optimal amount of debt to lower their weighted average cost of capital. This assumes the subject company can access a similar amount of debt. Iterative processes can be used for both minority and controlling interests but are more typically used in minority valuations. Clients will often have an anticipated capital structure that can also be employed. Risk Management Associates and book value information are all based on book values, not fair market values. The weights to be used in the weighted average cost of capital are fair market value weights, not book value weights.

EXERCISE 59   Explain the iterative process for determining the weights in the weighted average cost of capital.

ANSWER: The analyst will make an initial capital structure assumption to value the company. Then using the actual debt of the company, the analyst will calculate the percent of debt in the capital structure implied by the initial value conclusion. If the implied capital structure weighting is different than the assumed weighting, the analyst uses multiple reiteration calculations of the capital structure assumption until it reconciles to the capital structure that is in existence based on the value of debt. The use of spreadsheets makes this reiteration process easy to accomplish.

EXERCISE 60 Changing the amount of debt in the capital structure of the company has no effect on the return on equity.

a. True
b. False

ANSWER: b. False

As the assumption of capital structure of the company changes through an iterative process, increases in the level of debt may increase the rates of return on equity as well. The more debt the company assumes, the higher the return on equity. This can be reflected directly through the use of MCAPM by levering and unlevering betas based on the different debt levels. If the build-up method is used, the adjustment is based more on judgment.

EXERCISE 61 When valuing a controlling interest in a company, should you use the optimal capital structure based on public data or the capital structure anticipated to be employed by the owner of the company?

ANSWER: This answer depends on the type of valuation being performed. The valuation could be from the perspective of a sale to an owner that could employ a different capital structure. The company may be valued on a stand-alone basis, and the owners may want to know what it is worth to them with the existing or anticipated capital structure. In the valuation of Nova, the Company was valued using industry capital weights, which were consistent with management's expectations.

EXERCISE 62 Calculate the capitalization rate from the information in the text and calculate the value (add excess working capital) based on the most recent fiscal year cash flow.

ANSWER: $(13\% - 4.5\%) = 8.5\%$
$\$639,159/.85 = \$15,800,000$

EXERCISE 63 Items used to support growth rates in the capitalized cash flow method of the income approach include:

a. Inflation
b. Nominal gross domestic product
c. Industry growth rate
d. Actual historical company growth rate
e. All of the above

ANSWER: e. All of the above

The selection of the growth rate can have a tremendous impact on the value conclusion. Value is very sensitive to growth. Many analysts use the inflation rate as the perpetual growth rate in the capitalized capital cash flow method. Others use the average nominal (real and inflation) growth of the GDP of the United States (as considered in the case of Nova), which has been 6 to 6.5 percent when measured from 1926 to the present. Others also use prospective (10-year forecast) information (real GDP and inflation) from sources like the *Livingston Survey* (Federal Reserve Bank of Philadelphia), which has been about 5 percent. Still other analysts use what they believe to be the anticipated or long-term industry growth rate. Economic and industry information can be helpful in supporting the growth rate. A company's historical growth is also a consideration.

EXERCISE 64 Size is often a consideration in selecting guideline public companies. The general criterion for using size as a selection parameter is:

a. 2 times
b. 5 times
c. 10 times
d. None of the above

ANSWER: d. None of the above

There is really no general criterion for selecting guideline public companies based on size. A rule of thumb used by some analysts is no greater than 10 times revenue. However, this is not always applicable. Analysts adjust for size not so much because the guideline public companies are larger but because size typically indicates that the company is more diversified in product lines and geography. Furthermore, larger companies tend to have more management depth.

EXERCISE 65 In the valuation of Nova, only one company, P&F Industries, Inc., was comparable in size, but all the guideline companies operate in the same industry and were not considered too big to provide growth, margin, and multiple data for Nova. Given that fact, which option would probably result in the best presentation of the GPCM in the valuation of Nova?

a. Only use P&F Industries.
b. Use all guideline public companies.
c. Reject the guideline public company method.
d. Use the guideline public company method but only as a reasonableness test for the other approaches.

ANSWER: b. Use all guideline public companies.

The guideline public companies are somewhat larger than the subject company but were determined to be similar in terms of industry, products, operations, growth, and margin opportunities. As such, the guideline public company data was deemed to be reliable for application in the guideline public company method.

EXERCISE 66   Guideline public company methods are not applicable to smaller businesses such as Nova.

a. True
b. False

ANSWER: b. False

Some analysts believe that guideline public companies are not applicable to small businesses. Such analysts may be surprised by the number of potential publicly traded companies that are similar in size in certain industries. At the very least, in valuing a small company, a quick review of public companies should be undertaken to determine if there are any similar companies.

EXERCISE 67   Which initial selection criteria are generally used by analysts in choosing guideline public companies?

a. Size
b. Return on equity
c. Profit margin
d. Industry similarity
e. Similar products and services
f. Growth rates
g. Investors' similarities

ANSWER: a. Size
d. Industry similarity, and
e. Similar products and services

Analysts typically screen initially by industry similarity, including similar products and services, and then by size. Once an initial selection of companies is made, profit margins, return on equity, and growth rates may also be considered. However, these are typically not used in the initial screening. Some analysts will also look at similarity in terms of investor preferences. They believe that the selection process for guideline public companies can be expanded outside the particular industry in which the company operates. They will look for similar investment characteristics such as growth, return on equity, profit margin, and so forth. Their belief is that a prudent investor would invest in companies that have similar characteristics regardless of industry. Generally, the courts have been reluctant to accept companies outside the subject company's industry that are not at least somewhat similar in product, market, and so on.

EXERCISE 68   Which of these are commonly used guideline public company valuation multiples?

a. Price/earnings
b. Invested capital/revenues
c. Price/gross profits
d. Invested capital/book value of equity
e. Invested capital/EBITDA
f. Invested capital/EBIT
g. Price/assets
h. Invested capital/debt-free net income
i. Invested capital/debt-free cash flow

ANSWER: a. Price/earnings
b. Invested capital/revenues
e. Invested capital/EBITDA (widely used)
f. Invested capital/EBIT
h. Invested capital/debt-free net income, and
i. Invested capital/debt-free cash flow

A variety of multiples can be used to value a company. In the valuation of Nova, the analyst used invested capital to net revenues, EBITDA and EBIT, and price to equity. This is a judgment area, and the analyst should consider all potential multiples and decide which ones may be the best fit. It is preferable for the numerator and denominator to be similar. For example, if price of equity is in the numerator, then the earnings' parameters should be the earnings available to equity in the denominator. If the numerator is invested capital, then the denominator should be the earnings' parameters available for invested capital. Price/gross profit, invested capital/book value of equity, and price to assets would not be the best multiples to use here.

EXERCISE 69   When using the guideline public company method, at what point in time are the prices of the public companies' stock valued?

a. Thirty-day average
b. As of valuation date

c. Six-month average

d. Three-year average

ANSWER: b. As of valuation date

Valuation theory holds that the value should be at a single point in time, typically as of a single day. Whatever the day the valuation is, that is the day the stock price should be used. Some analysts develop multiples based on the current price divided by a projected income or cash flow figure. They believe that this multiple better represents the price of the stock to the anticipated performance of the company. This assumes reasonable unbiased projected income or cash flow.

ANSWER: e. All of the above

Some analysts use an average of multiples to derive a value. Some use a mean average that is the sum of the indications divided by the number of indications or a harmonic mean based on averaging the reciprocals of the data points. Others believe that the median average is a better fit because it excludes outliers because it is the midpoint. Still other analysts believe that you should look at each guideline company separately, decide which ones are more comparable, and rely on those multiples rather than an average of the multiples. Many analysts will use averages, then take a fundamental discount from the average to reflect the subject company's differences. This fundamental discount is often used to adjust for size and/or other factors.

EXERCISE 70 What type of value is the result of the application of the guideline public company method?

a. Control

b. Minority

c. Neutral

ANSWER: c. Neutral

Some analysts argue that the underlying stocks are minority such that the application of a valuation multiple would result in a minority value. Others argue that the valuation multiples are basically inverted capitalization rates (earnings, not net cash flow) derived from the public market. As such, the underlying theory about minority/control being in the cash flows for the income approach should also apply to the market approach. If that is true, then the application of valuation multiples would be neutral and control/minority would, like the income approach, be an adjustment to the earnings' parameter to which the valuation multiples are applied.

EXERCISE 71 In selecting multiples from guideline public companies for application to a subject company such as Nova, what options do analysts typically have?

a. Mean or harmonic mean average of the multiples
b. Median average of the multiples
c. Individual guideline company multiples
d. Average multiples with a fundamental discount
e. All of the above

ANSWER: e. All of the above

Some analysts use an average of multiples to derive a value. Some use a mean average that is the sum of the indications divided by the number of indications or a harmonic mean based on averaging the reciprocals of the data points. Others believe that the median average is a better fit because it excludes outliers because it is the midpoint. Still other analysts believe that you should look at each guideline company separately, decide which ones are more comparable, and rely on those multiples rather than an average of the multiples. Many analysts will use averages, then take a fundamental discount from the average to reflect the subject company's differences. This fundamental discount is often used to adjust for size and/or other factors.

EXERCISE 72 Which of these time periods can be used to derive valuation multiples from publicly traded companies?

a. Most recent four quarters
b. Most recent fiscal year-end
c. Three-year average
d. Five-year average
e. One-year projected
f. Five-year future average

ANSWER: a. Most recent four quarters
            b. Most recent fiscal year-end
            c. Three-year average
            d. Five-year average, and
            e. One-year projected

Analysts must decide whether the multiples derived from publicly traded companies should be the most recent multiples, typically based on an annual fiscal year-end or four-quarter trailing figure or a multiple of some average earnings such as a three-year or five-year average. If it is believed that an average multiple would be more indicative of future performance of a company, then that may be more appropriate. Many analysts use both—the most recent period as well as a historical period—and weight them according to what they think would be most indicative of the future value and performance of the company. Some analysts also use a multiple based on a one-year projected annual earnings parameter typically forecasted by investment banking houses that follow the company. Occasionally an analyst will use a multiple of a future amount over one year forward, but a multiple of a five-year average is not recommended.

EXERCISE 73 Which of these are general transaction databases considered by analysts in valuing companies?

a. *DealStats*
b. RMA
c. Bizcomps
d. *Mergerstat Review*

ANSWER: a. *DealStats*,
  c. Bizcomps, and
  d. *Mergerstat Review*

RMA provides book value ratios of companies, not pricing data.

EXERCISE 74 What is one of the most significant problems when attempting to use transaction data?

ANSWER: One of the common mistakes made in the application of transaction multiples is to aggregate the transactions from the different databases. This will result in an inaccurate valuation, because each of the databases collects and presents its data in a different format. Some of the databases use invested capital multiples, some use equity multiples, some include working capital, some include debt, some include inventory, and so on. When using these databases, if they are different, it is recommended that information from each database be used and applied separately to the subject company's earnings parameters. This will avoid any possible inaccuracies. The other major problem is the absence of meaningful detail about the transactions, which often makes the method unsupportable or to be used only as a corroborating method.

EXERCISE 75 Is a 100 percent controlling interest marketable or non-marketable?

ANSWER: The term *marketable*, as it applies to a 100 percent controlling interest, assumes the entire company can be sold in a reasonable amount of time. It does not mean the company is liquid. The price of the transaction should reflect some reasonable amount of time to sell the company such that marketability issues are included in the value. The marketability, or lack thereof, is already reflected in the transaction price(s) when using the guideline company transaction method.

Although many experts agree, in theory, on the need for a discount for lack of marketability/liquidity on controlling interests in a privately held company, no direct empirical evidence is available to support such a discount. The initial public offering and restricted stock studies used to develop discounts for lack of marketability are based on minority interests, not controlling interests.

EXERCISE 76   Discounts for lack of marketability/liquidity can be applied to 100 percent controlling interests in a company such as Nova.

  a. True
  b. False

ANSWER: a. True

There is continuing controversy about whether discounts for lack of marketability/ liquidity should be applied to controlling interests, particularly 100 percent controlling interests, as in National Fastener. Some analysts believe that a 100 percent interest is marketable and no discount would apply. Other analysts believe that it depends on the underlying methodology used to derive the pre-discount value. For example, when using valuation multiples or rates of return derived from public company data, the rates of return, or multiples, reflect the fact that the public stock can be sold in a very short amount of time, typically receiving cash within three days. You cannot sell a company and receive cash within three days. These analysts believe that the underlying method assumes such marketability or liquidity, which does not exist in a controlling interest in a private company. Thus, some level of discount may be appropriate. There are no known studies to determine discounts for lack of marketability/liquidity of a 100 percent controlling interest in a business. Many analysts rely on discount for lack of marketability studies for minority interests and, using their judgment, reduce the discount to reflect the 100 percent control. Option models and the time period differences for restricted stock may be useful here as well. No discount for lack of liquidity was taken for Nova.

EXERCISE 77   Which discount for lack of marketability studies and/or data are available in determining discounts?

  a. *Mergerstat Review*
  b. Restricted stock studies
  c. IPO studies
  d. Court cases

e. Flotation costs
f. CAPM
g. Kroll
h. Quantitative marketability discount model (QMDM)
i. Option pricing models

ANSWER: b. Restricted stock studies,
          c. IPO studies,
          e. Flotation costs,
          h. QMDM, and
          i. Option pricing models

Analysts typically rely on restricted stock studies, which compare restricted or letter stocks to their publicly traded counterparts. Some analysts also use IPO studies based on the comparison of transactions of interests in companies within months (or years) of when they went public. Flotation costs are sometimes considered when valuing much larger companies. However, their application assumes that the subject company is an IPO candidate. QMDM looks at holding periods for investments for minority interests in closely held companies. It is a present value technique that has gained increased acceptance currently. Option pricing models like Finnerty and Longstaff have gained visibility in recent years. *Mergerstat Review* reports control premiums, MCAPM is the model for deriving discount rates, and Kroll contains data for calculating risk premiums. Court cases will indicate discounts for lack of marketability, but they are very fact- and circumstance-specific and should seldom be relied on in determining discounts. Knowledge of court cases can be important, but they should not be used as the primary method for discounts.

EXERCISE 78   Although a 100 percent controlling interest is valued in Nova, numerous other levels of ownership interests can exist in a closely held company. Provide some examples of other levels of ownership.

ANSWER: 100 percent ownership
          Less than 100 percent ownership but greater than majority
          Majority interest
          Operating control
          Two 50 percent interests
          Largest minority block of stock
          Minority with swing vote
          Minority can elect board member
          Pure minority (no control rights)
          Each of these may have a different discount for lack of control and/or lack of marketability/liquidity.

EXERCISE 79 A discount for lack of marketability/liquidity should be applied to all of the valuation methods used in the valuation of Nova.

a. True
b. False

ANSWER: b. False

As previously mentioned, the discounted cash flow method, capitalized cash flow method, and the guideline public company method are based on pricing and rate of return data on securities that can be sold with cash received within three days. This option does not exist for Nova. As such, a small discount for lack of marketability/liquidity, subjectively derived and based on judgment, may be applied by some analysts. In the application of the transaction databases, the transaction prices already reflect any potential discount for lack of marketability. No discount is applied. A 100 percent control interest may be marketable, but it is not liquid.

EXERCISE 80   Which method can be used to correlate and reconcile value?

a. Straight average of the indications of value
b. Numerical weights assigned to each of the value indications
c. Qualitative judgment in selection of value
d. All of the above

ANSWER: d. All of the above

In correlating and reconciling values, many analysts simply average all of the indications of value. This implies that each method has equal weight, validity, and accuracy. This is seldom the case in a business valuation, including the situation here with Nova, in which the guideline company transaction method was given no weight. Other analysts will assign weights to each of the methods, such as 0.5 to the income approach, 0.2 to the guideline public company approach, 0.1 to transactions, and so on. However, this may again imply accuracy that does not exist. Also, applying only a 10 percent weight on a method may be indicating that the method may not be very supportable. In the valuation of Nova, the analyst considered each of the methodologies and decided that the discounted cash flow method under the income approach and the guideline public company method under the market approach were the most relevant.

2.1 ADDENDUM: DISCOUNT CASE STUDY EXERCISES

EXERCISE A Assume that we are determining the fair market value of a minority nonmarketable interest in a company for gift tax purposes. The minority marketable value derived by various methods is $100 per share. We are in a state where you need over 50 percent for full control. What is the relative discount for lack of marketability in these situations?

a. Value of a 10 percent interest with one 90 percent owner
b. Value of a 10 percent interest with nine other 10 percent owners
c. Value of a 50 percent interest with one other 50 percent owner
d. Value of a 33.33 percent interest with two other 33.33 percent owners
e. Value of a 2 percent interest with two 49 percent owners

ANSWER: a. This is a typical minority ownership with very few rights. The 90 percent owner has full control, and, absent any shareholder oppression or dissenting rights issues, can pretty much do what they want concerning the direction of the company, including selling the company and distributions. The 10 percent owner is almost completely at the mercy of the 90 percent owner.

b. This is a much better situation than *a* because no one has control. A 10 percent owner would need to team up with five other owners to control the company. As such, they have more potential for influence than the situation in *a*.

c. In owning a 50 percent interest with one other 50 percent owner, each owner possesses veto power. Although neither owner can do anything without agreement of the other owner, a single owner can veto anything the other owner does. This is a better situation than in *a* or *b*. A discount for lack of control and marketability would still be applicable, but not as great as in *a* and *b*.

d. In this situation, there is more ability to influence the company because a one-third owner would only have to team up with another one-third owner. There is some risk that two one-third owners could collaborate on the direction of the company.

e. This is the classic situation of swing value. Each one of the owners may be willing to couple with the 2 percent owner to direct the company. However, there are many situations where there are two major owners of a company with a small minority share where the two major owners collaborate. This may not necessarily be to the benefit of the small minority owner. The value of a 2 percent interest may go up when the two 49 percent owners are in a dispute.

EXERCISE B Again, assume we are determining the fair market value of a company for gift tax purposes. In this case study, we are valuing a 100 percent controlling interest on a stand-alone basis in a closely held company. What is the discount for lack of marketability/liquidity in these situations where the pre-discount value is determined by using:

a. P/E ratios from control transactions information (i.e., *DealStats*)
b. P/E ratios from guideline public companies
c. Discounted cash flow (DCF) with a discount rate determined using Kroll information
d. Capitalized cash flow method
e. Asset approach

ANSWER: a. Many analysts believe that the application of control transaction information results in a value that already reflects the marketability of the company. This is because most control transactions are of private companies.

b. Some analysts believe that when using P/E ratios from public companies, the marketability and liquidity of the public company stocks are inherent in the multiples when applied to a private company. That level of liquidity does not exist, even for a 100 percent interest. In those situations, some analysts will take a discount for lack of marketability based on the DLOM studies for minority interests, which are then reduced based on judgment.

c. This is similar to *b*. Because the discount rate is determined using Kroll information based on publicly traded company rates of return, they, too, reflect much greater marketability and liquidity than exists in a 100 percent controlling interest in a private company. Some analysts believe that some level of discount may be appropriate based on judgment.

d. Same situation for capitalized cash flow as for DCF when using Kroll information.

e. When valuing a company through an asset approach, the marketability of the asset is included in the individual values of those assets. A discount for lack of marketability may be appropriate because selling an entire company may be more difficult than selling individual assets. Some analysts will apply some level of discount, again usually based on DLOM studies based on minority interests reduced for the 100 percent controlling interest being valued.

CHAPTER 3

Financial Valuation
Applications and Models
Companion Exercises and
Test Questions

This chapter comprises exercise and test questions taken from the book *Financial Valuation Applications and Models*, 5th edition. You should read the book, answer the questions, and then proceed to the Answer Grid of this chapter. Good luck! The reader should note that questions are grouped according to chapter and similar subject matter but do not necessarily follow the chapter order of *FVAM*.

3.1 CHAPTER 1: INTRODUCTION TO FINANCIAL VALUATION

Note: Select the best answer(s) from the list of multiple-choice questions. Some multiple-choice questions have only one correct answer and some have several correct answers. Do not assume each question has only one correct answer. Circle the correct answer(s) for each question.

1. Which of the following is/are a purpose of a valuation?
   a. Income tax
   b. Divorce
   c. Corporate planning
   d. Litigation
   e. Going concern value
   f. Fair market value

2. Which of the following is/are considered a type of interest in a business that can be valued?
   a. 100 percent control
   b. 50 percent interest with one other 50 percent owner
   c. Minority
   d. Majority without control
   e. Minority with control

3. Articles of incorporation and bylaws are seldom useful in determining value.
   a. True
   b. False

4. Name the five organizations that have adopted the 2001 *International Glossary of Business Valuation Terms*.

   1. _____

   2. _____

   3. _____

   4. _____

   5. _____

5. Relying on the wrong standard of value can result in a very different value.
   a. True
   b. False

6. Which of the following is/are considered standards of value?
   a. Investment value
   b. Actual value
   c. Intrinsic value
   d. Going concern value
   e. Fair market value
   f. Fair value (state rights)
   g. Fair value (financial reporting)
   h. Liquidation value

7. Treasury regulations and Revenue Rulings define fair market value.
   a. True
   b. False

8. Which of the following is/are components of the fair market value definition?
   a. Willing buyer
   b. Most probable price
   c. Not under compulsion
   d. Control
   e. Willing seller
   f. Knowledge of relevant facts
   g. Normalization adjustments
   h. Lack of marketability

9. Fair market value is the standard of value in divorce.
   a. True
   b. False

10. Investment value is the value:
    a. To a particular investor
    b. To a hypothetical investor
    c. In the marketplace
    d. In tax valuations

11. ASC 820 requires which standard of value?
    a. Fair market value
    b. Fair value (financial reporting)
    c. Fair value (state rights)
    d. Investment value

12. All states have the same definition of fair value (state rights).
    a. True
    b. False

13. The SEC sets the standard of value for financial reporting.
    a. True
    b. False

14. Which of the following statements is/are true?
    a. Fair value (financial reporting) assumes a hypothetical buyer and seller.
    b. Fair market value assumes a hypothetical buyer and seller.
    c. Fair value (state rights) assumes a hypothetical buyer and seller.

15. Investment value always assumes that the investor has control.
    a. True
    b. False

16. Which of the following is/are considered a premise of value?
    a. Intrinsic value
    b. Going concern value
    c. Orderly liquidation value
    d. Depreciated value
    e. Fair market value
    f. Fair value
    g. Forced liquidation value

17. The intangible elements that result from factors such as having a trained work-force, an operational plant, and the necessary licenses, systems, and procedures in place is/are considered in what premises of value?
    a. Fair value (financial reporting)
    b. Fair market value
    c. Orderly liquidation value
    d. Going concern value

18. Investment value and intrinsic value are the same.
    a. True
    b. False

19. Forced liquidation value assumes an instant sale on the date of the valuation.
    a. True
    b. False

20. Which of the following statements is/are true?
    a. Price and cost equal value.
    b. Value is based on what a business's profits and cash flows are historically.
    c. Value is forward-looking, so a discounted cash flow method using expected projected cash flows must be used.

21. The valuation date is/are which of the following?
    a. The date the report is signed.
    b. The date the analysis is finished.
    c. The effective date of the valuation.
    d. The date the report is sent to the client.

22. Which of the following is/are approaches to value?
    a. Guideline public company
    b. Transactions
    c. Discounted cash flow
    d. Capitalized cash flow
    e. Excess cash flow
    f. Income
    g. Market
    h. Asset

23. Which of the following statements is/are true?
    a. All valuation approaches must be considered.
    b. All valuation approaches must be applied.
    c. All valuation methods must be applied.
    d. Indications of value should be averaged.
    e. There are four main approaches to value.

24. The income approach is always the preferred approach in valuing a business.
    a. True
    b. False

25. In valuing a business, most analysts agree that only facts known or knowable at the valuation date should be considered.
    a. True
    b. False

3.2 CHAPTER 2: STANDARDS OF VALUE

Note: Select the best answer(s) from the list of multiple-choice questions. Some multiple-choice questions have only one correct answer and some have several correct answers. Do not assume each question has only one correct answer. Circle the correct answer(s) for each question.

1. Which of the following are standards of value?
    a. Fair market value
    b. Subsequent value
    c. Fair value (financial reporting)
    d. Fair value (state rights)
    e. Fair value (federal)
    f. Intrinsic value
    g. Investment value

2. Standards of value and premises of value are the same.
    a. True
    b. False

3. The standard of value for estate and gift tax is fair market value.
   a. True
   b. False

4. The standard of value has no influence on the consideration and application of discounts.
   a. True
   b. False

5. Which of the following are general premises of value?
   a. Value in exchange
   b. Personal goodwill value
   c. Value to the holder
   d. Highest and best use value

6. Which of the following are operational premises of value?
   a. Practice goodwill value
   b. Value in the most likely market
   c. Going concern value
   d. Liquidation value

7. Most states do not recognize discounts in fair value cases.
   a. True
   b. False

8. Fair value for financial reporting is an entry value.
   a. True
   b. False

9. The standard of value in divorce is determined state by state.
   a. True
   b. False

10. Shareholder agreements should never be considered in a valuation for tax purposes.
    a. True
    b. False

3.3 CHAPTER 3: RESEARCH AND ITS PRESENTATION

Note: Select the best answer(s) from the list of multiple-choice questions. Some multiple-choice questions have only one correct answer and some have several correct answers. Do not assume each question has only one correct answer. Circle the correct answer(s) for each question.

1. Which of the following statements concerning research is/are true?
   a. Analysts should start with a plan.
   b. 10-Ks of public companies are good sources of industry information.
   c. The author and publisher of information are not important as long as the information is good.
   d. Trade associations are poor sources of information because they are biased.

2. Name four business financial databases that are sources of information for valuations.

    1. _____

    2. _____

    3. _____

    4. _____

3. Which of the following is/are external factors that can affect value?
    a. Interest rates
    b. Inflation
    c. Management competence
    d. Product or service diversification
    e. Technological changes
    f. Dependence on natural resources
    g. Inventory controls
    h. Legislation

4. The Federal Reserve's *Beige Book* contains economic information through reports from interviews with key business professionals, economists, and market experts.
    a. True
    b. False

5. Which of the following is/are important considerations in industry research?
    a. Growth prospects
    b. Dominant economic traits
    c. Competitive forces
    d. Potential market changes
    e. Profitability
    f. Regulations

6. Which of the following is/are sources for transaction information?
    a. *DealStats*
    b. Public company 10-Ks
    c. RMA
    d. Bizcomps
    e. Federal Reserve System
    f. Integra
    g. *Mergerstat Review*

7. EDGAR stands for Electronic Disclosure Government Analysis and Retrieval.
    a. True
    b. False

8. Which of the following statements concerning EDGAR is/are true?
    a. Contains information on thousands of companies.
    b. Includes more private companies than public companies.
    c. Established by the Department of Justice.
    d. All eligible companies must file on EDGAR unless they receive a hardship exemption.

9. Industry and economic research is informative but is seldom relied on in actually supporting values.
   a. True
   b. False

10. A canned management questionnaire should not be used in a valuation.
    a. True
    b. False

3.4 CHAPTER 4: FINANCIAL STATEMENT AND COMPANY RISK ANALYSIS

Note: Select the best answer(s) from the list of multiple-choice questions. Some multiple-choice questions have only one correct answer and some have several correct answers. Do not assume each question has only one correct answer. Circle the correct answer(s) for each question.

1. Which of the following is/are considered elements of valuation analysis?
   a. An estimate of the amount of future economic benefit
   b. Assessment of risk
   c. An assessment of the probability that projected future economic benefits will be realized

2. Which of the following is/are steps in financial statement analysis?
   a. Industry comparisons
   b. Ratios
   c. Common sizing
   d. Spreading
   e. Normalizing
   f. Key person discount
   g. Marketability discount
   h. Identifying guideline companies

3. Only audited statements can be relied on in a valuation.
   a. True
   b. False

4. CPA analysts must take responsibility for the financial statements relied on in a valuation even if they did not prepare them.
   a. True
   b. False

5. Analysts should spread five years of historical financial statements.
   a. True
   b. False

6. Which of the following statements concerning financial statement adjustments is/are true?
   a. Historical statements are used to help predict future performance.
   b. Historical statements should not be adjusted to cash flow if they are GAAP statements.

     c. Historical statements help analysts understand a company but are not helpful in projecting future performance.

     d. Adjustments are made to better reflect true operating performance.

     e. Historical statement analysis should enable a company to be compared to prior performance.

     f. Historical statement analysis should enable a company to be compared to industry peer data.

7. Which of the following is/are considered normalization adjustments?
   a. Unusual items
   b. Lack of marketability
   c. Nonoperating assets
   d. Control
   e. Nonconformance with GAAP
   f. Extraordinary items
   g. Change in accounting principles
   h. Nonrecurring items

8. Which of the following is/are considered unusual, nonrecurring, or extraordinary items?
   a. Gain or loss on a sale of a business unit or assets
   b. Losses
   c. High profits
   d. Interest income on operating cash
   e. Capital expenditures exceeding depreciation in any one year

9. Which of the following is/are typical nonoperating assets?
   a. Excess compensation
   b. Boat
   c. Condo
   d. Excess working capital
   e. Raw land not currently used
   f. Art
   g. Excess cash
   h. Planes
   i. Autos used in the business
   j. Antiques
   k. Cash reserves for bonding

10. Changing from LIFO to FIFO is normal so it is not considered a change in accounting principles.
    a. True
    b. False

11. The *Gross, Heck, Adams, Dallas, Wall,* and *Gallagher* tax court cases opined that:
    a. You tax-affect S corporations.
    b. You do not tax-affect S corporations.
    c. Facts and circumstances dictate whether you tax-affect S corporations or not.
    d. You tax-affect S corporations because the IRS Appeals Manual says to do so.

12. A change to a company's capital structure is considered a control adjustment.
    a. True
    b. False

13. Which of the following is/are true concerning common-sizing normalized financial statements?
    a. They provide insight into a company's historical operating performance.
    b. They facilitate an assessment of relationships between and among certain accounts.
    c. They identify trends or unusual items.
    d. They can be used to make comparisons to public companies or industry data.

14. Review Exhibits 4.4 through 4.9 and comment on any perceived trends for Ale's. Also, review these schedules and comment on any factors that may need to be considered in a valuation of Ale's.

15. Which of the following statements is/are true regarding financial ratios and ratio analysis?
    a. They are the most commonly used tools in financial analysis.
    b. They do little to help us understand the future prospects of a company.
    c. They include such groupings of ratios as liquidity, performance, profitability, leverage, and growth.
    d. They provide a quantitative method for calculating rates of return.
    e. Risk Management Association (RMA) calculates ratios based on year-end versus average beginning- and ending-year balances.
    f. Time series analysis compares a specified company's ratios to other companies or industry benchmarks.
    g. Cross-sectional analysis compares a company's ratios over a specified historical time period.

16. It doesn't matter whether you compare year-end ratios with information based on average beginning- and ending-year data.
    a. True
    b. False

17. Analysts should be familiar with how benchmark industry ratios are calculated, their scope, as well as limitations in the data.
    a. True
    b. False

18. Review Exhibits 4.10 through 4.12 and comment on any perceived trends for Ale's. Also, review these schedules and comment on any factors that may need to be considered in a valuation of Ale's.

19. Which of the following is/are considered specific company risk assessment models or analyses?
    a. Porter
    b. McKinsey 7-S
    c. Macro-environmental
    d. SWOT
    e. Normalization
    f. Ibbotson
    g. *Mergerstat Review*
    h. RMA

20. The DuPont model considers which factors?
    a. Current ratio
    b. Working capital turnover
    c. Growth
    d. Profit margins
    e. Asset turnover
    f. Leverage

3.5 CHAPTER 5: INCOME APPROACH

Note: Select the best answer(s) from the list of multiple-choice questions. Some multiple-choice questions have only one correct answer and some have several correct answers. Do not assume each question has only one correct answer. Circle the correct answer(s) for each question.

1. The income approach is probably the most widely recognized approach in business valuation.
    a. True
    b. False

2. An investment in the equity of a company will compensate the investor for which of the following factors?
    a. The time the funds are committed
    b. Inflation
    c. Uncertainty
    d. Risk
    e. The time value of money

3. The income approach has a numerator and a denominator.
    a. True
    b. False

4. Which of the following statements is/are true concerning the income approach?
    a. It is forward looking.
    b. Value is equal to future cash flow discounted at the opportunity cost of capital.
    c. Economic benefit is always cash flow.
    d. Investor expectations include the real rate of return, inflation, and risk.
    e. Net cash flow is net income after tax plus depreciation.

5. Name the three income approach methods.

    1. _____

    2. _____

    3. _____

6. The excess cash flow method is a hybrid of both the income approach and the asset approach.
    a. True
    b. False

7. CPA analysts must attest to and verify any financial information they rely on.
   a. True
   b. False

8. Normalizing adjustments result in a control value when using the income approach.
   a. True
   b. False

9. Which of the following categories is/are considered normalizing adjustments in the income approach?
   a. Ownership characteristics
   b. Taxes
   c. Marketability
   d. Key person
   e. Extraordinary, nonrecurring, and unusual items
   f. Nonoperating assets and liabilities
   g. Synergies, if applicable
   h. Trapped capital gains taxes
   i. Information access and reliability

10. Which of the following, when applicable, is/are considered control adjustments?
    a. Excess fringe benefits
    b. Nonbusiness expenses
    c. Related-party transactions at arm's length
    d. Purchases from a sister company owned by the same person at prices that were negotiated at arm's length
    e. Perquisites

11. The discount rate determines whether the application of the income approach results in a minority or control value.
    a. True
    b. False

12. Normalization adjustments are typically made pre-tax.
    a. True
    b. False

13. Which of the following is/are examples of potential nonoperating assets?
    a. Plane
    b. Boat
    c. Expensive cars
    d. Adjacent vacant land with no plans for future use
    e. Unsold and unused excess plant facilities

14. There is no adjustment to the income statement for unused raw land because it does not produce income.
    a. True
    b. False

15. Fair market value should always include synergistic value.
    a. True
    b. False

16. In many small companies, income and cash flow are the same or similar.
    a. True
    b. False

17. Only cash flow can be discounted or capitalized in the income approach.
    a. True
    b. False

18. Concerning net cash flow, which of the following statements is/are true?
    a. It is the most common measure of future economic benefit.
    b. It is equivalent to dividends or distributions paid.
    c. It is the measure that most rate-of-return data are based on.
    d. It should be used only in the direct equity method, not the invested capital method.

19. List the six components of net cash flow to equity.

    1. _____

    2. _____

    3. _____

    4. _____

    5. _____

    6. _____

20. Net cash flow direct to equity is a debt-inclusive model.
    a. True
    b. False

21. List the five components of net cash flow to invested capital.

    1. _____

    2. _____

    3. _____

    4. _____

    5. _____

22. Net cash flows to invested capital include interest expense and debt principal.
    a. True
    b. False

23. List the five most common methodologies by which to estimate future economic benefits from historical data.

    1. _____

    2. _____

    3. _____

4. _____

5. _____

24. Company A has the following historical normalized cash flows: 20X5 (most recent year) $500,000; 20X4 $480,000; 20X3 $400,000; 20X2 $200,000; 20X1 $380,000. Calculate the simple average, a weighted average, and the trend line static method. Which result gives the best indication of anticipated future cash flows? Explain your answer.
    a. Simple average
    b. Weighted average
    c. Trend line static method
    d. Current cash flow
    Best indication explanation:

    _____

    _____

    _____

25. Discounted cash flow (DCF) models should use five years of projections.
    a. True
    b. False

26. In a DCF model, the period beyond the projected discrete period is called the explicit period.
    a. True
    b. False

27. Which of the following statements concerning DCF models is/are true?
    a. For companies that have fairly even cash flows throughout the year, the mid-year convention is generally preferred.
    b. Some analysts believe that the end-of-year convention better reflects when dividends/distributions are paid.
    c. The midyear convention may not be as applicable in a seasonable business.
    d. The midyear convention generally results in a value similar to discounting monthly cash flows.

28. The terminal value in a DCF model is often the majority of the value.
    a. True
    b. False

29. The Gordon Growth Model can be used in a capitalized cash flow (CCF) model or a DCF model.
    a. True
    b. False

30. Which of the following statements is/are true regarding the excess cash flow model?
    a. The return on net tangible assets should be the debt rate after tax.
    b. Revenue Ruling 68-609 states that the excess earnings method should always be used in valuing a business.

c. There is no direct method for determining the cap rate to capitalize excess cash flow into intangible asset/goodwill value.

d. The cap rate developed in the capitalized cash flow method can be used to check the values and returns in the excess cash flow method.

3.6 CHAPTER 6: COST OF CAPITAL/RATES OF RETURN

Note: Select the best answer(s) from the list of multiple-choice questions. Some multiple-choice questions have only one correct answer and some have several correct answers. Do not assume each question has only one correct answer. Circle the correct answer(s) for each question.

1. The cost of capital is an expected rate of return that the market requires to attract funds to a particular investment.
   a. True
   b. False

2. The cost of capital depends on the investor, not the investment.
   a. True
   b. False

3. Which of the following statements concerning cost of capital is/are true?
   a. It is an opportunity cost.
   b. It involves the principle of substitution.
   c. It is investor-driven.
   d. It is market-driven.
   e. It includes risk.
   f. It includes a real rate of return.
   g. It excludes inflation.
   h. Cost of capital equals discount rate.
   i. It equals expected rate of return, which is expected dividends/distributions plus expected capital appreciation.

4. Which of the following is/are cost of capital methods?
   a. Build-Up model
   b. Modified capital asset pricing model
   c. Capital asset pricing model
   d. Weighted average cost of capital
   e. Price to earnings
   f. Excess earnings
   g. Specific company risk

5. Discount rate equals capitalization rate plus growth.
   a. True
   b. False

6. Long-term growth rates are used in both the DCF and CCF models.
   a. True
   b. False

7. Which of the following factors is/are typically considered in determining growth rates?
   a. Subject company historical growth
   b. Subject company projected growth as prepared by management
   c. Industry growth
   d. Inflation
   e. Gross domestic product
   f. Analyst judgment

8. Which of the following factors is/are considered a risk category in the cost of capital?
   a. Maturity risk
   b. Lack of marketability
   c. Minority
   d. Systematic
   e. Unsystematic

9. Systematic risk can be captured by beta.
   a. True
   b. False

10. Investors cannot diversify unsystematic risk away.
    a. True
    b. False

11. The calculation of unsystematic risk involves judgment.
    a. True
    b. False

12. Which of the following factors is/are primary sources of unsystematic risk?
    a. Size
    b. Lack of marketability
    c. Minority
    d. Industry (nonbeta)
    e. Specific company attributes

13. Which of the following resources is/are sources of size equity risk premiums for a discount rate?
    a. *Mergerstat Review*
    b. Kroll
    c. Emory
    d. FMV Opinions

14. Which of the following is/are considered macro-environmental forces?
    a. Economic
    b. Technological
    c. Company strengths
    d. Company weaknesses
    e. Company opportunities
    f. Company threats
    g. Sociocultural
    h. a. Demographic
    i. International
    j. Political

15. Name the five main industry-related risk factors according to Michael E. Porter.
    a. Threat of new entrants
    b. Bargaining power of suppliers
    c. Bargaining power of customers
    d. Company strengths
    e. Industry strengths
    f. Threat of substitutes
    g. Company threats
    h. Rivalry among existing firms

16. Which of the following factors is/are considered potential risks particular to a small business?
    a. Key person
    b. Thin management
    c. Access to financing
    d. Industry
    e. Economic
    f. Lack of marketability
    g. Minority
    h. Lack of diversification

17. List the four components of a build-up model for computing equity returns for a small private company. Include the formula inputs and the actual name. Exclude the industry risk premium.

    a. _____

    b. _____

    c. _____

    d. _____

18. The risk-free rate is typically based on a 10-year U.S. Treasury bond.
    a. True
    b. False

19. Which of the following size premiums and/or type of data can be considered based solely on Kroll information?
    a. Micro-cap NYSE and equivalent ASE and NASDAQ companies
    b. 10th-decile NYSE and equivalent ASE and NASDAQ companies
    c. 10A NYSE and equivalent ASE and NASDAQ companies
    d. 10B NYSE and equivalent ASE and NASDAQ companies
    e. In excess of CAPM with a OLS beta
    f. In excess of CAPM with an annual beta
    g. In excess of CAPM with sum beta
    h. Average return on the market (large stocks) minus the average return on micro-cap stocks since 1926

20. Some analysts include the Kroll industry risk premium in the modified CAPM but not the build-up model.
    a. True
    b. False

21. Kroll data can be used to directly determine specific company risk.
    a. True
    b. False

22. Which of the following statements concerning Kroll data is/are the general position of Kroll concerning its data?
    a. It is based on after-tax cash flows from the entities.
    b. It represents discount and capitalization rates as if publicly traded.
    c. Discount rates are neutral as to minority or control.
    d. It is based on earnings returns.
    e. Industry risk premiums can be used in MCAPM but not CAPM.

23. Theoretically, all securities would fall on the securities market line and the return reflects risk (beta).
    a. True
    b. False

24. Which two components is/are in the MCAPM but not the CAPM?

    1. _____

    2. _____

25. What is the only difference between MCAPM and build-up?

    _____

26. All betas are calculated the same so it doesn't matter which source of betas you use.
    a. True
    b. False

27. Given the formula for unlevering a beta (Bu) and using the following information, calculate the levered beta.
    - From guideline public company data:
      - Levered beta is .66.
      - Tax rate is 33 percent.
      - Market value capital structure is 10 percent debt, 90 percent equity.
    - For the subject company:
      - Tax rate is 33 percent.
      - Market value capital structure is 20 percent debt, 80 percent equity.
      - $Bu = Bl / \left[1 + (1 - t)(W_d / W_e) \right]$.

28. Given the following information, calculate the weighted average cost of capital (WACC).

    W_d = 200 percent
    W_e = 78 percent
    R_f = 4 percent
    RP_m = 6 percent
    RP_s = 5 percent
    RP_c = 3 percent
    Re-levered beta = 1.2
    Tax rate = 30 percent
    K_d(pre-tax) = 8 percent

29. Which of the following factors concerning the price-to-earnings (P/E) method is/are true?
    a. It is based on public company multiples.
    b. It is pre-tax.
    c. When inverted, the P/E ratio is a capitalization rate.
    d. The capitalization rate is an earnings rate, not a cash flow rate.
    e. It includes assumptions of growth.

30. Which of the following statements concerning the Kroll *Cost of Capital Navigator* portfolios data is/are true?
    a. It includes eight different measures of size.
    b. It allows for 25 magnitudes of size for the companies in the data.
    c. It includes both public and private company data.
    d. It goes back to 1963, not 1926 like CRSP data (previously published by Ibbotson).
    e. It includes risk measures including operating margin, coefficient of variation in operating margin, and coefficient of variation of return on equity.

3.7 CHAPTER 7: INTERNATIONAL COST OF CAPITAL

[This section left intentionally blank.]

3.8 CHAPTER 8: MARKET APPROACH

Note: Select the best answer(s) from the list of multiple-choice questions. Some multiple-choice questions have only one correct answer and some have several correct answers. Do not assume each question has only one correct answer. Circle the correct answer(s) for each question.

1. The use of statistics in valuation replaces qualitative judgment.
    a. True
    b. False

2. Statistics can be used in the following areas of valuation:
    a. Calculation of market multiples of public companies
    b. Picking market multiples of public companies
    c. Determining the effect of one variable on another variable
    d. Determining averages

3. Which of the following is/are considered an average?
    a. Mean
    b. Mode
    c. Median
    d. Correlation
    e. Regression
    f. R squared
    g. Harmonic mean

4. Which of the following statements is/are true?
   a. Correlation analysis summarizes the strength of the relationship between factors.
   b. Correlation coefficients (r) are between 0 and 1.
   c. An (r) of 0 denotes no relationship.
   d. Regression analysis (linear) shows how to predict one of the variables using the other one.
   e. Coefficient of determination says how much of the variability of Y is explained by X.
   f. R squared stands for regression analysis.
   g. Harmonic mean is a straight average.

5. Guideline companies generally have the following traits in the market approach:
   a. They are in the same or similar industry.
   b. They are the same in size.
   c. They should not be more than 10 times the revenue size of the subject company.
   d. They should have similar capital structures.
   e. They should have similar profit margins.
   f. They must be publicly traded.
   g. Sufficient information should exist for the guideline company for it to be used as a primary value indicator.

6. Which of the following is/are market approach methods?
   a. Guideline public companies
   b. Guideline company transactions
   c. Excess earnings
   d. Rules of thumb
   e. Subject company transactions
   f. Subject company acquisitions

7. Guideline company transactions are control values.
   a. True
   b. False

8. The application of the guideline public company method results only in a control value.
   a. True
   b. False

9. Which of the following statements is/are true concerning the guideline company transaction method?
   a. It results in a nonmarketable value.
   b. It results in a liquid value.
   c. It results in an illiquid value.
   d. The result is a value assuming the marketability of the guideline companies that were acquired.

10. Which of the following statements is/are true concerning the guideline public company method?
    a. It results in a marketable value.
    b. It results in a nonmarketable value.

c. It may result in a liquid value.
d. It results in an illiquid value.
e. The result is a value assuming the marketability of the guideline public companies' stock.

11. The application of the market approach includes intangible assets and goodwill to the extent they exist.
    a. True
    b. False

12. The market approach is forward looking.
    a. True
    b. False

13. The price of a public company stock includes anticipated growth.
    a. True
    b. False

14. Name four major sources of transaction data.

    1. _____

    2. _____

    3. _____

    4. _____

15. Which of the following statements is/are true concerning the guideline company transaction method?
    a. It generally relies on full disclosure of details about the transactions.
    b. It can include acquisitions of both public and private companies.
    c. Only P/E multiples are valid.
    d. Noncompete agreements are excluded.
    e. All the expenses are normalized.
    f. It is important to distinguish whether the transaction is an asset or stock deal.

16. The guideline company transaction method is generally (and relatively) a better method than the guideline public company method when valuing very small businesses.
    a. True
    b. False

17. You should always consider the guideline public company method when valuing any company.
    a. True
    b. False

18. The level of detailed information is the same for the guideline public company method and the guideline company transaction method.
    a. True
    b. False

19. Which of the following statements concerning the guideline public company method is/are correct?
    a. The prices of the stocks should be on or near the valuation date.
    b. The financial statement data of the public companies must match the date of the stock prices.
    c. Only audited statements of the public companies should be used.

20. 10-Ks and 10-Qs of public companies are audited.
    a. True
    b. False

21. Which of the following statements is/are true concerning the selection process for guideline public companies?
    a. Management of the subject company is often a good source for companies.
    b. Management often thinks their company is unique.
    c. If a small division of a diversified public company is the only part of that public company that is similar to the subject company, it should be used as a guideline company.
    d. Industry publications and websites can be good sources for potential guideline companies.
    e. After industry similarities, size is often the next most important selection criterion.

22. Low volume and/or infrequent trades may indicate that a public company's stock price may not be indicative of value.
    a. True
    b. False

23. It is better to have a larger number of guideline public companies that are only somewhat similar than a small number that are more similar.
    a. True
    b. False
    c. Based on facts and circumstances

24. Based on examination of Exhibits 8.1 and 8.2, determine the comparability of the subject company to the guideline public companies. Assume all are similar in terms of the industry. Decide how you would apply multiples based on these comparisons: specific companies, mean, median, percentiles, averages with fundamental discount, and so on. Write your comments in the following space.

_____

_____

_____

25. Which of the following financial information periods can be used in calculating guideline public company multiples?
    a. Trailing four quarters
    b. Most recent fiscal year end
    c. Three-year average
    d. Five-year average
    e. One-year forecast

26. List the two main numerators for deriving market multiples:

    1. _____

    2. _____

27. Which of the following multiples is/are correct?
    a. MVEq/net income after tax
    b. MVEq/pre-tax income
    c. MVIC/net income after tax
    d. MVIC/pre-tax income
    e. MVEq/book value of equity
    f. MVIC/EBITDA
    g. MVIC/EBIT
    h. MVIC/revenue
    i. MVIC/debt-free net income after tax

28. Rules of thumb are often a primary method for determining value.
    a. True
    b. False

29. Negative multiples should be relied on.
    a. True
    b. False

30. Based on your comparisons from Exhibit 8.1, choose multiples and values for the subject company based on the multiples presented in Exhibits 8.2 and 8.3. Again, assume all the guideline companies are equally similar based on the industry. Write your results in the following space.

    _____

    _____

    _____

3.9 CHAPTER 9: ASSET APPROACH

Note: Select the best answer(s) from the list of multiple-choice questions. Some multiple-choice questions have only one correct answer and some have several correct answers. Do not assume each question has only one correct answer. Circle the correct answer(s) for each question.

1. Which of the following statements is/are true concerning the asset approach?
    a. Book value equals fair market value.
    b. Book value balance sheets are often the starting point for the asset approach.
    c. The asset approach does not include intangible assets.
    d. Book value seldom equals fair market value.

2. Some asset book values on the balance sheet are often similar to fair market value.
    a. True
    b. False

3. Unless purchased as part of a transaction, intangible assets are usually not on the books.
   a. True
   b. False

4. Which of the following statements concerning the asset approach is/are true?
   a. The asset approach should be considered in every business valuation.
   b. The asset approach is more commonly applied in valuing operating companies that sell products and/or services.
   c. The asset approach is more commonly used in valuations for purchase price allocations for financial reporting purposes.
   d. The book value of real estate is usually pretty close to fair market value.
   e. The asset approach is sometimes used in valuing very small companies and/or professional practices where there is little or no company or practice intangible assets and goodwill value.
   f. When valuing a business, valuing intangible assets in an operating company is common and provides increased accuracy for the valuation conclusion.

5. Revenue Ruling 59-60 ignores the asset approach.
   a. True
   b. False

6. Control and minority issues are not a concern in applying the asset approach.
   a. True
   b. False

7. Notes to financial statements can contain useful information about contingent liabilities.
   a. True
   b. False

8. Which of the following statements is/are true concerning real estate and equipment appraisal?
   a. Market value equals fair market value in real estate appraisal.
   b. The income approach is often used in real estate but not equipment appraisal.
   c. The cost approach is the most common approach in real estate appraisal.

9. As in business valuation, there are three approaches to value for real estate and equipment appraisal.
   a. True
   b. False

10. Economic obsolescence reflects the fact that an asset is not earning a required rate of return.
    a. True
    b. False

3.10 CHAPTER 10: VALUATION DISCOUNTS AND PREMIUMS

Note: Select the best answer(s) from the list of multiple-choice questions. Some multiple-choice questions have only one correct answer and some have several correct answers. Do not assume each question has only one correct answer. Circle the correct answer(s) for each question.

1. The two main discounts are the discount for lack of marketability (DLOM) and the discount for lack of control (DLOC).
   a. True
   b. False

2. The DLOC and the minority discount are the same.
   a. True
   b. False

3. When applying the DLOM and the DLOC, you should add them together and then apply the aggregated discount.
   a. True
   b. False

4. General benchmark DLOCs are derived from control premium studies.
   a. True
   b. False

5. Which of the following statements is/are true concerning discounts and premiums?
   a. They are either entity-level or shareholder-level.
   b. They must all be applied sequentially.
   c. DLOMs and DLOCs are applied to all valuation methods.

6. Control premiums:
   a. Are based on public company acquisitions.
   b. Include synergistic or strategic premiums when present.
   c. Quantify the value of controlling the destiny of a company.

7. Which of the following statements is/are true?
   a. Control often means a lesser or no DLOM.
   b. DLOMs for control and minority are the same because a DLOM only reflects the lack of marketability of the entire company.
   c. There is no relationship between DLOCs and DLOMs.

8. Control adjustments to earnings/cash flow:
   a. Should be made in every valuation.
   b. Are often made when valuing a controlling interest.
   c. Are made before applying a control premium.

9. A 50/50 percent ownership arrangement contains which of the following rights?
   a. Swing vote
   b. Cumulative voting
   c. Veto power
   d. Right of first refusal

10. All other things being equal, in the same company, which of the following 25 percent interests is worth relatively less (i.e., would have greater discounts)?
    a. Four 25 percent interests
    b. One 25 percent interest with one 75 percent interest
    c. Two 25 percent interests with one 50 percent interest
    d. 25 percent interests with no other shareholder holding more than 10 percent

11. A greater-than-50-percent interest always gives full control.
    a. True
    b. False

12. When the interest being valued represents a minority position, nonvoting stock is generally valued slightly less than voting stock.
    a. True
    b. False

13. General benchmark minority and lack-of-control discounts is/are derived from which of the following sources?
    a. Court cases
    b. *Mergerstat Review* data
    c. Thin air
    d. Restricted stock studies

14. The formula for calculating a DLOC from control premium data is:
    a. 1 divided by control premium
    b. 1 divided by (1 + control premium)
    c. 1 minus [1 divided by (1 + control premium)]
    d. (1 divided by control premium) times 100

15. *Mergerstat Review* data allow the analyst to segregate the pure control premium and the synergistic/acquisition premium.
    a. True
    b. False

16. Which of the following valuation methodologies result(s) in a control value where the cash flows have been adjusted for control items?
    a. Discounted cash flow method
    b. Guideline company transaction method
    c. Guideline public company method
    d. Capitalized cash flow method

17. Which of the following statements is/are true?
    a. Actively traded public stock is marketable.
    b. Actively traded public stock is liquid.
    c. Minority stock is marketable.
    d. Minority stock is liquid.
    e. 100 percent control is marketable.
    f. 100 percent control is liquid.

18. There is direct empirical evidence supporting a DLOM for a controlling interest.
    a. True
    b. False

19. Which of the following studies can be relied on when selecting DLOMs?
    a. Restricted stock
    b. Quantitative marketability discount model (QMDM)
    c. Initial public offering
    d. Emory
    e. Willamette
    f. Hitchner
    g. Revenue Ruling 77-287
    h. Revenue Ruling 59-60

20. Which of the following statements is/are true concerning the Emory studies?
   a. They include transactions of a company within 12 months of an IPO.
   b. They include failed IPOs.
   c. They include only stock option transactions.
   d. They are adjusted to reflect the rise or fall of a company's stock price after the IPO.
   e. Discounts have typically been in the range of 60 percent to 65 percent.

21. Which of the following statements is/are true concerning restricted stock studies?
   a. They include only publicly traded companies.
   b. They are based on control transactions of a company's stock.
   c. Stocks are restricted for two years in all the studies.
   d. Recent studies have resulted in lower average discounts.

22. Name four option-pricing models for computing a DLOM?

   1. _____

   2. _____

   3. _____

   4. _____

23. Which of the following factors is/are considered in the QMDM?
   a. Control value of the stock
   b. Expected holding period
   c. Required rate of return over the holding period
   d. Expected dividend payments

24. Name at least five factors that can affect the marketability of a minority interest in a private business.

   1. _____

   2. _____

   3. _____

   4. _____

   5. _____

25. Which of the following tax court cases is/are famous for the method used to select a DLOM?
   a. *Branson*
   b. *Mandelbaum*
   c. *Sheffield*
   d. *Weinberger*

26. Some discounts are applied after the pre-discount value is determined, and some are incorporated into the cost of capital in the income approach or the multiples in the market approach.
   a. True
   b. False

27. Which of the following is/are discounts or affect discounts that can be considered in a valuation?
    a. Key person
    b. Restrictive agreement language
    c. Information access and reliability problems
    d. Trapped capital gains
    e. Blockage
    f. Market absorption
    g. Small company
    h. Lack of diversification

28. It is generally acceptable to take the average of various DLOM studies and apply that average to the subject company.
    a. True
    b. False

29. Dr. Mukesh Bajaj et al. have provided further support for the typical averages in the IPO and restricted stock DLOM studies.
    a. True
    b. False

30. A private company that pays substantial dividends/distributions would generally have a lesser DLOM than the same company that pays little or no dividends/distributions.
    a. True
    b. False

3.11 CHAPTER 11: REPORT WRITING

Note: Select the best answer(s) from the list of multiple-choice questions. Some multiple-choice questions have only one correct answer and some have several correct answers. Do not assume each question has only one correct answer. Circle the correct answer(s) for each question.

1. Reports must be prepared for every valuation.
   a. True
   b. False

2. Reports must contain sufficient detail to allow another qualified analyst to re-create or replicate the work.
   a. True
   b. False

3. Which of the following factors should be included in a report?
   a. What the analyst was asked to do
   b. The fee
   c. Standard of value
   d. Information relied on
   e. Names of all people who worked on the engagement
   f. Procedures that were performed
   g. Assumptions and limiting conditions
   h. Conclusion and reconciliation

4. Which of the following types of reports is/are allowed by the Uniform Standards of Professional Practice (USPAP) for a business valuation?
   a. Appraisal report
   b. Summary appraisal report
   c. Restricted appraisal report
   d. Limited appraisal report
   e. Other appraisal report

5. All valuation analysts are required to adhere to the reporting requirements of USPAP in every engagement.
   a. True
   b. False

6. Outside of USPAP, analysts generally produce two types of reports, complete/detailed and other.
   a. True
   b. False

7. SSVS VS Section 100 requires reports to contain enough information for the reader to be able to replicate all the information and data and calculations.
   a. True
   b. False

8. Revenue Ruling 59-60 contains detailed reporting requirements.
   a. True
   b. False

9. Which of the following factors is/are often considered in the analysis of industry conditions section of a report?
   a. Identity of the industry
   b. Description of the industry
   c. Suppliers
   d. Government regulations
   e. Marketability of the companies that make up the industry
   f. Key person issues
   g. Risks

10. The financial statement analysis should include at least five years of financial statement information.
    a. True
    b. False

11. Reports should include a quantitative method of reconciling various values derived by different valuation methods.
    a. True
    b. False

12. Which of the following types of reports is/are allowed in SSVS VS Section 100?
    a. Valuation engagement—detailed report
    b. Oral report
    c. Appraisal report
    d. Valuation engagement—summary report
    e. Restricted use report
    f. Calculation report

13. SSVS VS Section 100 dictates how long reports are supposed to be.
    a. True
    b. False

14. Summary or letter reports should not be relied on by clients.
    a. True
    b. False

15. Which of the following statements concerning assumptions and limiting conditions is/are true?
    a. They can reduce the risk to the analyst.
    b. They inform the reader of what the analyst did and did not do.
    c. They should not be provided in valuation reports prepared in a litigation setting.

3.12 CHAPTER 12: BUSINESS VALUATION STANDARDS

Note: Select the best answer(s) from the list of multiple-choice questions. Some multiple-choice questions have only one correct answer and some have several correct answers. Do not assume each question has only one correct answer. Circle the correct answer(s) for each question.

1. Name the three major U.S. associations that currently grant certifications in valuation:
    a. AICPA, ASA, CFA
    b. AICPA, ASA, CFE
    c. AICPA, NACVA, ASA
    d. AICPA, NACVA, CFA

2. CPAs are required to follow the Uniform Standards of Professional Practice (USPAP).
    a. True
    b. False

3. The IRS has recently adopted USPAP.
    a. True
    b. False

4. The AICPA SSVS VS Section 100 only applies to CPAs who are ABVs.
    a. True
    b. False

5. Which of the following organizations has/have adopted the original *International Glossary of Business Valuation Terms*?
    a. AICPA
    b. AIMR
    c. NACVA
    d. IBA
    e. CICBV
    f. IRS
    g. ASA
    h. Appraisal Foundation

6. Business valuation appraisers must abide by the specific standards for real estate and personal property in their business valuations.
   a. True
   b. False

7. USPAP Standard Rule 3, Review Appraisal, is applicable only to real estate and personal property appraisers.
   a. True
   b. False

8. Which of the following statements concerning USPAP is/are true?
   a. There are 10 standards rules.
   b. Statements on Appraisal Standards are only for explanatory purposes and do not have the weight of a standards rule.
   c. Advisory opinions are for explanatory purposes only and do not have the weight of a standards rule.
   d. Standards 9 and 10 address development and reporting for business valuation.
   e. The definitions, preamble, ethics rule, record keeping rule, competency rule, scope of work rule, jurisdictional exception rule, and the supplemental standards affect business appraisers.

9. The IRS has business valuation guidelines.
   a. True
   b. False

10. Name the two types of analyses/engagements covered under SSVS VS Section 100.

    1. _____

    2. _____

3.13 CHAPTER 13: VALUATION OF PASS-THROUGH ENTITIES

and

3.14 CHAPTER 27D: VALUATION ISSUES IN PREFERRED STOCK

and

3.15 CHAPTER 27E: RESTRICTED STOCK VALUATION

and

3.16 CHAPTER 27G: VALUATION ISSUES RELATED TO STOCK OPTIONS AND OTHER SHARE-BASED COMPENSATION

Note: Select the best answer(s) from the list of multiple-choice questions. Some multiple-choice questions have only one correct answer and some have several correct answers. Do not assume each question has only one correct answer. Circle the correct answer(s) for each question.

1. The biggest issue in valuing pass-through entities is taxes.
   a. True
   b. False

2. Which of the following Tax Court cases disallowed the application of taxes at the entity level?
   a. *Gross*
   b. *Wall*
   c. *Mandelbaum*
   d. *Jelke*
   e. *Adams*
   f. *Heck*
   g. *Dallas*

3. There is still some controversy concerning the application of taxes in control valuations and minority valuations.
   a. True
   b. False

4. In valuing a pass-through entity, the level of distributions can affect value.
   a. True
   b. False

5. Valuing a pass-through entity by capitalizing pre-tax cash flows at a pre-tax capitalization rate results in an after-tax value.
   a. True
   b. False

6. Which of the following statements concerning preferred stock is/are true?
   a. It is a hybrid security.
   b. Dividend rate is the yield rate.
   c. It can be cumulative or noncumulative.
   d. If redeemable, it is considered solely as an equity security.
   e. Preferred stock is never voting because it is not common stock.
   f. It can be convertible into common stock.
   g. It can contain put options or features.

7. Which of the following Revenue Rulings directly address(es) the valuation of preferred stock?
   a. 59-60
   b. 68-609
   c. 83-120
   d. 93-12
   e. 77-287

8. Which of the following factors should be considered when valuing preferred stock?
   a. Yield
   b. Lack of control
   c. Lack of marketability
   d. Dividend coverage
   e. Liquidation preferences

9. Given the following information, calculate the value of the preferred stock using the dividend discount model:
   Par value = $100
   Stated rate = $6
   Required yield = 10 percent

   _____

   _____

   _____

10. Employee stock options can be incentive stock options or nonqualified stock options.
    a. True
    b. False

11. Options that can be exercised only on the expiration date are called American options.
    a. True
    b. False

12. Which of the following statements is/are true concerning stock options?
    a. Call options give the holder the right to buy the stock.
    b. Put options give the holder the right to sell the stock.
    c. Exercise price typically changes over time.
    d. "In the money" occurs when a call option's strike price is less than the current price of the underlying stock.
    e. "Out of the money" options can never have value.

13. Name the two best-known option models.

    1. _____

    2. _____

14. There is never a distinct discount for lack of marketability of a stock option in a private company.
    a. True
    b. False

15. Which of the following factors is/are considered when applying the Black-Scholes option model?
    a. Underlying stock price
    b. Lack of control
    c. Exercise price
    d. Volatility
    e. Time to expiration
    f. Risk-free rate

16. Volatility has a significant impact on the value of a stock option.
    a. True
    b. False

17. Binomial models are sometimes referred to as lattice models.
    a. True
    b. False

18. Which of the following Revenue Rulings directly address(es) the valuation of restricted stock?
    a. 59-60
    b. 68-609
    c. 83-120
    d. 93-12
    e. 77-287

19. Restricted stocks are typically stocks in public companies that are restricted from public trading for a period of time.
    a. True
    b. False

20. Which of the following statements is/are true concerning restricted stocks?
    a. All the companies in the restricted stock studies had a two-year holding period.
    b. Rule 144 restrictions no longer apply.
    c. Volume limitations under Rule 144 include a restriction that no more than 1.0 percent of the outstanding shares of stock can be sold during any three-month period.
    d. Volume limitations under Rule 144 include a restriction that no more than the average weekly market trading volume in such securities during the four calendar weeks preceding a sale of stock can be sold during any three-month period.
    e. Dribble-out periods should be considered in valuing restricted stock.

3.17 CHAPTER 14: ESTATE, GIFT, AND INCOME TAX VALUATIONS

Note: Select the best answer(s) from the list of multiple-choice questions. Some multiple-choice questions have only one correct answer and some have several correct answers. Do not assume each question has only one correct answer. Circle the correct answer(s) for each question.

1. Revenue Ruling 59-60 is applicable only to tax valuations.
   a. True
   b. False

2. Revenue Ruling 59-60 addresses the concept of a key person.
   a. True
   b. False

3. Which of the following statements is/are included in Revenue Ruling 59-60?
   a. Use common sense, judgment, and reasonableness.
   b. Valuation must be based on the facts available at the required date of appraisal.
   c. Consider at least five years of income statements and two years of balance sheets.
   d. Valuation of securities is a prophecy as to the future.
   e. Valuation reflects the degree of optimism or pessimism of investors.
   f. The appraiser should include subsequent events after the appraisal date.

4. Which of the following statements is/are true regarding fair market value for tax purposes?
   a. Assumes a hypothetical buyer only
   b. Assumes a hypothetical seller only
   c. Assumes both a hypothetical buyer and seller
   d. Assumes specific buyers and sellers
   e. Assumes the most likely buyer and seller

5. Revenue Ruling 59-60 does not address excess compensation and its potential effect on value.
   a. True
   b. False

6. Which of the following statements concerning Revenue Ruling 59-60 is/are true?
   a. It requires reliance on historical averages of earnings.
   b. It is silent concerning intangible assets and goodwill and their value.
   c. It addresses the concept of control and minority.
   d. It gives consideration to the value of similar publicly traded company stock.

7. Revenue Ruling 59-60 presents standard capitalization rates.
   a. True
   b. False

8. Name the four main Revenue Rulings in valuation.
   a. 48-220
   b. 83-120
   c. 77-287
   d. 98-254
   e. 59-60
   f. 93-12
   g. 69-609

9. The IRS has adopted USPAP.
   a. True
   b. False

10. Which of the following statements concerning the definition of fair market value is/are true?
    a. Most likely buyer
    b. Willing buyer
    c. Willing seller
    d. Same knowledge of relevant facts
    e. No compulsion

11. Which of the following statements is/are most true regarding court cases?
    a. They can be used to determine discounts.
    b. They should not be used to determine discounts.
    c. They are informative only as to the court's view on discounts.
    d. They should be quoted in valuation reports.

12. Revenue Ruling 59-60 supports the use of the asset approach for valuing investment or holding companies.
    a. True
    b. False

13. Averaging the values from different methods is endorsed by Revenue Ruling 59-60.
    a. True
    b. False

14. Which of the following statements is/are true regarding Revenue Ruling 77-287?
    a. It can be used to determine discounts for lack of marketability for closely held stock.
    b. It can be used to value restricted stock.
    c. It can be used to value preferred stock.
    d. It replaces Revenue Ruling 68-609.

15. Revenue Ruling 93-12 addresses family attribution for gift and estate tax.
    a. True
    b. False

16. What is the single most important court case dealing exclusively with discounts for lack of marketability?
    a. *Lappo*
    b. *Mandelbaum*
    c. *Jelke*
    d. *Peracchio*

17. The IRS has business valuation guidelines.
    a. True
    b. False

18. Which of the following statements is/are true regarding Revenue Ruling 83-120?
    a. It expands on Revenue Ruling 59-60.
    b. It discusses yield, dividend coverage, and liquidation preferences.
    c. It addresses freeze transactions.
    d. It applies only to public companies.
    e. It is no longer relevant with the issuance of Revenue Ruling 93-12.

19. The IRS has regulations regarding the valuation of charitable contributions of closely held stock, including a definition of a qualified appraiser.
    a. True
    b. False

20. Which was one of the first tax court cases to allow a reduction in value due to trapped-in capital gains taxes?
    a. *Lappo*
    b. *Mandelbaum*
    c. *Jelke*
    d. *Davis*

3.18 CHAPTER 15: VALUATION OF FAMILY LIMITED PARTNERSHIPS

Note: Select the best answer(s) from the list of multiple-choice questions. Some multiple-choice questions have only one correct answer and some have several correct answers. Do not assume each question has only one correct answer. Circle the correct answer(s) for each question.

1. Which of the following statements is/are true concerning family limited partnerships (FLPs)?
   a. Discounts can be taken for more than 50 percent limited partner interests.
   b. Discounts can be taken only for less than 50 percent limited partner interests.
   c. The general partner interest can never be discounted.
   d. The partnership agreement is not considered in setting discounts.
   e. Discounts cannot be taken if there are high cash distributions.
   f. No discounts can be taken if the FLP holds only liquid marketable public securities.

2. The partnership agreement provisions concerning limited partner rights are not allowed to be considered in valuing an interest in an FLP.
   a. True
   b. False

3. Which of the following factors is/are included in Chapter 14 of the IRC?
   a. Taxation of certain transfers of corporate and partnership interests
   b. Sections 2701, 2702, 2703, and 2704
   c. Impact of buy-sell agreements
   d. Lapsing rights
   e. Applicable restrictions

4. Which of the following statements concerning section 2703 and buy-sell agreements is/are true?
   a. They are bona fide business arrangements.
   b. They must include a formula for valuation.
   c. They are not devices to transfer property for less than full and adequate consideration.
   d. Terms are comparable to similar arrangements entered into by persons in arm's-length transactions.

5. FLPs are often valued using the asset approach.
   a. True
   b. False

6. FLPs that hold marketable securities are discounted using mutual fund data.
   a. True
   b. False

7. Which of the following is/are typically relied on when determining discounts for limited partner interests in an FLP that holds marketable securities and real estate?
   a. Revenue Ruling 59-60
   b. Partnership Profiles
   c. Morningstar closed-end funds
   d. Restricted stock studies

8. Closed-end fund information is always used to determine the DLOM of a limited partner interest in an FLP.
   a. True
   b. False

9. Some marketability is implicit in the sales of partnerships referenced in Partnership Profiles.
   a. True
   b. False

10. Closed-end fund data reflect instant marketability/liquidity.
    a. True
    b. False

3.19 CHAPTER 16: SUMMARY OF COURT CASE VALUATION ISSUES

[This section left intentionally blank.]

3.20 CHAPTER 17: SHAREHOLDER DISPUTES

and

3.21 CHAPTER 18: EMPLOYEE STOCK OWNERSHIP PLANS

Note: Select the best answer(s) from the list of multiple-choice questions. Some multiple-choice questions have only one correct answer and some have several correct answers. Do not assume each question has only one correct answer. Circle the correct answer(s) for each question.

1. For dissenting stockholder suits, the standard of value and its definition are the same for each state.
   a. True
   b. False

2. Which of the following is/are typically shareholder disputes under state statutes?
   a. Dissenting shareholder
   b. Gift tax
   c. Estate tax
   d. Minority oppression
   e. Income tax
   f. ESOPs

3. Which of the following standards of value is/are the standard(s) of value for shareholder disputes under state statutes?
   a. Fair market value
   b. Investment value
   c. Intrinsic value
   d. Fair value
   e. Going concern value
   f. Orderly liquidation value

4. Fair value equals fair market value.
   a. True
   b. False

5. Which state(s) is/are the most influential in the area of dissenting rights nationally?
   a. Pennsylvania
   b. Texas
   c. Delaware
   d. Rhode Island
   e. California
   f. Georgia

6. In the dissenting shareholder area, all states disallow discounts for minority interest and lack of marketability.
   a. True
   b. False

7. The ultimate responsibility for obtaining an accurate valuation in an ESOP lies with the appraiser.
   a. True
   b. False

8. Every valuation in an ESOP must fulfill the regulations of both the IRS and the Department of Labor.
   a. True
   b. False

9. Which of the following statement(s) is/are true regarding ESOPs?
   a. Adequate consideration is the fair market value of the asset as determined in good faith by the trustee or named fiduciary.
   b. The analyst preparing the valuation must be independent of all parties to the transaction.
   c. ESOPs create greater liquidity for an ownership interest in a closely held company.
   d. ESOPs can own stock in C corporations only.
   e. Adequate consideration means that the ESOP cannot pay less than fair market value.
   f. Most ESOPs have put provisions that allow greater liquidity.
   g. ESOPs provide favorable tax treatment.
   h. Discounts for lack of marketability are not allowed because of put provisions.

10. Analysts should consider repurchase liabilities when considering the value of a company's shares pursuant to an ESOP.
    a. True
    b. False

3.22 CHAPTER 19: VALUATION IN THE DIVORCE SETTING

and

3.23 CHAPTER 20: VALUATION ISSUES IN SMALL BUSINESSES

and

3.24 CHAPTER 21: VALUATION ISSUES IN PROFESSIONAL PRACTICES

Note: Select the best answer(s) from the list of multiple-choice questions. Some multiple-choice questions have only one correct answer and some have several correct answers. Do not assume each question has only one correct answer. Circle the correct answer(s) for each question.

1. Fair market value is the standard of value in all states in divorce actions.
   a. True
   b. False

2. Which of the following statements is/are true concerning goodwill in a divorce valuation?
   a. All states allow goodwill value.
   b. All states allow entity goodwill but not personal goodwill.
   c. Generally, state case law will determine whether personal goodwill is considered a marital asset.
   d. Personal goodwill is usually more difficult to transfer than entity goodwill.
   e. In many professional practices and very small businesses, it is not unusual that personal goodwill makes up the majority of goodwill value.

3. Noncompete agreements completely protect the transfer of personal goodwill.
   a. True
   b. False

4. Which of the following is/are considered factors about the professional that can be considered in determining the amount of personal goodwill in a professional practice?
   a. Age and health
   b. Reputation
   c. Types of clients and services
   d. Source of new clients
   e. Location and demographics

5. Divorce courts never aggregate family interests because this violates the concept of hypothetical buyer and seller.
   a. True
   b. False

6. Small businesses tend to be highly dependent on their owner.
   a. True
   b. False

7. Which of the following is/are generally characteristics of small businesses?
   a. They have less access to capital.
   b. Their cost of borrowing is higher.
   c. There is a need for personal guarantees by owner.
   d. They have audited financial statements.
   e. They contain discretionary owner items.

    f. Only the guideline company transaction method of the market approach is valid.

    g. They have a higher failure rate.

    h. They may not contain any entity goodwill value.

    i. Guideline public company method of the market approach is never a valid method.

    j. Rules of thumb, particularly from business brokers, should be rejected for consideration.

8. Discretionary earnings are usually defined as earnings before interest, taxes, depreciation, and amortization and one owner's compensation.

    a. True

    b. False

9. In preparing a reasonableness test for the value of a small business, which of the following is/are typical financing assumptions?

    a. 25 percent to 30 percent down payment.

    b. Seller financing.

    c. Repayment over 10 years.

    d. Owner must stay for at least three years.

    e. All-cash deals.

10. Analysts should consider all three approaches to value when valuing an interest in a professional practice.

    a. True

    b. False

3.25 CHAPTER 22: REASONABLE COMPENSATION

[This section left intentionally blank.]

3.26 CHAPTER 23: THE VALUATOR AS EXPERT WITNESS

[This section left intentionally blank.]

3.27 CHAPTER 24: FAIR VALUE MEASUREMENT AND THE VALUATION OF INTANGIBLE ASSETS

Note: Select the best answer(s) from the list of multiple-choice questions. Some multiple-choice questions have only one correct answer and some have several correct answers. Do not assume each question has only one correct answer. Circle the correct answer(s) for each question.

1. Goodwill is an intangible asset.

    a. True

    b. False

2. The standard of value for the valuation of intangible assets is fair market value.

    a. True

    b. False

3. Intangible assets receiving legal protection are often referred to as intellectual property.
   a. True
   b. False

4. Which of the following is/are major categories of intangible assets as defined by the Financial Accounting Standards Board (FASB)?
   a. Marketing related
   b. Customer related
   c. Artistic related
   d. Contract based
   e. Technology based
   f. Assembled workforce

5. Rates of return on many intangible assets are generally higher than rates of return on tangible assets.
   a. True
   b. False

6. Fair value is the same for financial reporting and dissenting rights actions.
   a. True
   b. False

7. ASC 805 addresses business combinations including allocating the purchase price to intangible assets.
   a. True
   b. False

8. ASC 350 addresses the treatment of intangible assets and goodwill and how to test them for impairment.
   a. True
   b. False

9. ASC 820 defines fair value.
   a. True
   b. False

10. Indefinite-life intangibles cannot be valued separately and are included in goodwill.
    a. True
    b. False

11. Which of the following statements is/are true regarding goodwill impairment for public companies?
    a. If necessary, it is a two-step process.
    b. Step 2 requires the valuation of all intangible assets as if the reporting unit was just acquired and purchase accounting applied.
    c. There is no impairment if carrying value is less than fair value.
    d. Fair value assumes a market participant in a hypothetical transaction.
    e. It is calculated after ASC 360 impairments.

12. Intangible assets are generally valued after tax.
    a. True
    b. False

13. The amortization tax benefit recognizes the value of the tax shield as a result of the 15-year tax amortization of most intangible assets and goodwill.
    a. True
    b. False

14. Goodwill typically has the highest rate of return assigned to it.
    a. True
    b. False

15. Which of the following statements is/are true regarding the valuation of intangible assets for financial reporting?
    a. Net cash flows attributable to a specific intangible asset must be after returns on other contributory assets, both tangible and intangible.
    b. Returns on contributory assets are all at the same discount rate.
    c. FASB Concept 7 presents two present-value approaches, the expected cash flow approach and the traditional approach.

16. The amount of value to be allocated under ASC 805 is the purchase price paid for the invested capital of a business.
    a. True
    b. False

17. Where applicable and feasible, the income approach is often the preferred approach in valuing intangible assets.
    a. True
    b. False

18. The three approaches to value should be applied in the valuation of any intangible asset.
    a. True
    b. False

19. Internally used software not for resale is often valued using the cost approach.
    a. True
    b. False

20. Individual returns on assets can be reconciled to the company's weighted average cost of capital.
    a. True
    b. False

3.28 CHAPTER 25: MARKETING, MANAGING, AND MAKING MONEY IN A VALUATION SERVICES GROUP

[This section left intentionally blank.]

3.29 CHAPTER 26: BUSINESS DAMAGES

[This section left intentionally blank.]

3.30 CHAPTER 27: OTHER VALUATION SERVICE AREAS

This section left intentionally blank.]

3.31 CHAPTER 28: VALUATION OF HEALTHCARE SERVICE BUSINESSES

[This section left intentionally blank.]

3.32 CHAPTER 29: DETERMINATION OF COMPENSATION IN THE HEALTHCARE INDUSTRY

[This section left intentionally blank.]

3.33 CHAPTER 30: SPECIAL INDUSTRY VALUATIONS

[This section left intentionally blank.]

3.34 CHAPTER 31: BUY-SELL AGREEMENTS

Note: Select the best answer(s) from the list of multiple-choice questions. Some multiple-choice questions have only one correct answer and some have several correct answers. Do not assume each question has only one correct answer. Circle the correct answer(s) for each question.

1. In tax valuations, values in buy-sell agreements are:
   a. Determinative of value for gift tax purposes
   b. Determinative of value for estate tax purposes
   c. Only a consideration for gift and estate tax purposes
   d. Determinative for value for estate tax purposes and a consideration of value for gift tax purposes

2. What are the names of the three types of buy-sell agreements?
   a. Restrictive, hybrid, cross-purchase
   b. Hybrid, restrictive, repurchase
   c. Hybrid, entity-purchase, cross-purchase
   d. First refusal, restrictive, hybrid

3. Buy-sell agreements should be customized for each company.
   a. True
   b. False

4. Which of the following statements is/are true concerning buy-sell agreements?
   a. The greater the selling restrictions, the greater the possible impact on a DLOM.
   b. They should include the standard of value and a definition of the standard of value.
   c. Discounted values are not acceptable for tax purposes. It is good practice to have a mechanism for the value.
   d. Funding of a buyout should be excluded.

5. Buy-sell agreements are not typically legal agreements under state law.
   a. True
   b. False

3.35 CHAPTER 32: VALUATION VIEWS AND CONTROVERSIAL ISSUES: AN ILLUSTRATION

[This section left intentionally blank.]

CHAPTER 1: INTRODUCTION TO FINANCIAL VALUATION

1. a, b, c, d
2. a, b, c, d
3. b. False
4. American Institute of Certified Public Accountants
   American Society of Appraisers
   Canadian Institute of Chartered Business Valuators
   Institute of Business Appraisers
   National Association of Certified Valuators and Analysts
5. a. True
6. a, c, e, f, g
7. a. True
8. a, c, e, f
9. b. False
10. a
11. b
12. b. False
13. b. False
14. b
15. b. False
16. b, c, g
17. d
18. b. False
19. b. False
20. none
21. c
22. f, g, h
23. a
24. b. False
25. a. True

CHAPTER 2: STANDARDS OF VALUE

1. a, c, d, f, g
2. b. False
3. a. True
4. b. False
5. a, c
6. c, d
7. a. True
8. b. False
9. a. True
10. b. False

CHAPTER 3: RESEARCH AND ITS PRESENTATION

1. a, b
2. Bloomberg
   Proquest Dialog
   Factiva
   Lexis-Nexis
   Avention
   Alacra
   Thomson Reuters
3. a, b, e, f, h
4. a. True
5. a, b, c, d, e, f
6. a, b, d, g
7. b. False
8. a, d
9. b. False
10. b. False

CHAPTER 4: FINANCIAL STATEMENT AND COMPANY RISK ANALYSIS

1. a, b, c
2. a, b, c, d, e
3. b. False
4. b. False
5. b. False
6. a, d, e, f
7. a, c, d, e, f, g, h
8. a
9. b, c, d, e, f, g, h, j
10. b. False
11. b
12. a. True
13. a, b, c, d
14. Potential comments:
    - Total assets, total liabilities, and total equity have increased each year.
    - They have made capital expenditures each year.
    - Revenues and gross profit are up each year.
    - EBITDA and operating income are up each of last four years with a dip from the first to second year.
    - Officers' compensation is up $500,000 or one-third increase over the five-year period.
    - There is a steady use of liabilities
    - Gross margin is steady.
    - There is some fluctuation in operating income margin (low of 2.5 percent to high of 4.5 percent; however, margin is up each of last four years).
    - Ale's seems to be growing although down from year one to two in margin and profits.

15. a, c, e
16. b. False
17. a. True
18. See Addendum of Chapter 4 of *Financial Valuation Applications and Models*, 5th edition, for detailed explanation.
19. a, b, c, d
20. d, e, f

CHAPTER 5: INCOME APPROACH

1. a. True
2. a, b, c, d, e
3. a. True
4. a, b, d
5. Discounted cash flow
   Capitalized cash flow
   Excess cash flow
6. a. True
7. b. False
8. b. False
9. a, b, e, f, g
10. a, b, e
11. b. False
12. a. True
13. a, b, c, d, e
14. b. False
15. b. False
16. a. True
17. b. False
18. a, c
19. Net income after tax
    Plus: depreciation/amortization and other noncash charges
    Less: incremental working capital needs
    Less: incremental capital expenditure needs
    Plus: new debt principal in
    Less: repayment of debt principal
20. a. True
21. Net income after tax
    Plus: interest expense (tax-affected)
    Plus: depreciation/amortization and other noncash charges
    Less: incremental debt-free working capital needs
    Less: incremental capital expenditure needs
22. b. False
23. Current earnings
    Simple average
    Weighted average
    Trend line static
    Formal projection

24. a. $392,000
    b. $426,667
    c. $496,000
    d. $500,000
    e. $500,000
    f. 20X2 seems like an aberration. The last three years show growth as well. A management interview would help make the proper selection. A simple average doesn't recognize the upward trend. If an average were used, the weighted average would be better. The trend line static method recognizes the trend but is based on only five periods. May be okay, though.
25. b. False
26. b. False
27. a, b, c, d
28. a. True
29. a. True
30. c, d

CHAPTER 6: COST OF CAPITAL/RATES OF RETURN

1. a. True
2. b. False
3. a, b, d, e, f, h, i
4. a, b, c, d, e
5. a. True
6. a. True
7. a, b, c, d, e, f
8. a, d, e
9. a. True
10. b. False
11. a. True
12. a, d, e
13. b
14. a, b, g, h, i, j
15. a, b, c, f, h
16. a, b, c, h
17. a. R_f: Rate of return available on a risk-free security as of the valuation date
    b. RP_m: Equity risk premium (ERP) for the market as a whole
    c. RP_s: Risk premium for smaller size
    d. RP_u: Risk premium attributable to other company risk factors
18. b. False
19. a, b, c, d, e, f, g
20. b. False
21. b. False
22. a, b, c
23. a. True
24. a, b
25. MCAPM relies on an explicit beta, while build-up may or may not reflect RP_i—industry risk premium (also based on industry betas).

26. b. False
27. a.

$Bu = .66/(1+(1-.33)(.10/.90))$

$Bu = .66/1+.67(.11)$

$Bu = .66/1.074$

$Bu = .61$

b.

$Bl = .61(1+(1-.33)(.20/.80))$

$Bl = .61(1+(.67)(.25))$

$Bl = .61(1.1675)$

$Bl = .71$

28. MCAPM = 4% + (1.2 × 6%) + 5% + 3% = 19.2%
    WACC = .2(1 − .30) 8% + .8(19.2%)
    WACC = 16.5%
29. a, c, d, e
30. a, b, d, e

CHAPTER 8: MARKET APPROACH

1. b. False
2. b, c, d
3. a, b, c, g
4. a, c, d, e
5. a, g
6. a, b, d, e, f
7. a. True
8. b. False
9. c, d
10. a, c, e
11. a. True
12. a. True
13. a. True
14. Bizcomps
    DoneDeals
    Mergerstat Review
    DealStats
    GF Data Resources
    PitchBook
    SDC Platinum
15. b, f
16. a. True
17. a. True
18. b. False
19. a
20. b. False

21. a, b, d, e
22. a. True
23. c
24. See explanation in Chapter 8 of *Financial Valuation Applications and Models*, 5th edition
25. a, b, c, d, e
26. Equity, Invested capital
27. a, b, e, f, g, h, i
28. b. False
29. b. False
30. See explanation in Chapter 8 of *Financial Valuation Applications and Models*, 5th edition

CHAPTER 9: ASSET APPROACH

1. b, d
2. a. True
3. a. True
4. a, c, e
5. b. False
6. b. False
7. a. True
8. b
9. a. True
10. a. True

CHAPTER 10: VALUATION DISCOUNTS AND PREMIUMS

1. a. True
2. b. False
3. b. False
4. a. True
5. a
6. a, b, c
7. a
8. b
9. c
10. b
11. b. False
12. a. True
13. b
14. c
15. b. False
16. a, b, c, d
17. a, b, e
18. b. False
19. a, c, d, e, f
20. none

21. a, d
22. Black-Scholes
    Finnerty
    Chaffe
    Longstaff
23. b, c, d
24. Dividend policy
    Stock restrictions
    Redemption policy
    Number of shareholders
    Size of block of stock
    State law
25. b
26. a. True
27. a, b, c, d, e, f, g, h
28. b. False
29. b. False
30. a. True

CHAPTER 11: REPORT WRITING

1. b. False
2. b. False
3. a, c, d, f, g, h
4. a, c
5. b. False
6. a. True
7. b. False
8. b. False
9. a, b, c, d, g
10. b. False
11. b. False
12. a, b, d, f
13. b. False
14. b. False
15. a, b

CHAPTER 12: BUSINESS VALUATION STANDARDS

1. c
2. b. False
3. b. False
4. b. False
5. a, c, d, e, g
6. b. False
7. b. False
8. a, c, d, e
9. a. True
10. Valuation, Calculation

CHAPTER 13: VALUATION OF PASS-THROUGH ENTITIES

and

3.14 CHAPTER 27D: VALUATION ISSUES IN PREFERRED STOCK

and

CHAPTER 27E: RESTRICTED STOCK EVALUATION

and

CHAPTER 27G: VALUATION ISSUES RELATED TO STOCK OPTIONS AND OTHER SHARE-BASED COMPENSATION

1. a. True
2. a, b, e, f, g
3. a. True
4. a. True
5. a. True
6. a, c, f, g
7. c
8. a, b, c, d, e
9. $6 ÷ 0.10 = $60
10. a. True
11. b. False
12. a, b, d
13. Black-Scholes
    Binomial
14. b. False
15. a, c, d, e, f
16. a. True
17. a. True
18. e
19. a. True
20. c, d, e

CHAPTER 14: ESTATE, GIFT, AND INCOME TAX VALUATIONS

1. b. False
2. a. True
3. a, b, c, d, e
4. c
5. b. False
6. c, d
7. b. False
8. b, c, e, f

9. b. False
10. b, c, e
11. b, c
12. a. True
13. b. False
14. a, b
15. b. False
16. b
17. a. True
18. a, b, c
19. a. True
20. d

CHAPTER 15: VALUATION OF FAMILY LIMITED PARTNERSHIPS

1. a
2. b. False
3. a, b, c, d, e
4. a, c, d
5. a. True
6. b. False
7. a, b, c, d
8. b. False
9. a. True
10. a. True

CHAPTER 17: SHAREHOLDER DISPUTES

and

CHAPTER 18: EMPLOYEE STOCK OWNERSHIP PLANS

1. b. False
2. a, d
3. d
4. b. False
5. c
6. b. False
7. b. False
8. a. True
9. a, b, c, f, g
10. a. True

CHAPTER 19: VALUATION IN THE DIVORCE SETTING

and

CHAPTER 20: VALUATION ISSUES IN SMALL BUSINESSES

and

CHAPTER 21: VALUATION ISSUES IN PROFESSIONAL PRACTICES

1. b. False
2. c, d, e
3. b. False
4. a, b, c, d, e
5. b. False
6. a. True
7. a, b, c, e, g, h
8. a. True
9. a, b
10. a. True

CHAPTER 24: FAIR VALUE MEASUREMENT AND THE VALUATION OF INTANGIBLE ASSETS

1. True
2. b. False
3. a. True
4. a, b, c, d, e
5. a. True
6. b. False
7. a. True
8. a. True
9. a. True
10. b. False
11. a, b, c, d, e
12. a. True
13. a. True
14. a. True
15. a, c
16. b. False
17. a. True
18. b. False
19. a. True
20. a. True

CHAPTER 31: VALUATION ISSUES IN BUY-SELL AGREEMENTS

1. c
2. c
3. a. True
4. a, b, c
5. b. False

CHAPTER 4

ValTips

4.1 INTRODUCTION

In the companion book, *Financial Valuation Applications and Models (FVAM)*, numerous ValTips are presented to highlight important concepts, application issues, and pitfalls to avoid. These ValTips are reproduced in this chapter with slight modification for presentation on a stand-alone basis. The ValTips are organized and identified by *FVAM* chapter.

4.2 CHAPTER 1: INTRODUCTION TO FINANCIAL VALUATION

1. Relying on the wrong standard of value can result in a very different value than would have been concluded under the proper standard of value. In a dispute setting, the use of the wrong standard of value for the jurisdiction can result in a possible dismissal of the value altogether.
2. Although state courts may use the term *fair market value* in marital dissolution cases, no states have specific and detailed definitions of fair market value.
3. Some companies are worth more dead than alive. It is important for the analyst, particularly when valuing an entire company, to determine if the going concern value exceeds the liquidation value. For a minority interest, there are situations where the going concern value is less than the liquidation value. However, the minority shareholder cannot force a liquidation if the controlling shareholder desires to continue the business as a going concern.
4. Price and cost can equal value but don't necessarily *have to* equal value. Furthermore, value is future-looking. Although historical information can be used to set a value, the expectation of future economic benefits is the primary value driver. Investors buy tomorrow's cash flow, not yesterday's or even today's.

4.3 CHAPTER 2: STANDARDS OF VALUE

1. Although selecting a standard of value in a valuation assignment seems like a straightforward concept, different standards may have different meanings in different contexts. Defining *value* and adhering to the assumptions inherent in a particular standard of value, especially in connection with a valuation for tax, judicial, or regulatory purposes, is often not an easy task.

2. *Fair market value* is perhaps the most well-known standard of value and is commonly applied in judicial and regulatory matters. Fair market value applies to virtually all federal and state tax matters, including estate, gift, inheritance, income, and ad valorem taxes, as well as many other valuation situations.[1]

3. In many instances the reported value of a controlling interest for financial statement reporting purposes (fair value) is the same as fair market value. This is relevant in 409a valuations for which the client needs to know the value of stock compensation for tax and financial statement reporting.

4. In judicial appraisals, *fair value* is a legally mandated standard that applies to specific transactions and is commonly used in matters involving dissenters' rights and shareholder oppression.

5. Investment value can be measured, for example, as the discounted net cash flow that a particular investor would expect a company to earn in the way that particular (owner) investor would operate it.

6. Intrinsic value and investment value may seem like similar concepts, but they differ in that *intrinsic value* represents an estimate of value based on the perceived characteristics adhering to the investment itself, and *investment value* is more reliant on characteristics adhering to a particular purchaser or owner.[2]

7. Although allowed in some jurisdictions, application of a control premium is controversial. When aspects of control are reflected in the cash flow, many analysts consider application of a control premium as double counting, which creates a potential problem when a court believes it should be applied. See the addendum to Chapter 17, "Testing for an Implied Minority Discount in Guideline Company Prices," by Gilbert E. Matthews, CFA, *Financial Valuation and Litigation Expert*, issue 19, at www.wiley.com/go/FVAM5E.

8. Because states view property differently, no one consistent business valuation model can be used across the nation. States treat various issues such as professional goodwill, buy-sell agreements, and shareholder-level discounts differently.

4.4 CHAPTER 3: RESEARCH AND ITS PRESENTATION

1. Because of the complexity of the data-assembling process, many professionals use checklists that detail the types of information they are seeking. See online addenda for this chapter at www.wiley.com/go/FVAM5E and in the companion workbook. Addendum 1, "Valuation Information Request (VIR) General," presents a sample list of documents requested and questions to be asked in the course of a valuation engagement. Addenda 2 and 3 contain sample management interview questionnaires. Using these tools can help ensure that the valuation analyst covers the necessary bases in gathering internal information.

2. Before looking for information, valuation analysts should have a plan.

3. The 10-Ks of public companies often have detailed analyses of the industry.

4. Google is great, but it doesn't cover every resource you may need. Also consider database services such as Bloomberg, Dialog, Factiva, Lexis-Nexis, and Refinitiv, which offer extensive collections of periodicals, legal information, and financial data.

---

[1] Shannon P. Pratt and ASA Educational Foundation, *Shannon Pratt's Valuing a Business*, 6th ed. (McGraw-Hill, 2022), pp. 28–31.

[2] Ibid., p. 30.

5. Analysts consider the key external factors that affect value, such as interest rates, inflation, technological changes, dependence on natural resources, and legislation.
6. The Federal Reserve's *Beige Book* contains information on current economic conditions in each district gathered through reports from interviews with key business professionals, economists, and market experts.
7. The investor relations section of the websites of public companies operating in the same industry as the subject company is often a source of free industry data. Such websites typically provide access to public filings with the Securities and Exchange Commission, which include management's assessment of the current and future market and industry risks. Such public information can provide a highly useful source for understanding the industry.
8. Yahoo Finance (https://finance.yahoo.com) is a quick, free place to check data on individual publicly traded companies.
9. A common mistake by inexperienced valuation analysts is to wait until the last minute to do the industry and economic analysis and then to drop it into the text without any discussion of how it relates to the valuation conclusion.

4.5 CHAPTER 4: FINANCIAL STATEMENT AND COMPANY RISK ANALYSIS

1. The CPA analyst who is an ABV must take special care to set expectations in both the engagement letter and the valuation report regarding the degree of responsibility assumed for financial statements presented within the report because of accounting standards for attest services. CPAs performing valuation services must not violate the AICPA Code of Professional Conduct.
2. Financial statements may be necessary for more or fewer than five years if the subject company's business cycle does not coincide with a five-year time frame or if certain earlier years are not relevant (e.g., period of recession or unusual operating activity) or available.
3. Extraordinary and unusual items used to be identified in financial statements, but in accordance with ASU No. 2015-01, such transactions may no longer be segregated out. Valuation analysts may need to inquire about these types of items in discussions with management.
4. The valuation report should provide reasonable commentary regarding methods and ratios chosen and results of the analysis.
5. Analysts should be careful when mixing year-end data with beginning- and ending-year average data when preparing comparisons of the subject company to industry benchmark data and ratios.
6. To use benchmark industry ratios appropriately, analysts must be familiar with their scope and limitations as well as with the differences among them regarding data presentation and computation methods.

4.6 CHAPTER 5: INCOME APPROACH

1. Failure to develop the appropriate normalizing adjustments may result in a significant overstatement or understatement of value.

2. Compensation adjustments are made to differentiate the portion of the owner's compensation for their personal service rendered to the subject company (return on labor) and the portion of the compensation attributed to their equity investment (return on investment).

3. By choosing to make certain adjustments to the future economic benefit (i.e., the numerator), the analyst can develop a control or noncontrolling value. A control value is also referred to as a controlling value, and a noncontrol value is also referred to as a minority value or a noncontrolling value. These terms are used interchangeably.

4. Normalization adjustments affect the pre-tax income or cash flow of the entity being valued. Consequently, the adjustments will result in a corresponding modification in the income tax of the entity, if applicable.

5. Adjustments to the income and cash flow of a company are the primary determinants of whether the resulting value from the income approach is minority or control.

6. When the benefit stream or operations of the subject entity are affected by the influence of controlling interests and a minority interest is being valued, it may be preferable to provide a minority value directly by not making adjustments. Doing this will avoid the problems related to determining and defending the application of a minority discount.

7. Depending on the situation, statements prepared on a "tax basis" or "cash basis" may have to be adjusted to be closer to generally accepted accounting principles (GAAP) and/or normalized cash flow.

8. As with the control-oriented adjustments, extraordinary, nonrecurring, or unusual item adjustments affect the profit or loss accounts of a company on a pre-tax basis. Therefore, certain income tax–related adjustments may be necessary.

9. Specialists in the valuation of particular nonoperating assets may need to be hired. Engagement letters should clearly set out these responsibilities and the related appraisal expenses.

   Permission should be obtained from any third-party appraiser before relying on their appraisal conclusions and incorporating them into the valuation report. The valuation date, purpose, and standard of value for the related appraisal should be consistent with the valuation.

10. Synergistic value is investment value, which may not be fair market value.

11. In many small companies, income and cash flow can be the same or similar.

12. Cash flows presented on the financial statements are generally not used in business valuations. Because cash flows are normalized to estimate cash flows into perpetuity, specific changes in current assets and liabilities, specific purchases, and specific borrowings and repayments are ignored.

13. There are only four general types of analyses for application of the income approach.

14. Regardless of the method employed, dialogue with or information from management can provide insight into future projections.

15. Projections are used when variability in growth can be, or needs to be, accounted for in the benefit stream. When static growth is accounted for in the discount (risk) rate, a single sum projection (historical earnings) may be used. In deciding how long to project into the future, project until growth is estimated to be static, at which point growth is accounted for in the risk (capitalization) rate.

16. Theoretically, the length of the explicit period is determined by identifying the year when all the following years will change at a constant rate. Practically,

however, performance and financial position after three to five years often are difficult to estimate for many closely held companies. Lesser periods are sometimes used as well.

17. Often, the management of the business provides financial projections. In this case, the analyst typically discusses those projections with the management and tests them for reasonableness before they are used in the income approach.

18. In some circumstances, the past is not indicative of the future. Analysts must exercise care in analyzing projected performance in these situations. Adequate support must exist for the assumptions on which the projections are based.

19. The valuation analyst uses normalized historical data, management insights, and trend analysis to analyze formal projections for the explicit period. These projections consider balance sheet and income statement items that affect the defined benefit stream and involve not only projected income statements but also may include projected balance sheets and statements of cash flow.

    CPAs preparing projections may be subject to AICPA standards and reporting requirements for prospective financial statements.

20. The CCF formula includes the assumption that the NCF_1 can be "distributable" to the owners of the enterprise.

21. All other things being equal, the more certain the future streams of cash flow are, the more valuable the asset or entity.

22. The terminal value often represents a substantial portion of the total value of an entity, particularly when using a three- to five-year explicit forecast period. Longer explicit projections will result in a lesser impact from the terminal year value.

23. The Value Driver Model can result in a lower terminal value than the Gordon Growth Model.

24. The Advanced Growth Model is shown here for informational purposes only. Currently, it does not have widespread use in the valuation community.

25. Property (i.e., real estate) may be segregated from tangible assets at the outset and added back in separately. Rent expense can be substituted for real estate–related expenses.

26. If the control excess cash flow method is used and a minority value is the interest that is being valued, if appropriate, a discount for lack of control may be determined and applied.

27. Excess cash and cash equivalents are nonoperating assets and can be isolated from the operating assets during normalization.

28. The company's lending rates may be different if personal guarantees are required from the company's owners/officers. Lending rates will also vary based on the type of assets.

29. Whatever rate of return is used for goodwill, the aggregate return on all net assets should approximate the weighted average cost of invested capital for the entity.

30. The CCF method (also the Gordon Growth Model) is applicable when the interest-bearing debt (IBD) is in the form of a line of credit that grows at the same constant growth rate applied.

4.7 CHAPTER 8: COST OF CAPITAL/RATES OF RETURN

1. Unlike with publicly traded companies, the cost of capital of a private company is not observable and therefore is always an estimate.

2. The value of a company can be expressed as the present value of the future economic benefits expected to be generated by the company. This value can be either for equity, in which case the future benefits are those accruing directly to equity and an equity discount rate must be used, or for the overall company, including its debt, in which case a weighted average cost of capital (WACC) must be used.

3. The cost of capital depends on the risk characteristics of the investment, not those of the investor.

4. Remember, potential investors in the subject company are free to invest in one or more of the alternative investments on the risk spectrum. Therefore, it is useful to consider which of the type of investments serves as the best "proxy" for the subject company as a starting point.

5. The estimation of company-specific risk is one of the more difficult aspects of calculating rates of return.

6. Arbitrage Pricing Theory (APT) is not widely used in business valuation assignments for cost of capital determinations due to the unavailability of usable data for the components of the model.

7. Do not blindly rely on numbers from sources for the elements of the cost of equity. Understand the source of the data and how the numbers are derived. Mixing components from different sources without adjustment can lead to errors.

8. Under fair market value, the horizon may be that of the investment, not the investor.

9. No direct source for returns on 20-year Treasury bonds for all the years going back to 1926 is available. The Board of Governors of the Federal Reserve System publishes an online database of historical Federal Reserve Statistical Releases, which includes yields on 20-year Treasury constant maturities. The St. Louis branch of the Federal Reserve Bank publishes an extensive inventory of historical yield rates on all types of government securities, including the 20-year constant maturity Treasury bond. Analysts can consult the *Wall Street Journal* to find the quoted market yields on 30-year bonds with approximately 20 years of maturity left.

10. Kroll recommends that the normalized Rf be used only with the Kroll-recommended ERP.

11. The risk-free rate is a forward-looking concept, although historical data are often relied on to estimate the risk-free rate.

12. The ERP is a forward-looking concept, although historical data are often relied on to estimate the ERP. The ERP is an estimate of expected future market returns, and this must be considered in choosing an appropriate ERP for each circumstance.

13. For publicly held companies, beta is a measure of systematic risk.

14. Betas calculated using stock price data for public companies that are thinly traded may not be a reliable measure of risk.

15. It is common to assume a privately held company's beta as 1.0 and develop separate risk factors to include in its overall rate of return calculations or to use a beta for an industry group or from guideline public companies.

16. Published betas from multiple sources can display different results due to differing time periods, methodologies, and adjustments. Although several sources may be consulted or considered, the valuation analyst should not mix betas from different sources when estimating the beta in a valuation.

17. The commonly used Hamada formulas assume that debt remains at a constant amount, not a constant percentage of the capital structure.

18. Analysts who simultaneously rely on the industry risk premium (IRP) for developing cost of equity and argue the lack of comparable guideline public companies should be aware of the inconsistency in that statement. The industry premia are based on betas for a standard industrial classification (SIC) or global industry classification standard (GICS) code that may include guideline public companies previously rejected by the analyst.

19. In some cases and for certain industries, the industry risk premium data may be materially different from year to year. The inclusion of the industry risk premium as a component of the build-up model (BUM) remains questionable and is affected by the quality and comparability of the data.

    Alternatively, some analysts evaluate the risk premia provided for SIC and GICS codes related to the valuation target under consideration and then use such information inferentially to adjust the company-specific risk component of the BUM under the premise that industry risk is an element thereof. To avoid double-counting, when using the industry risk premium, eliminate consideration of industry risks within the company-specific risk adjustment.

20. The size premium is different from the small-stock risk premium, which is not beta adjusted and is simply the arithmetic return on small stocks less the arithmetic return on the market.

21. Per the *Cost of Capital Navigator*, the Risk Premium Size Study or Risk Study should not be used to estimate cost of equity for a financial services company (i.e., companies with an SIC Code beginning with 6).[3]

22. Lists of small-company risk factors can be used to analyze the attributes of a specific subject company and to select the level of adjustment for size and other company-specific risk. Because adjustments for size may implicitly include adjustments for other operating attributes, it is important to avoid double counting in the company-specific risk premium adjustment.

23. Every business enterprise will have its own unique attributes and risks, which can be incorporated into the rate of return.

24. Analysts must use caution when working with a methodology that assigns specific numerical adjustments to the build-up or CAPM rate. Due to the subjective nature of the numerical assignments for each category, the analyst may be asked if it is reasonable for each of the factors to be, say, a half percentage point higher or lower, thereby in summation causing a significant change in the resulting capitalization or discount rate being developed. These numerical adjustments are not as exact as they appear and are not based on any empirical data. Also, these lists may not be all-inclusive.

    Analysts should avoid "false precision" (e.g., carrying an estimate of company-specific risk to more than one decimal place).

25. The format and content of an analytical framework for analyzing company-specific risk will vary considerably depending on the nature of the assignment and the depth of analysis required. The articulation of the analyst's thought process by use of diagnostic tools can be a means of competitive differentiation, whether the tools are included in the final report or in engagement work papers.

26. Because traditionally derived discount and capitalization rates are cash flow rates and not earnings rates, for comparability an upward subjective adjustment

---

[3] Kroll, *Cost of Capital Navigator,* "Risk Premium Report Study." https://www.kroll.com/en/cost-of-capital.

would typically have to be made to convert the implied rate of return on earnings from the P/E multiple. If appropriate, to make the adjustment an assumption may be made that the historical relationship of net income to net cash flow is expected to continue.

4.8 CHAPTER 7: INTERNATIONAL COST OF CAPITAL

[This section left intentionally blank.]

4.9 CHAPTER 8: MARKET APPROACH

1. Comparability relates to similar operating characteristics; therefore, companies within the same industry are not always comparable to the subject company.
2. The prices paid for businesses and business interests reflect investor expectations. Consequently, any valuation methods that use stock or sales prices of businesses, including the market approach, are prospective in nature.
3. Multiples derived from the market approach include future growth expectations. Similar companies with different expected future growth rates will have different multiples.
4. Sales transaction data are available only for companies that have sold and reported pricing information, but the entire universe of companies includes those that were never sold or were sold in transactions for which data were unreported. Therefore, the multiples from databases of transactions may be overstated because the companies for which data are reported may be more saleable than those not reported.
5. Adjustments to the subject interest for lack of marketability or liquidity depend on the facts and circumstances related to the subject company valuation, the industry, and the selected multiple(s).
6. The values derived from both the market and income approaches implicitly include the value of all operating assets, both tangible and intangible.
7. When relying on databases of transaction information, analysts should use caution. Some of the databases calculate multiples excluding working capital. Thus, working capital must be added to the value indication to calculate the operating value of the company.
8. Investors' assumptions about growth are implicit in the prices of publicly traded companies and transactions. Generally, the higher the expected growth, the higher the value, all else being equal.

   Analysts' reports may be available for publicly traded companies and will often discuss expected growth, whereas no such information is available for private transaction companies.
9. Examining detailed business descriptions of the possible guideline companies is an essential step in the analysis. Some data vendors provide good descriptions of a company's business(es). For publicly traded companies or those subject to SEC reporting requirements, the most detailed description data are published in a company's 10-K filing or annual report.
10. Presenting potential guideline companies to subject company management can be challenging because managers frequently believe their company is "truly unique" and that none of the guideline companies are comparable. Assuming

the guideline companies have been properly vetted with regard to industry, markets, size, margins, and growth, the guideline companies may often still be used to provide insight into the pricing for similar companies. The analyst should be prepared to explain the reasons why the guideline companies are comparable to the subject company.

Alternatively, management may insist that a particular company is comparable because it is a competitor, but the division that offers a product or service similar to the subject company may be just one of many larger lines of business.

11. The Institute of Business Appraisers (IBA) cautioned analysts that the P/E ratios in the database are less reliable than revenue multiples due in part to the "different interpretations by persons who furnish the data as to what constitutes earnings."

12. When using the market approach to value a very small business, the guideline company transactions method can be a relatively better method than guideline publicly traded company analysis. Some transaction information is often available even for very small businesses, but the smallest guideline publicly traded company may be much larger than the subject. Also, the stock of some small publicly traded companies may not be traded frequently, in which case its market pricing may not be reliable for valuation multiples.

13. The lack of detailed information is the major disadvantage of this method when using private company transactions. It is difficult to know the structure of the transactions or the motivation of the buyer or seller.

14. Because detailed financial statements of the acquired company are usually not available, it is impossible to make certain adjustments to the data underlying the pricing multiples, if necessary.

15. When analyzing guideline company transactions, the lack of data on which to compute growth rates or to track trends in operations limit the confidence in the results obtained from this method.

16. Use caution when using SIC codes, North American Industry Classification System (NAICS) codes, GICS codes, or other industry classifications for searches. Often, these classifications do not reflect a change in the focus of a business. On occasion, companies are misclassified.

17. The valuation analyst may have to consult publicly traded company SEC filings to obtain detailed financial information. Electronic databases are a good starting point, but the data may have to be adjusted for comparability of financial position and performance across the companies analyzed.

18. It is good practice to review the SEC filings of selected guideline public companies, even when using a data vendor to populate valuation models. In addition to understanding the financial data, the notes to the financial statements can provide insights into major events and expectations for the company.

19. Some analysts believe that publicly traded companies are much too large to be used as guidelines in many situations. Although this may be true for the smallest of subject companies, such as mom-and-pop operations, small professional practices, or sole proprietorships, there is generally enough size variation among publicly traded companies that they should at least be considered for most other valuations.

20. One of the most important indicators of comparability is size, which can be expressed in terms of revenue, total assets, or market capitalization. Numerous studies have indicated that, on average, smaller companies have lower pricing

multiples than larger companies. The primary reason for this is that smaller companies typically have more business and financial risk than large companies.[4]

21. Many analysts believe that valuation multiples should not be adjusted for differences in profit margins between the guideline public companies and the subject company because of a potential for double counting by adjusting the multiple downward to reflect the lower margins of the subject company and then applying those lower multiples to that lower profit. They consider the anticipated growth of those profits to be the more important criterion.

22. Another issue is whether the volume of trading in a guideline company's stock is sufficiently active to give meaningful and realistic values for that company. Although companies with low trading volumes may be very similar to the subject in terms of business and financial characteristics, infrequent trades may not reflect the fair market value of the stock. As such, valuation multiples based on these prices may not be sufficiently reliable to value a subject company.

23. Valuation analysts may have to choose between a very small group of companies whose business descriptions and operating characteristics are quite similar to that of the subject or an expanded group of companies, some of whose business descriptions and operating characteristics are not as good a match.

24. Interest-bearing debt should be reflected at market value; however, on a practical basis, analysts frequently use book value of debt as a proxy for market value.

25. Using percentiles rather than simple averages or composites provides a range of values and helps protect the information from the effects of outliers.

26. Market multiples capture investment expectations of the likelihood of these types of conditions continuing into the future. Inappropriate adjustments could cause the multiple to reflect expectations of the actual earnings base less accurately.

27. Different assets, including different business operations within a company, may have different rates of return. When a company operates in multiple business segments or industries, it may be necessary to segregate operations and value them separately.

28. If the subject company owns real estate used in the business, the real estate may need to be segregated to properly reflect its rate of return. This determination should be made based on how real estate is treated in the selected guideline companies. If it is included in the calculation of the multiple for the guideline companies, the analyst will not need to segregate it in the valuation. Also, if the highest and best use of the real estate is its current use, then it may be part of the operating assets.

29. The analyst may consult with a recruiter to assist in determining the qualifications for a particular position and market compensation. Recruiters understand the market and the available pool of applicants. This information may help assess how many positions will be necessary to replace an owner and the market level of compensation.

    Another source of data for executive compensation is the proxy statements for the selected guideline public companies. Executive compensation with benefits is reported annually. It is important to have an accurate job description as a basis for determining the market salary for the relevant positions.

30. When using private transactions as guideline companies, some databases report the type of entity, making it possible to analyze pass-through entities separately from entities taxable at the corporate level.

---

[4] More risk means investors will require a higher rate of return on their investment, and the way to achieve a higher rate of return is by lowering the price.

31. For public companies, it is important to refer to the SEC filings to determine whether nonrecurring items, such as changes in product lines, mergers, and discontinued operations, are included in the historical financial statements on which the analyst is relying. Not all data vendors incorporate restated financial statements into their data.
32. Deficiencies in working capital may be an indicator that short-term debt should be reclassified as long-term debt. In other words, disguised permanent funding may be causing the subject company's working capital to be low or negative.
33. Excess working capital can be identified by comparing the working capital ratio of the subject to those of the guideline companies or by comparisons to industry norms. However, the analyst should use caution and take into consideration information from management regarding the future operating requirements of the subject company. For example, a company may be accumulating working capital to pay for capital improvements in the near future, or its lenders may require minimum working capital reserves above the level observed in the guideline companies.
34. Certain adjustments to the cash flow can change the level of value resulting from the analysis—many times from a noncontrol to a control level of value.
35. The quality and quantity of the guideline publicly traded company information will affect the reliability of the results of the guideline public company method of the market approach and how it factors into the analyst's conclusion of value.
36. Check definitions used by your sources. Some vendors of publicly traded stock information define MVIC as equity value less cash plus interest-bearing debt.
37. The choice of whether to use market value to equity (MVEq) or market value to invested capital (MVIC) is a function of the purpose of the valuation, the capital structures of the subject and guideline companies, and the analyst's preference.
38. The term *capital structure* refers to the relationship between the market values of debt and equity, never the book value of equity.
39. In theory, the best denominator to use is one that reflects expectations (i.e., using next year's expected revenues or income). It is an appropriate match with the numerator because the value of equity or invested capital is a prospective concept, containing the market's best assessment of the prospects for the future.
40. Even though the analyst uses the LTM to calculate a guideline company multiple, the price used in the calculation is based on investors' future growth expectations for the guideline company. Therefore, the multiple incorporates growth expectations.
41. Earnings before interest, taxes, depreciation, and amortization (EBITDA) multiples tend to be frequently used across many industries and are commonly used by investment bankers.
42. Although rules of thumb seldom, if ever, should be used as the sole way of valuing a business, they can offer insight into the way investors view the industry.
43. Rules of thumb for smaller businesses may not provide reliable guidance for selecting the types of multiples to rely on from guideline public companies.
44. Negative valuation multiples, which usually arise from losses, are not meaningful and should be ignored. In such cases, a different positive guideline company multiple can be used.
45. The final determination of which pricing multiple(s) to rely on must be based on an understanding of how the subject compares to the guideline companies in terms of the important factors discussed previously (i.e., growth, size, longevity, profitability, etc.). The coefficient of variation may be useful in determining how much weight to assign each of the various multiples.

46. An analysis using guideline company transactions is essentially the same as the analysis of the guideline public companies except there are considerably less data available to support its use as a primary method. Furthermore, the application of valuation multiples from each of the transaction databases may result in a different type of value, for example, with or without inventory or working capital.
47. If necessary adjustments are not made to guideline public company multiples, the analyst may not be accounting for differences in growth, size, or company-specific risk factors. If substantial adjustments are made, it may leave the impression that the "comparable" companies are really not that comparable to the subject company.
48. Sometimes differences in growth assumptions between the guideline companies and the subject can explain large differences between values derived from the income approach and those from the market approach.

Addendum 3: Adjusting Market Multiples: The Final Decision Is Still a Matter of Professional Judgment

1. Mathematical models and formulas to determine fundamental discounts to public company multiples still require professional judgment.

4.10 CHAPTER 9: ASSET APPROACH

1. Book value, which pertains to cost-basis accounting financial statements, is not fair market value.
2. The asset approach also is sometimes used in the valuation of very small businesses and/or professional practices where there is little or no practice goodwill.
3. The asset approach is seldom used in the valuation of operating companies. The time and costs involved in valuing individual tangible and intangible assets typically are not justified, because there is little, if any, increase in the accuracy of the valuation. The value of all tangible and intangible assets is captured, in aggregate, in the proper application of the income and market approaches. In many valuations, there is no real need to break out the amount of value associated with individual assets, including goodwill. However, the asset approach is sometimes used as a floor value. Other times it may be a value that is too high if the net asset values do not have income support as a going concern.
4. If the asset approach is used in valuing a minority interest of a closely held company, the value indication derived usually will have to be adjusted from control to minority and, depending on the facts and circumstances, from a marketable to a nonmarketable basis.
5. Notes to the financial statements often contain useful information concerning contingent liabilities.

4.11 CHAPTER 10: VALUATION DISCOUNTS AND PREMIUMS

1. Discounts and premiums may be applied at the entity level or shareholder level depending on whether the premium or discount is driven by factors affecting the entity as a whole, such as an environmental discount, or whether the driver is characteristic of a specific ownership interest.

2. Control premiums quantify the value of the right to control the destiny of the company and/or the ability to divert cash flows and value to the controlling ownership. Acquisition or strategic premiums quantify the incremental value of a particular investment as viewed by a specific investor(s). Empirical evidence of the size of combined control and strategic premiums is available but does not separate the premiums into these components.

3. Frequently, control premiums have been overstated by the use of acquisition premium data that reflect synergistic and strategic premiums as a proxy.

4. Lack of control and marketability are not unrelated. A majority shareholder may be able to affect marketability in ways that a minority shareholder cannot by, for example, pursuing a sale, a merger, or an initial public offering. Thus, the two discounts, although separate, should be considered in conjunction.

5. From the point of view of the minority shareholder, the majority shareholder's ability to control can reduce or eliminate the return on the minority shareholder's investment.

6. Quantification of the amount of the discount for lack of control (or the minority discount) is difficult due to the lack of empirical evidence.

7. The *Mergerstat* data include synergistic and acquisition premiums along with the control premium, and segregation of these premiums is difficult.

8. "The Working Group anticipates that in many instances such benefits will not be reliably identifiable, resulting in either no, or a small, premium . . . It is inconsistent with best practices to rely solely on benchmark premium data to evaluate the reasonableness of the MPAP in a fair value measurement."[5]

9. The use of minority cash flows in the income approach produces a minority interest value. As discussed in Chapter 5, minority cash flows are those cash flows without any adjustments due to controlling shareholders' actions, such as excess compensation, rent payments, or perquisites.

10. Consistency is important. Whether you start with control cash flows or minority cash flows, it is important to apply the same methodology throughout your minority value engagements.

11. Marketability expresses the relative ease and promptness with which a security or commodity may be sold when desired, at a representative current price, without material concession in price merely because of the goal of a prompt sale.

12. Although many experts agree, in theory, on the need for a discount for lack of marketability/liquidity on controlling interests in a privately held company, no direct empirical evidence is available to support such a discount. The initial public offering and restricted stock studies used to develop discounts for lack of marketability are based on minority interests, not controlling interests.

13. To address the issue of valuing restricted stocks, the IRS issued Revenue Ruling 77-287 "to provide information and guidance to taxpayers, Internal Revenue Service personnel, and others concerned with the valuation, for Federal tax purposes, of securities that cannot be immediately resold because they are restricted from resale pursuant to Federal securities laws."

14. The QMDM represents continued theoretical development of the concept of the marketability discount. This method is gaining in visibility and use, and numerous appraisers have adopted some form of the framework for analyzing discounts that Mercer/Harms have presented.

---

[5] *VFR Valuation Advisory 3, The Measurement and Application of Market Participant Acquisition Premiums,* The Appraisal Foundation (September 6, 2017), 7.

15. In addition to the discounts for lack of control and marketability, other potential discounts may apply to a minority interest in a closely held company. Some analysts consider these discounts in the calculation of a discount or capitalization factor and others separately quantify and apply the discounts.
16. Restrictions under certain agreements limit the ability to sell or transfer ownership interests.
17. In valuing a closely held company, an adjustment for information access and reliability may be in order.
18. An ongoing disagreement between the IRS and many tax practitioners is based on the treatment of the costs to liquidate the assets in estates.
19. A key person or *thin* management entity-level discount would be appropriate in the valuation of a closely held company where an owner or employee is responsible for generating a significant portion of the business's sales or profits. This key person may be a revenue generator, possess technical knowledge, or have close relationships with suppliers, customers, or banks.
20. Blockage discounts are based on the theory that, ordinarily, a large block of publicly traded stock cannot be sold as readily as a few shares of stock.
21. Blockage or market absorption discounts can also be considered when valuing other assets, such as real estate. In the valuation of a closely held real estate investment holding company, a discount for potential market absorption should be considered.
22. When a smaller closely held company is being compared to a larger publicly traded company, an adjustment for size may be appropriate.
23. Small companies often have limited access to capital, limited ability to weather a market downturn, limited resources to develop and market new products, and so on. Smaller companies also can have a higher cost of capital than larger companies.
24. Care should be exercised to avoid overlaps or "double discounting" with thin management discounts, small-company risk discounts, lack-of-diversification discounts, or others.

4.12 CHAPTER 11: REPORT WRITING

1. A detailed written report should provide the details necessary to permit another qualified analyst to use similar information and to understand the work done and the valuation conclusion reached.
2. Draft reports provided to attorneys or other appropriate parties are to be marked "draft" or "preliminary" and should not contain a signed certification.
3. Although many analysts often comply with Uniform Standards of Professional Appraisal Practice (USPAP) as a general rule, many of the reports that analysts write are not conducted under the services specified by USPAP for compliance. Only the American Society of Appraisers requires its members to comply with USPAP.
4. In certain engagements, such as litigation, or the recent COVID pandemic, the analyst might not be granted access to the facilities. If so, the introduction section can explain this and also what was done to obtain the knowledge usually gained during a site visit.
5. Financial statement adjustments may be of two different types. Normalizing adjustments convert the statements into economic financial statements. Control

adjustments reflect prerogatives of control and adjust the statement to conditions only the control interest may realize.

6. Analysts usually do not audit or perform reviews or any other assurance procedures on the historical financial information provided by the entity. They typically accept the information as accurate and state this in the assumptions.

7. Some analysts include the assumptions and limiting conditions in the engagement letter as well. See Appendix A of the sample valuation report for an example of assumptions and limiting conditions.

4.13 CHAPTER 12: BUSINESS VALUATION STANDARDS

1. The Internal Revenue Service has not officially adopted USPAP or any other organization's standard.

2. Terminology used in standards is not uniform across the professions performing appraisals. For example, USPAP Standards 3 and 4 discuss the "review" of another appraiser's work. To certified public accountants doing business valuation, the term *review* carries a meaning that is unique to the accounting profession and represents a level of service related to financial statements.

3. The pertinent sections of USPAP for the business appraiser include definitions, the preamble, the ethics rule, the record-keeping rule, the competency rule, the scope of work rule, the jurisdictional exception rule, the standards and standards rules, and applicable advisory opinions. Standard 9 covers Business Appraisal, Development; Standard 10 covers Business Appraisal, Reporting; Standard 3 covers Appraisal Review, Development; and Standard 4 covers Appraisal Review, Reporting.

4. Certain engagements, such as deal pricing and litigation, require the analyst or appraiser to sign a nondisclosure agreement. The analyst must be comfortable that adherence to the nondisclosure agreement does not violate the record-keeping rule of USPAP.

5. "An appraiser must not allow assignment conditions to limit the scope of the work to such a degree that the assignment results are not credible in the context of the intended use. An appraiser must not allow the intended use of an assignment or a client's objectives to cause the assignment results to be biased."[6]

6. For CPAs, the word *certify* has special meaning concerning attestation of financial information. Some CPAs will add a sentence in their report that they are not certifying any financial information but are adhering to the appraisal certification requirements of USPAP. In the business valuation standards of the AICPA, the word *certification* is replaced with *representation*.

7. The FASB provides guidance for how to measure fair value of financial and nonfinancial assets and liabilities under authoritative accounting pronouncements. Fair value measurement guidance provided by FASB is for financial statement purposes and should not be confused with fair value in dissenting shareholder cases that is determined according to state laws and court decisions in the respective states.

---

[6] Uniform Standards of Appraisal Practice (USPAP) 2020–2021 (extended through December 31, 2023), The Appraisal Foundation, https://appraisalfoundation.org/imis.

4.14 CHAPTER 13: VALUATION OF PASS-THROUGH ENTITIES

1. Depending on the characteristics of the company and ownership rights of the interest, valuation of a controlling versus a minority interest in a pass-through entity may require different approaches.
2. The Tax Court rejected many, if not most, of the reasons put forth by analysts for their deduction of taxes. Thus, if analysts are still providing these same reasons for the deduction of income taxes in their valuation reports, then they should either examine their reasoning or provide a better explanation as to why they believe such logic to be well founded.
3. In theory, diligent application of each model with attention to the specific facts relating to the subject interest should result in fairly similar conclusions, no matter which model is used.
4. A clear trend supported by the literature on the valuation of S corporations and by various models has been to value the shares from the perspective of the investor. This includes following the cash all the way into the investor's pockets. This approach makes sense because it is common knowledge that investors take taxes into consideration when pricing any investment. More recently, some authors suggest taking additional care to understand the taxes—investor-level as well as entity-level—embedded in the discount rates used to value pass-through entities and adjusting those rates accordingly.
5. The vast majority of the discussion of the existence of an "S corporation premium" is under the fair market value standard in the context of estate and gift taxes. The perspective would be the same as the marketplace, which assumes a buyer would consider the flow of benefits from ownership of the interest.
6. Nearly everyone agrees that tax benefits at the corporate level can create shareholder value; however, the issue of whether tax benefits enjoyed at the election of the shareholder also create value has historically been the subject of some debate.
7. Relative to S corporations, privately held C corporations have a greater incentive to pay out earnings to owners as a bonus in order to lower their EBT. As such, in comparing the multiples of S corporations and C corporations, the sales multiple is the more reliable measure. Privately held C corporations generally bonus out salaries rather than pay dividends. Although the ability to distribute cash flow through bonuses is limited by tax regulations on excessive compensation, the practice contributes to the notion that double taxation for privately held C corporations is myth rather than reality.
8. When using market data for transaction pricing for either S or C corporations, analysts must be careful to understand the data and at a minimum, identify the following characteristics of the transaction:
   - Asset or stock sale
   - Assets transacted
   - S or C corporation
   - Size of the transaction
   - Capital structure and liabilities assumed

   Failure to take these factors into consideration when using market data to value a pass-through entity could result in inappropriate valuation conclusions.
9. There is no conclusive market transactional evidence that S corporation values are different from private C corporation values on a control basis. However, if the analyst has used publicly traded C corporation data to value the S corporation,

if possible the differences between the expectations of the investor in a public C corporation and a private S corporation should be taken into consideration.

10. Many analysts still prefer simpler, more qualitative methods to valuing S corporations than the models presented here. Assuming the analysis is well conceived, qualitative methods are acceptable.

11. Some analysts have interpreted Treharne's articles as recommending consideration of all three scenarios for each valuation project. However, Treharne presented the three scenarios solely for the purpose of emphasizing the possible range of value conclusions attributed to the three possible input scenarios. Typically, all three scenarios do not need to be considered in each valuation project.

12. Each of the two theories considers the following issues:
    - Amount and timing of distributions
    - Retained net income
    - Holding period and exit strategy
    - Tax rates—personal, corporate, and capital gains
    - Further effect of minority or marketability discounts
    - Possible ability to participate in step-up-of-basis transaction

13. It is important to note that there are still many analysts who prefer simpler, more qualitative methods to valuing S corporations than the models presented here. Assuming a well-thought-out analysis, this is acceptable.

4.15 CHAPTER 14: ESTATE, GIFT, AND INCOME TAX VALUATIONS

1. Often events that would otherwise affect a subject company's value occur subsequent to the valuation date. Such events generally should not be considered for purposes of estate and gift tax valuations. The key to determining what events should be considered is what facts were known or knowable as of the valuation date.

2. Many analysts make the mistake of focusing on a subject company's past historical performance as the primary determinant of value. The expectation of the company's future performance as of the valuation date is what determines value. Past performance is only relevant to the extent that it is indicative of the company's future performance.

3. Value is dependent on investors' expectations of a company's future earnings capacity. If an unprofitable operation can be discontinued without adversely affecting the company's other lines of business, then the future earnings capacity (and hence the value) of the remaining lines of business may be materially greater than if the values of all operating lines were aggregated. In other words, the sum of some of the parts may be greater than the whole.

4. Dividend-paying capacity is equivalent to equity net cash flows, which is defined as "those cash flows available to pay out to equity holders (in the form of dividends) after funding operations of the business enterprise, making necessary capital investments, and increasing or decreasing debt financing."[7]

5. Sometimes analysts fail to consider the use of the guideline public company method of the market approach because they believe that publicly traded

---

[7] 2001 *International Glossary of Business Valuation Terms*. Note: This term is not defined in the 2022 *International Valuation Glossary—Business Valuation*.

companies are too large to be truly comparable. Although the size of many public companies may eliminate them as guidelines, the size of some public companies may approximate that of the closely held company being valued.

6. Revenue Ruling 59-60 does not specifically address the use of the guideline company transactions method of the market approach in valuing closely held companies because such data were not widely available at the date of publication of the Revenue Ruling. Revenue Ruling 59-60 guidance relating to comparability of the business lines and consideration of other relevant factors in the application of the guideline public company method may also be applicable to the guideline company transactions method.

7. Revenue Ruling 59-60 supports the use of an asset approach for valuing investment or holding companies. Therefore, use of an asset approach when valuing family limited partnerships and limited liability companies (LLCs) with similar characteristics is considered reasonable in view of this ruling.

8. Inexperienced analysts often make the mistake of arbitrarily averaging each of the various valuation approaches/methodologies used in valuing a closely held company. For example, if three approaches are used, each approach may be routinely assigned an equal one-third weighting. As noted in Revenue Ruling 59-60, such practice would be inappropriate. Rather, each valuation is subject to particular facts and circumstances, and these must be considered in selecting the most appropriate approach(es) and level of reliance when determining the final estimate of value.

4.16 CHAPTER 15: VALUATION OF FAMILY LIMITED PARTNERSHIPS

1. Once a valuation analyst has an understanding of the bundle of rights, they can determine how to capture the positive or negative impact of the bundle of rights (or lack of rights) on the benefit stream, rate of return, discount applied to enterprise value, or a combination of these as regards the subject interest.

2. If assets are not transferred on formation in return for the same percentage of partnership interest in relation to the assets, the value differential between the assets transferred and the interest received may result in an unintended gift.

3. Term restriction is important from a valuation perspective because it defines the inability of the limited partners to receive a return on their investment prior to the completion of the partnership term.

4. This type of provision provides rights for limited partners in certain circumstances that may enable them to affect some operations of the partnership. As such, the impact of this type of provision is partially dependent on the size of the limited partnership interest being valued.

5. If the provisions in the agreement are anything other than fair market value between family members, it may be disregarded under § 2703.

6. Most partnership agreements have a clearly stated restriction on transferability of partnership interests, primarily to protect all partners from finding themselves legally bound to a partnership with individuals not of their choice. From a valuation perspective, such restrictions on transferability may have a material impact on the degree of discount for lack of control and lack of marketability. The amount of the discount for lack of control and lack of marketability may be mitigated by provisions that moderate restrictions in transferability.

7. All contributions are to be credited to the partners' accounts to avoid the "gift on formation" issues previously discussed.

8. The provisions concerning amendments to the partnership agreement provide a substantial level of authority to the general partner with input by the limited partners. However, many partnership agreements provide for a "power of attorney" clause whereby the limited partners specifically provide the authority for the general partner to act on their behalf. In addition, a restriction on transferability provides some level of protection to the limited partners regarding possible changes in management of the partnership. These restrictions may allow for some level of discount for lack of control when valuing a general partner interest.

9. Like the provision for the general partner capital accounts, this provision makes it clear that all contributions are to be credited to the partners' account to avoid the "gift on formation" issues previously discussed.

10. One of the benefits to a limited partnership structure is the protection afforded the limited partners from the debts and obligations of the partnership or other partners.

11. The previous provisions are the foundation for selecting appropriate discounts for lack of control and lack of marketability for two reasons:

    a. A limited partner, by definition, does not have any right to manage or control the partnership, thus eliminating their ability to determine the amount and timing of any distributions or asset liquidations of the partnership. This effectively eliminates some of the sources of return on the partner's investment.

    b. In addition, the inability to readily transfer the interest or withdraw from the partnership eliminates the other avenue for a limited partner to receive a return on their investment.

12. To avoid the negative impact § 2704(a) can have on the estate tax value of a limited partnership interest, it is better if the limited partner does not own a general interest in the partnership at death. Alternatively, the limited partner can gift all of their limited interest before death. The general partner can also be a separate entity.

13. Whether an asset is income producing or not will affect value. For instance, if an FLP is holding undeveloped land instead of an income-producing property, the value of an investment in the FLP will be influenced by the inability of the undeveloped land to generate a return to partners other than through ongoing appreciation and possible liquidation of the asset.

14. The closed-end funds to be used as a source of pricing data should match as closely as possible the specific portfolio structure of the FLP. For instance, if the FLP holds only technology stock and some blue chips, the closed-end funds selected should have a similar asset mix to appropriately reflect the market perception of risk for the type of portfolio being held by the FLP.

15. Analysis of closed-end funds with similar investment characteristics to the subject FLP can provide an indication of the adjustment to net asset value that the market would require.

16. For closed-end funds that are actively publicly traded, the difference between the trading price and net asset value has nothing to do with marketability. Funds that are thinly traded would be less reliable indicators of market dynamics.

4.17 CHAPTER 16: SUMMARY OF COURT CASE VALUATION ISSUES

[This section left intentionally blank.]

4.18 CHAPTER 17: SHAREHOLDER DISPUTES

1. State statutes and judicial precedent control this area of valuation. Although analysts should not be acting as attorneys, it is important that they become generally familiar with the statutes and case law in the jurisdiction in which the lawsuit has been filed. The analyst should consult with legal counsel to ensure that they have a proper understanding of jurisdictional precedent, specifically as it relates to their valuation as well as any legal interpretations.
2. Shareholder dispute cases typically arise under two different state statutes: dissenting shareholder actions and minority oppression (dissolution) actions.
3. In both dissenting and oppressed shareholder disputes, the statutes are clear—the standard of value is *fair value* in almost all states.
4. The standard of value is important in determining both the methodology that will be applied and the discounts and premiums that will or will not be applied, and the courts have demonstrated that they do not equate fair value and fair market value.
5. The attorney should be consulted regarding the appropriate standard of value. That may mean the attorney provides statutes and case law requesting assistance from the valuation expert interpreting it. The standard of value and definition of value, if known, should be stated in the engagement letter to avoid a potential misunderstanding.
6. When preparing a fair value analysis, the valuation analyst should consult the attorney on the engagement who will consider the state statute and case law to establish the valuation date because this date influences the information that may be considered in conjunction with the valuation.
7. Valuation experts are vital in these cases. Courts look to the valuation analyst to provide a well-reasoned, objective valuation to aid them in their findings. To do so requires that analysts maintain objectivity and independence. Analysts present their professional opinions rather than their clients' opinions.
8. Currently, the three approaches to value—market, income, and asset—are all acceptable in the shareholder dispute arena, although it is important to confer with the attorney in the particular jurisdiction. Methodologies (or preferred methods) vary from one jurisdiction to another.
9. Various courts interpret the methodologies differently and refer to commonly known methods by other names.

4.19 CHAPTER 18: EMPLOYEE STOCK OWNERSHIP PLANS

1. In an S corporation owned 100 percent by an employee stock ownership plan (ESOP), cash retention can be significant because no payments are required for federal income taxes on its earnings.
2. It is prudent for the trustees to engage the valuation analyst to participate in the process of analyzing transaction proposals and counterproposals in negotiations and not impair the valuation analyst's independence and objectivity.

3. An objective analyst providing valuation services and a valuation report to a plan trustee of an ESOP is not a fiduciary. This is not to be confused with an independent plan trustee fiduciary who is independently providing a valuation.

4. As a practical matter, and assuming the sponsoring company is paying the fee, it is appropriate to have the trustee of the ESOP engage the analyst and to have an officer of the sponsoring company sign that same engagement as obligor for the analyst's fee.

5. A thorough understanding of the source and application of loan proceeds is necessary because the analyst's valuation analysis will treat the use of ESOP loan proceeds and debt repayment differently from other non-ESOP debt obligations.

6. A common misconception of sellers to the ESOP is that after the ESOP share transaction, the share earnings and operating benefits continue to accrue to the former shareholder in much the same manner as before the ESOP made the acquisition of those shares.

7. When an ESOP owns Subchapter S shares, it is the ESOP that is exempt from federal taxation as a qualified plan under ERISA. The shares themselves have no such exemptions; thus, the tax-exempt status is only applicable while those shares are held by the ESOP as a qualified plan asset.

8. Reporting the sponsoring company's ERISA-required buyback of ESOP shares (the put obligation) on financial statements as contingent liability is not supported by GAAP, the accounting community, or appraisers.

9. As the ESOP owns a greater percentage of the sponsoring company's stock and the plan ages, the repurchase obligation becomes more material to valuation considerations.

10. Analysts should be careful not to double count the impact of ESOP acquisition debt on the value of equity. If higher benefit plan contributions required to pay down the ESOP acquisition debt are included in compensation expense, and the total book value of the debt is deducted from MVIC, the impact of the debt has been accounted for twice: once in the higher compensation expenses and again in the subtraction of debt from MVIC.

11. The level of value for an ESOP valuation is of a noncontrolling, minority interest, unless compelling requisite relevant factors, empirical evidence, and support in both form and substance indicate otherwise.

12. Often, in a 100 percent–owned ESOP company, the only control/liquidity adjustment required is for the put right.

13. The put right does not create a ready market for the ESOP shares, but it does provide a mechanism for potential marketability that can significantly reduce an adjustment for a lack of marketability in a private company.

14. Discussions about compensation practices should be rational, reasonable, and in accordance with the reality that it takes money to attract and keep quality, qualified talent.

15. Assess whether the compensation arrangement is aligned with enhanced operating performance conducive to equity growth and not diminishing equity value.

16. Various methods may be used to analyze scenarios of diminishing equity value in an ESOP, but often a simple test of the purchase price may suffice. For example, assume a sale of 100 percent of equity to an ESOP. Fair market value assumed a capital structure representative of the industry in which the subject company operates at approximately 30 percent equity and 70 percent debt at an appropriate interest rate. Using the expected operating cash flow, the post-acquisition value could be tested in a discounted cash flow analysis to equity, reflecting the amortization of debt repayment to normalized levels.

17. In an ESOP environment, the default discount period convention is end-of-year.
18. Anticipated debt leverage to an initial ESOP purchase of shares is not considered in the initial valuation of those shares because the debt leverage event did not exist as of the date of valuation.
19. Example of an annotated subsequent event disclosure: Six weeks after the company's fiscal year-end, the company's primary manufacturing plant suffered a catastrophic uninsured loss due to a tsunami.

4.20 CHAPTER 19: VALUATION IN THE DIVORCE SETTING

1. The analyst must know the specific definition of *value* that is to be used in determining a value in a divorce setting. Failure to do so could result in the valuation being excluded, discredited, or ignored by the judge if challenged. The attorney should provide guidance on the law to the analyst.
2. The state-specific definitions and components of *goodwill* often cause confusion. It is important to fully understand the term's meaning in the context it is being used.
3. Because of the differences in state laws, analysts should be aware of the espoused standard of value in a particular jurisdiction and variations imposed by judicial decisions. Consultation with an attorney is advised.
4. *Personal goodwill* is attached to the persona and the personal efforts of the individual. It is generally considered to be difficult to transfer, even if possible. *Entity goodwill* is attached to the business enterprise and can be transferred or sold.
5. No "average" percentage can be assumed to be either personal or enterprise goodwill, reinforcing the variability of facts and circumstances from matter to matter as well as the need for the analyst to carefully review and understand the respective facts and circumstances at hand.
6. If the analyst presents their case appropriately and supports the allocations with sound logic, the court will be more likely to accept the analyst's conclusions as a reasonable approximation and allocation of personal and enterprise goodwill.
7. The analyst should be cautious not to assume there is automatically enterprise goodwill associated with a particular factor such as location without looking at the facts and circumstances of the case.
8. Analysts should consider the number of employees, the job titles and job descriptions, the pay scale, the length of service, and the nature of their relationships to the clients.
9. The issue of nonowner professionals and their impact on value is one that moves beyond the issue of separation of personal and entity goodwill. In determining the fair market value of a professional practice, the issue of control of clients, patients, and customers relates to the transferable value of the practice, before consideration of personal and entity goodwill of the owner.
10. If applicable in the jurisdiction, the valuation analyst should consider the issue of a trifurcation of goodwill when valuing a business interest in a divorce case and discuss the pros and cons with the attorney prior to concluding on a value for the subject business interest.
11. The arguments set forth by proponents of a personal goodwill element for commercial businesses sound similar to a key person discount. However, in reality, personal goodwill, if present, even in a commercial business, is likely

separate and distinguishable from a key person discount. A key person discount is an entity-level discount that purports to measure the loss of value to a business as a result of a loss of a particular person. However, the analyst should focus on the facts and circumstances at hand and be cautious of overcounting the risk plus reflecting a personal goodwill allocation, unless it is appropriate. The goal is to determine the earnings attributable to the individual.

12. The analyst should be aware of the double-dipping concept and its application to the jurisdiction in which the divorce case is being litigated and be prepared to provide an analysis to the court of the application of the concept.

13. Although compliance with an appropriate business valuation standard is not a requirement of a court for an acceptable value for divorce purposes, the cross-examining attorney can nevertheless use noncompliance as a tool for impeachment.

14. Noncompliance to standards does not necessarily invalidate a valuation report for the court (that decision is up to the judge), but it can provide fodder for cross-examination.

4.21 CHAPTER 20: VALUATION ISSUES IN SMALL BUSINESSES

1. Small businesses tend to have lower-quality financial statements that are less likely to have been prepared by an outside accountant. Their statements tend to be structured on tax reporting requirements rather than oriented to stockholder disclosure, as in larger companies.

2. Adjustments from cash-basis accounting to accrual-basis accounting can be made, as necessary, for valuation assignments. However, such adjustments may be unnecessary when valuing a small business.

3. The characteristics of small businesses tend to result in overall higher risk than is found in larger businesses. These risk characteristics can be extreme in the smallest of businesses. Risk tends to increase as size decreases.

4. It may be necessary to make certain adjustments to improve comparability of the subject company to industry norms, publicly traded companies, or companies involved in market transactions considered in the valuation process.

5. When valuing a control interest in a small business, it is appropriate to adjust for discretionary items. When valuing a minority/noncontrolling interest, it may not be appropriate to adjust for discretionary items because the owner of a minority/noncontrolling interest is not in a position to change these items. However, a minority/noncontrolling shareholder may be in a position to force an adjustment as an oppressed shareholder. In this regard, one may need to consider the external stakeholders reviewing the valuation. In certain litigation venues, many triers of fact still like to see a traditional valuation of the entire 100 percent interest before discounts applied for lack of marketability and lack of control for an interest without attributes of control. Also, operational control issues may have an impact on how the analyst values the interest.

6. Business brokers can provide insight into the qualitative factors buyers consider in a particular market.

7. Earnings in the latest 12 months and average earnings in recent years tend to be given the most weight in establishing prices for the smallest businesses. Capitalization of earnings/cash flow is often an appropriate method for valuing these small businesses.

8. Many analysts assume that the guideline public company method is never applicable to small businesses. For the mom-and-pop very small business, this is often

a safe assumption. However, data are available for many publicly traded companies with market capitalization below \$50 million, which may be a reasonable size range for comparability with some small businesses.

9. The analyst must exercise caution in using transaction databases because they define variables in different ways.

10. *Revenue* and *discretionary earnings* are two of the most common multiples used in the guideline company transactions method when applied to small businesses.

11. Revenue multiples are used most often for service businesses or when reliable data on earnings are not available. Using this multiple implies that the subject company and the acquired companies have similar asset ratios and have or can achieve similar profit margins, which may not be the case. Valuation analysts should take caution when using this methodology.

12. Value indications derived from the guideline company transactions method are on a control basis.

13. The AICPA *Statements on Standards for Valuation Services VS Section 100 (SSVS)* note that a rule of thumb is "technically not a valuation method. A rule of thumb is typically a reasonableness check against other methods used and should generally not be used as the only method to estimate the value of the subject interest."

14. The excess earnings/cash flow method is widely used for small businesses, but analysts frequently misuse it.

4.22 CHAPTER 21: VALUATION ISSUES IN PROFESSIONAL PRACTICES

1. Many professional practices obtain most of their patients or clients through referrals based on the reputation of specific professionals.

2. In some jurisdictions, an important issue in valuing professional practices is distinguishing between the goodwill that is solely attributable to the professional (personal goodwill, which is difficult to transfer) and the goodwill that is attributable to the practice (practice or enterprise goodwill, which may be transferable).

3. Litigation (including disputes among principals and marital dissolutions) and transactions (including the sale of a practice, an associate buying in, and buy-sell formulas) account for a large portion of valuation engagements.

4. Goodwill may be the primary intangible asset found in professional practices, but the definition of goodwill differs based on the purpose of the valuation.

5. When a professional practice is being valued for transaction or litigation purposes, it may be important to identify professional and practice goodwill separately and to discuss the likelihood that a portion of the professional goodwill can be transferred in a transaction.

6. The professional's earnings and/or the practice's economic income should be calculated in the same manner as the comparative compensation data.

7. In a small professional practice, value may be greater if a successor for the key professional is in place. Bringing in an associate and introducing the associate to clients or patients may facilitate the transfer of some "professional goodwill" and may increase the price received by the exiting professional.

8. When valuing professional practices, it is important to analyze and make appropriate adjustments to the financial statements. The widespread use of cash-basis accounting may require several adjustments.

9. If using a cash flow to equity benefit stream, there is no need to adjust to accrual-basis financial reporting. Professional practices are generally valued on cash

flow. Balance sheet adjustments are only relevant to the extent they affect cash flow or for the determination of nonoperating assets or debt.

10. If the practice owns material amounts of nonoperating assets, such as art collections and antiques in excess of what is customary in the decor of comparable offices, it may be necessary to value these assets separately from practice operations.

11. If the economic benefits stream being discounted or capitalized is pre-tax earnings or pre-tax earnings plus owners' compensation and benefits, the discount rate or the capitalization rate should be higher than if the benefits stream is net cash flow after tax.

12. Guideline company transactions sometimes are used as a reasonableness test for values obtained by other methods.

13. The usefulness of past transactions in the subject company often is limited by the structure of the transactions. Post-transaction compensation to the seller is often a significant economic benefit. In prior transactions, it may be difficult to distinguish the portion of value attributed to this benefit compared to the value attributable to the practice.

   In some cases, the withdrawal terms of a shareholder or partnership agreement may provide buyout terms that are artificially low as an incentive not to leave the practice.

14. Although rules of thumb may provide insight on the value of a professional practice, it is usually appropriate to use them only for reasonableness tests of the value conclusion.

4.23 CHAPTER 22: REASONABLE COMPENSATION

1. Treas. Reg. § 1.162–7(b)(3) defines reasonable compensation as the "amount that would ordinarily be paid for like services by like organizations in like circumstances."

2. When bonuses paid to individuals are not contingent on any identified factors, the analyst may need to evaluate such payments further to confirm that they are not actually distributions disguised as compensation.

3. When catch-up pay is being deducted, for tax purposes especially, the business should have documentation from prior years of the amount of under-compensation and the intent of repayment.

4. On completion of analysis, consider whether the level of compensation would be acceptable to all parties if the transaction were in an arm's-length relationship; if so, the conclusion is likely fair and reasonable.

4.24 CHAPTER 23: THE VALUATOR AS EXPERT WITNESS

1. Experts must consciously avoid being advocates; they must be careful not to alter the objectivity of a valuation conclusion simply to advance the client's interest. The only thing that should be advocated by experts is their opinion—not the client's position.

2. An important caveat is that when the expert is formulating questions in the courtroom for counsel to put to the opposing expert in cross-examination, it should not appear to the judge that the expert is part of the client's or lawyer's litigation team. If the valuator is perceived as being a member of the team, their perceived independence and objectivity may be questioned by the judge.

3. Once certain evidence has been excluded by a *Daubert* motion because it fails to meet the relevancy and reliability standard, it will likely be challenged when reintroduced in another trial. Even though a *Daubert* motion is not binding on other courts of law, if something was found untrustworthy by one court, other judges may choose to follow that precedent.
4. The expert's role is to the assist the court with respect to technical issues that are beyond the knowledge of the layperson and to explain how the expert arrived at their conclusions.

4.25 CHAPTER 24: FAIR VALUE MEASUREMENT AND THE VALUATION OF INTANGIBLE ASSETS

1. In addition to fair value accounting related to business combinations and impairment testing, intangibles may be valued for merger and acquisition activity, licensing purposes, bankruptcy, sale of the individual intangible asset, or litigation, among other reasons. In general, the methodology applied for such purposes will be similar to that used for fair value accounting.
2. Intangible assets receiving legal protection become intellectual property, which may be generally categorized into five types: patents, copyrights, trade name (trademarks and trade dress), trade secrets, and know-how.
3. Transaction costs are specific to the transaction and represent the incremental direct costs to sell the asset or transfer the liability; thus, the price should not be adjusted for transaction costs because they are not an attribute of the asset or liability. However, transportation costs from the current location to the market may be included in the fair value measurement of an asset if location is a characteristic of the asset.[8]
4. A fair value measurement assumes that a transaction occurs in the principal market, or in the absence of a principal market, in the most advantageous market for the asset or liability.[9]
5. A business combination is a transaction or other event in which an acquirer obtains control of one or more businesses. Transactions sometimes referred to as true mergers or mergers of equals also are business combinations.[10]

   FASB provides the following definition for the term *identifiable*:
   An asset is identifiable if it meets either of the following criteria:
   a. It is separable, that is, capable of being separated or divided from the entity and sold, transferred, licensed, rented, or exchanged, either individually or together with a related contract, identifiable asset, or liability, regardless of whether the entity intends to do so.
   b. It arises from contractual or other legal rights, regardless of whether those rights are transferable or separable from the entity or from other rights and obligations.[11]

---

[8] Financial Accounting Standards Board, Accounting Standards Codification (2023), ASC 820-10-35-9C.
[9] Ibid., at 820-10-35-5.
[10] Ibid., Master Glossary.
[11] Ibid., Master Glossary.

6. Because return requirements increase as risk increases and because intangible assets are usually inherently more risky for a company than tangible assets, it is reasonable to conclude that the returns expected on intangible assets typically will be at or above the average rate of return (discount rate) for the company as a whole.

7. Some analysts have advocated that the direct and indirect costs be adjusted to reflect developer's profit and entrepreneurial incentive/opportunity cost. Application of these adjustments is currently inconsistent in the valuation profession.

8. The royalty is typically expressed as a pre-tax percentage of revenues. The relief from royalty method relies on two general types of inputs: the royalty rate and the revenue forecast.

9. The risk premium assessed to a new-product launch should decrease as a project successfully proceeds through its continuum of development because the uncertainty related to each subsequent stage typically diminishes.

10. The valuation method known as the multi-period excess earnings method (MPEEM) is generally reserved for the value drivers, the intangible assets with the most direct relationship to the revenue and cash flow streams of an enterprise.

11. The MPEEM measures the present value of the future earnings to be generated during the remaining lives of the subject assets.

12. The weighted average return on assets (WARA) calculation employs the rate of return for each asset weighted according to its fair value relative to the whole. The WARA should approximate the overall WACC for the business.

13. By its nature, goodwill is the riskiest asset of the group, and therefore should require a return much higher than the overall business return, and at times, even higher than venture capital returns.

14. The valuation of noncompete agreements is typically performed by preparing two discounted cash flow models—one that is based on the market participant business enterprise analysis and assumes a noncompete agreement is in place and a second that assumes that the noncompete agreement is not in place.

15. Including such tax effects in the valuation process is more common in the income approach but is not typical in the market approach because any tax benefit should be factored into the quoted market price. The cost approach may be prepared pre-tax, so no adjustment is required.

16. The tax amortization benefit is calculated as the present value of the tax savings resulting from the 15-year amortization of the asset under Internal Revenue Code Section 197, assuming market participants in the United States.

17. The tax amortization benefit calculation may be expressed in the following formula:

$$AB = PVCF \times \left(n / \left(n - \left((PV(Dr,n,-1) \times (1+Dr)^{\wedge}0.5) \times T \right) \right) - 1 \right)$$

Where:

$$AB = \text{Amortization benefit}$$
$$PVCF = \text{Present value of cash flows from the asset}$$
$$n = \text{15-year amortization period in the U.S.}$$
$$Dr = \text{Discount rate}$$

$PV(Dr,n,-1) \times (1+Dr)^{\wedge}0.5 =$ Present value of an annuity of \$1 over 15 years, at the discount rate, using a mid-year convention

$$T = \text{Tax rate}$$

18. Under the acquisition method, in-process research and development is capitalized if it is acquired as part of a business combination, rather than expensed at the acquisition date.

19. The Financial Accounting Standards Board is continually updating accounting standards and has made many changes related to fair value accounting over the years. It is imperative that analysts be familiar with the most up-to-date guidance before preparing an analysis for fair value financial reporting.

20. Impairment of goodwill is the condition that exists when the carrying amount of a reporting unit that includes goodwill exceeds its fair value. A goodwill impairment loss is recognized for the amount that the carrying amount of a reporting unit, including goodwill, exceeds its fair value, limited to the total amount of goodwill allocated to that reporting unit.[12]

21. Application of the income approach using a present value technique is often an appropriate way to estimate the fair value of a group of assets (such as a reporting unit).[13]

22. In most applications, the appropriate rate of return for determining the business enterprise value is the WACC, which is the weighted average of the return on equity capital and the return on debt capital. The rate must be a rate that market participants would use in discounting enterprise cash flows.

23. The ASC specifically prohibits the recognition of the assembled workforce as an intangible asset apart from goodwill.

24. The value of the assembled workforce is represented by the assemblage cost avoided. Therefore, the cost approach is the most appropriate valuation technique to value this asset.

25. Trade names and trademarks must be considered individually to determine their remaining useful life. Trade names and trademarks that are associated with a company name or logo (e.g., McDonald's) typically have indefinite lives. Many product trade names and trademarks also will have an indefinite life if no reasonable estimate can be made of the end of the product life (e.g., Coca-Cola). However, the analyst must be careful to find out whether there is a planned phase-out of a product or ascertain whether it can be estimated with reasonable certainty that a name will lose value or be abandoned over time. In such a case, a finite life is suggested and, therefore, an amortization period is warranted. For tax purposes, generally all intangibles are amortizable over a 15-year life.

4.26 CHAPTER 25: MARKETING, MANAGING, AND MAKING MONEY IN A VALUATION SERVICES GROUP

Addendum 1: Marketing, Managing, and Making Money in a Valuation Services Group

1. Some practices whose revenues are based primarily on fixed fees make the mistake of failing to maintain or to evaluate time records and other information about efficiency and profitability that would indicate problem areas that need corrective action.

2. It is desirable that staff chargeable hours for engagements should, on average, result in billings equal to 90 percent or more of the recorded hours.

---

[12] Ibid., at 350-20-35-2.
[13] Ibid., at 820-10-55-4.

3. On average, a group practice should be charging billable hours to engagements for more than 70 percent of the standard hours available for work.
4. Despite the higher profits offered by litigation services, some practitioners find that being an expert witness is disruptive to the processes needed to direct a practice that must deliver valuation reports on a regular basis.
5. Because a business valuation engagement is a consulting project, proactive planning and control are key to maximization of the efficiency, quality, and profitability of the work process and product.
6. Resource flexibility is a rich area for practice leaders to explore as they seek to smooth the peaks and valleys of the workflow.
7. Unless the practice has a culture toward quality and client value, there is less chance for good economics, at least for any sustained period of time.
8. Litigation services engagements in particular need an organized and disciplined approach because frequently the initial engagement criteria are augmented and revised over the life of the project. It is not unusual at the start of some litigation service engagements that the engagement criteria are vague and specific tasks are undefined.
9. A practice may not want to accept engagements for individuals (as opposed to companies) as clients without receiving substantial retainers.
10. In most situations, if you are good enough to be engaged, you are good enough to be paid a portion of the fee in advance.
11. Work plans and budgets, where appropriate, can be valuable tools that aid in the supervision and control of the engagement team, and can help in obtaining efficiency on the job. These can be detailed or general and in writing or oral.
12. Sometimes the best approach to take with an engagement that is floundering economically is to take the practice's best people and put them on the job to finish it up.
13. The old adage "People do what you inspect, not what you expect" applies to valuation engagements, because team members may not know or admit on a timely basis that they are off track about the direction their work is headed.
14. A very general rule of thumb for frequency of inspection by a practice leader or engagement manager is that the work of novices should be reviewed every two hours or so. The work of all other professionals should be inspected on a time interval of three hours, increasing for each year of their experience. This is particularly affected by the type and complexity of the engagement, the staff person, and the practice leader. Some senior analysts require only periodic discussions of the engagement progress and issues.
15. Preparing a work plan and budget (whether written or oral) for known tasks and obtaining approval aids the client and the attorney to understand the likely fee levels required.
16. Do not assume anything without frequent and clear communication with the client and the client's attorney.

4.27 CHAPTER 26: BUSINESS DAMAGES

1. Although financial experts are not necessarily expected to know the law, having contextual knowledge of relevant legal principles can help ensure that the expert's calculations are relevant and applicable to the case at hand.

2. Experts should communicate with legal counsel regarding statutory or legal standards as well as any contractual definitions that may affect measures of business damages.

3. Rather than use the term *causation* as a stand-alone term, financial experts should consider using the term *loss causation* or *economic loss causation* when addressing the issue of how, and to what extent, the damages computed were caused by the alleged wrongful conduct as opposed to other unrelated factors.

4. Although it may be appropriate for an expert to assume legal liability, it is not appropriate for an expert to simply assume loss causation, concluding that the results of a calculation are damages, without considering other contributing factors.

5. The concept of *economic loss causation* makes sense from an economic perspective given that a damages award is intended to put a party in the position it would have been in had the alleged wrongful conduct not occurred.

6. Establishing reasonable certainty involves rigorous analysis of which the identification and testing of key assumptions may be an important part.

7. Damages calculations should only include damages caused by the wrongful conduct. Typically, such calculations should not include as damages any losses by a plaintiff due to other factors not alleged as wrongful conduct.

8. *Daubert,* and other comparable cases in state courts, established trial judges as "gatekeepers" over the admissibility of expert testimony in order to avoid admitting "junk science" into evidence.

9. The methodology to estimate what revenue would have been is a critical assessment in a lost profits calculation because the rest of the computation is often revenue- (or volume-)dependent.

10. Cost analysis is an important element of a damages calculation. Identification of incremental expenses may be complex. Not all costs are simply either fixed or variable, especially when considering a large proportion of a company's or plant's production volume or a long time horizon.

11. One important aspect of a damages calculation is determining how far into the future to project the ongoing profits lost by the plaintiff or the gains realized by the defendant. The period of recovery depends on the facts and circumstances of the case and on the consideration of reasonable certainty and economic loss causation.

12. Using hindsight, the fact that an event ultimately took place does not mean that it was reasonably foreseeable as of the valuation date.

13. The financial expert may be asked to calculate prejudgment interest, which is acceptable, but it should be presented in a transparent manner, separate from the calculation of other aspects of damages.

14. In many cases, the rate and method of applying prejudgment interest are determined by statute. Whether or how prejudgment interest should be calculated is not generally a question for the financial expert; that is a legal issue. However, the financial expert may be asked to perform the calculations.

15. In a reasonable royalty analysis, establishing the date of the hypothetical negotiation is an important first step. The financial expert should carefully consider when infringement first occurred and the parties that would have been involved.

16. In evaluating the comparability of existing license agreements in a hypothetical negotiation analysis, the financial expert should carefully consider how terms of the agreements and the economic conditions compare to those of the hypothetical license. Factors such as additional rights being included or licenses resulting from settlement of litigation may impair comparability and should be accounted for.

4.28 CHAPTER 27: OTHER VALUATION SERVICE AREAS

4.28.1 A: Valuations for Public Companies and/or Financial Reporting

1. Unlike most other valuation assignments, the need for public company valuation services is often dictated by GAAP.
2. The standard of value used most often in financial reporting valuations is fair value. This is different from the "fair value" used in shareholder disputes.
3. When engaged to provide an opinion regarding the fair value of a particular public company's assets or liabilities, the items to be valued should be clearly identified with confirmation from management and the auditor.
4. Although a public corporation's traded stock has a readily determinable value and its options may be publicly traded, distinct differences between employee stock options and publicly traded stock options influence their value. Corporations may grant employee stock options on shares that are not publicly traded, including shares in subsidiaries and shares with voting rights different from those of the publicly traded stock.
5. In certain businesses, the lines are blurred between the intangible assets and income-producing real estate (e.g., hotels, motels, hospitals, and skilled nursing centers). By performing a purchase price allocation, the analyst can separate intangible assets from the real property. The client can then amortize intangibles over a much shorter life than the real property.
6. Clients typically are not versed in the differences among standards of value, so early communication and active listening are the keys to a successful engagement.

4.28.2 B: Valuation of Debt

1. A key to understanding and valuing debt is reviewing underlying loan documentation, such as the original loan agreement, promissory note, personal loan guarantees, amendments, emails, or additional correspondence between the lender and borrower.
2. The value of a convertible bond should account for two components. First consider the value of the bond as a debt instrument only. This would be considered the floor value. A second component is the incremental value above the floor value associated with the conversion feature. The value of the common stock of the company must be known to determine this amount.
3. Because a bond with a long period until maturity may be more volatile than a bond that will mature in the near future, the bond with the longer term to maturity usually has a higher discount rate than the bond with the shorter term to maturity, except for when yield curves are inverted (i.e., short-term interest rates are higher than longer-term rates).

4.28.3 C: Valuation of Preferred Stock

1. Preferred stock is a "hybrid" security with features similar to both common stock and bonds. Similar to common stock, it represents equity ownership and, much like a bond and, similar to debt, it may receive fixed income distributions and preferential treatment.
2. Dividends on preferred stock are typically stated as a fixed percentage of the par value.

3. Investors, especially in early-stage companies, may acquire preferred shares with the right to assign a specific number of board seats, which may increase the value of such securities.
4. "Preferred stock with noncumulative dividend features will normally have a value substantially lower than a cumulative preferred stock with the same yield, liquidation preference and dividend coverage."[14]
5. The protection ratio can be compared to the ratios of publicly traded preferred stocks and should be greater than 1.0, indicating that the total liquidation preference can be covered.

4.28.4 D: Valuation of Restricted Stock

1. The Longstaff analysis indicates that the greater the volatility, the greater the discount; the marketability discount is not a linear function of time because the greatest risks—and therefore the largest increases in percentage discount—occur early in the restriction period.

4.28.5 E: Valuation Issues in Early-Stage Companies

1. To avoid excess compensation charges, companies are required to set the grant price of employee stock options equal to or greater than the underlying common stock's fair market value at the time of issuance.
2. The analyst may need to focus on the timing when the company expects to achieve sustainable profit margins and work backward to the valuation date.
3. As with more traditional companies, the largest impediment to properly using the guideline transactions method in the technology arena is lack of information. Information on the bundle of assets and liabilities acquired, the true price and terms, and inclusion of strategic considerations, if any, is difficult to obtain.
4. Analysis of subject company transactions is the preferred market approach method when a contemporaneous or fairly recent transaction in the subject company's securities exists.
5. Simultaneous gifts made by the same donor in the same security can have different fair market values.
6. Due to the potential for abnormally high growth in the scale of operations, revenue, and cash flows, the discounted cash flow method, in conjunction with the H-model, is the income approach method of choice when valuing early-stage technology companies that have achieved some semblance of product or technical feasibility.
7. One of the first decisions the valuation analyst will face in implementing the income approach is whether to accept management projections as representing the most likely potential outcome or whether multiple scenarios should be projected and a probability of occurrence assigned to each. In theory, the latter approach is best, but due to practical considerations, most often projection risk is addressed in the discount rate and not through multiple outcome scenarios.
8. Forecast losses that result from pre-revenue-phase expenditures (e.g., research and development and brand building) can be discounted at a rate different from the profits.

---

[14] Rev. Rul. 83-120, 1983-2 C.B. 170.

9. If venture capital rates of returns are referenced in selecting an appropriate discount rate, the valuation analyst may need to adjust the lack of marketability discount applied later because many VC discount rates are predicated on investments in nonmarketable securities.

4.28.6 F: Stock Options and Other Share-Based Compensation

1. Employee stock options (ESOs)[15] can be attractive because they generally do not involve cash. Vesting rights often are embedded in ESOs to promote employee retention by rewarding longevity.
2. Employee stock options are classified as either incentive stock options or nonqualified stock options. Incentive stock options are governed by strict governmental requirements whereas nonqualified stock options are not.
3. If not exercised before the expiration date, the option simply expires with no value.
4. As a result of dilution, the value of a warrant may vary somewhat from the value of a call option with identical terms.
5. Even without being in the money, an option may have value. This value is created by the possibility that the option could be exercised profitably in the future. Three factors determine time value:
   a. Volatility of the stock underlying the option
   b. Risk-free rate of interest over the option period
   c. Length of time before the option expires
6. A key limitation of the Black-Scholes model is that it was developed to price European call options in the absence of dividends.
7. ESOs are characterized as incentive stock options or nonqualified stock options.
8. Warrants often are sold in connection with other financial instruments as a "sweetener" to enhance the attractiveness of the placement of the financial instrument with which they are bundled or to obtain favorable terms on another financial instrument.
9. If the underlying stock is lightly traded or not publicly traded, volatility can be estimated using a representative sampling of guideline companies or an industry benchmark.
10. If an intervening event is identified in the analysis, it may be appropriate to exclude it from the volatility.
11. No studies are available regarding the lack of marketability of closely held stock options.

4.28.7 G: Real Option Valuations

1. The traditional discounted cash flow (DCF) model may also fail to capture the existence of any flexibility that a financial executive maintains as the decision-maker of a project or strategic initiative. Once an investment decision is initiated, a financial executive may expand it, terminate it, defer additional work until later and then restart it, or even convert the investment entirely into another strategic purpose.
2. The benefit of real option analysis is its ability to apply a positive indication of value to uncertainty or volatility. Financial executives have many options in

---

[15] ESOs are sometimes referred to as incentive stock options (ISOs).

reacting to changes throughout the investment's economic life by adapting or revising their decisions in response to unexpected developments. This flexibility clearly provides companies with value, and the real option analysis assesses the value of this flexibility.

3. The analysis behind real option theory is the valuation of opportunities associated with management's flexibility and is derived from the relationship connecting the methods in valuing financial options and the methods in valuing flexibility.
4. Real options exist in most businesses and may be more representative of the manner in which businesses operate, although they are not always very readily identifiable.
5. Real option analysis can become an important measurement tool in management's strategic decision-making. Although many analysts still predominantly use DCF, as real option analysis becomes better understood and properly applied, it may be more prevalent in the future.

4.28.8 H: Maximizing Shareholder Value[16]

1. Economic value added (EVA) is a well-known metric that attempts to better measure value creation.
2. The EVA concept, which is a value-driven financial performance measure, attempts to charge earnings with an expense for the cost of capital employed. In other words, it is simply a measure of what is left to the shareholders over the cost of capital.
3. The principle behind the EVA concept is that if a corporation's net income is positive after applying a charge for the cost of capital employed, the corporation has added shareholder value. If a corporation's net income is negative after applying a charge for the cost of capital employed, the corporation has destroyed shareholder value.
4. Similar models such as market value added, return on invested capital, and cash flow return on investment are also value-based concepts that claim to parallel the interests of shareholders with those of management.
5. Value drivers can be identified in almost any company. Here are some of the more widely recognized value drivers:
   - Sales growth
   - Key people
   - Optimal profit margins
   - Effective capital controls
   - Broad and varied customer base
   - Optimal cash flow

4.29 CHAPTER 28: VALUATION OF HEALTHCARE SERVICE BUSINESSES

1. The level of reimbursement is a critical assumption in the financial projections of healthcare organizations. Many analysts make the inaccurate assumption that reimbursement will continue to increase at the national inflation rates. Analysts

[16] Many of the concepts explained here are from Tim Koller, Marc Goedhart, and David Wessels *Valuation: Measuring and Managing the Value of Companies*, 7th ed. (John Wiley & Sons, 2020).

must understand and consider the payer mix of the business being valued, including how specific payers reimburse for services and the prospect for future changes in those reimbursements.

2. The volatility of reimbursement for individual procedures can be very high. It is important to consider prospective reimbursement changes when performing the valuation analysis.

3. Individual physicians exert a significant amount of control over the direction of patient referrals to healthcare service providers.

4. Opinions of fair market value that could be subject to the anti-kickback laws could receive high levels of scrutiny from regulators. Many transactions are subject to the anti-kickback regulations.

5. It is important to identify applicable situations and possibly seek advice from healthcare attorneys about the fraud and abuse implication of valuations performed in the healthcare services industry.

6. Violations of the anti-kickback law are subject to criminal fines and possible imprisonment, whereas violations of the Stark law are punishable only by civil penalties (as of the date of publication).

7. Appropriately factoring the regulatory environment into the valuation is important when valuing healthcare businesses.

8. It may be necessary to consult a qualified tax lawyer to understand how to appropriately consider the tax laws when valuing a business that involves a tax-exempt enterprise.

9. If a valuation is being performed as a result of regulatory requirements, the valuation must apply the fair market value standard of value.

10. It is important to understand the source of fees included in the revenue stream of the subject entity because the generation of professional versus technical revenue can involve different valuation dynamics.

11. A negative reimbursement trend for certain healthcare services is not uncommon. Unless supported by a reimbursement analysis, it may be erroneous to assume that reimbursement will increase at inflationary rates.

12. One of the erroneous assumptions sometimes made in healthcare valuations is that variable expenses are always solely a function of revenue.

13. The net result of volatile reimbursement levels for some healthcare entities is declining margins. Valuation professionals must carefully track variable costs.

14. Historically, public healthcare companies have been acquisitive and have had high valuation multiples. As a result, the multiples generated by public companies are generally not comparable to those of small private businesses.

15. Many analysts feel compelled to use the guideline company transaction multiples in every valuation. Unfortunately, transaction information is rarely provided at the level of detail necessary to perform a supportive guideline company transaction analysis as a primary method of value. Depending on the situation, the information can sometimes be used as a general reasonableness test for the value indications from other methods.

16. Many minority interests in healthcare partnerships do not exhibit the general characteristics that would require the magnitude of discounts in other closely held businesses.

17. The analyst should read the operating and/or partnership agreement to identify characteristics that would affect the level of minority or marketability discount.

18. A common oversimplification is using limited market transaction data without understanding the transactions, a situation that can lead to faulty conclusions.

Transaction data may be used as a reasonableness test for the results of other valuation methods.

19. Understanding the dialysis center's relationship with the nephrologist is critical in assessing risk.

4.29.1 Addendum 1—Mountain Surgery Center, LLC

1. It is important to understand the underlying components of the case mix because the reimbursement rates for each specialty are not homogenous.
2. The analyst must ascertain the likelihood that the top 10 surgeons will continue to perform cases at a center, which affects the specialty growth rates used in the projections.
3. Analysts can review a sample of the surgery center's explanation of benefits (EOB) for the most recent surgical cases to understand the dynamics of the payer mix. An adequate sampling of 25 to 30 EOBs with the associated gross and net charges per procedure will provide an understanding of the main procedures performed under each specialty as well as help assess the reasonableness of the facility's overall charge rates.

4.29.2 Addendum 2—Valuation of Walnut Hospital

1. Simply adding inpatient days plus outpatient cases would be erroneous because patients who are treated on an outpatient basis in the hospital are not measured in terms of days. The hospital applies an adjustment factor to convert the patient days into adjusted patient days equal to (Inpatient Gross Revenue + Outpatient Gross Revenue/Inpatient Gross Revenue). This is necessary to arrive at a standard volume metric for measuring a hospital's occupancy rate and capacity.

4.30 CHAPTER 29: DETERMINATION OF COMPENSATION IN THE HEALTHCARE INDUSTRY

[This section left intentionally blank.]

4.31 CHAPTER 30: SPECIAL INDUSTRY VALUATIONS

4.31.1 A: Construction

1. Construction contractors can engage in several types of contracts that differ in the way the contactor is compensated and the level of risk assumed. These contracts include fixed-price contracts, time-and-materials contracts, and unit-price contracts.
2. The three most common methods of accounting are the cash-basis method, the completed-contract method, and the percentage-of-completion method.
3. The amount of retention is typically between 5 percent and 10 percent of each billing. Once a project is complete to the satisfaction of the customer, the retention will be released. The retention period can last months if not years after the project is complete. The purpose of the retention is to provide an incentive to the contractor to complete a project to the final satisfaction of the customer.

4. Recomputing the job schedule using historical gross profit data can be a useful analytical tool in assessing the accuracy of management's current job estimates.
5. Because of intense price competition in the industry, many construction contractors have little, if any, goodwill value. This stems from the low margins that result from the competitive bidding process. Contractors who do have goodwill tend to have more negotiated contracts than competitively bid contracts and may have a good reputation and/or good relationship with customers.
6. There are three types of surety bonds:
   - *Bid bond.* Provides a financial guarantee that the bid has been submitted in good faith and that the bidder intends on entering into the contract at the bid price.
   - *Performance bond.* Protects the owner of a project from financial losses if the contractor should fail to perform under the contract.
   - *Payment bond.* Guarantees that the contractor will pay subcontractors.
7. Rules of Thumb[17]
   General rules of thumb for construction valuations:
   - Book value
   - Book value plus a multiple of backlog
   - 10 to 30 percent of annual revenues
   - 2 to 3.5 times cash flows

   General contractors would tend to be on the low end. Specialty contractors would tend to be on the high end. Conclusions will vary based on region, name recognition, financial strength, and other factors.

   Rules of thumb are provided only as a broad benchmark. The facts and circumstances of each individual company should be considered in determining the value of that particular company.

4.31.2 B: Oil and Gas Exploration and Production Valuations

1. The oil and gas industry uses a variety of specific terminology and abbreviations that are not common in other industries (e.g., dry holes, barrel of oil equivalent [BOE], spud, etc.). Take care to learn these terms and abbreviations because they are essential for understanding the industry.
2. Ask management about its required use of tangible assets in the extraction of reserves from a given area. The extent of use can vary considerably from one location to another and from one company to another. The degree of tangible asset use will affect the concluded valuation of an exploration and production company's reserves.
3. Oil and gas reserves are commonly classified into various reserve categories. Different reserves will have substantially different value conclusions depending on their category due to the varying probabilities of extracting each particular reserve category.
4. The following items are not covered in a reserve report:
   - Independently supportable commodity price forecasts (commonly referred to as a *price deck*)
   - Whether a reasonable discount rate falls within the range of discount rates presented; the analyst must calculate their own supportable discount rate (or range of discount rates)

---

[17] Based on author's industry experience.

- The appropriate level of depreciation, depletion, and amortization (DD&A) in the valuation of reserves on a post-tax basis
- As reserve reports are generally reported on a pre-tax basis, the analyst must use their knowledge to incorporate an appropriate level of DD&A

5. The analyst should have a strong understanding of the units and conversion factors used to measure and analyze reserves.

4.31.3 C: Restaurants

1. At first glance, restaurants appear similar and the valuation process would seem cookie-cutter. In reality, each restaurant has unique characteristics that require individual analysis and assessment. Generally, restaurants can be lumped into certain groups: fast food, fast casual, casual dining, fine dining, and family style. Restaurants can be single location, multi-location, or chains. Appraising groups of franchised restaurants can be lucrative but also can be complex, requiring analysis of different cities and regions with different wage structures and licensing requirements. Although this section covers many of the nuances and complexities, the analyst should consider the specifics of the restaurant that is being valued.

2. The restaurant industry is highly competitive because barriers to entry and customer loyalty are low.

3. Analyze leases and franchise royalties for future increases that may be buried in contractual agreements.

4. After food and beverage costs, labor costs are a significant expense of a restaurant.

5. Pressure to increase the minimum wage at the federal and state levels is a threat to restaurant profitability.

6. Seldom, if ever, does a buyer assume an existing loan. In a typical acquisition, a "hypothetical buyer" obtains a new loan and makes a down payment in cash of 20 percent to 25 percent.

7. Two ratios used by a majority of restaurant lenders are the debt/EBITDA ratio (sometimes debt/EBITDAR, which is pre-rent expense) and the debt-service coverage ratio.

8. Analysts should carefully question management during their interviews to establish what reinvestment is planned in the coming years. Do not assume that a five-year average of capital expenditures is reliable for predicting future expenses. What if an $800,000 remodel is planned two years in the future?

9. Often rents or franchise fees are stepped to reflect increases over time. Read the contracts to understand the rights of the restaurant as a lessor and as a franchisee.

10. A major risk in restaurant valuation is the "risk of the unknown." Topping the list of unknowns is the risk of a competitor arriving shortly after a purchase.

11. Few restaurant managers know their breakeven point by year, by month, or by day.

12. A big secret of restaurant valuation is that variable expenses can fall dramatically as volume increases.

13. Management is another secret of restaurant valuation. Are their results consistent? Do they manage turnover well? Do they implement and monitor training programs, including food safety? How experienced are they? Enthusiastic? Customer friendly? Profit focused?

14. Although an analyst cannot be expected to be a food safety expert, the analyst should carefully document actual safety performance and restaurant procedures. This is an important component of the restaurant's risk premium.
15. Generally, franchise restaurants are worth more than stand-alone restaurants.
16. The hypothetical seller of a group or chain of restaurants will not usually allow a hypothetical buyer to exclude a restaurant that is generating negative cash flow.
17. Every restaurateur has a memorized rule of thumb. They are all different. They seldom are correct. Readers of most valuation texts are aware of all the problems, limitations, and flaws in applying a rule of thumb.

4.31.4 D: Bars and Nightclubs

1. Cash flow is cash flow, whether for a restaurant or a bar. However, much like restaurants, be aware that on the accounting/internal control side, reported cash flow does not always represent actual cash flow. Theft, unreported sales, or other items affecting cash flow are more likely to surface in this segment of the industry. Lacking reliable financial data reduces the valuator's confidence in the information being provided and subsequently can affect the estimated value conclusion.
2. Two bars have food and alcoholic beverage sales of $800,000 each. The mix of sales is different for each of the entities. Sales are composed of $250,000 in alcohol sales at one bar versus $400,000 in alcohol sales at the other. All else being equal, the bars will have different values. The same multiple would not apply to each of the entities.

4.32 CHAPTER 31: BUY-SELL AGREEMENTS

1. Periodic reviews of the buy-sell agreement between the owners, legal counsel, and a valuation specialist can help prevent unforeseen issues and unintended value results when—not if—the agreement is triggered.
2. The definitions of changes in employment status should be unambiguous, leaving no room for misunderstandings. The application methodology of the discount(s) should also be clearly outlined, especially if other discounts are included in the valuation process.
3. Business owners often do not understand the distinction between fair market value and fair value, which can lead to a standard of value used and defined in the buy-sell agreement that is different from what the owners intended.
4. Valuation analysts can help business owners understand the need for their buy-sell agreements to be thorough to avoid costly litigation or transactions that provide a windfall to one party at the expense of another by reviewing their buy-sell agreement. The best time to review the agreement is before a triggering event occurs.
5. Business owners often incorrectly attribute simplicity to fixed prices and formula clauses without considering the risks and complexities associated with them.
6. Through the periodic valuation process, shareholders learn to understand their company's value drivers and what future transactions might look like. The appraiser also gains valuable experience with the company that may streamline the valuation process when a triggering event occurs.

7. It is advisable that a firm not otherwise associated with the company and/or shareholders be selected to perform the valuation work for a triggering event.
8. If the parties to the agreement want a requirement rather than an option to purchase in some circumstances, the agreement should outline a process to protect the financial security of the company in the event of multiple triggering events occurring within a short time period.
9. If a buy-sell agreement entered into after October 8, 1990, contains a clause that would value the stock at less than fair market value, it will be disregarded for tax purposes.
10. Shareholders who have signed agreements that value the company's stock at something less than fair market value may find themselves in the unfortunate position of having transferred the stock for the price set by the agreement, only to find that the IRS values it at something greater. This may result in an unexpected tax liability.

4.33 CHAPTER 32: VALUATION VIEWS

[This section left intentionally blank.]

CHAPTER 5

Income Approach Valuation Process Flowchart

5.1 INTRODUCTION

The Income Approach Valuation Process Flowchart presented here provides valuation analysts with a structured process to assist in the proper application of the income approach. For less experienced analysts, it provides guidance in selecting and supporting the various methods and assumptions used in the income approach. Use of this flowchart will encourage good documentation of the reasons the approach was applied in the manner ultimately determined.

The Income Approach Valuation Process Flowchart is presented in outline form for ease of adaptation to a checklist for compliance. It suggests a series of questions to answer and concepts to consider when preparing the income approach. The cost of capital topic is not part of this guide.

5.2 INCOME APPROACH VALUATION PROCESS FLOWCHART

Disclaimer Excluding Any Warranties: This Income Approach Valuation Process Flowchart is designed to provide guidance to analysts, auditors, and management, but it is not to be used as a substitute for professional judgment. This guide does not include nor address all the considerations and assumptions in a valuation. These procedures must be altered to fit each assignment; the various factors listed in this flowchart may not be necessary for every valuation. The practitioner takes sole responsibility for implementation of this guide. The implied warranties of merchantability and fitness of purpose and all other warranties, whether express or implied, are excluded from this transaction and shall not apply to this guide.

Business Name: _____

Date of Valuation: _____

    I. Input five years of financial statements or tax returns.

        A. If five years do not exist, number of years input _____

        B. Reason for inputting fewer than or more than five years _____

II. Is a minority or control valuation being performed?

_____ Minority _____ Control

A. Make all appropriate normalization adjustments, including nonrecurring, nonoperating, and extraordinary items.

B. If control value, list and explain all adjustments.

1. Excess compensation

2. Other perquisites

3. Capital structure

4. Other

III. Analyze historical trends and compare to industry information, economic information, and projected/anticipated performance.

A. Revenue growth rates

1. Investigate reasons for each year's growth.

2. Explain all fluctuations.

a. Generally upward

b. Generally downward

c. Erratic (up and down)

3. Is historical growth in line with projected/anticipated performance? If not, explain the differences.

4. Are historical growth and projected performance in line with industry and general economic growth rates? Explain.

B. Gross margin

1. Investigate reasons for each year's gross margins.

2. Explain all fluctuations.

a. Generally upward

b. Generally downward

c. Erratic (up and down)

3. Is historical gross margin in line with projected/anticipated performance? If not, explain the differences.

4. Are historical gross margin and projected performance in line with industry and general gross margins? Explain.

C. Selling, general, and administrative (SG&A) expenses as a percent of revenue

1. Investigate reasons for each year's expenses.

2. Explain all fluctuations.

a. Generally upward

      b. Generally downward

      c. Erratic (up and down)

   3. Are historical SG&A expenses in line with projected/anticipated performance? If not, explain the differences.

   4. Are historical SG&A expenses and projected performance in line with industry and general SG&A expenses? Explain.

D. Operating income margin

   1. Investigate reasons for each year's operating income margin.

   2. Explain all fluctuations.

      a. Generally upward

      b. Generally downward

      c. Erratic (up and down)

   3. Are historical operating income margins in line with projected/anticipated performance? If not, explain the differences.

   4. Are historical operating income margins and projected performance in line with industry and general operating income margins? Explain.

E. Pre-tax income margin

   1. Investigate reasons for each year's pre-tax income margin.

   2. Explain all fluctuations.

      a. Generally upward

      b. Generally downward

      c. Erratic (up and down)

   3. Are historical pre-tax income margins in line with projected/anticipated performance? If not, explain the differences.

   4. Are historical pre-tax income margins and projected performance in line with industry and general pre-tax income margins? Explain.

F. Taxes

   1. Are taxes anticipated to change? _____ Yes _____ No

   2. Include both federal and state taxes.

   3. If net operating losses exist, explain how they were handled.

G. Net income growth rates

   1. Investigate reasons for each year's net income growth.

   2. Explain all fluctuations.

      a. Generally upward

      b. Generally downward

      c. Erratic (up and down)

3. Are historical net income growth rates in line with projected/anticipated performance? If not, explain the differences.

4. Are historical net income growth rates and projected performance in line with industry and general net income growth rates? Explain.

H. Working capital

1. If using a discounted cash flow (DCF) to invested capital method, make sure you are using debt-free working capital, which excludes short-term interest-bearing debt, including notes and the current portion of long-term debt.

2. Investigate each year's working capital requirements, including typical days' sales outstanding, inventory turnover, and days payable outstanding.

3. Explain all fluctuations.

 a. Generally upward

 b. Generally downward

 c. Erratic (up and down)

4. Are historical working capital requirements in line with projected/anticipated performance? If not, explain the differences.

5. Are historical working capital requirements and projected performance in line with industry and general working capital requirements? Explain.

I. Depreciation

1. Investigate changes in annual depreciation, which should relate to capital expenditure investments.

2. Explain all fluctuations.

 a. Generally upward

 b. Generally downward

 c. Erratic (up and down)

3. Is historical depreciation in line with projected/anticipated performance? If not, explain the differences.

4. Are historical depreciation and projected performance in line with industry and general depreciation? Explain.

5. Was book or tax depreciation used? Explain.

J. Capital expenditures

1. Investigate reasons for each year's capital expenditures and discuss future requirements with management.

2. Explain all fluctuations.

 a. Generally upward

 b. Generally downward

 c. Erratic (up and down)

3. Are historical capital expenditures in line with projected/anticipated performance? If not, explain the differences.

4. Are historical capital expenditures and projected performance in line with industry and general capital expenditures? Explain.

IV. Are there any nonoperating or excess assets? Explain why they are nonoperating or excess assets.

A. Identify all such assets, value separately, and make sure both income statement and balance sheet are adjusted both historically and projected. Remove the effect of nonoperating assets from the operating cash flows. Consider whether to discount nonoperating assets when valuing a minority interest.

1. Cars, boats, condos, houses

2. Real estate

3. Idle machinery and equipment

4. Working capital

5. Cash

6. Receivables

7. Inventory

8. Other

V. Are earnings and cash flow anticipated to continue consistent with past trends?

A. Yes

1. Consider using a capitalized cash flow (CCF) method instead of a DCF.

2. If using a CCF method, choose the period(s) on which the cash flow relies and explain your choice.

a. Five-year straight average

b. Three-year straight average

c. Five-year weighted average

d. Three-year weighted average

e. Most recent 12 months trailing

f. Most recent four quarters trailing

g. Most recent fiscal year-end

h. One-year forward

i. Trend analysis

j. Other

B. No

1. If the future performance of the company is expected to change, consider using a DCF method. This usually means growth rates, profit margins,

or both are anticipated to change, or a normalized level of cash flow has not been achieved currently. It may also mean that the business itself may be changing.

2. Has the client prepared projections of future cash flows?

_____ Yes _____ No

3. If no, who prepared projections? _____

4. Decide whether to use an equity or invested capital model and explain your decision.

_____ Equity Model _____ Invested Capital

5. Do projections include:

   a. Revenue

   b. Gross profits

   c. Depreciation

      1. Book (remember to consider deferred taxes)

      2. Tax (deferred taxes are not considered)

   d. SG&A

   e. Operating income

   f. Other income/expenses

      1. Interest expense

      2. Interest income

      3. Nonoperating income or expenses, such as real estate, securities

   g. Pre-tax income

   h. Net income after tax

   i. Capital expenditure needs

   j. Incremental working capital needs (If using an invested capital model, working capital must be meaning that all interest-bearing, short-term debt is removed from the working capital calculation. This usually includes the current maturity of long-term debt.)

   k. Debt principal to be repaid, if equity model

   l. New debt principal in, if equity model (must be normalized in CCF and terminal year of DCF)

   m. Deferred taxes if using book depreciation

   n. Terminal-year value (What is the future anticipated perpetuity growth rate?)

VI. Is future growth rate greater than historical nominal gross domestic product (GDP) growth of approximately 6 percent?

_____ Yes _____ No _____ Same. Explain.

A. Is future growth rate greater than forecasted nominal GDP growth, for example, the *Livingston Survey*?

1. What is forecasted nominal GDP growth?

2. Explain.

B. Test growth rates in revenue versus earnings versus cash flow. If different, explain why.

C. Is there a large difference between the terminal-year growth rate and the growth rate in the last year of the discrete period?

_____ Yes _____ No

1. Explain.

2. Do not mix revenue growth rates with cash flow growth rates. They are often the same, but the terminal-year growth assumption is based on expected growth in normalized cash flow.

D. If using the Gordon Growth Model (GGM), calculate the implied value in the terminal year as a multiple of EBITDA or EBIT.

_____ EBITDA _____ EBIT

1. Is this consistent with the multiples used in the market approach?

Yes _____ EBITDA

No _____ EBITA

2. Explain. It is sometimes justified to test the terminal-year implied multiple against the market multiples adjusted downward to reflect the risk of projecting a multiple in future years.

E. Is the working capital assumption into perpetuity driven by the perpetuity growth rate?

_____ Yes _____ No. Explain.

VII. Are capital expenditures and depreciation similar in the terminal year (typically, due to cost increases, capital expenditures can exceed depreciation into perpetuity)?

A. If yes, no further adjustment is necessary.

If no, normalize them to be similar, or

1. If there is a material depreciation overhang, present value it separately and add it to the value.

2. If there is a material capital expenditure overhang, present value it separately and deduct it from the value.

VIII. Are projections and resultant value minority or control?

        _____ Minority _____ Control

A. Explain. If all discrete expenses have been added back—excess compensation, perquisites, capital structure—the value is on a control stand-alone value. If such expenses have not been added back, then the resultant value is on a minority stand-alone basis because the cash flows reflect the diminished cash flows and value. If the company has no discrete expenses to add back, then the value is the same for both minority and control. In this situation, some practitioners will apply a smaller minority discount when valuing a minority interest to reflect the fact that, although the controlling stockholder is not taking cash out today, that policy could change in the future, resulting in added risk that diminishes value. Be careful using minority discounts derived from control premium studies (*Mergerstat Review*) to discount for stand-alone minority value, because those studies reflect mostly synergized premiums paid by strategic buyers of public companies.

B. Is the resultant value a marketable or liquid value?

        _____ Yes _____ No

1. Explain. If using Kroll data, the value is a marketable/liquid value and assumes cash in less than three days. A further discount for marketability/liquidity may be warranted for both a minority and control value. Some practitioners will discount a minority interest at a greater amount than a controlling one. However, even a controlling interest cannot usually be sold with cash in three days.

C. Optional: Check terminal-year value using the Value Driver Formula (VDF).[1]

1. VDF assumes that the company will always earn a return on new invested capital equal to its cost of capital and thus no increase in value. This is true regardless of the growth rate, because both returns on capital and the actual costs of new capital will grow at the same rate under this formula. VDF is sometimes used to check the individual components of the GGM for reasonableness.

2. VDF = NOPLAT / WACC (NOPLAT is net operating profit less adjusted taxes)

3. To check the components of GGM, we consider the value driver model:

    a. Continuing Value = FCF / (WACC − g) = [NOPLAT (1 − g / ROIC)] / (WACC − g)

        1. FCF = Free cash flow, or (DFNI + Depr. − CAPEX − ΔW / C)

        2. NOPLAT = Net operating profit less adjusted taxes (this is the same as DFNI)

        3. g = Expected growth rate in NOPLAT in perpetuity

        4. r = Expected rate of return on net new investment (also ROIC)

---

[1] Tim Koller, Marc Goedhart, and David Wessels, *Valuation: Measuring and Managing the Value of Companies*, 6th ed. (John Wiley & Sons, 2015), 28–33.

b. Using algebra, we deduce: FCF = NOPLAT $(1 - g / r)$, or FCF = DFNI $(1 - g / r)$

c. Restating the formula:

1. DFNI + Depr. − CAPEX − $\Delta W / C$ = DFNI $(1 - g / r)$

2. As we know the individual components of the formula, we can test our conclusion of value by solving for g or r, such that:

a. $g = r [1 - ((DFNI + Depr. - CAPEX - \Delta W / C) / DFNI)]$, and

b. $r = g / [1 - ((DFNI + Depr. - CAPEX - \Delta W / C) / DFNI)]$

4. If the calculated r is much greater or less than the discount rate used in the conclusion of value, maybe reconsider the Depr., CAPEX, or $\Delta W / C$ growth, or even discount rate.

5. What is VDF value?

a. Is it higher or lower than GGM value?

1. If VDF is higher, then the company is destroying value by growing because the costs of capital must then be exceeding the return on capital.

2. If the VDF is lower, then the company is earning a return on capital higher than its cost of capital into perpetuity.

6. Conclusion: If used, correlate with other values derived from other valuation approaches/methods.

CHAPTER 6

Marketing, Managing, and Making Money in Valuation Services

Caveat: Most of the following information is presented in a best-case scenario where everything is almost perfect. It may not be possible or relevant to adopt all of these procedures, policies, and ideas. Each professional and firm should choose the resources that fit the firm/group, its philosophy, and its culture.

Disclaimer: For discussion and educational purposes only. Some topics may not be relevant to every practice. Valuation and litigation services are very much affected by specific facts and circumstances. As such, the views expressed in this chapter do not necessarily reflect the professional opinions or positions that the authors would take in every assignment or practice, or in providing valuation or litigation services in connection with an actual engagement, matter, or practice. Every situation and practice is unique, and differing facts and circumstances may result in variations of the information presented. Jim Hitchner, and Valuation Products and Services, LLC assume no responsibility for any errors in this information, use of this information, or reliance on the information. Use at your own risk.

6.1 SMART "MULTI-MARKETING": LEVERAGING YOUR EFFORT—SELLING AND NETWORKING BEYOND ONE-ON-ONE

The following point list is designed to assist the professional firm in planning an effective marketing strategy.

- Decide on what target market you want to reach:
  - Attorneys
  - Business owners
  - CPAs
  - Bankers
  - Other advisors
- Publish an article:
  - Look back at the last two years and do something different.
  - Court cases are popular and very low risk.

- Cap rates and discounts are popular, but practice what you preach:
  - Remember, articles are discoverable.
- Write on a subject that is leverageable and of interest to your target market.
- Publishers are always in need of articles.
- Send a pitch letter.
- Tell them the subject has not been addressed in the last two years.
- Call them.
- Get a commitment for an article, assuming it is acceptable to the publisher and editor.
  - Leverage the article:
    - Speak on the article:
      - Appraisal/valuation society meetings
      - State CPA society meetings
      - National conferences
    - Send article to clients.
    - Send article to prospects, for example, attorneys.
      - Invest in Martindale & Hubbell
  - Court case E-Flashes:
    - Very inexpensive except for initial setup of database
    - Email
    - Should come from practice leader
    - Subject line important
    - Court cases a good start
    - Keep it simple and short
    - Provide some advertising:
      - A little up front (e.g., banners) (Appendix 6.1)
      - More at the end
    - Attached Adobe files can also be used
      - See Gibraltar Business Valuations, Sample (Appendix 6.2)
    - Sources:
      - AICPA
      - ASA
      - Financial Consulting Group, LLC (FCG) (authored by Chris Treharne and his firm)
      - Other local, state, or national society
  - Advertising:
    - Must be continuous
    - Takes a while to be effective
    - Must be classy
    - Use color and images
    - Stay away from clutter
  - Speeches:
    - Contact state CPA society groups
    - Contact local appraisal/valuation chapters
    - Contact bar associations
    - Contact law firms:
      - Breakfasts and lunches at law firm good
      - Cocktail parties at law firm or in same building good

- National conferences:
  - AICPA
  - ASA
  - NACVA
- Industry associations:
  - All business owners interested in valuation
  - Always looking for speakers
  - Rules of thumb a big hook
- Make sure the participants learn at least two terrific new pieces of information as a takeaway
- Teaching:
  - Volunteer for national BV organizations
  - Teach what you are comfortable with
  - Keeps you up to speed
  - Good networking
  - May be time-consuming, depending on the commitment
  - Good for resume
- Random thoughts:
  - The talk meter sales call:
    - Just the questions, man, just the questions (let the client talk)
  - Keep a manageable target list of prospects/clients:
    - Much work can come from a lesser number that you keep in constant contact with
    - *Nifty Fifty* technique (50 main contacts)
  - Marketing is not a fancy word for selling
  - Good work travels fast, bad work travels faster
  - It's expensive to keep a client, but it's more expensive to gain a client
  - Prospects who choose based on fee will continually choose on fee; it's hard to raise fees later
  - Good work should be paid for
  - Good work sometimes goes unnoticed
  - Your bad work rarely goes unnoticed
  - Love what you do and do what you love
  - Get rid of difficult clients
  - Do everything, well . . . almost everything, to keep "pay on time" clients
  - Stay in front of clients . . . they sometimes forget about you
  - Most of your competitors hate to market and sell
  - The phone never rings unless you make it ring
  - Cold calls are just that: cold
  - Use warm-call techniques (get someone you know to help)
  - Be patient
  - Be diligent
  - Be different
  - And always be good

6.2 RISK MANAGEMENT: ENGAGEMENT LETTERS, REPORTS, AND TURNING DOWN WORK

The following list is intended to provide the professional with those items they should consider when establishing assignment guidelines and practices.

- Risk . . . not all purposes are created equal
- Riskier engagements:
  - ESOPs
  - Transactions
  - Fair value reporting work for public clients
  - Seat-of-the-pants valuations for any reason
  - Any purpose without an engagement letter
  - Any purpose without the proper protection in an engagement letter
- Engagement letters (see Engagement Letter and Report Language Examples section):
  - Must be written, bilateral, and signed
    - One-way communication is not a binding contract
  - Restrictions on:
    - Who can see it
    - Who can rely on it
    - Purpose and use
    - No other use
    - Sometimes who is not allowed to see it
    - Only good as of a single date
    - Scope
  - Protective language:
    - Indemnification
    - Corporate/entity only without any liability to individuals
    - Fees:
      - Retainer applied against last bill . . . stay ahead
      - Client cannot sue unless fees paid up front
      - Must be paid regardless of outcome of matter
      - Must be paid regardless of what the court awards in fees
      - Timing of billings and expected collections
      - Interest on unpaid balances
      - Can quit if not paid timely
      - Caveat that you will inform client of higher fees due to unexpected events or information problems
      - No report or testimony unless paid in full
      - Require retainer before testimony
      - Mediation/arbitration provision for disputes
      - Disclaimers:
        - Not an attest service
        - Reliability of data used
- Relationship check
- Form of work product/report
- Work paper retention policy
  - Standards abided by:
    - USPAP, AICPA, NACVA, ASA

- Confidentiality section:
  - May help protect clients in later litigation cases when asked about other clients
- Other services and additional fees
- Expiration date on engagement letter
- Reports:
  - Type:
    - USPAP
      - Appraisal Report
      - Restricted Appraisal Report
    - SSVS VS Section 100
      - Detailed
      - Summary
    - Calculation
    - Oral
    - Other?
  - Protective language:
    - Repeat much of what is in engagement letter
    - Belt and suspenders
- Don't eat bad food
  - When you're hungry, you'll be tempted to eat anything . . . don't
  - Signs of a possibly difficult client:
    - Retainer resistance
    - Fee or rate resistance
    - Many suggested changes to engagement letter
    - Unresponsive when you try to contact them
    - Gruff and unpleasant
    - Does not treat you with respect
    - Does not listen
  - Bad jobs will:
    - Upset your staff
    - Take a lot of energy
    - Take away from your ability to work on good engagements and good clients
    - Possibly cause billing and collection problems
    - Make you miserable

6.3 ENGAGEMENT LETTER AND REPORT LANGUAGE EXAMPLES

6.3.1 Caution for Using Engagement Letter and Report Language Examples

These selected engagement letter and report language examples are to be adjusted to the facts and circumstances of each assignment/engagement. The examples presented here are only a tool that is subordinate to the judgment of the valuation professional in charge of the engagement. This language should not be used unless the valuation professional understands each term and phrase in the language examples and has verified that the facts of an engagement were properly captured.

Users *must* have an attorney review the terms of these engagement letter and report language examples to make sure that they reflect the particular needs of each firm. Jim Hitchner, Financial Valuation Solutions, LLC, and Valuation Products and Services, LLC, assume no responsibility for any errors in the language, use of the language, or reliance on the language. Use at your own risk.

6.3.2 Purpose and Objectives

The valuation is provided for the sole purpose of _____ planning.

The objective of the valuation is to provide an independent valuation analysis and report to assist you in your determination of the fair market value of (a minority, a majority, a controlling interest, a percent interest) in (COMPANY NAME) ("_____" or "Company") as of _____.

6.3.3 Disclaimer

We will read and analyze, to the extent available and relevant, financial statements, income tax returns, contracts, agreements, property schedules, and such other records or other documents we deem appropriate. In addition, outside research sources and knowledgeable individuals will be consulted as necessary. Factual information provided will be relied on as being true and correct. We will not perform an audit, review, or compilation of financial statements in the capacity of certified public accountants under the standards promulgated by the American Institute of Certified Public Accountants (AICPA). Our work cannot be relied on to discover errors, irregularities, or illegal acts, including fraud or defalcations. As part of the valuation process, projections and/or forecasts of future operating results and related balance sheets may be used if deemed practical in the circumstances. If so, such projections and forecasts will be performed by management and represented as being management's best estimate of such future results and balance sheets. The Firm will not perform procedures prescribed by the AICPA that would otherwise be required were we to be engaged specifically to compile or examine such forecasts. Accordingly, the Company and its owners understand and accept that the Firm is not being employed in the capacity of examining certified public accountants and will not therefore express any form of comfort or assurance in the achievability of the forecasts or projections or the reasonableness of underlying assumptions.

6.3.4 Form of Work Product

6.3.4.1 (Option 1) Our valuation will be presented in a report for your use. Our analysis and report will meet the development and reporting requirements of the AICPA's Statement on Standards for Valuation Services (SSVS) VS Section 100, and the Uniform Standards of Professional Appraisal Practice (USPAP) of the Appraisal Foundation. (Insert other association standards as appropriate, e.g., ASA, NACVA, IBA.) (Option) Our report will be subject to the assumptions and limiting conditions contained as Appendix B.

6.3.5 Fees and Billing

Our total fee for the valuation services and report will be $ _____ to $ _____, plus expenses. Expenses include travel and meals, document and report reproduction, telephone, mail, computer charges, research information, and related overhead. An initial retainer fee is due on acceptance of this contract. Accordingly, an invoice for our (nonrefundable) retainer fee of $ _____ is attached. The retainer will be applied to the last invoice.

Following the receipt of the retainer and the commencement of work on this project, fees and expenses will be billed to you (*insert time period*—monthly, quarterly, etc.) and are due on presentation of statements. Our final bill must be paid prior to the issuance of our final report. If for any reason the transaction is terminated prior to its consummation and the Firm is requested to terminate work, then the Firm's fee shall not be less than the Firm's total time and costs at the normal rate for such projects, plus out-of-pocket expenses.

Our fee is based on our knowledge of the facts and circumstances as of the date of this engagement letter. This fee is also contingent on our receiving all data and information in a timely manner. Any changes that require additional professional time will be discussed before proceeding.

Any invoice not paid within thirty (30) business days following presentation shall bear interest at the rate of 1.5 percent compounded each month. Should it be necessary to refer any invoice for collection or arbitration, you shall be responsible for all costs of collection and arbitration, including attorneys' fees. In the event that you disagree with or question any amount due under an invoice, you agree that you shall communicate such a disagreement to us in writing within thirty (30) days of the invoice date. Any claim not made within that period shall be deemed waived.

When initiated by the Client and as a condition precedent to mediation, arbitration, or suit, the parties agree that all invoices billed by the Firm shall be paid in full, including accrued but unpaid interest.

6.3.6 Additional Options for Hourly Billing Where Attorney Retains Firm

Company acknowledges its obligation to pay the Firm for services rendered, whether arising from you or your attorney's request or otherwise necessary as a result of our efforts in this engagement, regardless of the outcome of this matter, at our billing rates for personnel used. We will notify you with respect to those activities and related fees as the engagement progresses. Our billing rates for staff that we expect to use currently range from $ _____ to $ _____ per hour. Mr./Ms. [Responsible Analyst's] rate is $ _____ per hour. Our billing rates will usually increase effective January 1 of each year to reflect increases in our costs. We will advise you of any such increases, should they occur, prior to providing additional services at increased rates. Our billing rates will not increase prior to _____. Company is solely responsible for payment of all of our fees and expenses.

It is the Firm's policy to require a retainer prior to the commencement of our engagement. Please send us a retainer of $ _____ following the signing of this engagement letter. This retainer will be applied against our final invoice. We will bill periodically for services rendered and expenses incurred on this engagement. Such expenses, for example, may be those directly incurred for travel, business meals, delivery, photocopies, telephone calls, graphics, data charges, and overhead applicable to this engagement. We may use administrative support personnel in the performance of certain tasks for this engagement; if so, we will charge for such time at their hourly rates. All invoices are payable on receipt. All bills will be paid prior to testimony of any kind or the delivery of written analyses or reports. If we do not hear to the contrary within a 30-day period of time, it is understood that our invoice is accepted as presented.

All fees associated with the preparation for, and the actual attendance of, any depositions concerning our analysis will be paid by the Company. You agree that it is your responsibility to collect any fees from opposing counsel and that failure to collect such fees has no bearing on your responsibility to pay the Firm.

6.3.7 Arbitration Provision (Could Be Mediation Provision)

The parties agree that any claims, disputes, or controversies arising out of or relating to this engagement letter, or its breach, that cannot be resolved by the parties shall be submitted to arbitration in [City, State], in accordance with the applicable rules, regulations, policies, and procedures of the Commercial Arbitration Rules of the American Arbitration Association (AAA) and the Federal Arbitration Act. The arbitration shall be conducted before a neutral arbitrator mutually agreed on by the parties. If the parties do not promptly agree on an arbitrator, either party may request that an arbitrator be appointed by the AAA. The decision before the arbitrator shall be final and binding. (Caution: Consult with your attorney.)

(Option)

6.3.8 Representations

Our report will be subject to the representations attached hereto as Appendix A. At the conclusion of the engagement, we may require you to sign an additional representation letter on these and various other assumptions and information relied on in the valuation.

(Option)

6.3.9 Statement of Assumptions, Contingent, and Limiting Conditions

Our report will be subject to the Statement of Assumptions, Contingent, and Limiting Conditions or something similar to, as attached hereto as Appendix B.

6.3.10 Indemnity

(Caution: See your attorney and/or the AICPA guide on engagement letters. Highly recommended in certain types of valuations.) The indemnity might also include the following statements with consideration to *Daubert* challenges.

6.3.11 *Daubert* Challenges

(Caution: Consult with your attorney.) Because of the adversarial nature of any dispute, it is not uncommon that parties in litigation challenge the admissibility of experts (e.g., *Daubert* challenge). Prior to the release of any opinions to opposing counsel and the rendering of any testimony in this engagement, you and your attorneys agree to review the facts and circumstances on which our work and opinions are based. You and your attorneys hereby acknowledge that the Firm is being retained because its professionals satisfy the necessary requirements of knowledge, skill, experience, training, or education.

You and your attorneys retain sole responsibility for assessing other factors or assumptions that may bear on the question of admissibility. As such, even if testimony is excluded as a result of a challenge to the admissibility of our testimony, all fees and expenses are still due, and owing on presentation of an invoice, the Company is not relieved of liability of such fees and expenses. You further agree to compensate us for any time or out-of-pocket expenses incurred in defending such challenges. Additionally, should a trier of fact determine that the testimony to be offered by a member of our Firm be excluded, you and your client agree to indemnify and hold harmless the Firm and its personnel from any claims, liabilities, costs, and expenses arising from this exclusion, except to the extent it is finally determined that such exclusion resulted solely from the Firm's gross negligence or willful misconduct. (Caution: Consult with your attorney.)

6.3.12 Relationships

We have undertaken a limited review of our records to determine the professional relationships of the Firm with the persons and entities you identified in connection with this matter. We have not identified any such relationships at this time. (Option: We have relayed all such relationships to you.) Although we will notify you immediately of any relationships that come to our attention, we cannot assure you that all such relationships will come to light.

6.3.13 Confidentiality and Work Papers

We agree to hold in strict confidentiality all proprietary information provided by you in connection with this project. We agree not to share any confidential information with persons outside the Firm. The working papers for this engagement will be retained in our files and are available for your reference. We would be available to support our valuation conclusion(s), should this be required. Those services would be performed for an additional fee. (Option: The ownership of schedules, information, and other work papers developed during the assignment by the Firm or supplied by the Company are the sole property of the Firm and are not subject to examination or production to the client at any time during or after the engagement.)

6.3.14 Termination

Failure to make the payments required by this agreement, or failure by you to comply with the terms of this agreement, will release the Firm from this agreement.

6.3.15 Other Services

If the Firm is called on to render services, give testimony, produce documents, answer depositions or interrogatories, or otherwise become involved in connection with any administrative or judicial proceedings, investigations, or inquiries relating to the engagement, the Company will pay, in addition to other fees here, for the time reasonably required to be expended by any officers or employees of the Firm, at their standard hourly rates as then in effect, plus out-of-pocket expenses relating thereto. Professional fees for such services are independent of this engagement.

6.3.16 Corporate Obligation

The obligations of the Firm are solely corporate obligations, and no officer, principal, director, employee, agent, shareholder, subcontractor, or controlling person shall be subjected to any personal liability whatsoever to any person or entity, nor will any such claim be asserted by or on behalf of any other party to this agreement or any person relying on the opinion.

6.3.17 Distribution of Analysis, Conclusions, and Report

Our analysis, conclusions, and report, which are to be used only in their entirety, are for the use of the Company, their accountants and attorneys, solely to assist them in their determination of the value of the Company for (*insert purpose*). They are not to be used for any other purpose, or by any other party for any purpose, without our express written consent. (Option: Our report may be furnished to the [example—Internal Revenue Service]). No third parties are intended to be benefited.

Any summary of, or reference to, the opinion, any verbal presentation with respect thereto, or other references to the Firm in connection with the transaction will be, in each instance, subject to the Firm's prior review and written approval, except as may be required by a governmental agency or court. The opinion will not be included in, summarized, or referred to in any manner in any materials distributed to the public without the Firm's express prior written consent.

6.3.18 Acceptance

If this engagement letter is satisfactory to you, please indicate approval of the terms set forth herein and attached hereto by signing and dating the engagement letters and returning one of the originals. Retain the other original for your file. This offer for engagement will expire if not accepted within _____ days.

6.4 ASSUMPTIONS AND LIMITING CONDITIONS EXAMPLES

6.4.1 Caution for Using Assumptions and Limiting Conditions Language Example

This selected assumptions and limiting conditions language is to be adjusted to the facts and circumstances of each assignment/engagement. The language example presented here is only a tool that is subordinate to the judgment of the valuation professional in charge of the engagement. This language should not be used unless the valuation professional understands each term and phrase in the language example and has verified that the facts of an engagement were properly captured.

FVW readers and language example users *must* have an attorney review the terms of this assumptions and limiting conditions language example to make sure that it reflects the particular needs of each firm. Jim Hitchner, Financial Valuation Solutions, LLC, and Valuation Products and Services, LLC, assume no responsibility for any errors in the language, use of the language, or reliance on the language. Use at your own risk.

6.4.2 Language Examples

6.4.2.1 Assumptions, Limiting Conditions, and Valuation Representation/Certification Valuation Engagement
Note: Items 1 to 17 are taken directly from SSVS, either exactly or with slight modifications. Items 18 to 42 are an illustrative list of additional assumptions and limiting conditions that each analyst, along with their attorney, can decide to use in whole or in part. These can be modified and used in reports and engagement letters.

The primary assumptions and limiting conditions pertaining to the value estimate conclusion(s) stated in this [identify type of report] appraisal report (report) are summarized here. Other assumptions are cited elsewhere in this report.

1. The conclusion of value arrived at herein is valid only for the stated purpose as of the date of the valuation.
2. Financial statements and other related information provided by [ABC Company] or its representatives, in the course of this engagement, have been accepted without any verification as fully and correctly reflecting the enterprise's business conditions and operating results for the respective periods, except as specifically noted herein. [Valuation Firm] has not audited, reviewed, or compiled the financial information provided to us and, accordingly, we express no audit opinion or any other form of assurance on this information.
3. Public information and industry and statistical information have been obtained from sources we believe to be reliable. However, we make no representation as to the accuracy or completeness of such information and have performed no procedures to corroborate the information.
4. We do not provide assurance on the achievability of the results forecasted by [ABC Company] because events and circumstances frequently do not occur as expected; differences between actual and expected results may be material; and achievement of the forecasted results is dependent on actions, plans, and assumptions of management.
5. The conclusion of value arrived at herein is based on the assumption that the current level of management expertise and effectiveness would continue to be maintained and that the character and integrity of the enterprise through any sale, reorganization, exchange, or diminution of the owners' participation would not be materially or significantly changed.
6. This report and the conclusion of value arrived at herein are for the exclusive use of our client for the sole and specific purposes as noted herein. They may not be used for any other purpose or by any other party for any purpose. Furthermore, the report and conclusion of value are not intended by the author and should not be construed by the reader to be investment advice in any manner whatsoever. The stated valuation represents the considered conclusion of value of [Valuation Firm], based on information furnished to them by [ABC Company] and other sources.

7. Neither all nor any part of the contents of this report (especially the conclusion of value, the identity of any valuation specialist(s), or the firm with which such valuation specialists are connected or any reference to any of their professional designations) should be disseminated to the public through advertising media, public relations, news media, sales media, mail, direct transmittal, or any other means of communication, including but not limited to the Securities and Exchange Commission or other governmental agency or regulatory body, without the prior written consent and approval of [Valuation Firm].
8. Future services regarding the subject matter of this report, including but not limited to testimony or attendance in court, shall not be required of [Valuation Firm] unless previous arrangements have been made in writing.
9. [Valuation Firm] is not an environmental consultant or auditor, and it takes no responsibility for any actual or potential environmental liabilities. Any person entitled to rely on this report, wishing to know whether such liabilities exist, or the scope and their effect on the value of the property, is encouraged to obtain a professional environmental assessment. [Valuation Firm] does not conduct or provide environmental assessments and has not performed one for the subject property.
10. [Valuation Firm] has not determined independently whether [ABC Company] is subject to any present or future liability relating to environmental matters, (including but not limited to CERCLA/Superfund liability) nor the scope of any such liabilities. [Valuation Firm]'s valuation takes no such liabilities into account, except as they have been reported to [Valuation Firm] by [ABC Company] or by an environmental consultant working for [ABC Company], and then only to the extent that the liability was reported to us in an actual or estimated dollar amount. Such matters, if any, are noted in the report. To the extent such information has been reported to us, [Valuation Firm] has relied on it without verification and offers no warranty or representation as to its accuracy or completeness.
11. [Valuation Firm] has not made a specific compliance survey or analysis of the subject property to determine whether it is subject to, or in compliance with, the American Disabilities Act of 1990, and this valuation does not consider the effect, if any, of noncompliance.
12. [Sample wording for use if the jurisdictional exception is invoked.] The conclusion of value in this report deviates from the Statement on Standards for Valuation Services as a result of published governmental, judicial (legal), or accounting authority. [State difference and that only the part(s) that differ are void and of no force or effect.]
13. No change of any item in this appraisal report shall be made by anyone other than [Valuation Firm], and we shall have no responsibility for any such unauthorized change.
14. Unless otherwise stated, no effort has been made to determine the possible effect, if any, on the subject business due to future federal, state, or local legislation, including any environmental or ecological matters or interpretations thereof.
15. If prospective financial information approved by management has been used in our work, we have not examined or compiled the prospective financial information and, therefore, do not express an audit opinion or any other form of assurance on the prospective financial information or the related assumptions. Events and circumstances frequently do not occur as expected, and there

will usually be differences between prospective financial information and actual results, and those differences may be material.

16. We have conducted interviews with the current management of [ABC Company] concerning the past, present, and prospective operating results of the company.

17. Except as noted, we have relied on the representations of the owners, management, and other third parties concerning the value and useful condition of all equipment, real estate, investments used in the business, and any other assets or liabilities, except as specifically stated to the contrary in this report. We have not attempted to confirm whether or not all assets of the business are free and clear of liens and encumbrances or that the entity has good title to all assets.

18. The approaches and methodologies used in our work did not comprise an examination in accordance with generally accepted auditing standards, the objective of which is an expression of an opinion regarding the fair presentation of financial statements or other financial information, whether historical or prospective, presented in accordance with generally accepted accounting principles. We express no opinion and accept no responsibility for the accuracy and completeness of the financial information or other data provided to us by others. We assume that the financial and other information provided to us is accurate and complete, and we have relied on this information in performing our valuation.

19. The valuation may not be used in conjunction with any other appraisal or study. The value conclusion(s) stated in this appraisal is based on the program of utilization described in the report, and may not be separated into parts. The appraisal was prepared solely for the purpose, function, and party so identified in the report. The report may not be reproduced, in whole or in part, and the findings of the report may not be used by a third party for any purpose without the express written consent of [Valuation Firm].

20. Unless otherwise stated in the appraisal, the valuation of the business has not considered or incorporated the potential economic gain or loss resulting from contingent assets, liabilities, or events existing as of the valuation date.

21. The working papers for this engagement are being retained in our files and are available for your reference. We would be available to support our valuation conclusion(s) should this be required. Those services would be performed for an additional fee.

22. Any decision to purchase, sell, or transfer any interest in the subject company or its subsidiaries shall be your sole responsibility, as well as the structure to be used and the price to be accepted.

23. The selection of the price to be accepted requires consideration of factors beyond the information we will provide or have provided. An actual transaction involving the subject business might be concluded at a higher value or at a lower value, depending on the circumstances of the transaction and the business, and the knowledge and motivations of the buyers and sellers at that time. Due to the economic and individual motivational influences that may affect the sale of a business interest, the appraiser assumes no responsibility for the actual price of any subject business interest if sold or transferred.

24. All facts and data set forth in our letter report are true and accurate to the best of the Appraiser's knowledge and belief.

25. All recommendations as to fair market [other standard] value are presented as the Appraiser's conclusion based on the facts and data set forth in this report.

26. During the course of the valuation, we have considered information provided by management and other third parties. We believe these sources to be reliable, but no further responsibility is assumed for their accuracy.

27. We made [did not make] an on-site visit to selected Company facilities. We did [did not] interview Company management.

28. This valuation analysis and report, which are to be distributed only in their entirety, are intended solely for use by you and your client, solely to assist you and your client in the determination of the fair market value [other standard] of the subject interest for tax [other] purposes. It should not be used for any other purpose or distributed to third parties for any purpose, in whole or in part, without the express written consent of [Valuation Firm].

29. If applicable, we have used financial projections approved by management. We have not examined the forecast data or the underlying assumptions in accordance with the standards prescribed by the American Institute of Certified Public Accountants and do not express an opinion or any other form of assurance on the forecast data and related assumptions. The future may not occur as anticipated, and actual operating results may vary from those described in our report. This would not affect our conclusion of value as of the valuation date of this valuation.

30. We have no responsibility or obligation to update this report for events or circumstances occurring subsequent to the date of this report.

31. Our report is based on historical and/or prospective financial information provided to us by management and other third parties. This information has not been audited, reviewed, or compiled by us, nor has it been subjected to any type of audit, review, or compilation procedures by us, nor have we audited, reviewed, or compiled the books and records of the subject company. Had we audited, reviewed, or compiled the underlying data, matters may have come to our attention that would have resulted in our using amounts that differ from those provided; accordingly, we take no responsibility for the underlying data presented or relied on in this report.

32. Our valuation judgment, shown herein, pertains only to the subject business, the stated value standard (fair market value), as at the stated valuation date, and only for the stated valuation purpose(s).

33. The various estimates of value presented in this report apply to the valuation report only and may not be used out of the context presented herein.

34. In all matters that may be potentially challenged by a court or other party we do not take responsibility for the degree of reasonableness of contrary positions that others may choose to take, nor for the costs or fees that may be incurred in the defense of our recommendations against challenge(s). We will, however, retain our supporting work papers for your matter(s), and will be available to assist in defending our professional positions taken, at our then current rates, plus direct expenses at actual, and according to our then current Standard Professional Agreement.

35. No third parties are intended to be benefited. An engagement for a different purpose, or under a different standard or basis of value, or for a different date of value, could result in a materially different opinion of value.

36. [Valuation Firm] retains all exclusive rights to copyrights to the report and to control the issuance of copies by others, and the client has no right of diffusion, reproduction, distribution, or sale. The client may reproduce ten (10) [other]

copies of the report solely for its internal use. Otherwise, the client may not reproduce the report without the prior written consent of [Valuation Firm].

37. Our report will not be used for financing, or included in a private placement or other public documents, and may not be relied on by any third parties.
38. The report assumes all required licenses, certificates of occupancy, consents, or legislative or administrative authority from any local, state, or national government, or private entity or organization have been or can be obtained or reviewed for any use on which the opinion contained in the report is based.
39. The obligations of [Valuation Firm] are solely corporate [Entity] obligations, and no officer, director, employee, agent, contractor, shareholder, owner, or controlling person shall be subject to any personal liability whatsoever to any person, nor will any such claim be asserted by or on behalf of any other party to this agreement or any person relying on the report.
40. [Valuation Firm] does not consent to be "expertised" with respect to matters involving the Securities and Exchange Commission. For purposes of this report, the foregoing sentence means that [Valuation Firm] shall not be referred to by name or anonymously in any filing or document. Should you breach this stipulation and refer to [Valuation Firm] by name or anonymously, you will amend such filing or document on the written request of [Valuation Firm].
41. We express no opinion for matters that require legal or other specialized expertise, investigation, or knowledge beyond that customarily employed by business appraisers.
42. Unless stated otherwise in this report, we express no opinion as to (1) the tax consequences of any transaction that may result, (2) the effect of the tax consequences of any net value received or to be received as a result of a transaction, and (3) the possible impact on the market value resulting from any need to effect a transaction to pay taxes.

6.4.2.2 Valuation Representation/Certification   I [we] represent/certify that, to the best of my [our] knowledge and belief:

- The statements of fact contained in this [type of report] report are true and correct.
- The reported analyses, opinions, and conclusions of value are limited only by the reported assumptions and limiting conditions, and are my personal, impartial, independent, unbiased, objective professional analyses, opinions, and conclusions.
- I have no present or prospective/contemplated financial or other interest in the business or property that is the subject of this report, and I have no personal financial or other interest or bias with respect to the property or the parties involved.
- I have performed no services, as an appraiser or in any other capacity, regarding the property that is the subject of this report within the three-year period immediately preceding acceptance of this assignment.
- My engagement in this assignment was not contingent on developing or reporting predetermined results.
- My compensation for completing this assignment is fee-based and is not contingent on the development or reporting of a predetermined value or direction in value that favors the cause of the client, the outcome of the valuation, the amount of the value opinion, the attainment of a stipulated result, or the occurrence of a subsequent event directly related to the intended use of this appraisal.

- The economic and industry data included in the valuation report have been obtained from various printed or electronic reference sources that the valuation analyst believes to be reliable. The valuation analyst has not performed any corroborating procedures to substantiate those data.
- My analyses, opinions, conclusions (valuation engagement), and this [type of report] appraisal report were developed in conformity with the American Institute of Certified Public Accountants Statements on Standards for Valuation Services VS Section 100 and the [if appropriate] 2024 Uniform Standards of Professional Appraisal Practice as promulgated by the Appraisal Foundation and the ethics and standards of the American Society of Appraisers [state other association standards as appropriate].
- The parties for which the information and use of the valuation report is restricted are identified; the valuation report is not intended to be and should not be used by anyone other than such parties.
- The valuation analyst has no obligation to update the report or the opinion of value for information that comes to my attention after the date of the report.
- No one provided significant business and/or intangible asset appraisal assistance to the person signing this certification. [OR] The valuation analyst used the work of one or more outside specialists to assist during the valuation engagement. The specialist is Mr./Ms. _____ with the firm _____. [The valuation report should include a statement identifying the level of responsibility, if any, the valuation analyst is assuming for the specialist's work].
- This report and analysis were prepared under the direction of [Lead Appraiser] with significant professional assistance from [Name]. [Lead Appraiser] is a Certified Public Accountant licensed in the State [State(s)] of and [if appropriate] is accredited in business valuation by the American Institute of Certified Public Accountants. [if appropriate] He or she is also an accredited senior appraiser with the American Society of Appraisers, a certified business appraiser with the Institute of Business Appraisers, and a certified valuation analyst with the National Association of Certified Valuators and Analysts.
- [if appropriate] The American Society of Appraisers has a mandatory recertification program for its Senior Members. [Appraiser(s)] is [are] in compliance with that program.

_____   _____

[Lead Appraiser]   [Valuation Firm]

6.4.2.3 NACVA This valuation and report were completed in accordance with the National Association of Certified Valuators and Analysts' Professional Standards.

_____

© Copyright 2025 Financial Valuation Solutions, LLC. All rights reserved. Used with permission.

6.5 KEEPING UP TECHNICALLY

The following list is intended to provide industry professionals with resources and suggestions for maintaining their professional designation(s) and keeping up to date with the valuation industry.

- Attend one or two national conventions per year
- Attend all local events
- Join state CPA society valuation/litigation sections or local ASA, IBA, NACVA chapters:
  - Good information/resources
  - Good for mentoring
- Read:
  - At least two to four different periodicals per year
  - At least one valuation book per year
  - Organization E-Flashes or Alerts:
    - Financial Consulting Group (FCG)
    - AICPA
    - ASA
    - Business Valuation Resources
  - Once a year, review:
    - Revenue Ruling 59-60
    - *Kroll Cost of Capital Navigator*
    - USPAP
    - Standards of the BV associations to which you belong
    - The construction of transaction databases relied on
- Volunteer for committee work
- Join FCG

6.6 PRACTICE BENCHMARKS FOR PRODUCTIVITY, BILLINGS, REALIZATION, AND THE BOTTOM LINE

The following list is intended to demonstrate basic items that should be considered when a professional firm establishes internal productivity and billing procedures. Some information is based on a best-case model.

- Productivity:
  - General annual benchmarks depend on practice and type of work.
    - Staff above 90 percent
    - Managers (non-selling) above 80 percent
    - Partners above 50 percent
    - Group must understand that some months are way up and some way down depending on work volume and staff availability
  - Billings:
    - High-end, efficient practice can bill an hourly rate three to four times raw cost hourly rate of staff
    - Should bill between 90 percent and 100 percent of billable hours generated by staff
      - May be lower for firms with heavier reliance on fixed-fee engagements
    - Should collect between 90 percent and 100 percent of what is billed to client

- Realization:
  - Overruns should be investigated and managed with client before final billing and preferably earlier
  - Engagement letter language important here
- Bottom Line:
  - High-end, efficient practice should be over 50 percent profit margin before partner compensation
  - Over 30 percent acceptable depending on the type of practice and type of work
- Golden Rule:
  - Seldom really followed
  - Very easy . . .
  - Tie performance measures *directly* to pay

6.7 FINDING, TRAINING, AND RETAINING THE RIGHT STAFF FOR YOUR PRACTICE

The following list is intended to list basic items that should be considered for a professional firm's workforce.

- Finding staff:
  - Use your staff to find staff:
    - Provide incentives
  - Post at the local universities:
    - Full time
    - Interns
  - Competition
  - ASA, BVR, or e-letter
  - State CPA Society
- Training staff:
  - In-house always the best
    - Staff should constantly be asking questions
    - Partners should always be asking staff why they did what they did
    - AICPA
    - ASA
    - NACVA
- Retaining staff:
  - Treat them with respect
  - Fear-based leadership is not leadership:
    - Only effective in the short term
    - Learning in a fear-based environment takes an emotional toll
  - Keep them informed
    - Team players know what is going on
  - Pay them above market
    - Much more expensive to replace staff than to keep them
    - Don't worry; your competition won't do this

- Provide growth opportunities.
  - Transfer existing relationships to staff
  - Partner/principal can get new clients much easier than staff
- Where feasible, offer flexible work arrangements

6.8 DELEGATE LITIGATION ENGAGEMENTS TO STAFF

The following list is intended to demonstrate partner and staff traits and practices that are critical in delegating litigation engagements.

- What it takes:
  - A change in leadership philosophy:
    - Cannot be control freak
    - Must want to grow your practice
    - Type of staff matters but it's you, not the staff
    - Must have trust but rely on controls and checks
  - Access to leader:
    - A five-minute conversation with staff can save hours and sometimes even days of work
    - Must not get annoyed when constantly asked questions and direction from staff
    - It really takes only one to three hours a day of leader time
    - Leader can be chargeable through inspection and direction (depends on engagement)
    - Each staff person should have the leader's cell phone
  - The right staff:
    - Again, leadership is critical, but the right staff members are important
    - Detail orientation . . . no shooting from the hip
    - Must feel comfortable asking questions
    - Cannot be afraid to admit they are puzzled or do not understand what they are doing
    - Up to leader to set the tone
    - The model works best with more senior staff but will work with less experienced staff as well
    - Willingness to ask each other questions as well as the leader
  - Controls and checks:
    - People do what you inspect, not what you expect
      - Check each person at least once daily
      - Effective in smaller groups
      - Larger organizations: Check direct reports
      - Rough rule of thumb: Check junior staff at a time interval of two hours or so for each year of experience
      - Tell them to bring their work and explain the task they are working on, how long they expect to be working on that task, and what their next two tasks are

- Make sure they understand the big picture and not just the specific piece they are working on
- More senior staff should also check in at least once a day or so
- Schedule detailed reviews of work completed to date at reasonable intervals
- When feasible, make staff take notes and tell you what was agreed on at the meeting before they move on
- At the next meeting, make sure they have their notes
- Use control sheets where possible
  - This is a list of who reviewed it and when it was reviewed (Appendix 6.3)
  - Use of cold reviews
  - It is up to the leader to determine how detailed these control sheets need to be
- Summary of findings binder:
  - Standardize it
  - Everything important summarized with copies of the major backup items
  - Should point to where everything is and where it came from, including other file binders
  - Use it to prepare for trial, if necessary
- Footing, proofing, and comparing:
  - Done by another staff member
  - Signed off by leader
  - Recheck changes at end of engagement because such changes are often made under deadline pressure
- Bottom line:
- Should go up
- Leader must still get into the details, but if engagement is organized properly, that will happen
- Know the strengths and weaknesses of each staff member
  - Remember, you can change habits but not personalities
- Leader must be disciplined and consistent

6.9 APPENDIX 6.1: SAMPLE GIBRALTAR E-FLASH COVER SHEET

Welcome to
The Gibraltar Business Appraisals Court E-Flash,
easily accessible information on important tax court information.

Please click on the attached PDF file to access news you can use.
We encourage you to forward this E-Flash, with attribution intact,
to other interested parties.
For the full text of this case or more information on Gibraltar, visit our
website at www.4avalue.com.

****

Gibraltar Business Appraisals, Inc.
provides Business Valuation, Business Brokerage, and Corporate Financial
Consulting Services.

****

Chris D. Treharne, ASA, MCBA, BVAL
Gibraltar Business Appraisals, Inc.
1325 Dry Creek Drive
Suite 201
Longmont, CO 80503
(303) 532-2545
ctreharne@4avalue.com
www.4avalue.com

****

To unsubscribe from E-Flash distribution, please respond to this email and
include your email address and the word UNSUBSCRIBE in the subject line.
Thank you.

6.10 APPENDIX 6.2: SAMPLE GIBRALTAR E-FLASH

1325 Dry Creek Drive, Suite 201
Longmont, CO 80503
Local   303.532.2545
Toll Free 888.428.2583
888 4-A-Value

BUSINESS APPRAISALS, INC.
www.4aValue.com

Financial Consulting Group *E-Flash* Vol. 12:4

The Ringgold Telephone Company v. Commissioner

T.C. Memo 2010-103

By Chris D. Treharne, ASA, MCBA, BVAL and Fawntel Romero, AM
Gibraltar Business Appraisals, Inc.

Post Valuation Date Transaction Relevant

The Tax Court determined whether a post valuation date sale of a partnership interest should be included as evidence of fair market value.

Additionally, the Tax Court decided the taxpayer's expert (who had a business valuation designation) was more credible and persuasive than the IRS' expert (who was not accredited in business valuation and had never appraised a company in the telecommunications industry).

BV TAKEAWAY

In a telephone conversation with the taxpayer's expert, the authors confirmed that **both experts tax affected the subject S corporation's income using C corporation income tax rates.** According to the taxpayer's expert, the trial occurred during December 2008, well after the controversial Tax Court decisions asserting that tax affecting S corporation income is inappropriate, yet the issue was not discussed at trial. The absence of an IRS challenge on this issue should not be overlooked.

Telephone Company Converts to S Corporation

The Ringgold Telephone Company ("Taxpayer" or "Ringgold") provides telecommunication services. On January 1, 2000, Ringgold converted from a C corporation to an S corporation for federal tax purposes.

Ringgold, Bell South Mobility, Inc. ("BellSouth"), Trenton Telephone Co., and Bledsoe Telephone Co. each owned 25% partnership interests in Cellular Radio of Chattanooga ("CRC").

CRC's primary asset was a 29.54% limited partnership interest in Chattanooga MSA Limited Partnership ("CHAT"). Accordingly, Ringgold indirectly owned a noncontrolling interest in CHAT.

On November 27, 2000, Ringgold sold its 25% partnership interest in CRC to BellSouth for $5,220,043.

BellSouth wholly owned Chattanooga CGSA, the sole general partner of CHAT and its controlling owner. Chattanooga CGSA's combined general and limited partner interest in CHAT was 55.31%.

A business valuation report was issued by Warinner, Gesinger & Associates, L.L.C., on February 15, 2000, which estimated the value of the CRC interest to be approximately $2,600,000 ("February 2000 Report").

Taxpayer's Position

On Ringgold's 2000 Form 1120S, the February 2000 Report's value, $2,600,000, was used to calculate the IRC § 1374 built-in gain attributable to the CRC interest as of January 1, 2000.

IRS Position

The IRS determined the January 1, 2000, fair market value of the CRC interest was $5,243,602 (based on its November 27, 2000, sale to BellSouth) - instead of the February 2000 Report's $2,600,000 - and asserted a tax deficiency and IRC § 6662(a) taxpayer penalty based on the difference.

Court's Ruling

With regard to the value of the subject ownership interest, the court considered the following:

• The sale price of Ringgold's partnership interest in CRC was evidence of value.

• The Taxpayer, court, and IRS all agreed that the November 2000 sale occurred within a reasonable time of the valuation date (i.e., no significant events that would affect the share price occurred between January and November 2000) and was an arm's-length sale in the normal course of business.

• The sale price should be adjusted to reflect "special circumstances surrounding the buyer, the seller, or the transaction generally that could have skewed the sale price from a measure of true fair market value that would have been reached between a hypothetical buyer and seller absent those circumstances."

• The Taxpayer argued that a controlling interest holder would place a greater value on a minority interest compared to a hypothetical buyer who lacks control. Therefore, the purchase price reflects a control value. The IRS argued that because BellSouth already indirectly owned a controlling interest in CHAT, it would not have paid a control premium for the interest. The court recalled that the Taxpayer's own expert indicated BellSouth had no incentive from a control perspective to purchase the CRC interest. The court disagreed that a lack of control discount should be applied to the purchase price.

• In addition, the Taxpayer argued that BellSouth paid a premium for the CRC interest to discourage the other partners from exercising their rights of first refusal. As part of the argument, the Taxpayer's expert testified that if the sale was a strategic acquisition, BellSouth would pay a premium for the CRC interest. The court found the Taxpayer's expert to be a credible witness and found no evidence contradicting his testimony.

Based on the preceding, the court concluded that the sale price was probative, but not conclusive, evidence of the fair market value of the CRC interest on the valuation date.

The court also provided insightful information with regard to the two experts:

- The Taxpayer's witness, William E. King, CPA/ABV, is accredited in business valuation by the American Institute of Certified Public Accountants. Additionally, he has extensive experience in telecommunications valuations.
- The IRS' witness, Steven C. Hastings, CPA, is not accredited in business valuation and had never performed a business valuation for a telecommunications company prior to the subject appraisal.

The court found Mr. King to be a more persuasive expert relative to Mr. Hastings. In particular, his experience in valuing telecommunication companies allowed him to factor in industry specific conditions. Unlike Mr. Hastings, Mr. King also considered the distribution history of CHAT in his valuation analysis. The court recognized the importance of the distribution paying history to a minority shareholder who is unable to force the company to pay distributions.

To determine the fair market value of the CRC interest, the court considered the sale price of the CRC interest, the King Report, and the Hastings Report, in addition to all other relevant factors.

The court found the taxpayer's expert credible and relied on his expert report rather than the IRS' expert report. However, Mr. King failed to consider the post-valuation date sale of the partnership interest to BellSouth in his analysis, a factor the court concluded should have been considered. To determine the value of the CRC interest, the court gave equal weighting to Mr. King's business valuation analysis, Mr. King's distribution yield analysis, and the BellSouth sale price.

6.11 APPENDIX 6.3: SAMPLE CONTROL SHEET

Valuation Group
Engagement Log Sheet

Client _____   Fee (range) _____

Client Contact _____

Address _____   Budget _____

_____

Phone _____

Facsimile _____

Subject Company _____

Nature of Business _____

Interest Valued _____

Purpose of Valuation _____

Date of Valuation _____

	Initial	Date	W/P Reference

Engagement Selection

Independence Relationship Check Performed _____ _____ _____

Proposal Issued _____ _____ _____

Engagement Letter Issued _____ _____ _____

Engagement Letter Executed _____ _____ _____

Indemnification Obtained, if applicable _____ _____ _____

Engagement Preparation

Date Report Due _____ _____ _____

Information Request Sent _____ _____ _____

Information Received from Client _____ _____ _____

	Initial	Date	W/P Reference

Analysis/Report Technical Review

Staff   _____ _____ _____

Manager   _____ _____ _____

Shareholder   _____ _____ _____

Review Engagement Letter for Changes in Scope   _____ _____ _____

Draft Analysis/Report Reviewed

Staff   _____ _____ _____

Manager   _____ _____ _____

Shareholder   _____ _____ _____

Draft Analysis/Report Edit   _____ _____ _____

Draft Analysis/Report P & C   _____ _____ _____

Draft Analysis/Report Issued   _____ _____ _____

Final Analysis/Report Reviewed

Staff   _____ _____ _____

Manager   _____ _____ _____

Shareholder   _____ _____ _____

Cold Review, if applicable   _____ _____ _____

Working Papers Signed Off   _____ _____ _____

Final Analysis/Report Issued   _____ _____ _____

CHAPTER 7

Practice Management Workflow Procedures

7.1 INTRODUCTION

These workflow procedures are designed to assist midsize firms in maintaining the continuity of the client report and exhibits and will eliminate unnecessary draft files. The purpose of these procedures and checklists is to define the checks and balances that are needed to reduce exposure. These procedures are also completely dependent on each firm's internal policies, which can be and often are different from what is presented here. For example, policies concerning notes and drafts can and do differ by firm. In most cases, large firms will have already established procedures and policies. Conversely, small firms may not have the staff to implement these procedures with the appropriate degree of independence. However, both large and small firms may find the checklists useful in their practice.

In order to comply with the procedures, emails and drafts can be created according to the appropriate templates that exist within the system. Correspondence with the client, including emails both sent and received, can be retained in the Client folder. Additionally, verbal conversations can be logged on the appropriate form and filed in the client's folder.

If a report draft is created and sent to the attorney, any changes that the attorney recommends may be retained in the Client's file and may potentially be used in future litigation. (Note: There are some exceptions.) Additionally, drafts sent to the client may be retained both electronically and in the Client's file.

The initial section presents summary flowcharts. The remaining section introduces an example of detailed practice management workflow processes. The process shown here is copyrighted by The Financial Valuation Group of Florida, Inc., and is used with permission. Certain revisions have been made by the authors.

7.2 SECTION I—PRACTICE MANAGEMENT FLOWCHARTS

**Practice Management
Workflow Procedures
Summary Flowcharts**

1

● **Overall Caveat:** Most of the information is presented in a best-case scenario where everything is almost perfect. It will not be possible or relevant to adopt all of the procedures, policies, and ideas. Each professional and firm should choose the resources that fit the firm/group, its philosophy, and culture.

● **Caveat:** For discussion and educational purposes only. Valuation and litigation services are very much affected by specific facts and circumstances. As such, the views expressed in these written materials do not necessarily reflect the professional opinions or positions that the presenter would take in every assignment or practice, or in providing valuation or litigation services in connection with an actual engagement, matter, or practice. Every situation and practice is unique, and differing facts and circumstances may result in variations of the information presented. The authors assume no responsibility for any errors in this information, use of this information, or reliance on the information. Use at your own risk.

2

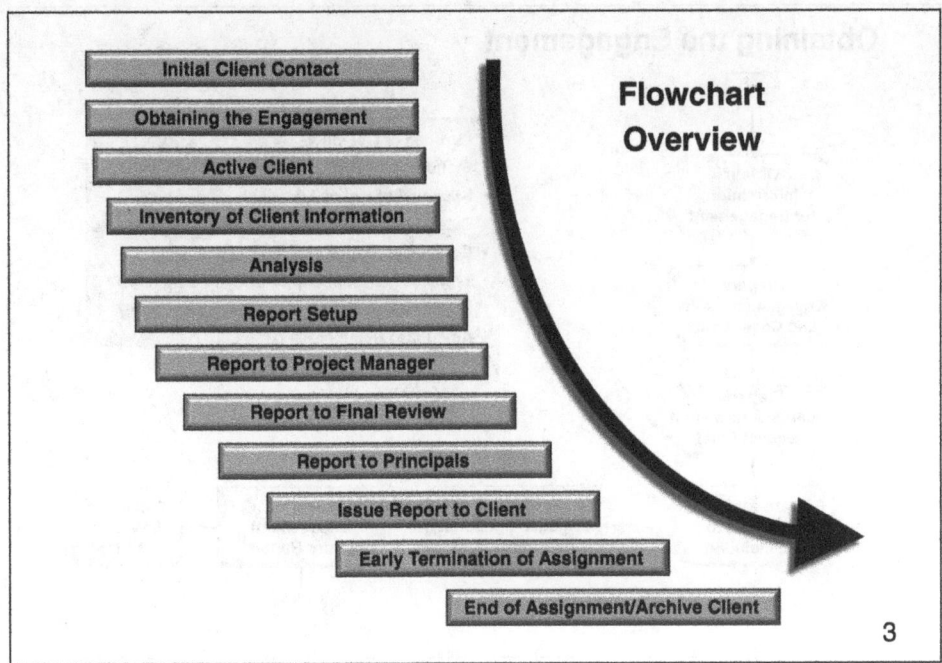

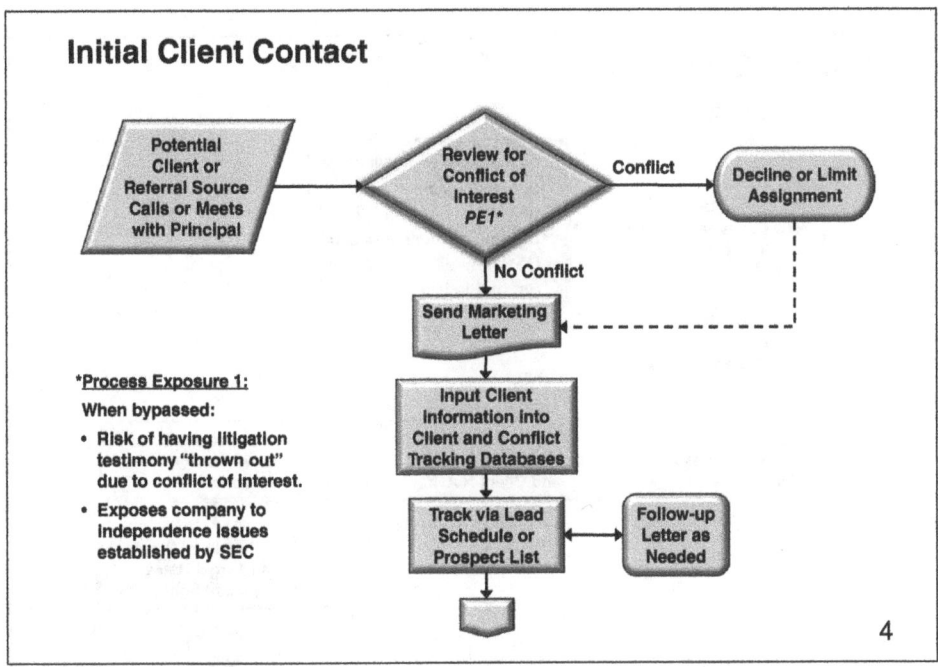

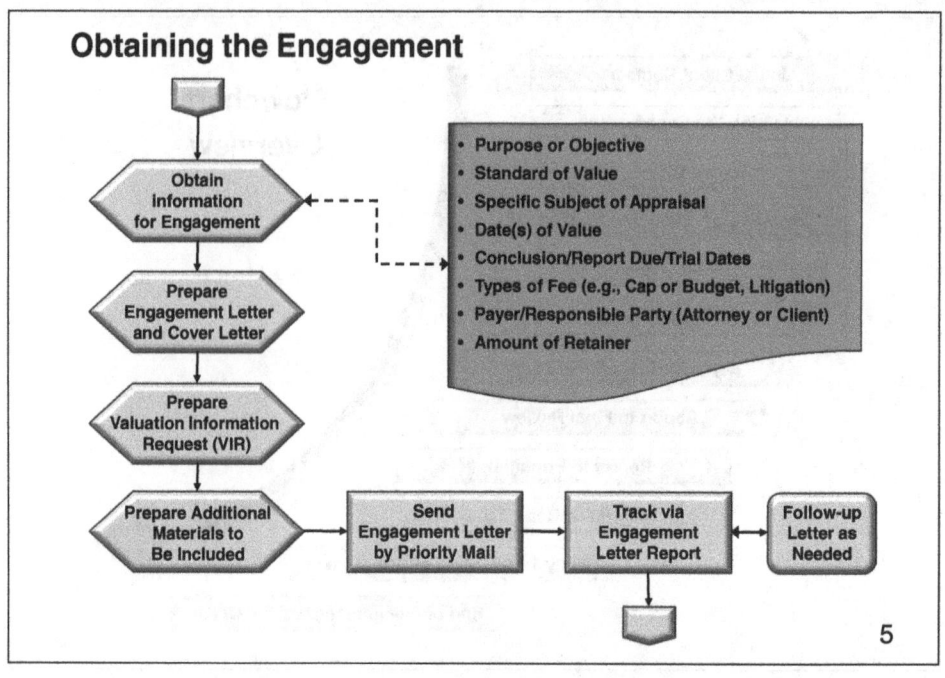

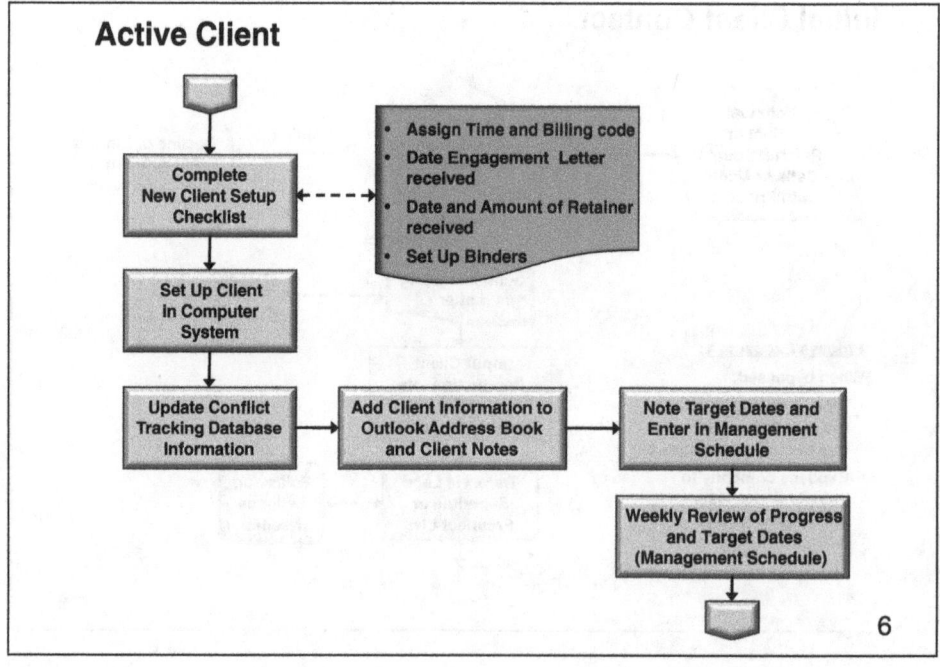

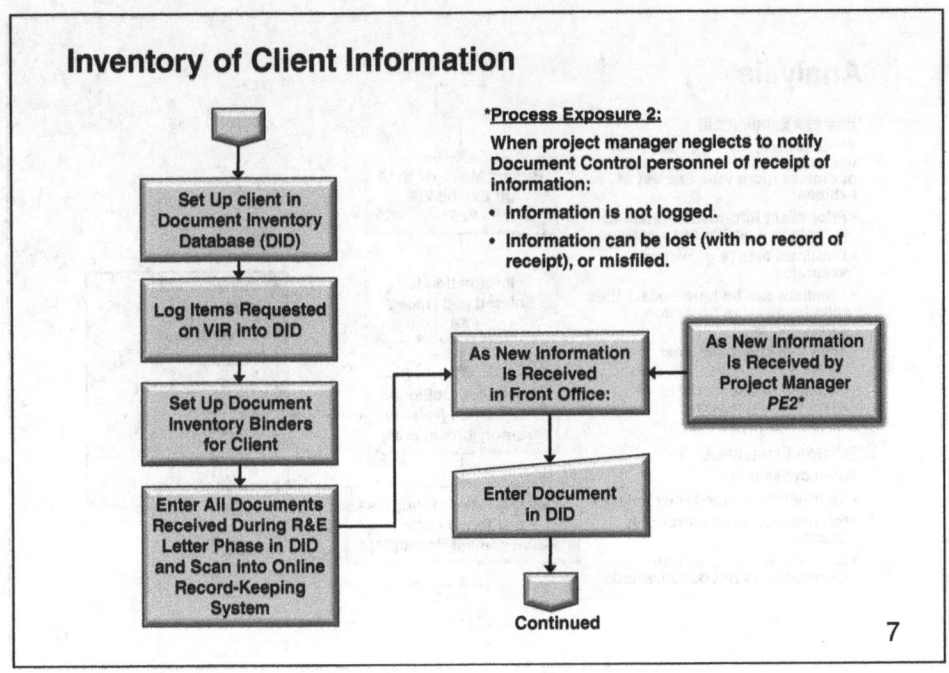

Inventory of Client Information

*Process Exposure 2:

When project manager neglects to notify Document Control personnel of receipt of information:

- Information is not logged.
- Information can be lost (with no record of receipt), or misfiled.

Set Up client in Document Inventory Database (DID)

Log Items Requested on VIR into DID

Set Up Document Inventory Binders for Client

Enter All Documents Received During R&E Letter Phase in DID and Scan into Online Record-Keeping System

As New Information Is Received in Front Office:

As New Information Is Received by Project Manager PE2*

Enter Document in DID

Continued

7

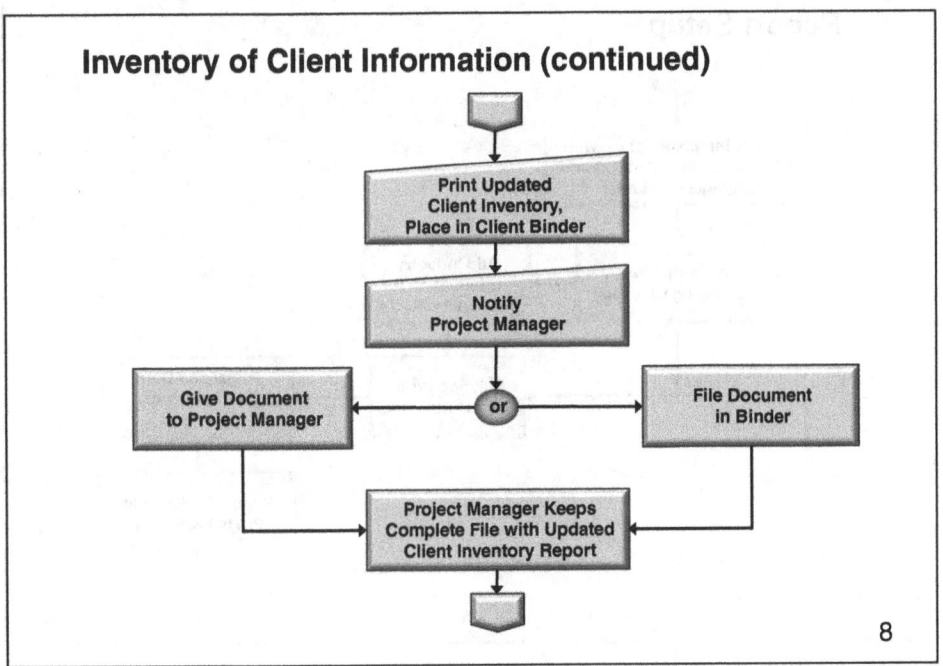

Inventory of Client Information (continued)

Print Updated Client Inventory, Place in Client Binder

Notify Project Manager

Give Document to Project Manager

or

File Document in Binder

Project Manager Keeps Complete File with Updated Client Inventory Report

8

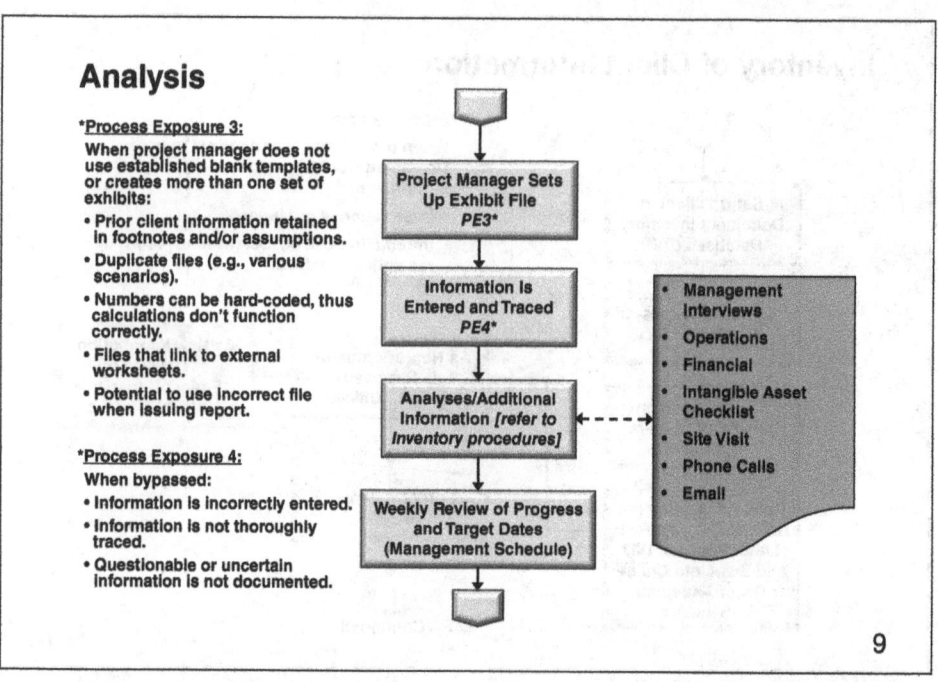

Analysis

*Process Exposure 3:

When project manager does not use established blank templates, or creates more than one set of exhibits:

- Prior client information retained in footnotes and/or assumptions.
- Duplicate files (e.g., various scenarios).
- Numbers can be hard-coded, thus calculations don't function correctly.
- Files that link to external worksheets.
- Potential to use incorrect file when issuing report.

*Process Exposure 4:

When bypassed:

- Information is incorrectly entered.
- Information is not thoroughly traced.
- Questionable or uncertain information is not documented.

Project Manager Sets Up Exhibit File PE3*

Information Is Entered and Traced PE4*

Analyses/Additional Information [refer to Inventory procedures]

Weekly Review of Progress and Target Dates (Management Schedule)

- Management Interviews
- Operations
- Financial
- Intangible Asset Checklist
- Site Visit
- Phone Calls
- Email

9

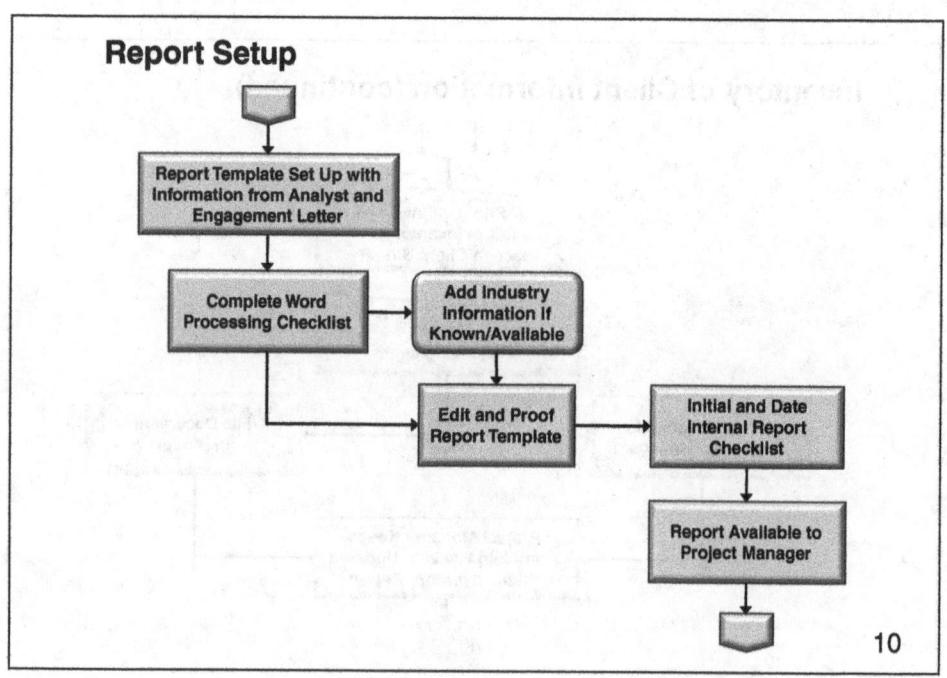

Report Setup

Report Template Set Up with Information from Analyst and Engagement Letter

Complete Word Processing Checklist

Add Industry Information if Known/Available

Edit and Proof Report Template

Initial and Date Internal Report Checklist

Report Available to Project Manager

10

Report to Project Manager

*Process Exposure 5:

When bypassed:

- Communication breakdown between project Manager and principal.
- Unnecessary billable hours or budget overage (due to work having to be redone or more extensive review required by principal).
- Possible write-down on invoice.

*Process Exposure 6:

When project manager does not use established blank templates:

- Prior client information retained in text.
- Duplicate reports (Save As).
- Numbers in exhibits are not verified with numbers in text.

*Process Exposure 7:

When bypassed or not completed timely:

- Incorrect assumptions/methodologies used.
- Most recent information not used (financial, industry, company).
- Increased billable hours, invoicing due to work involved to correct assumptions/methodologies.
- Inaccurate report issued.

Complete Analysis

Track Workflow via Work Program Checklist PE5*

Write Report with Supporting Exhibits PE6* ↔ Consult with Principal as Needed

Complete Development Review Checklist PE7*

Continued

11

Report to Project Manager (continued)

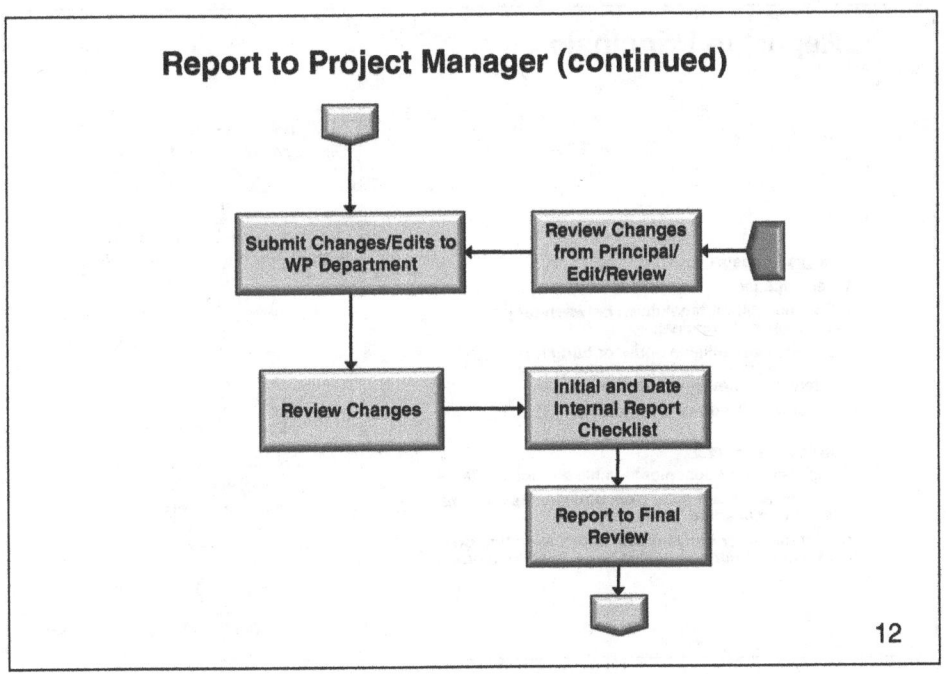

Submit Changes/Edits to WP Department ← Review Changes from Principal/ Edit/Review

Review Changes → Initial and Date Internal Report Checklist

Report to Final Review

12

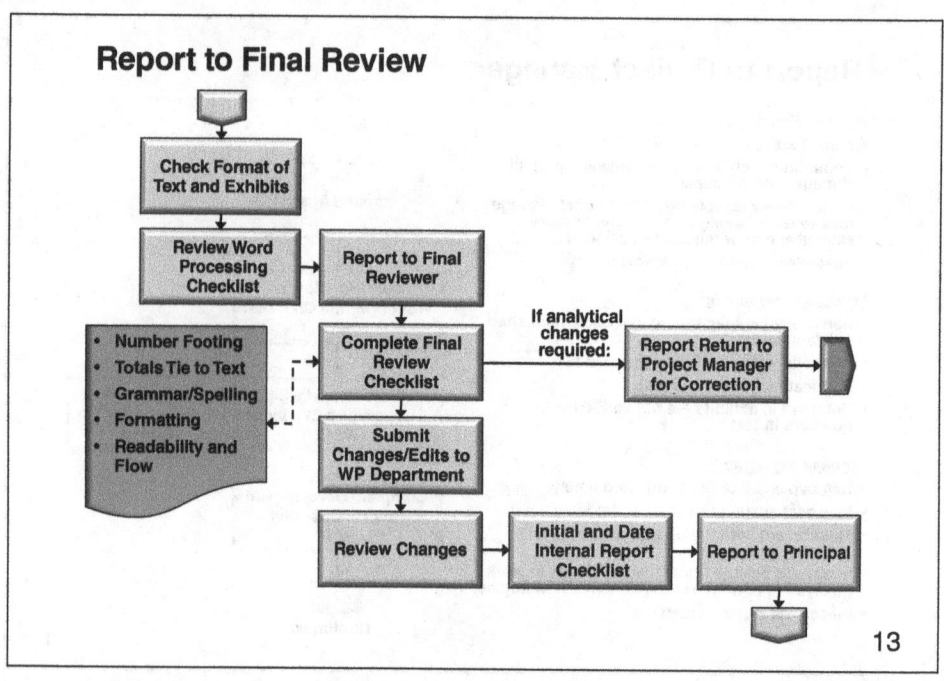

Report to Final Review

- Check Format of Text and Exhibits
- Review Word Processing Checklist
- Report to Final Reviewer
- Number Footing
- Totals Tie to Text
- Grammar/Spelling
- Formatting
- Readability and Flow
- Complete Final Review Checklist
- If analytical changes required: Report Return to Project Manager for Correction
- Submit Changes/Edits to WP Department
- Review Changes
- Initial and Date Internal Report Checklist
- Report to Principal

13

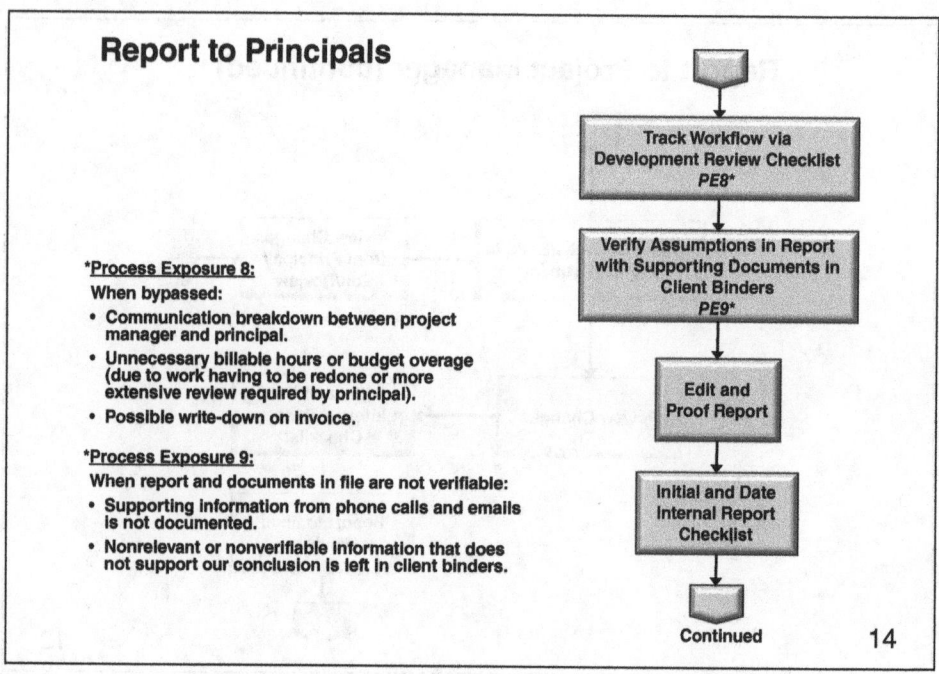

Report to Principals

*Process Exposure 8:
When bypassed:
- Communication breakdown between project manager and principal.
- Unnecessary billable hours or budget overage (due to work having to be redone or more extensive review required by principal).
- Possible write-down on invoice.

*Process Exposure 9:
When report and documents in file are not verifiable:
- Supporting information from phone calls and emails is not documented.
- Nonrelevant or nonverifiable information that does not support our conclusion is left in client binders.

- Track Workflow via Development Review Checklist PE8*
- Verify Assumptions in Report with Supporting Documents in Client Binders PE9*
- Edit and Proof Report
- Initial and Date Internal Report Checklist

Continued   14

Report to Principals (continued)

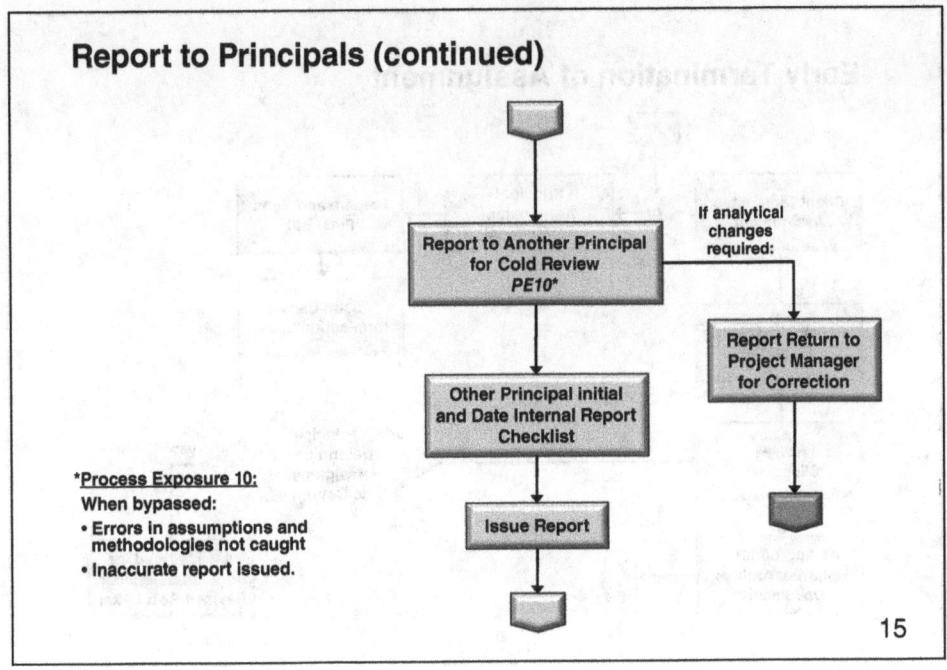

Report to Another Principal for Cold Review
PE10*

If analytical changes required:

Report Return to Project Manager for Correction

Other Principal initial and Date Internal Report Checklist

***Process Exposure 10:**
When bypassed:
• Errors in assumptions and methodologies not caught
• Inaccurate report issued.

Issue Report

15

Issue Report

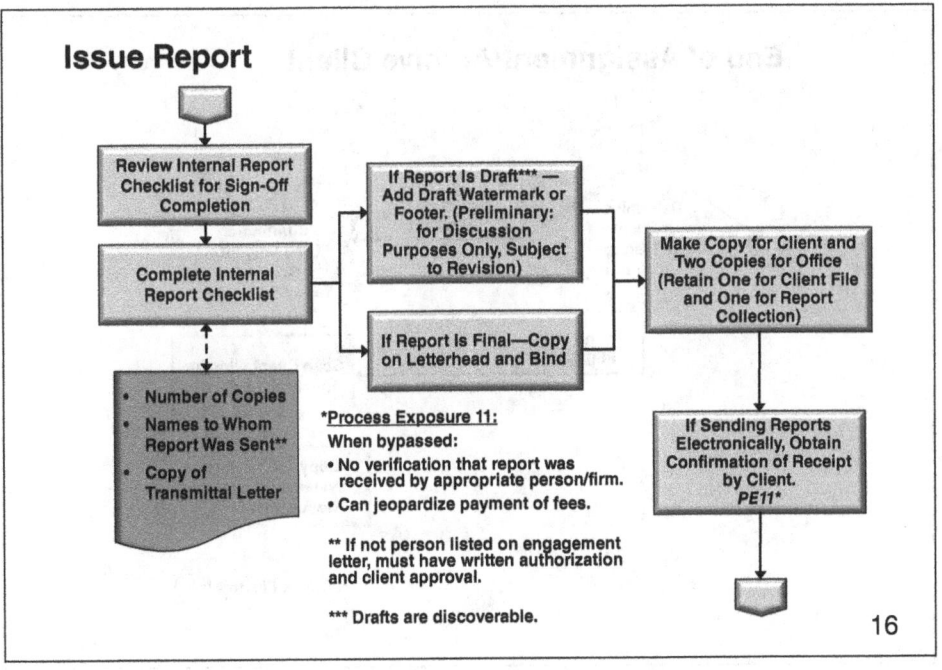

Review Internal Report Checklist for Sign-Off Completion

Complete Internal Report Checklist

If Report Is Draft* — Add Draft Watermark or Footer. (Preliminary: for Discussion Purposes Only, Subject to Revision)**

If Report Is Final—Copy on Letterhead and Bind

Make Copy for Client and Two Copies for Office (Retain One for Client File and One for Report Collection)

• Number of Copies
• Names to Whom Report Was Sent**
• Copy of Transmittal Letter

***Process Exposure 11:**
When bypassed:
• No verification that report was received by appropriate person/firm.
• Can jeopardize payment of fees.

** If not person listed on engagement letter, must have written authorization and client approval.

*** Drafts are discoverable.

If Sending Reports Electronically, Obtain Confirmation of Receipt by Client.
PE11*

16

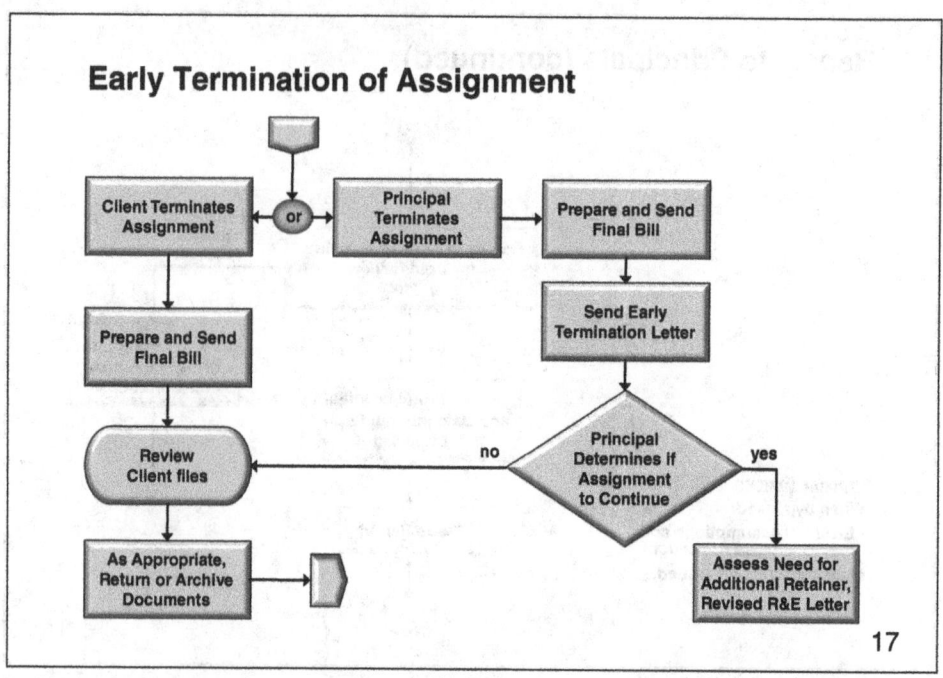

Early Termination of Assignment

17

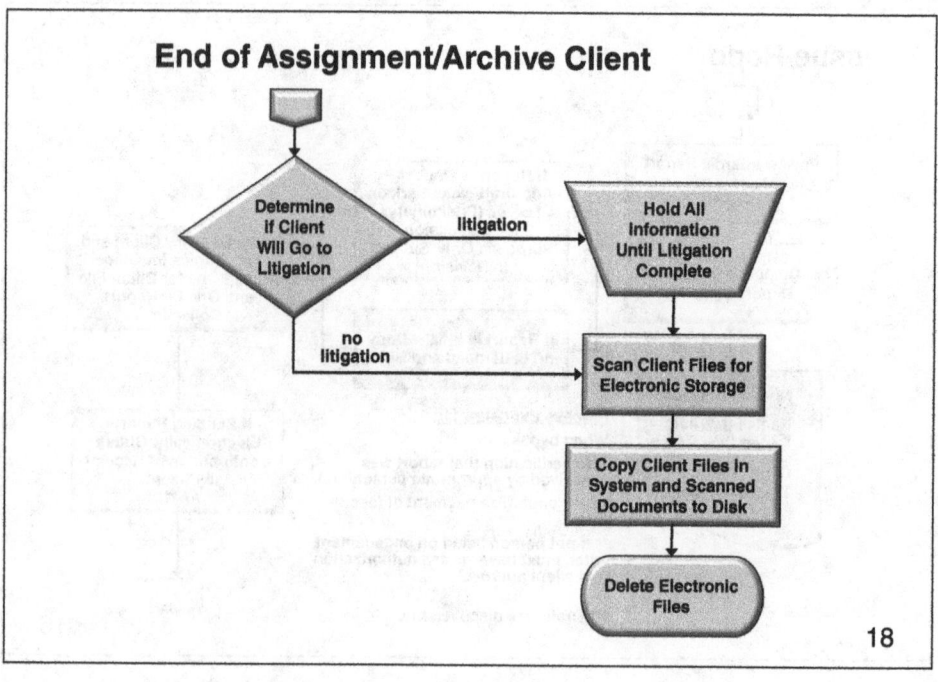

End of Assignment/Archive Client

18

7.3 SECTION II—PRACTICE MANAGEMENT WORKFLOW PROCESS

7.3.1 Initial Client Contact

Note: All client/prospect information is to be stored in the appropriate folder on the server. Local computer hard drives are not available.

I. Potential Client or Referral Source calls or meets with firm Principal.
   A. Principal completes blue **Contact Information Sheet** (Exhibit 7.1).
   B. Contact Information Sheet is given to Support Staff by Principal for Relationship Review.

II. Support Staff dates receipt of Contact Information Sheet and completes Relationship Review.
   A. Support Staff searches Relationship Tracking Database (or other record-keeping method) to determine if potential relationship exists.
   B. If no potential relationship found in Relationship Tracking Database, Support Staff completes **Relationship Review Checklist** (Exhibit 7.2).
      1. Support Staff emails other Company offices with prospective client information to check for potential relationship with other Company offices.
      2. Support Staff follows up with phone calls to those offices that do not respond to email.
      3. Support Staff indicates if there is or is not a potential relationship between other offices and prospective client.
      4. If potential relationship exists, Support Staff indicates reason for potential relationship on Relationship Review Checklist.
      5. Support Staff initials and dates completion of Relationship Review.
      6. Support Staff attaches Relationship Review Checklist to Contact Information Sheet.
   C. Results are relayed via email or written documentation to Principal.
   D. If Principal determines relationship exists using either Relationship Review Checklist or other means of determination, Principal notifies Client or Referral Source by **Engagement Declination Letter** (Exhibit 7.3) indicating if engagement is declined or limited.
      1. Engagement Declination Letter is stored electronically on server in the client's electronic file.
      2. A copy of the letter is placed in the client's folder.

III. Principal defines potential engagement and completes Lead section of green **Lead and Project Information Sheet** (Exhibit 7.4), including:
   A. Type
   B. Name(s) of Client(s)
   C. Name(s) of Company(ies)
   D. Name(s) of Attorney(ies)

IV. If Principal requests **Marketing Letter** (Exhibit 7.5) be sent to potential client:
   A. Support Staff designated by Principal creates new marketing letter from template.
      1. Support Staff stores the electronic copy of the marketing letter on server.
      2. Support Staff places a copy of the marketing letter in client's folder.
      3. Client's folder is labeled with blue label designating a lead/prospect.

      B. Support Staff mails marketing package via First Class mail.

      C. Principal follows up with potential client within 10 days.

   V. Schedule Controller inputs information into Client Database (or other Client Management System), including:

      A. Client Name(s)

      B. Contact Name(s)

      C. Company Name(s)

      D. Date of Contact

      E. Type of Engagement

      F. Assigned Principal

  VI. Schedule Controller inputs information into Relationship Tracking Database, including:

      A. Client Name(s)

      B. Contact Name(s)

      C. Company Name(s)

      D. Date of Contact

      E. Type of Engagement

      F. Responsible Company office

 VII. Weekly on Friday, Schedule Controller generates **Lead Schedule** (Exhibit 7.6), which contains a list of existing leads and new leads generated during the week.

VIII. Weekly on Monday, Lead Schedule is reviewed for follow-up during Monday staff meeting.

      A. Leads marked for follow-up by Principal are contacted via **Lead Follow-up Letter** (Exhibit 7.7) generated by Support Staff. Support Staff creating letter communicates with Schedule Controller via email or verbally that letter is sent.

        1. Support Staff enters date of follow-up on Lead Schedule.

        2. Support Staff stores Lead Follow-up Letter on the server.

        3. Support Staff places a copy of the Lead Follow-up Letter in client's folder.

      B. If Lead is marked inactive by Principal:

        1. Schedule Coordinator indicates "Inactive" status in Client Database.

        2. Support Staff moves potential client's marketing folder to inactive file drawer.

7.3.2 Obtaining the Engagement

Note: All client/prospect information is to be stored in the appropriate folder on the server. Local computer hard drives are not available.

   I. Principal obtains information from client and updates Engagement section of Lead and Project Information Sheet.

      A. Such information will include:

        1. Purpose or Objectives of valuation

        2. Standard of Value

        3. Specific Subject of Appraisal

        4. Date(s) of Value

        5. Conclusion/Report Due/Trial Dates

        6. Types of Fee (i.e., cap or budget, litigation)

       7. Payer/Responsible Party (Attorney or Client)

       8. Amount of Retainer required

  B. Verbal Communication

     1. The Principal having the verbal exchange with the client is responsible for documenting pertinent information from the conversation on a blue-colored Contact Sheet. If it is determined that a new Client Contact exists, Principal will notify Support Staff by indicating same in area on Contact Sheet.

     2. The contact sheet is given to the Support Staff by the Principal for inclusion into the Client Database and Relationship Tracking Database. Contact sheets may be accumulated by the Principal; however, they must be delivered to the Support Staff frequently.

     3. Contact Sheet is placed in Client folder by Support Staff.

  C. Written Correspondence

     1. Written correspondence created or requested by Principal to a client can be copied and filed into the client's folder.

     2. If the correspondence is sent using a form of mail that creates a tracking record, the tracking slip can be filed in the client's folder.

     3. If correspondence was generated by Support Staff, Support Staff notifies Principal that task is complete.

II. Support Staff creates **Representation and Engagement Letter** (See Chapter 6) and **Representation and Engagement Letter Cover Letter** (Exhibit 7.8) from Template.

  A. Support Staff stores the electronic Representation and Engagement Letter and the electronic Representation and Engagement Letter Cover Letter on the server.

  B. Support Staff places a copy of the Representation and Engagement Letter in client's folder.

  C. Client's folder is labeled with a red label.

  D. Schedule Coordinator updates Client Database with new information.

III. Project Manager prepares initial **Valuation Information Request** (VIR) General (see Chapter 8, Checklist 8.5).

  A. Support Staff generates the VIR to send to the client based on information received from the Project Manager.

  B. Support Staff stores the electronic Valuation Information Request on the server.

  C. Support Staff places a copy of the Valuation Information Request and the Engagement Letter Cover Letter in client's folder.

  D. Support Staff prepares additional materials to be included as indicated by Principal. Such materials may include:

     1. Firm brochure

     2. Articles

     3. Books

     4. Marketing package

IV. Support Staff sends Representation and Engagement Letter with VIR and additional materials by Priority Mail (for tracking).

  A. Receipt for priority mail is placed in client's folder.

  V. Schedule Controller updates information in Client Database, including:
  A. Date of Contact
  B. Date Engagement Letter Sent
  C. Amount of Retainer Requested
  D. Assigned Project Manager
 VI. Weekly on Friday, Schedule Controller generates **Engagement Letter Schedule** (Exhibit 7.9). The Engagement Letter Schedule lists all outstanding engagement letters.
VII. Weekly on Monday, Engagement Letter Schedule is reviewed for follow-up during Staff Meeting.
  A. If follow-up is required as determined by Principal, Schedule Controller marks follow-up date on Engagement Letter Schedule.
    1. Engagement Letters marked for follow-up are contacted via **Representation and Engagement Letter Follow-up Letter** (Exhibit 7.10).
      a. Support Staff creates the Representation and Engagement Letter Follow-up Letter (RELFL).
      b. Support Staff stores the electronic copy of the RELFL on the server.
      c. Support Staff places a copy of the RELFL in client's folder.
  B. If engagement is deemed inactive by Principal:
    1. Representation and Engagement Letter, Valuation Information Request, and Representation and Engagement Letter Cover Letter are moved to disk by Support Staff for storage.
    2. Representation and Engagement Letter, Valuation Information Request, and Representation and Engagement Letter Cover Letter are deleted from server by Support Staff.
    3. The client's physical folder is saved for six months.
    4. If requested by the client, information sent by the client relating to the valuation is returned to the client.
    5. After six months, the client's physical folder is destroyed out by Support Staff.

7.3.3 Active Client

Note: All client/prospect information is to be stored in the appropriate folder on the server. Local computer hard drives are not available.
   I. Project Manager is assigned by Principal (if not already assigned).
  II. Client Production Coordinator (CPC) is assigned by Principal.
 III. CPC completes **New Client Setup Checklist** (Exhibit 7.11), including:
  A. Assign Time & Billing Code using first 12 characters of client name.
  B. Indicate the date the Representation and Engagement Letter was received.
  C. Indicate amount of retainer and date received.
  D. Set up client binders and deliver them to Project Manager, including:
    1. Labels
    2. File Index
    3. Blank Internal Report Signoff sheet
    4. Blank New Client Report Request
    5. Blank New Client Exhibit Request
    6. Blank Math Review checklist
    7. Blank Development Review checklist
    8. Blank Report Compliance checklist
    9. Blank Management Questionnaires

10. Copy of Representation and Engagement Letter and VIR sent to client, or blank VIR

E. Add client to Time and Billing software.

F. Assign Copier and Phone code if applicable.

1. Update code list on copier.

2. Update phone system.

IV. CPC creates Client folder in computer using the following protocol:

A. A main Client folder is created on the server in the following location: F:/Clients/Active/xCLIENTx.

B. If there is more than one valuation for a client, the file will contain a folder for the year in which the valuation was performed. (Example: F:/ Clients/Active/xCLIENTx/2010)

C. If there is more than one valuation for a client in a particular year, the file will contain a folder for each individual valuation name by type and/ or date of valuation within the year folder. (Example: F:/Clients/Active/ xCLIENTx/2010/Business Comb (or DOV 4-15-10))

D. In the final valuation folder created using the previous criteria, create one (1) subfolder for each of the following:

- Correspondence
- Billing
- Analysis
- Report
- Engagement Letter
- Information from Client

E. Move all information from Engagement Letter folders and Marketing folder on server to client Engagement Letter folder.

V. CPC updates Conflict Tracking Database information with additional information received on VIR, correspondence, and conversations with client as additional information is received by CPC, Project Manager, or Principal.

VI. CPC adds Client information to Address Book (Microsoft Outlook or other tracking system).

VII. Target Dates are entered in the Client Database and/or Company Calendar by CPC. Target dates include:

A. Date report is due

B. Date(s) of depositions

C. Date of trial

D. Date(s) of upcoming meetings, site visits, or phone calls

VIII. Schedule Controller generates **Management Schedule Report** (Exhibit 7.12) weekly on Friday, which includes a list of all Active clients, On-hold clients, and outstanding Engagement Letters. This report shows:

A. Name of client

B. Principal and Project Manager(s) assigned to client

C. Target Dates

D. General comments about assignment status

IX. Management Schedule Report is reviewed weekly on Monday during Staff meeting.

A. New Target Dates and other assignment information revealed during management meeting are reviewed and noted as appropriate.

X. After the weekly Staff meeting, CPC updates Client Database for each assigned client with new information and target dates (Schedule Controller updates unassigned clients).

7.3.4 Inventory of Client Information

Note: All client/prospect information is to be stored in the appropriate folder on the server. Local computer hard drives are not available.

    I. CPC sets up client in Document Control System (or other tracking system) as part of Client Setup Checklist.

    II. DCP records items requested on the initial VIR in the Document Control System, including:

        A. Description of item requested

        B. Date requested

    III. On a frequent basis, DCP enters items received in the Document Control System, including:

        A. Section and Type of document

        B. Date received

        C. Year of information (ex: 2010 Interim Financial Statements)

        D. Description of information if different from Type

        E. Location of document in binder (if more than one binder or section)

    IV. On a frequent basis, DCP notifies primary Project Manager and Principal that information has been received.

    V. DCP files document in Client Binder, or gives document to Project Manager (per Project Manager's verbal or written request).

    VI. DCP prints updated **Document Control System Report** (Exhibit 7.13) each time new information is received or requested.

        A. DCP files updated Document Control System Report in the front of the client's Administrative binder.

7.3.5 Analysis

Note: All client/prospect information is to be stored in the appropriate folder on the server. Local computer hard drives are not available. Project Manager will not copy previous exhibits. If Project Manager requires a template from a previous exhibit to use on the current client, Project Manager can submit a request to the CPC for template creation by completing the New Client Exhibit Request form.

    I. Project Manager requests Analysis File from CPC by completing a **New Client Exhibit Request** (Exhibit 7.14).

        A. If a standard template is requested, the finished template is due in four hours.

        B. If a new template (from previous exhibits) is requested, the finished template is due in the amount of time specified by Project Manager (typically one to two days). Once a new template is created, a copy of that new template is maintained for use in the future. Future requests for that same template would be considered standard template requests.

    II. CPC creates new Exhibit File in Client folder in computer from Analysis Template. Analyses are conducted within this Exhibit File.

    III. Project Manager enters/processes financial and operational information for assignment in accordance with **Work Program Checklist** (see Chapter 8, Checklist 8.37).

    IV. Information entered in Exhibit File is verified by nonprimary Project Manager or staff by completing **Math Review Checklist** (Exhibit 7.15). The nonprimary Project Manager or staff is assigned by Principal.

    A. Each number in Exhibit File is verified against the source document.

    B. Calculations are manually recomputed for confirmation.

    C. Information that populates other exhibits is verified.

    D. Individual who verifies information initials and dates the **Internal Report Sign-off Sheet** (Exhibit 7.16) for the Math Review task.

Note: No staff member is to initiate contact with the client except at the direction of the Project Manager.

  V. During the analysis, the Project Manager may require additional information. This may be obtained through:

    A. Management Interviews

      1. Operations (see Chapter 8, Checklist 8.13)

      2. Financial (see Chapter 8, Checklist 8.14)

    B. Site Visit (using Management Interview checklists)

    C. Emails

      1. Email correspondence by ANY staff member can be printed by that staff member and filed into the Client's file. This includes both emails to and from the staff member. Items can be printed and filed AS THEY ARE RECEIVED AND/OR SENT and not accumulated to be printed at a later date.

        a. Any email that is a request for information from the Client MUST BE COPIED TO THE DOCUMENT CONTROL PERSONNEL (DCP). The email may be blind copied at the Project Manager's request.

          1. After receiving a copied email that is a request for information, the DCP will enter the request in the Document Control System for tracking.

          2. The Project Manager is still responsible for copying and filing the email.

      2. Once an email is printed and filed, it can be deleted from electronic storage. Electronic retention of email communications is not allowed—systems can be periodically reviewed during the regularly scheduled review.

    D. Faxes or Letters

      1. Written correspondence created by ANY staff member to a client can be copied and filed into the client's folder.

      2. If an electronic copy of the correspondence is retained, it can be saved into the appropriate Client folder on the server.

      3. If the correspondence is sent using a form of mail that creates a tracking record, the tracking slip can be filed in the client's folder.

      4. Support Staff notifies Project Manager that task is complete.

    E. Verbal Communication

      1. The staff member at the direction of the Project Manager (support, Project Manager, or Principal) having the verbal exchange with the client can document pertinent information from the conversation on a blue Contact Sheet. If it is determined that a new Client Contact exists, Project Manager will notify CPC by indicating same in area provided on Contact Sheet.

      2. The Contact Sheet is then given to the CPC by the Project Manager for inclusion into the Client Database, Conflict Tracking Database, and Outlook Address List. Contact sheets may be accumulated by the Project Manager; however, they must be delivered to the CPC frequently.

3. Blue Contact Sheet is placed in client binder by CPC.

VI. CPC prints new **Contact Information Summary** (Exhibit 7.17) after each update and places it in the front of the client's Administrative binder.

VII. Requests for information are given to DCP for entry into Document Control System.

A. Support Staff mails original request to client.

1. Project Manager may send request for information directly to client.
2. Project Manager can copy or blind copy ALL Email Information Requests to DCP.

B. DCP can file copy of Information Request in appropriate client binder.

VIII. Principal, Project Manager, CPC, and DCP review weekly (during the Staff Meeting) the status of the assignment, including any new target dates.

7.3.6 Report Setup

Note: All client/prospect information is to be stored in the appropriate folder on the server. Local computer hard drives are not available. Project Manager may not copy previous reports. If Project Manager requires a template from a previous report to use on the current client, Project Manager can submit a request to the CPC for template creation by completing the New Client Report Request form.

I. Project Manager can request Report framework from CPC by completing a **New Client Report Request** (Exhibit 7.18).

A. If a standard template is requested, the finished template is due in four hours.

B. If a new template (from previous report) is requested, the finished template is due in the amount of time specified by Project Manager (typically one to two days). Once a new template is created, a copy of that new template can be maintained for use in the future. Future requests for that same template would be considered standard template requests.

II. CPC creates new Report Framework in Client folder in computer from Report Template.

A. This report framework includes information obtained from the Engagement Letter, such as Company name(s) and Date(s) of value.

B. If known, CPC includes general and economic industry information in Appendices of report framework.

III. CPC carefully edits and proofs Report template using **Word Processing Checklist** (Exhibit 7.19).

IV. CPC initials and dates Initial Report Format task on Internal Report Sign-off Sheet.

V. Report is delivered to Project Manager by CPC.

7.3.7 Report to Project Manager

Note: All client/prospect information is to be stored in the appropriate folder on the server. Local computer hard drives are not available. Project Manager will not copy from previous reports. If Project Manager would like to use information from a previous report, Project Manager will print the appropriate section from the previous report's PDF file and submit to CPC with clear handwritten notes. CPC will incorporate the information into the appropriate section of the client's report and return both original and notes to Project Manager for review.

    I. Project Manager conducts analysis.

    II. Principal, Project Manager, and CPC review weekly (during the Management Meeting) the status of the assignment, including any new target dates.

    III. Project Manager and Principal track workflow via **SSVS VS Section 100 Compliance Checklist—Valuation Engagement** (see Chapter 8, Checklist 8.38). As each milestone is completed, Project Manager and Principal initial and date the checklist.

    IV. Project Manager completes Report with supporting Exhibits, consulting with Principal as needed.

Note: From this point on, unless otherwise indicated, *Report* will refer to the complete hard copy of the report, including exhibits and appendices.

In order to eliminate the possibility of Project Managers and reviewers editing multiple copies of the same report, hard-copy editing can take place from this point on. The CPC will be responsible for maintaining the status of the report during the Edit and Review Process. The following steps are necessary to ensure that the Edit and Review Process is properly sequenced.

    V. Project Manager gives Report and Internal Report Sign-off Sheet to CPC for hard-copy editing process. Once this process is begun, Project Manager may no longer make changes to the electronic report files or exhibits.

        A. CPC locks electronic files so they cannot be changed.

        B. If Project Manager needs to make further changes to electronic report, Project Manager will notify CPC.

            1. CPC will unlock electronic files for the duration of the editing.

            2. After being notified by the Project Manager that said editing is complete, CPC will relock file.

    VI. CPC prints Report.

    VII. Project Manager completes **SSVS VS Section 100 Compliance Checklist— Detailed Report (Valuation Engagement)** (see Chapter 8, Checklist 8.39), editing hard-copy report as necessary.

        A. Project Manager submits changes and edits to CPC.

        B. CPC makes changes and edits as indicated by Project Manager.

        C. CPC reprints Report.

        D. Edited Report and clean Report are returned to Project Manager by CPC.

        E. Project Manager reviews changes and edits for accuracy and completion.

        F. In the event that additional edits are necessary, Project Manager will submit changes and edits to CPC and continue with step VII. A.

    VIII. Once all changes and edits are completed, Project Manager initials and dates Internal Report Sign-off Sheet for SSVS VS Section 100 Compliance Checklist—Valuation Engagement.

    IX. Project Manager returns Report to CPC.

7.3.8 Report to Final Review

Note: All client/prospect information is to be stored in the appropriate folder on the server. Local computer hard drives are not available. CPC is responsible for monitoring report throughout the review process.

   I. Before Final Review, CPC performs the following tasks:
     A. Checks format and spelling of text and exhibits of electronic Report.
     B. Assigns unique report number (if final report).
     C. Prints clean Report (if necessary).
     D. Prints **Cover Page for Report** (Exhibit 7.20) using template on plain paper with assigned report number in footer.
   II. CPC delivers Report to Final Reviewer.
  III. Final Reviewer checks hard-copy Report for elements listed on **Final Review Checklist** (Exhibit 7.21), including:
     A. Number footing
     B. Totals from exhibits agree with report text
     C. Grammar and spelling accuracy
     D. Formatting and Word Processing Checklist items
     E. Readability and flow
  IV. If analytical changes are required, Final Reviewer meets with Project Manager to review.
   V. Final Reviewer submits changes and edits to CPC.
     A. CPC completes changes and edits, including Exhibits and Appendices.
     B. CPC returns report to Final Reviewer.
     C. Final Reviewer reviews report.
     D. In the event that additional changes and/or edits are deemed necessary by Final Reviewer, Final Reviewer will submit changes to CPC. The process will Continue with step V. A.
  VI. Final Reviewer initials and dates Internal Report Sign-off Sheet for Final Review.
 VII. Report is delivered to Principal for Review by CPC.

7.3.9 Report to Principals

Note: All client/prospect information is to be stored in the appropriate folder on the server. Local computer hard drives are not available.

   I. Principal tracks workflow via **SSVS VS Section 100 Compliance Checklist—Valuation Engagement** (see Chapter 8, Checklist 8.38). As each milestone is completed, Principal initials and dates the checklist.
   II. Principal verifies assumptions in hard-copy Report with supporting documents in Client binders.
  III. Principal reviews assumptions in hard-copy Report to ensure compliance with appropriate standards.
  IV. Principal edits and proofs hard-copy Report.
     A. If corrections need to be made:
       1. Principal meets with Project Manager.
       2. Project Manager revises Exhibits and Report to ensure accuracy.
       3. Changes on hard-copy Report are conveyed to CPC by Principal or Project Manager.
       4. CPC makes changes and edits.
       5. Project Manager or Principal verifies that edits and changes are correct.
         a. In the event that additional edits and/or changes are necessary, Project Manager or Principal will convey said changes to CPC. The process will continue with step IV.

  6. Project Manager or Principal returns report to CPC.

  7. Report is sent back to Final Review (see Report to Final Review).

 B. If Report is accurate:

  1. Principal initials and dates Internal Report Sign-off Sheet as Approved by Principal.

V. Report is delivered to CPC by Principal or Project Manager.

VI. CPC delivers report to alternate Principal for Cold Review, if applicable or requested.

7.3.10 Cold (Concept) Review

Note: All client/prospect information is to be stored in the appropriate folder on the server. Local computer hard drives are not available. All references made to Principal in the following section refer to the alternate Principal listed in Section 7.3.9 Report to Principals.

 I. Principal reviews assumptions in hard-copy Report to ensure compliance with appropriate standards.

 II. Principal reviews:

  A. Text flow

  B. Methodologies

  C. Discounts

  D. Conclusions

  E. Other subjective areas of analysis or assumptions

 III. Principal edits and proofs hard-copy Report.

  A. If corrections need to be made:

   1. Principal meets with Project Manager.

   2. Project Manager revises Exhibits and Report to ensure accuracy.

   3. Changes on hard-copy Report are conveyed to CPC by Cold Reviewer or Project Manager.

   4. CPC makes changes and edits.

   5. Project Manager or Cold Reviewer verifies that edits and changes are correct.

    a. In the event that additional edits and/or changes are necessary, Project Manager or Cold Reviewer will submit said changes to CPC. The process will continue with step 4.

   6. Project Manager or Cold Reviewer returns report to CPC.

   7. Report is sent back to Final Review (see Report to Final Review).

  B. If Report is accurate:

   1. Principal initials and dates Internal Report Sign-off Sheet as Cold Review—Principal.

 IV. Report is delivered to CPC by Principal or Project Manager.

7.3.11 Issue Report to Client[1]

Note: All client/prospect information is to be stored in the appropriate folder on the server. Local computer hard drives are not available.

---

[1] These procedures depend on each firm's Draft and Report Retention policies, and, if appropriate and applicable, jurisdictional rules.

I. CPC reviews Internal Report Sign-off Sheet for completion. Each item is initialed and dated prior to issuance of Report.

II. If items on Internal Report Sign-off Sheet are not initialed and dated:
   A. CPC verbally notifies Principal and Project Manager.
   B. Report is returned to Project Manager or Principal for completion of Sign-off Sheet item(s).

III. If all items on Internal Report Sign-off Sheet are initialed and dated:
   A. CPC finalizes Internal Report Checklist, including:
      1. Names to whom report was (is to be) sent (individuals, entities, corporations)
      2. Copy of Transmittal Letter

IV. CPC creates **Report Cover Letter** from template (Exhibit 7.22).

V. If a Preliminary written report is to be issued to the client or attorney:
   A. CPC prints report with Draft.
   B. CPC sends copy of Draft report to client and confirms receipt.
   C. CPC retains copy of Draft report in client's electronic folder.
   D. If Draft report is returned:
      1. Report is sent back to Project Manager (see Report to Project Manager).

VI. If a Final Report is to be issued to the client or attorney:
   A. CPC prints electronic copy of report for client as indicated on Internal Report Checklist.
   B. CPC sends copy of report to client and confirms receipt.
   C. CPC retains one copy of bound report in client's binder and in client's electronic file.
   D. CPC stores one copy of report in the appropriate Report Collection drawer.

7.3.12 Early Termination of Assignment

Note: Client/prospect information is to be stored in the appropriate folder on the server. Local computer hard drives are not available. Regardless of reason for early termination of assignment, no work product is released to the client. All work product is proprietary to OUR COMPANY NAME. Only that information provided by the client is returned to the client.

I. Termination by client
   A. Client indicates end of assignment via letter or verbal notification (from attorney) that case has settled.
   B. Principal notifies staff to stop all work on assignment and authorizes final bill.
   C. Accounts Payable prepares final bill.
      1. If final bill exceeds retainer received, invoice is created for client.
      2. If retainer exceeds final bill, Accounts Payable submits a request to Administration for refund check to be sent to client.
   D. Accounts Payable sends final bill/refund check to responsible party.
   E. Principal reviews client file. As appropriate:
      1. Client's documents are returned to sender.
      2. Client files (work product) are archived.

II. Termination by COMPANY
   A. During management meeting, Principal indicates client is to be notified of termination.

   B. Principal notifies staff to stop all work on assignment and authorizes final bill.
   C. Accounts Receivable prepares final bill.
      1. If final bill exceeds retainer received, invoice is created for client.
      2. If retainer exceeds final bill, Accounts Receivable submits a request to Administration for refund check to be sent to client.
   D. CPC sends **Early Termination Letter** (Exhibit 7.23) to client with final bill/refund check.
   E. Principal will review file and authorize collection or write-off of any outstanding balance.
   F. If at any time Principal determines assignment is to continue, Principal:
      1. Ensures account is current.
      2. Assesses need for a revised R&E Letter and additional retainer.

7.3.13 End of Assignment/Archive Client

Note: All client/prospect information is to be stored in the appropriate folder on the server. Local computer hard drives are not available.
   I. If litigation client, maintain client's active status.
   II. CPC prints one copy of Report and Exhibits to PDF format.
      A. CPC places PDF report and exhibits in server file.
   III. CPC moves Client folder on server to INACTIVE CLIENTS folder.
      A. Use same naming structure as that used in the CLIENTS folder.
   IV. Inactive Client files will be maintained in the Inactive Clients folder for one quarter.
      A. During the third week of the quarter, Inactive Client folders from the previous quarter will be copied onto a CD-ROM by the CPC (two copies).
      B. CPC deletes the Inactive Client files from the computer.
   V. CPC stores one CD-ROM in Client Archive file.
   VI. Administration stores one CD-ROM in off-site storage location.
   VII. CPC archives hard-copy documents.

EXHIBIT 7.1   Contact Information Sheet

Client or Contact: _____

Date of Contact: _____

In Reference To: _____

Contacted By: _____

If new contact, complete this information and give sheet to Support Staff

Name: _____ Title: _____

Company: _____

Address: _____

City, State, Zip: _____

Telephone: _____ Fax: _____

Email: _____

Additional Comments: _____

_____

_____

_____

_____

SUPPORT STAFF USE (DATE AND INITIAL WHERE INDICATED)

Date/Time Received: _____/_____ Response to Principal: _____/_____

Purpose:

Consulting   Corporate Planning   Financial Reporting   Tax   Lit   M&A   Int'l

Type:

Public Company	Private Company	
____ ASC 805	____ ESOP	____ Shareholder Dispute
____ Arbitration/Arbitrator	____ Estate Tax	____ S Corp Election
____ Broker Services	____ Financial Reporting Other	____ Stock Purchase
____ Business Valuation	____ Gift Tax	____ Transfer Pricing
____ Buy/Sell	____ Intellectual Property	
____ Charity Contribution	____ International	
____ Commercial Damages	____ IRS	
____ Consulting	____ Lost Profits	
____ Corporate Planning	____ Merger/Acquisition	
____ Derivatives	____ Offering Memo	
____ Divorce	____ Other _____	
____ Eminent Domain	____ Purchase Price Analysis	
____ ESBP	____ Rebuttal	

SIC/Market _____
Industry _____

Entered:
PCL # _____
C/I _____
Outlook _____
Mailing List _____
Archive _____

EXHIBIT 7.2 Relationship Review Checklist Instructions

Instructions:

1. Email relationship information to all offices.
2. Follow up with phone call those who do not respond to email. Note: Only one response per office is required.
3. Indicate if relationship exists, and if so, reason for relationship.
4. Attach this form to Contact Information Sheet.

Office Contact Information:

Office Location	Contact Name	Response		Relationship	
		Email	Phone	Yes	No
Phone #	Email Address				
Office Location	Contact Name	Response		Relationship	
		Email	Phone	Yes	No
Phone #	Email Address				
Office Location	Contact Name	Response		Relationship	
		Email	Phone	Yes	No
Phone #	Email Address				
Office Location	Contact Name	Response		Relationship	
		Email	Phone	Yes	No
Phone #	Email Address				

Reason for Relationship:

_____

_____

_____

_____

EXHIBIT 7.3 Engagement Declination Letter

Date

Name
Firm
Address
City, State ZIP

Re: Matter

Dear Name:

I am returning the information you sent in connection with the above matter. Regrettably, we have a business conflict that precludes our involvement.

Sincerely,

PRINCIPAL
TITLE

Enclosures

EXHIBIT 7.4   Lead and Project Information Sheet

Items in Bold are required

LEAD	Lead Date: _____
Contact Name: _____	F/U Date: _____
Firm/Title: _____	F/U Date: _____
Lead Name: _____	_____
Address: _____	**Bus. Unit:** _____
_____	**Principal:** _____
Phone: _____	Analyst: _____
Email: _____	DOV: _____
Notes: _____	
(attach call log) _____	

Entered:
- PCL # _____
- C/I _____
- Outlook _____
- Mailing List _____
- Archive _____

Purpose   Consulting   Corp. Plan   Fin. Reporting   Tax   Lit   M&A   Int'l

ENGAGEMENT	PROJECT NAME: _____

ENGAGEMENT LETTER ADDRESSEE: **EL DATES:**

Name/Title: _____	EL SENT: _____
Firm: _____	EL F/U Sent: _____
Address: _____	EL Received: _____
_____	EL Signed: _____
Phone: _____	**Retainer Amt:** _____
Email _____	Retainer Rcvd: _____

BILLING CONTACT (IF DIFFERENT FROM EL ADDRESSEE):

BILLING:

Name/Title: _____	Actual ____ Fixed ____
Firm: _____	Est. or Cap Amt: $ ____
Address: _____	Retainer: $ ____
_____	Draft: $ ____
Phone: _____	Final: $ ____
Email _____	____

EXHIBIT 7.5   Marketing Letter

Date

Contact
Company
Address1
Address2
City, State ZIP

Dear CONTACT:

I enjoyed speaking with you [**TODAY**]. I trust you received my email and have reviewed our website. Enclosed as you requested is our marketing packet, including:

- My Curriculum Vitae
- Firm brochures describing our services
- Information on our recent publications

Briefly, [OURCOMPANY] is a business valuation and consulting firm that in [twenty] years has provided valuation services for hundreds of clients. Our corporate clients have come in all sizes from small companies to large, closely held and public companies exceeding one billion dollars in revenues. Our firm has been retained to provide independent valuation opinions for many purposes. Among them are:

1. Appraisals for financial reporting, which include the valuation of intangible assets such as customer lists, technology, and depositor relationships.
2. Intellectual property appraisals, including trademarks, copyrights, and patents.
3. Litigation support testimony, including dissenting minority shareholder cases, corporate disputes, and marital dissolution.
4. Estate and other tax-related matters, including gifting, family limited partnerships, and other tax purposes.
5. Mergers, acquisitions, and other forms of corporate sales and reorganizations.

Our fees are based on our standard staff rates, which are $300 to $400 per hour for principals, $150 to $300 per hour for technical analysts, and $75 to $150 per hour for paraprofessionals. The fee usually averages around $200 per hour.

(continues)

Please call if you have any questions. I look forward to receiving the requested information and speaking with you further.

Sincerely,

PRINCIPAL, DESIGNATIONS
TITLE

Enclosures

EXHIBIT 7.6   Lead Schedule

Company	Contact	Purpose	Principal	Initial Contact	Marketing Sent	Follow-up Sent
Company	Contact Name	Shareholder Dispute	Initial	01/01/X0	1/15/X0	
Company	Contact Name	Divorce	Initial	12/13/X9	1/01/X0	01/15/X0
Company	Contact Name	Estate Tax	Initial	01/15/X0	1/25/X0	
Company	Contact Name	Business Val.	Initial	12/01/X9	12/18/X9	1/10/X0
Company	Contact Name	Litigation	Initial	01/01/X0	1/15/X0	
Company	Contact Name	Fin. Reporting	Initial	01/01/X0	1/15/X0	01/31/X0

EXHIBIT 7.7   Lead Follow-Up Letter Date

Date

Client
Company
Address1
Address2
City, State ZIP

RE:

Dear CLIENT,

On DATE, we spoke about the possible need for our services in connection with the above-referenced matter. I realize these matters take time to develop and hope your strategy is proceeding smoothly. Please keep me informed if you think our services will be needed and feel free to call if you have any questions.

I appreciate your consideration and hope to hear from you soon.

Sincerely,

PRINCIPAL, DESIGNATIONS.
TITLE

EXHIBIT 7.8 Representation and Engagement Letter Cover Letter Date

Date

Name
Company
Address
City, State ZIP

Re:

Dear CONTACT;

It was a pleasure talking with you DAY and I look forward to working with you. Enclosed as you requested are:

- Representation and Engagement Letter
- Retainer invoice for $XX,000

If you decide to retain me, please read and sign both copies of the Representation and Engagement Letter, returning one copy to OURCOMPANYNAME. Additionally, please send as soon as possible the following items so we can begin our analysis:

- Federal and State Corporate Income Tax Returns for the last five years
- Financial (audited or reviewed) statements for the last five years
- Corporate Charter, Articles of Incorporation, and/or Bylaws

As the assignment progresses, additional information will be necessary. We will send a tailored Valuation Information Request (VIR) for those items at that time.

If you have any questions, please give me a call.

Sincerely,

PRINCIPAL
TITLE

Enclosures

EXHIBIT 7.9   Engagement Letter Schedule

Company		Purpose		Retainer
Company		Shareholder Dispute		$10,000
Contact		**Contact Phone**		**Comments**
Contact Name		123-456-7890		Court Appointed, Joint Hire
Principal	**Initial Contact**	**R & E Letter Sent**		**Follow-up Sent**
Initials	1/01/X0	1/25/X0		02/15/X0

Company		Purpose		Retainer
Company		Business Valuation		$10,000
Contact		**Contact Phone**		**Comments**
Contact Name		123-456-7890		Multiple companies
Principal	**Initial Contact**	**R & E Letter Sent**		**Follow-up Sent**
Initials	1/15/X0	2/01/X0		

Company		Purpose		Retainer
Company		Financial Reporting		$5,000
Contact		**Contact Phone**		**Comments**
Contact Name		123-456-7890		Impairment Testing
Principal	**Initial Contact**	**R & E Letter Sent**		**Follow-up Sent**
Initials	12/22/X0	1/10/X0		1/28/X0

EXHIBIT 7.10 Representation and Engagement Letter Follow-Up Letter

Date

Client
Company
Address1
Address2
City, State ZIP

RE:

Dear CLIENT:

On DATE we sent you a Representation and Engagement Letter in connection with the above matter. As we have not received the signed Representation and Engagement Letter, we need to know if the case is still active and if our services will be needed.

If we can be of any assistance or if you have any questions, please feel free to call.

Sincerely,

PRINCIPAL
TITLE

EXHIBIT 7.11 New Client Set-up Checklist

PROJECT:_____

Initial each step when complete:

_____ INFORMATION TRACKING (Add/Update):
    ____ Time and Billing software Client #: _____ Project #: _____
    ____ Project Tracking database   Tracking #: _____
    ____ Relationship database
    ____ Mailing list
    ____ Outlook
    ____ Copier code

_____ ELECTRONIC FILE:
    ____ Set up folders in F:/CLIENT/ACTIVE
       - Analysis
       - Billing and Engagement
       - Correspondence
       - Report
       - Data from Client
    ____ Move prior correspondence to appropriate folder

_____ BINDER TO ANALYST (Includes the following):
    ____ Copy of signed Representation and Engagement Letter
    ____ Information received from Client
    ____ Checklists
       - Internal Report Signoff sheet
       - Math Review checklist
       - Developmental Review checklist
       - Prospective Financial Information checklist
       - Report Compliance/USPAP checklist
       - Management Interview—Financial
       - Management Interview—Operations
       - Report Request
       - Exhibit Request

_____ ENGAGEMENT FILE/FRONT OFFICE (Includes the following):
    ____ Original Representation and Engagement Letter
    ____ Billing folder
    ____ New Project checklist

EXHIBIT 7.12 Management Schedule Report

Client/Project	Next Critical Date	Traced	Math	Development (Analyst)	PFI	Development (Principal)	Report Compliance	Draft Review	Final Review	Critical Action
Project	01/30/X0									
Project	02/02/X0									
Project	02/02/X0	x	x							
Project	02/02/X0									
Project	02/02/X0	x	x							
Project	02/02/X0									
Project		x	x	x	x	x	x	x		
Project		x	x	x	x	x	x	x		Need EL Amend

EXHIBIT 7.13   Document Control System Report

Document Inventory for:

zzzzsample

Year	Type	Date of Document	Description	Binder
ADMINISTRATIVE				
	ENGAGEMENT LETTER	6/1/20X0		1
	INFORMATION REQUEST			1
FINANCIAL INFORMATION				
20X0	FINANCIAL PROJECTIONS			3
20X9	INTERIM STATEMENTS		CURRENT AND PRIOR YEAR	3
20X9	TAX RETURN			3
OPERATIONS				
	FRANCHISE AGREEMENTS			2
20X0	PERMITS		LAND USE PERMIT	2
FACILITIES				
	FIXED ASSET APPRAISALS			2
PERSONNEL/BENEFITS				
	PAYROLL/SALARIES		PAST TWO YEARS	2
STOCK				
	STOCK LEDGER		CURRENT	2
LEGAL				
0	AFFIDAVITS			1
	DEPOSITIONS			1
0	NOTICES, SUBPOENAS, PETITIONS, AFFIDAVITS			1
OPPOSITION EXPERTS				
	REPORT			3
NONRELEVANT INFORMATION				
				4

EXHIBIT 7.14 New Client Exhibit Request

In order to control workflow, it is necessary that the Analyst request client files be set up by the Support Staff. All requests for new files from templates must be submitted on this form.

This form is to be given directly to Support Staff. Do not place on desk or in tray.

Name of Client: _____

Note: Typical turnaround time for standard templates is two to four hours.

STANDARD TEMPLATES	MODIFICATIONS TO TEMPLATE	
_____ 1-Year Analysis	_____ Black-Scholes	_____ QM Discount
_____ 2-Year Analysis	_____ Blockage Discount	_____ RMA
_____ 3-Year Analysis	_____ Discount Rate Summary	_____ Software
_____ 4-Year Analysis	_____ Double Black-Scholes	_____ Tax
_____ 5-Year Analysis	_____ Growth Rate	_____ Voting Premium Analysis
	_____ Lifing	_____ Debt-free Working Capital
_____ CPR Only	_____ Options	_____ Working Capital

NEW TEMPLATE (Note: Turnaround time for new templates is one to two days)

Please create a new template from previous client   _____

Requested by: _____   Date: _____

Needed by: _____

SUPPORT STAFF USE (DATE AND INITIAL WHERE INDICATED)
Date/Time Received: _____/_____   Completed: _____/_____
Analyst Notified: _____/_____

Retain this form on file until Final Report has been issued to client.

EXHIBIT 7.15   Math Review Checklist

Subject Interest _____

Analyst in Charge _____

Principal in Charge_____

Purpose of the Math Review Checklist is to ensure/document that financial input (all Exhibits) have been independently traced, recomputed/verified. A traced, paper copy should be retained in the front of the binder.

> **STANDARD TICK MARKS:**
> ✓   Checked/traced to source document (including prior report)
> ¢   Checked for internal consistency within report
> v   Verified math (multiplication/division correct)
> Ø   Totaled/footed (addition/subtraction correct)
> e   Name/title/dates agree to Eng. Letter (SALC; Representations)
>
> ___   _____
>
> ___   _____

Tracer   Date

Second Principal Consultation/Review

___ ___ 1. Cold review completed by independent principal (can occur any time during the engagement)

Review 1: Financial Statement Analysis

___ ___ 2. Trace input (Exhibits 1–10) to source documents (financial statements and/or tax returns)

___ ___ 3. Verify internal consistency of numbers (Depreciation Expense on Cash Flow equals Operating Expense Detail) (Exhibits 1–10)

___ ___ 4. Trace RMA industry data to source document

___ ___ 5. Manually recompute randomly selected ratios, including growth rates (Exhibits 1–10)

___ ___ 6. Manually foot/total all columns; check for rounding errors

___ ___ 7. Verify internal consistency of ratios (e.g., ROE on Exhibit 6 equals ROE on Exhibit 10)

Review 2A: Asset-based Approach (Econ Balance Sheet)

___ ___ 8. Trace interim balances to source documents

___ ___ 9. Recompute randomly selected ratios; foot/total all columns

___ ___ 10. Trace asset value adjustments to appraisal/source documents in file; determine if tax liability adjustment from gain on sale is necessary

___ ___ 11. Trace information to Summary Valuation Exhibit

___ ___ 12. Trace relevant amount(s) to narrative section(s) of engagement report

Review 2B: Market Approach—Guideline Public Companies Method

__ __ 13. Verify accuracy of input (trace financial spreads to source)

__ __ 14. Trace information to Summary Valuation Exhibit

__ __ 15. Trace multiples to report; review report explanations to be sure they are supported by the work in the Exhibits

__ __ 16. Trace Appendix Guideline Public Company disclosures to source documents

Review 2C: Market Approach—External Transactions Method

__ __ 17. Trace market comps to the source documents

__ __ 18. Recompute financial ratios and final pricing multiples; foot/total all columns

__ __ 19. Trace information to Summary Valuation Exhibit

__ __ 20. Trace multiples to report; review report explanations to be sure they are supported by the work in the Exhibits

Review 2D: Income Approach

__ __ 21. Trace rate build-up components to source documents

__ __ 22. Trace and recompute ongoing earnings base and/or projections

__ __ 23. Trace and recompute all WACC components (debt/equity rate components)

__ __ 24. Trace info to Summary Schedule for conclusion of value

Review 2E: Allocation of Intangible Assets

__ __ 25. Complete Intangible Asset Checklist

Review 3: Conclusion Issues

__ __ 26. Recompute final valuation amount; agree to exhibit; first and last page of report; report valuation/calculation summary page, etc.

__ __ 27. Agree weighting of different valuation approaches from Valuation Summary Exhibit to written report

EXHIBIT 7.16   Internal Report Sign-Off Sheet

Draft _____   Final _____

CLIENT: _____

EL RECEIVED: _____   RETAINER RECEIVED: _____

REPORT DUE: _____   REPORT LOCATION: _____

Initial and date as each step is completed

	DRAFT	FINAL
Initial Report Format	_____	_____
Math Review	_____	_____
Developmental Review Checklist (Analyst)	_____	_____
Developmental Review Checklist (Principal)	_____	_____
Prospective Financial Information Checklist	_____	_____
Report Compliance Checklist	_____	_____
Cold Review	_____	_____
Verify Billing Current (Fixed or Actual)	_____	_____
Document Inventory Review	_____	_____
Approved by Principal for Final Edit	_____	_____
Final Edit	_____	_____
Approved by Principal to Client	_____	_____
Bound Copy Review	_____	_____
Report Signed	_____	_____
Billing to Client (if applicable)	_____	_____
Report Sent to Client	_____	_____
Update Databases	_____	_____
No. of Copies or Electronic (pdf)	_____	_____
Report Tracking No.	_____	_____

Copies Sent To: _____

_____

_____

EXHIBIT 7.17   Contact Information Summary

PLAINTIFF		DEFENDANT	
Atty:	_____	**Atty:**	_____
Company	_____	Company	_____
Address	_____	Address	_____
Tel/Email	_____	Tel/Email	_____
Plaintiff:	_____	**Defendant:**	_____
Company	_____	Company	_____
Address	_____	Address	_____
Tel/Email	_____	Tel/Email	_____
Experts:	_____	**Experts:**	_____
Company	_____	Company	_____
Address	_____	Address	_____
Tel/Email	_____	Tel/Email	_____
Experts:	_____	**Experts:**	_____
Company	_____	Company	_____
Address	_____	Address	_____
Tel/Email	_____	Tel/Email	_____
Other Contacts:	_____	**Other Contacts:**	_____
Company	_____	Company	_____
Address	_____	Address	_____
Tel/Email	_____	Tel/Email	_____
Other Contacts:	_____	**Other Contacts:**	_____
Company	_____	Company	_____
Address	_____	Address	_____
Tel/Email	_____	Tel/Email	_____

**IF YOU HAVE UPDATED INFORMATION, COMPLETE A CONTACT SHEET
AND PLACE IN TOP TRAY OF CPC**

Which side are we working for, or for which side were we contacted?   P   D

EXHIBIT 7.18   New Client Report Request

In order to control workflow, it is necessary that the Analyst request client files be set up by Support Staff. All requests for new files from templates must be submitted on this form.

Name of Client: _____

STANDARD TEMPLATES (Note: Turnaround time for standard templates is 2–4 hours)

___ Blockage Discount   ___ Multicompanies   ___ ASC 805 Business Combination
___ Calculation   ___ Multi-Dates   ___ Impairment Testing
___ Fractional Interest   ___ Offering Memorandum   ___ Short
___ FRCP 26   ___ Patent   ___ Standard
___ Restricted Appraisal   ___ Practice   ___ Stock Option
___ Mediation Fair Value   ___ Preliminary Value Letter   ___ Supplemental Analysis Letter
___ Mediation Fair Market Value

ADDITIONAL NARRATIVE TEMPLATES

___ Adjusted Net Worth   ___ Intangibles
___ Asset Valuation   ___ Option Valuation
___ Black-Scholes Narrative   ___ Practice Goodwill
___ Black-Scholes with Graph   ___ Qualification Language
___ Estimation of Blockage Discount   ___ S Corp Considerations
___ Hypothetical Appraisal Blurb   ___ S Corp Language
___ Income Approach

APPENDICES

Standard: *Additional:*
___ Assumptions and Limiting Conditions   ___ Controlling Interest
___ Analyst's Representations   ___ Minority Interest/Lack of Control
___ Economic Outlook   ___ Lack of Marketability/Studies
   Year _____, Qtr _____   ___ Voting Premium
   Short _____ Long _____ Graphs _____ ___ S Corp Issues
___ Industry Review   ___ Key Person
___ SIC _____ NAICS _____   ___ REITS
___ CV   ___ Guideline Companies

NEW TEMPLATE (Note: Turnaround time for new templates is one to two days)
___ Please create a new template from previous client _____

Requested by: _____   Date: _____
                                         Needed by: _____

SUPPORT STAFF USE (DATE AND INITIAL WHERE INDICATED)
Date/Time Received: _____/_____   Completed: _____/_____
Analyst Notified: _____/_____

Retain this form on file until Final Report has been issued to client.

EXHIBIT 7.19 Word Processing Checklist

CLIENT _____

WORD PROCESSOR _____

DATE _____

✓	N/A	ITEM
—	—	Copy appropriate template as indicated on New Client Report Request Form and save in Client Report folder.
—	—	Copy appropriate template as indicated on New Client Exhibit Request Form and save in Client Analysis folder.
—	—	Copy Cover Page for Report template and save in Client Report folder.
—	—	Insert in Cover Page (from Representation and Engagement Letter unless otherwise stated).
—	—	___ Client Name—Spelled and punctuated exactly as shown on Company Articles of Incorporation, if available, or other Company Document (see Client at top of this checklist).
		___ Date of Valuation: _____
		___ Purpose of Valuation: _____
		Assigned report tracking number.
—	—	Insert in Report (from Representation and Engagement Letter unless otherwise stated).
—	—	___ Client Name—Spelled and punctuated exactly as shown on Company Articles of Incorporation, if available, or other Company Document (see Client at top of this checklist).
		___ Client Name consistent throughout report.
		___ Name and Title—Spelled and punctuated exactly as shown on R&E: _____
		___ Date of Valuation—Consistent throughout report: _____
		___ Purpose of Valuation—Consistent with EL: _____
		___ Name and Title of Principal
—	—	Update Table of Contents:
		___ Text Titles and Page Numbers
		___ Exhibits—Numbers and Names
		___ Appendices—Letters and Titles
—	—	Insert in Appraisal Summary of Report:
		___ Standard of Value—correct: _____
		___ Basis of Value—correct: _____
		___ Premise of Value—correct: _____
—	—	Insert Appendix A—Statement of Contingent and Limiting Conditions—Same as Client R&E.
		Insert Appendix B—Representations.
		___ Single or Plural
		___ Company Name
		___ Assisted by name and title
		___ Compliance statement (single or plural)

✓	N/A	ITEM
—	—	Insert Other Appendices as indicated on New Client Report Request form:

    __ Economic Outlook Period:_____

    __ Industry Review

    __ Discount for Lack of Marketability

    __ Discount for Control

    __ Control Premium

    __ Voting Premium

    __ Other: _____

    __ Other: _____

    __ Other: _____

—   —   Include Industry Section with source information.

—   —   Text agrees with Exhibit Name and Number.

—   —   Text agrees with SIC/NAICS Number in Exhibits: _____

—   —   SIC/NAICS Description for this Client is the same in text and exhibit.

—   —   Agree Value Indications, Text to Exhibits:

    __ Asset Approach

    __ Market Approach

    __ Income Approach

    __ Value Conclusion

—   —   Exhibits:

    __ Verbiage for every footnote

    __ Percentage exhibits verbiage agrees with dollar exhibits verbiage line by line.

    __ Company, Partnership, or Member terminology is consistent throughout.

    __ Source Dates at bottom agree with Top Dates.

    __ Correct Exhibit numbers on Summary Exhibit.

—   —   Appendix A—Statement of Contingent and Limiting Conditions—Same as Client R&E.

—   —   Appendix B—Representations

    __ Single or Plural

    __ Company Name

    __ Assisted by name and title

    __ Compliance statement (single or plural)

—   —   Appendices for, if necessary:

    __ Economic Outlook Period: _____

    __ Industry Review

    __ Discount for Lack of Marketability

    __ Discount for Control

    __ Control Premium

    __ Voting Premium

    __ Other

(continues)

✓	N/A	ITEM

— — Appendix Conclusion agrees with Exhibit in
    __ Discount for Lack of Marketability: _____%
    __ Discount for Control: _____%
    __ Control Premium: _____%
    __ Voting Premium: _____%
    __ Other

— — Read report for content and flow of information.

— — Discuss changes with Project Manager.

— — Review requested changes.

— — Internal Report Sign-Off Form
    __ Initial at Final Approval

— — Update Exhibits:
    __ Insert additional Exhibit pages as requested on New Client Exhibit Request.
    __ Client Name—Spelled and punctuated exactly as shown on Company Articles of Incorporation, if available, or other Company Document (see Client at top of this checklist).
    __ Date of Valuation: _____
    __ Percentage exhibits verbiage agrees with dollar exhibits verbiage line by line.
    __ Company, Partnership, or Member terminology is consistent throughout.
    __ Check Margins
    __ Review Spacing
    __ Consecutive Page Numbers (if Litigation, number Exhibits)
    __ Consistent Style and Font ($, %, Underline)

— — Spell Check
    __ Internal Report Sign-Off Form
    __ Initial at Initial Format

EXHIBIT 7.20   Cover Page for Report

FAIR MARKET VALUE
OF
COMPANY NAME
AS OF
VALUATION DATE

T-XXX-09-1###

EXHIBIT 7.21   Final Review Checklist

CLIENT _____

REVIEWER _____

REVIEW DATE_____

REPORT TYPE _____

✓	N/A	ITEM
___	___	Initials on Internal Report Sign-Off Form

    ___ Math Review
    ___ Developmental Review, Analyst #1
    ___ Developmental Review, Principal, if necessary
    ___ Report Compliance
    ___ Approved by Principal to Final Edit

___ ___ Initials on Math Review Checklist
    ___ Traced to client documents and RMA
    ___ RMA data have transferred correctly to Exhibits
    ___ Check all formulas; add all columns
    ___ Correct amounts (dollars and percents) and dates flow from Exhibit to Exhibit

___ ___ Engagement Letter
    ___ Client Name—Spelled and punctuated exactly as shown on Company Articles of Incorporation, if available, or other Company Document (see Client at top of this checklist)
    ___ Client Name consistent throughout report and exhibits
    ___ Name and Title—Spelled and punctuated exactly as shown on R&E: _____
    ___ If signed R&E Letter shows a different name and title, an addendum to the R&E needs to be sent.
    ___ Date of Valuation—Consistent throughout report and exhibits:

    _____
    ___ If signed R&E shows a different date, an addendum to the R&E needs to be sent.
    ___ Purpose of Valuation—Consistent with EL: _____
    ___ If signed R&E shows a different purpose, an addendum to the R&E needs to be sent.

___ ___ Check for accuracy the signature(s) and title at bottom of Report Letter: _____

___ ___ Value Conclusion—Same in: _____
    ___ Report Letter (1st or 2nd page)
    ___ Appraisal Summary
    ___ Valuation Summary of Text
    ___ Summary Exhibit

___ ___ Table of Contents:
    ___ Text Titles and Page Numbers
    ___ Exhibits—Numbers and Names
    ___ Appendices—Letters and Titles

✓	N/A	ITEM

   —   —   Appraisal Summary
                 — Standard of Value—correct: _____
                 — Basis of Value—correct: _____
                 — Premise of Value—correct: _____
   —   —   For Text, Exhibits, and Appendices:
                 — Check Margins
                 — Review Spacing
                 — Consecutive Page Numbers (if Litigation, number Exhibits)
                 — Consistent Style and Font ($, %, Underline)
                 — Spell Check
   —   —   Include Industry Section with source information
   —   —   Text agrees with Exhibit Name and Number
   —   —   Text agrees with SIC/NAICS Number in Exhibits: _____
   —   —   SIC/NAICS Description for this Client is the same in text and exhibit
   —   —   Agree Value Indications, Text to Exhibits:
                 — Asset Approach
                 — Market Approach
                 — Income Approach
                 — Value Conclusion
   —   —   Exhibits:
                 — Verbiage for every footnote
                 — Percentage exhibits verbiage agrees with dollar exhibits verbiage line by line
                 — Company, Partnership, or Member terminology is consistent throughout
                 — Source Dates at bottom agree with Top Dates
                 — Correct Exhibit Numbers on Summary Exhibit
   —   —   Appendix A—Statement of Contingent and Limiting Conditions—Same as Client R&E
   —   —   Appendix B—Representations
                 — Single or Plural
                 — Company Name
                 — Assisted by name and title
                 — Compliance statement (single or plural)
   —   —   Appendices for, if necessary:
                 — Economic Outlook Period: _____
                 — Industry Review
                 — Discount for Lack of Marketability
                 — Discount for Control
                 — Control Premium
                 — Voting Premium
                 — Other
   —   —   Appendix Conclusion agrees with Exhibit in
                 — Discount for Lack of Marketability: _____%
                 — Discount for Control: _____%
                 — Control Premium: _____%
                 — Voting Premium: _____%
                 — Other

(continues)

✓	N/A	ITEM
—	—	Read report for content and flow of information
—	—	Discuss changes with Project Manager
—	—	Review requested changes
—	—	Internal Report Sign-Off Form
		__ Initial at Final Approval

EXHIBIT 7.22   Report Cover Letter Date

Date

Client Name
Firm/Company
Address
City, State ZIP

Dear CLIENT,

Enclosed is/are a copy/copies of the draft/final valuation report of the fair market
value of _____. A copy of the report has
been forwarded to NAME. Please note, in order to comply with appropriate standards and
case law, draft reports will be retained by OURCOMPANYNAME in the client file.

I look forward to receiving your comments so we can finalize the report. All draft reports
must be returned to this office in their entirety before the final report will be issued. If you
have any questions, please call.

Sincerely,

Principal, Designations
Title

Enclosure(s)

EXHIBIT 7.23   Early Termination Letter Date

Date

Client Name
Company
Address
City, State ZIP

Re: NAME OF ENGAGEMENT/CASE INFORMATION (FROM ENGAGEMENT
   LETTER)

Dear CLIENT:

To date, we have sent numerous billings in connection with the above matter. The only
payment we have received is the retainer of $X,XXX on DATE. Due to the sensitive
nature of the assignment, I have proceeded on good faith without further payments.
The balance due as of DATEDUE was $X,XXX. To bring the billing current, enclosed
is the invoice, in summary and detail, for work performed through DATEEND.
The balance due is now $X,XXX.

Pursuant to the Representation and Engagement Letter dated ENGDATE, FEE, AND
BILLING, I am exercising paragraph 9, which reads:

   9. OURCOMPANYNAME reserves the right to withdraw from or stop work on this
      engagement if fees have not been paid as agreed.

Please expedite full payment immediately so that work may resume.

Sincerely,

PRINCIPAL
TITLE

Checklists

Chapter 8 presents the checklists that can be used by analysts to run a valuation process. Not all analysts use checklists. However, for those who do, these checklists should be very helpful.

CHECKLIST 8.1: BUSINESS VALUATION OR REAL ESTATE APPRAISAL?

This checklist helps determine which discipline—business valuation or real estate appraisal—is the pertinent discipline when valuing an entity.

YES	NO	*Is the entity:*
☐	☐	A commercial, industrial, or service organization pursuing an economic activity?
☐	☐	An equity interest (such as a security in a corporation or partnership interest)?
☐	☐	A fractional interest, minority interest (i.e., less than 100 percent of the entity)?
☐	☐	Difficult to split up (perhaps because the owners do not have a direct claim on the assets)?

YES	NO	*Does the entity:*
☐	☐	Derive its revenues from providing goods or services?
☐	☐	Primarily use assets such as machinery, equipment, employee skill and talent in providing goods or services?
☐	☐	Depend on assets other than or in addition to real estate to generate earnings?
☐	☐	Conduct an economic activity that is more important than the location of the real estate where the economic activity is being conducted?
☐	☐	Likely have a value that fluctuates with conditions in its industry (as opposed to fluctuations in the real estate market)?

YES	NO	*Does the entity have:*
☐	☐	Intangible assets such as patents, trademarks, copyrights, franchises, licenses, customer lists, employment contracts, noncompete covenants, and goodwill that the entity uses to generate earnings?
☐	☐	Substantial assets that can be moved?
☐	☐	A variety of tangible and intangible assets that interact to produce economic activity?
☐	☐	Significant operating expenses such as marketing, advertising, research, and transportation?
☐	☐	Substantial labor expenses?
☐	☐	Management that substantially adds to the profit of the company?

Yes answers in the majority—Business Valuation
No answers in the majority—Real Estate Appraisal
Mix of yes and no answers—May need both disciplines

CHECKLIST 8.2:   KEY INFORMATION REQUIREMENTS

Financial

❑ Historical and prospective financial information on:
  ❑ Turnover
  ❑ Contribution
  ❑ Marketing
  ❑ Manufacturing/production
  ❑ R&D/marketing/capital expenditure
❑ Unusual, nonrecurring events
❑ Accounting principles and methods
❑ Contingent assets/liabilities
❑ Details of acquisition of assets
❑ Licensing arrangements
❑ Serious offers received for the asset

Market Characteristics

❑ Product/service awareness:
  ❑ Spontaneous
  ❑ Prompted
❑ Market share/position
❑ Consumer loyalty
❑ Image/esteem
❑ Geographical coverage
❑ Extension potential (products, markets, channels)
❑ Product history and life cycle
❑ Buyer purchase criteria
❑ Marketing mix
❑ Demographics

Industry Structure
❑ Structure of industry ❑ Nature of competition ❑ Barriers to entry ❑ Availability of substitutes ❑ Bargaining leverage of buyers ❑ Availability of supply ❑ Distribution arrangements ❑ Major industry trends ❑ Social, political, regulatory, environmental, and economic factors

Legal

❑ Registered or statutory rights
  ❑ Categories of goods or services
  ❑ Jurisdictions
  ❑ Pending applications
❑ Common law or similar rights (including assessment of legal protection)
❑ Duration of property rights
❑ Details of licensing arrangements
❑ Legal matters outstanding (e.g., infringements)

CHECKLIST 8.3: INDUSTRY RESEARCH FORM

Industry Name: _____

_____

Industry SIC CODE: _____ NAICS CODE: _____

Trade Associations in This Industry: _____

_____

Key Words, Industry Terms, Jargon: _____

_____

Leading Public Companies in This Industry:

_____

_____

_____ Checked 10-K for industry discussion

_____ Checked for analyst reports

_____

Trade Publications in This Industry:

_____

_____

_____ Checked periodical databases for relevant articles

_____ Checked publications by industry analysts (First Research, Standard & Poor's, etc.)

_____

CHECKLIST 8.4: IRS BV GUIDELINES CHECKLIST, INTERNAL REVENUE SERVICE, ENGINEERING PROGRAM, BUSINESS VALUATION GUIDELINES 4.48.4

Business Name		Subject Interest	
Valuation Date		Valuation Purpose	
Standard of Value		Premise of Value	
Analyst (sign and date)		Manager (sign and date)	
Principal (sign and date)			

Answering the following questions will help determine whether the development and reporting of a business valuation complies with IRS Business Valuation Guidelines. Preceding each section of questions is a reference to the section or page of the IRS BV Guidelines from which the question is drawn.

All "No" or "N/A" answers should be individually explained in the space provided on the last page of this checklist.

Yes	No	N/A	
			Purpose
❑	❑	❑	1. Is the Valuator aware of the [then] new IRM 4.48.4, Engineering Program, Business Valuation Guidelines dated July 1, 2006?
			Background
❑	❑	❑	1. Is the Valuator aware that this material is the product of the Valuation Policy Council (VPC), a cross-functional committee with executive representation from LMSB, SBSE, and Appeals?
❑	❑	❑	2. Is the Valuator aware that the VPC was established in 2001 to assist IRS leadership in setting direction for valuation policy that cuts across functional lines, and in identifying process improvements to improve compliance and better use resources?
			Nature of Materials
❑	❑	❑	1. Is the Valuator aware that this IRM provides specific guidelines for the following:
❑	❑	❑	Developing the valuation issue?
❑	❑	❑	Resolving the issue when possible?
❑	❑	❑	Preparing reports?
❑	❑	❑	2. Is the Valuator aware that this document provides specific instructions to examiners with respect to the following:
❑	❑	❑	Planning the valuation assignment?
❑	❑	❑	Analyzing relevant information?
❑	❑	❑	Preparing workpapers?
❑	❑	❑	Reviewing a third-party valuation?
			Effect on Other Documents
❑	❑	❑	1. Is the Valuator aware that this document has no effect on other documents?

(continues)

Yes	No	N/A	
			Audience
❏	❏	❏	1. Is the Valuator aware that the intended audience for this document is all IRS employees who provide valuation services or review the valuations and appraisals prepared by others?
			Introduction 4.48.4.1
❏	❏	❏	1. Is the Valuator aware that the purpose of this document is to provide guidelines applicable to all IRS personnel engaged in valuation practice (hereinafter referred to as "Valuators") relating to the development, resolution, and reporting of issues involving business valuations and similar valuation issues?
❏	❏	❏	2. If the Valuator departed from these guidelines, are they able to reasonably justify that departure?
❏	❏	❏	3. Is the Valuator aware that this document incorporates, by reference, the ethical and conduct provisions contained in the Office of Government Ethics (OGE) Standards of Ethical Conduct, applicable to all IRS employees?
❏	❏	❏	4. Is the Valuator aware that valuations of assets owned and/or transferred by or between controlled taxpayers (within the meaning of Treasury Regulation section 1.482-1[i][5]) may present substantive issues that are not addressed in these guidelines?
			Development Guidelines, 4.48.4.2
❏	❏	❏	1. Did the Valuator successfully complete a valuation assignment by including the following:
❏	❏	❏	Planning?
❏	❏	❏	Identifying critical factors?
❏	❏	❏	Documenting specific information?
❏	❏	❏	Analyzing the relevant information?
❏	❏	❏	Are all relevant activities documented in the workpapers?
❏	❏	❏	2. Was a review appraisal the best approach to the assignment?
			Development Guidelines, 4.48.4.2.1 Planning
❏	❏	❏	1. Did the Valuator adequately plan the valuation assignment?
❏	❏	❏	2. Did the Valuator's managers supervise the staff involved in the valuation process?
❏	❏	❏	3. Is the Valuator aware that quality planning is a continual process throughout the valuation assignment?
			Development Guidelines, 4.48.4.2.2 Identifying
❏	❏	❏	1. In developing a valuation conclusion, the Valuator should define the assignment and determine the scope of work necessary by identifying the following:
❏	❏	❏	Property to be valued?
❏	❏	❏	Interest to be valued?
❏	❏	❏	Effective valuation date?
❏	❏	❏	Purpose of valuation?
❏	❏	❏	Use of valuation?
❏	❏	❏	Statement of value?
❏	❏	❏	Standard and definition of value?
❏	❏	❏	Assumptions?
❏	❏	❏	Limiting conditions?
❏	❏	❏	Scope limitations?
❏	❏	❏	Restrictions, agreements, and other factors that may influence value?
❏	❏	❏	Sources of information?

Yes	No	N/A	
			Development Guidelines, 4.48.4.2.3 Analyzing
❏	❏	❏	1. In developing a valuation conclusion, the Valuator should analyze the relevant information necessary to accomplish the assignment, including:
❏	❏	❏	The nature of the business and the history of the enterprise from its inception?
❏	❏	❏	The economic outlook in general and the condition and outlook of the specific industry in particular?
❏	❏	❏	The book value of the stock or interest and the financial condition of the business?
❏	❏	❏	The earning capacity of the company?
❏	❏	❏	The dividend-paying capacity?
❏	❏	❏	Existence or nonexistence of goodwill or other intangible value?
❏	❏	❏	Sales of the stock or interest and the size of the block of stock to be valued?
❏	❏	❏	The market price of stocks or interests of corporations or entities engaged in the same or a similar line of business having their stocks or interests actively traded in a free and open market, either on an exchange or over-the-counter?
❏	❏	❏	Other relevant information?
❏	❏	❏	2. Did the Valuator give consideration to all of the three generally accepted valuation approaches, which are the asset-based approach, the market approach, and the income approach?
❏	❏	❏	3. Did the Valuator use professional judgment to select the approach(es) ultimately used and the method(s) within such approach(es) that best indicate the value of the business interest?
❏	❏	❏	4. Did the Valuator analyze and, if necessary, adjust historical financial statements to reflect the appropriate asset value, income, cash flows, and/or benefit stream, as applicable, to be consistent with the valuation methodologies selected by the valuator?
❏	❏	❏	5. Did the Valuator select the appropriate benefit stream, such as pre-tax or after-tax income and/or cash flows, and select appropriate discount rates, capitalization rates, or multiples consistent with the benefit stream selected within the relevant valuation methodology?
❏	❏	❏	6. Did the Valuator determine an appropriate discount and/or capitalization rate after taking into consideration all relevant factors such as:
❏	❏	❏	The nature of the business?
❏	❏	❏	The risk involved?
❏	❏	❏	The stability or irregularity of earnings?
❏	❏	❏	Other relevant factors?
❏	❏	❏	7. As appropriate for the assignment, and if not considered in the process of determining and weighing the indications of value provided by other procedures, the Valuator should separately consider the following factors in reaching a final conclusion of value:
❏	❏	❏	Marketability, or lack thereof, considering the nature of the business, business ownership interest or security, the effect of relevant contractual and legal restrictions, and the condition of the markets?
❏	❏	❏	Ability of the appraised interest to control the operation, sale, or liquidation of the relevant business?
❏	❏	❏	Other levels of value considerations (consistent with the standard of value in Section 4.48.4.2.2 [1] list item g), such as the impact of strategic or synergistic contributions to value?
❏	❏	❏	Such other factors which, in the opinion of the Valuator, are appropriate for consideration?

(continues)

Yes No N/A

			Development Guidelines, 4.48.4.2.4 Workpapers
			1. The workpapers should:
❏	❏	❏	Document the steps taken?
❏	❏	❏	Document the techniques used?
❏	❏	❏	Provide the evidence to support the facts and conclusions in the final report?
❏	❏	❏	2. Did the Valuator maintain a detailed case activity record (Form 9984, Examining Officer's Activity Record) that:
❏	❏	❏	Identifies actions taken and indicates time charged?
❏	❏	❏	Identifies contacts, including name, phone number, subject, commitments, and so on?
❏	❏	❏	Documents delays in the examination?
❏	❏	❏	3. The case activity record, along with the supporting workpapers, should justify that the time spent is commensurate with work performed?

			Development Guidelines, 4.48.4.2.5 Reviewing
❏	❏	❏	1. In reviewing a business valuation and reporting the results of that review, did the Valuator form an opinion as to the adequacy and appropriateness of the report being reviewed?
❏	❏	❏	2. Did the Valuator clearly disclose the scope of work of the review process undertaken?
❏	❏	❏	3. In reviewing a business valuation, did the Valuator do the following: Identify the:
❏	❏	❏	Taxpayer?
❏	❏	❏	Intended use of the Valuator's opinions and conclusions?
❏	❏	❏	The purpose of the review assignment?
❏	❏	❏	The report under review?
❏	❏	❏	The property interest being valued?
❏	❏	❏	The effective date of the valuation?
❏	❏	❏	The effective date of the review?
❏	❏	❏	Scope of the review process conducted?
❏	❏	❏	Determine the completeness of the report under review?
❏	❏	❏	Determine the apparent adequacy and relevance of the data and the propriety of any adjustments to the data?
❏	❏	❏	Determine the appropriateness of the valuation methods and techniques used and develop the reasons for any disagreement?
❏	❏	❏	Determine whether the analyses, opinions, and conclusions in the report under review are appropriate and reasonable, and develop the reasons for any disagreement?
❏	❏	❏	4. In the event of a disagreement with the report's factual representations, underlying assumptions, methodology, or conclusions, did the Valuator conduct additional fact-finding, research, and/or analyses necessary to arrive at an appropriate value for the property?

			Resolution Guidelines 4.48.4.3
❏	❏	❏	1. Did the Valuator make efforts to obtain a resolution of the case after fully considering all relevant facts?

			Resolution Guidelines, Objective 4.48.4.3.1
❏	❏	❏	1. Is the Valuator aware that the objective is to resolve the issue as early in the examination as possible?
❏	❏	❏	2. Did the Valuator perform credible and compelling work that will facilitate resolution of issues without litigation?
❏	❏	❏	3. Did the Valuator work in concert with the internal customer and taxpayer to attempt to resolve all outstanding issues?

Yes	No	N/A	

Resolution Guidelines, Arriving at Conclusions 4.48.4.3.2

❏ ❏ ❏   1. Once the Valuator has all the information to be considered in resolving the issue, did the Valuator use their professional judgment in considering this information to arrive at a conclusion?

❏ ❏ ❏   2. If the Valuator did not have all of the information that they would have liked to have to definitively resolve the issue, which may happen, did the Valuator decide when they had substantially enough information to make a proper determination?

❏ ❏ ❏   3. Did the Valuator employ independent and objective judgment in reaching conclusions and decide all matters on their merits, free from bias, advocacy, and conflicts of interest?

Reporting Guidelines, 4.48.4.4

❏ ❏ ❏   1. Did the Valuator prepare reports of their findings?

❏ ❏ ❏   2. Is the Valuator aware that this section requires specific information to be included or addressed in each report?

Reporting Guidelines, Overview 4.48.4.4.1

❏ ❏ ❏   1. Did the Valuator meet the primary objective of a valuation report, which is to provide convincing and compelling support for the conclusions reached?

❏ ❏ ❏   2. Did the valuation report contain all the information necessary to allow a clear understanding of the valuation analyses?

❏ ❏ ❏   3. Did the valuation report demonstrate how the conclusions were reached?

Reporting Guidelines, Report Contents 4.48.4.4.2

❏ ❏ ❏   1. Is the Valuator aware that the extent and content of the report prepared depends on the needs of each case?

❏ ❏ ❏   2. Did the valuation report clearly communicate the results and identify the information relied on in the valuation process?

❏ ❏ ❏   3. Did the valuation report effectively communicate the methodology and reasoning, as well as identify the supporting documentation?

❏ ❏ ❏   4. Subject to the type of report being written, did the valuation reports generally contain sufficient information relating to the items in Identifying and Analyzing to ensure consistency and quality?

❏ ❏ ❏   5. If the report was written with respect to Reviewing, did the report contain, at a minimum, information relating to those items in Identifying and Analyzing necessary to support the revised assumptions, analyses, and/or conclusions of the Valuator?

Reporting Guidelines, Statement 4.48.4.4.3

❏ ❏ ❏   1. The written valuation report should contain a signed statement that is similar in content to the following:

❏ ❏ ❏   To the best of my knowledge and belief:

❏ ❏ ❏   The statements of fact contained in this report are true and correct.

❏ ❏ ❏   The reported analyses, opinions, and conclusions are limited only by the reported assumptions and limiting conditions.

❏ ❏ ❏   I have no present or prospective interest in the property that is the subject of this report, and I have no personal interest with respect to the parties involved with this assignment.

❏ ❏ ❏   I have no bias with respect to the subject of this report or to the parties involved with this assignment.

❏ ❏ ❏   My compensation is not contingent on an action or event resulting from the analyses, opinions, or conclusions in, or the use of, this report.

❏ ❏ ❏   My analyses, opinions, and conclusions were developed, and this report has been prepared in conformity with the applicable Internal Revenue Service Valuation Guidelines.
Explain any "No" or "N/A" answers on the next page.

Explanation of "No" or "N/A" Answers	
Item #	Explanation
_____	_____
_____	_____
_____	_____
_____	_____
_____	_____
_____	_____
_____	_____
_____	_____
_____	_____
_____	_____
_____	_____
_____	_____

CHECKLIST 8.5:   VALUATION INFORMATION REQUEST (VIR) GENERAL

Business Name	Valuation Date

This is a generalized information request. Some items may not pertain to your company, and some items may not be readily available to you. In such cases, indicate N/A or notify us if other arrangements can be made to obtain the data. Items already provided are indicated.

Provided	N/A	
		Financial Information
❏	❏	1. Financial statements for fiscal years ending FIVE YEARS (order of preference: audited, reviewed, compiled, and internal).
❏	❏	2. Interim financial statements for the month-end DATE OF VALUATION and one year prior.
❏	❏	3. Financial projections, if any, for the current year and the next three years. Include any prepared budgets and/or business plans.
❏	❏	4. Federal and State Corporate Income Tax Returns and supporting schedules for fiscal years ending FIVE YEARS.
❏	❏	5. Explanation of significant nonrecurring and/or nonoperating items appearing on the financial statements in any fiscal year if not detailed in footnotes.
❏	❏	6. Accounts payable aging schedule or summary as of DATE OF VALUATION.
❏	❏	7. Accounts receivable aging schedule or summary and management's general evaluation of quality and credit risk as of DATE OF VALUATION.
❏	❏	8. Restatement of inventories and cost of goods sold on a FIFO basis for each of the past five fiscal years if LIFO accounting is used for inventory reporting purposes.
❏	❏	9. Fixed asset and depreciation schedule as of DATE OF VALUATION.
❏	❏	10. Amortization schedules of mortgages and notes payable; and terms of bank notes, credit lines, and/or debt agreements as of DATE OF VALUATION.
❏	❏	11. Current financial statements for any ESOP, profit-sharing, pension, or other employee benefit trust at DATE OF VALUATION.
❏	❏	12. Current level of over- (under-)funding for any defined benefit plan at DATE OF VALUATION.
❏	❏	13. Description of any compensation, salaries, dividends, or distributions received by persons not active in the operations of the business, including the year and respective compensation.
❏	❏	14. Estimated total revenue, gross profit, and net income for the current fiscal year.
❏	❏	15. Explanation of fluctuations, growth, or decline in revenue of the business during the past five years.
❏	❏	16. Explanation of expected failure of the business to meet this year's budget based on the year-to-date financial data, if applicable.
❏	❏	17. Description of any anticipated significant rate increases in the cost of labor or materials.
❏	❏	18. Estimate of revenues, gross profits, and earnings before interest and tax (EBIT) for the next five years if revenue growth, gross margins, or net margins are expected to be significantly different as compared to the past five years.
❏	❏	19. Explanation of expected changes in the amount of capital expenditures during the next five years if expectations differ from those incurred during the past five years, including the anticipated new levels of capital expenditures.

(continues)

Provided	N/A	

Financial Information (*continued*)

❏ ❏ 20. Average borrowing rate for the business and financial ratios that must be maintained to comply with lenders' credit terms.

❏ ❏ 21. Description of any assets with stated net book value on the balance sheet that differ significantly from the fair market value that could be realized if the business were liquidated (i.e., appreciated real estate, obsolete inventory, or equipment).

❏ ❏ 22. Description of any assets owned by the business that are not being used in the operations of the business (i.e., excess land, investments, excess cash, unused equipment, etc.).

Products and Markets

❏ ❏ 23. List of the major products, services, or product lines of the business and copies of marketing materials, including sales brochures, catalogs, or other descriptive sales materials.

❏ ❏ 24. Sales and profit contributions analysis by product, product line, service category, customer, subsidiary, and/or location (whichever is applicable).

❏ ❏ 25. Unit volume analyses for existing product lines for the past five years.

❏ ❏ 26. Description of major products or services added in the last two years (or anticipated) and current expectations as to sales potential.

❏ ❏ 27. Description of the features, if any, that distinguish the business's products or services from the competition.

❏ ❏ 28. Causes for the cost of products and services supplied to your business to fluctuate, and list of alternative suppliers available at similar rates, if any.

❏ ❏ 29. Description of new products under development, with expectations as to potential.

❏ ❏ 30. List of the top 10 customers of the business, indicating sales (or sales on which commissions were earned) and unit volumes for each of the past three fiscal years if customers are consolidated.

❏ ❏ 31. Summary of major accounts gained (lost) in the last year, indicating actual sales in the current year and beyond.

❏ ❏ 32. List of major competitors (full name, location, size, and estimated market share of each).

❏ ❏ 33. List of trade association memberships and industry publications of interest to management.

❏ ❏ 34. Classification of the business's industry (SIC No. or NAICS No.).

❏ ❏ 35. Description of any significant business operations that have been discontinued in recent years or are expected to be discontinued in the future (i.e., sale of facility or business line, closed-out product line, etc.), including date of discontinuation and impact on revenues and profits.

❏ ❏ 36. Description of any significant business operations that have been added in recent years or are expected to be added in the near future (i.e., purchase of facility, business acquisition, introduction of new product line, etc.), including date of addition and financial impact.

❏ ❏ 37. List of the names of all principal suppliers accounting for over 10 percent of total purchases.

❏ ❏ 38. Summary of terms of any existing purchase agreements with principal suppliers.

❏ ❏ 39. Summary of importance of research and development to the success of the business.

❏ ❏ 40. Characteristics of customers (i.e., industries served, demographics).

❏ ❏ 41. Approximate number of customers that the business has and percentage that are repeat clientele.

Provided	N/A	
		Products and Markets (*continued*)
❏	❏	42. Approximate time the average customer has been purchasing from the business.
❏	❏	43. Description of customers that account for over 10 percent of annual revenue or gross profit of the business.
❏	❏	44. Summary of any contractual agreements with customers and/or distributors.
❏	❏	45. Description of any contracts or agreements with customers, suppliers, or distributors that would be nontransferable if the business were sold.
❏	❏	46. Number of clients that would discontinue relations with the business if the business were sold, including reason(s) and the estimated impact on revenues.
❏	❏	47. Summary of factors that stimulate demand for the business's products or services.
❏	❏	48. Description of seasonal or cyclical factors, if any.
❏	❏	49. Reason for increases or decreases of major competitors during the past five years, including their respective market share.
❏	❏	50. Approximate percentage of the market the subject business holds.
❏	❏	51. Description of level of difficulty to enter into the market or industry by potential competitors.
❏	❏	52. Description of the differences of the subject business from its competitors, including price, quality, strengths, and weaknesses.
❏	❏	53. List of any publicly held companies or subsidiaries known to operate in your industry.
❏	❏	54. Name, address, and phone number of contact at industry organization that assists with market data, if any.
		Operations
❏	❏	55. In a paragraph or so, complete this statement: "Our company is in the business of . . ."
❏	❏	56. Name and description of the operations of all major operating entities, whether divisions, subsidiaries, or departments.
❏	❏	57. List of the top 10 suppliers (or all accounting for 5 percent or more of total purchases) and the level of purchases in each of the past two years (include total purchases by the business in each year).
❏	❏	58. List of product(s) on which the business is single-sourced or suppliers on which the business is otherwise dependent.
❏	❏	59. Dividend policy, dividend history, and prospect for future dividends.
❏	❏	60. Copy of any existing employee stock ownership plan (ESOP).
❏	❏	61. Copies of all other stock option plans or option agreements, or any other plan providing vested benefits in business stock. Also list number of options granted and to whom, and the stated exercise price(s) and expiration date(s).
❏	❏	62. Basis for business contributions (contribution policy), contributions in each of the past five years, and projection for future contributions to the ESOP, pension plan, and/or profit-sharing plan.
❏	❏	63. The most recent projection of emerging ESOP repurchase liability. If no study has been done, list known ESOP liquidity requirements during the next three years (e.g., known retirements during period).
❏	❏	64. Description of any services performed for, or by, a related party or business, including services provided, dollar amounts, nonmonetary benefits, and if transactions are at market rates.

(continues)

Provided / N/A

		Facilities
❑	❑	65. Location, age, and approximate size of each facility. Provide or estimate business volume by major facility.
❑	❑	66. Ownership of each facility and other major fixed assets. If leased, include name of lessor and lease terms or agreements. If owned by the business, include: ▪ Date purchased; ▪ Purchase price; ▪ Recent appraisals; ▪ Insurance coverage; and ▪ Book values.
❑	❑	67. Estimated depreciation of all assets on a straight-line depreciation basis if accelerated depreciation is used for financial statement purposes.
❑	❑	68. Copies of any appraisals of real estate or personal property owned by the business.
❑	❑	69. Copies of any appraisals of any company-owned real property or personal property performed during the last three years.
❑	❑	70. Comparison of rates of leases to market rates if facilities are rented from a related party.
❑	❑	71. Description of the terms of the real estate lease, including date of expiration, anticipated lease rate changes, and whether it is renewable.
❑	❑	72. Estimate of the cost to relocate business operations, including lost profits from business interruption.
❑	❑	73. Percentage of total capacity (expressed as percentage of total revenue) of the current business operations.
❑	❑	74. Description of changes in total operating capacity during the past five years (i.e., physical expansion, technological improvement), including related expenditures.
❑	❑	75. Based on future expected growth, description of when additional facilities or expansion (if foreseeable) will be needed, including approximate cost.
❑	❑	76. Approximate current and historical backlog (in revenues) or waiting list (number of customers).
		Personnel
❑	❑	77. Current organization chart.
❑	❑	78. Number of employees (distinguish full-time and part-time) at year-end for the last six years, including current employee classifications, general wage scales, and approximate rate.
❑	❑	79. List of all union relationships, including name of union, date of current agreement, workers and facilities covered.
❑	❑	80. Number of part-time and full-time business-employed salespersons, including compensation arrangements or schedules. If there are none, describe how sales are obtained and by whom.
❑	❑	81. Description of the management team, including current title, age, length of service, background, annual salary, and bonus for the current year and each of the last two years.
❑	❑	82. Full names of the board of directors, including occupation of outside members.
❑	❑	83. Summary of employee turnover (i.e., below average, average, or above average) compared to your industry.
❑	❑	84. Adequacy of supply of labor.
❑	❑	85. Summary of employee compensation (i.e., below average, average, or above average) compared to your industry.
❑	❑	86. Description of any significant staffing changes or increases anticipated during the next three to five years.
❑	❑	87. Description of terms of any contracts with personnel, such as noncompete agreements or employment contracts.

Provided	N/A	
		Personnel (*continued*)
❑	❑	88. Description of significant adverse effect on the operating performance of the business due to the loss of a key employee or manager, including potential revenue losses.
❑	❑	89. Specify succession of management, if determined.
❑	❑	90. Description of staff members who would not be retained if the business were sold, including their respective current compensation and position with the business.
		Corporate Documents and Records
❑	❑	91. Corporate charter, articles of incorporation, and/or bylaws.
❑	❑	92. Minutes of board of directors and shareholders' meetings for the most recent three years (may be reviewed by us on-site).
❑	❑	93. Summary of major covenants or agreements binding on the business (e.g., union contracts, capital leases, employment contracts, service contracts, product warranties, etc.).
❑	❑	94. Description of any pending litigation, including parties involved, date of filing, description and nature of the lawsuit or claim, current status, expected outcome, and financial impact.
❑	❑	95. List of all subsidiary companies and the percentage ownership in each.
❑	❑	96. Name of any "related" companies (common ownership, common shareholders, etc.) and brief description of the relationship(s).
❑	❑	97. Stock ledger.
❑	❑	98. All closing statements and purchase agreements related to all purchases of the business's stock over the history of the business.
❑	❑	99. All closing statements and purchase agreements related to all mergers or acquisitions by the business up to the valuation date.
❑	❑	100. Copies of any appraisals of the stock or assets of the business made during the last three years.
❑	❑	101. State(s) and year of incorporation or registration.
❑	❑	102. Form of ownership (C corporation, S corporation, general partnership, limited partnership, sole proprietorship).
❑	❑	103. List of the largest ownership interests in the business, including name of owner, percentage of shares held and position with business or inactive in business, total shares authorized, total shares issued, and total shares outstanding.
❑	❑	104. Description of any unusual stock features (i.e., voting or nonvoting, preferred or convertible, class A and class B).
❑	❑	105. Description of any restrictions on the sale or transfer of ownership interests (buy-sell agreement, lettered stock option to buy, stock options, etc.).
❑	❑	106. Description of familial or other relationships among owners.
❑	❑	107. Description of sales or transfers of any ownership interests in the business in the past five years, including how the price or value was determined.
❑	❑	108. Description of any bona fide offers to purchase the business during the past five years.
❑	❑	109. Analysis of adequacy of the current business insurance.
❑	❑	110. Description of any subsidiaries, joint ventures, or investments of a material nature in other companies.

CHECKLIST 8.6:   VALUATION INFORMATION REQUEST (VIR) BANK/HOLDING COMPANY

Company Name	Valuation Date

This is a generalized information request. Some items may not pertain to your company, and some items may not be readily available to you. In such cases, indicate N/A or notify us if other arrangements can be made to obtain the data. Items already provided are indicated. If you have any questions on the development of this information, please call.

Provided   N/A

Financial Statements (Banks Only)

☐ ☐ 1. Financial statements for fiscal years ending FIVE YEARS (order of preference: audited, reviewed, compiled, and internal).

☐ ☐ 2. Federal and State Corporate Tax Returns (if not consolidated) for fiscal years ending FIVE YEARS at DATE OF VALUATION.

☐ ☐ 3. Call Reports (include all schedules) as of DATE OF VALUATION.

☐ ☐ 4. Uniform Bank Performance Reports as of DATE OF VALUATION.

☐ ☐ 5. Internally prepared financial statements. (Audits are sometimes presented in abbreviated form and with supplementary schedules. Please provide copies with supplementary schedules. Also, please provide copies of auditors' management letters for most recent two years.)

Financial Statements (Holding Company If Applicable)

☐ ☐ 1. Financial statements for fiscal years ending FIVE YEARS (order of preference: audited, reviewed, compiled, and internal).

☐ ☐ 2. Federal and State Corporate Tax Returns (if not consolidated) for fiscal years ending FIVE YEARS at DATE OF VALUATION.

☐ ☐ 3. Holding Company Form Y-9 filed with Federal Reserve as of DATE OF VALUATION.

☐ ☐ 4. Holding Company Performance Reports as of DATE OF VALUATION.

☐ ☐ 5. Internally prepared financial statements as of DATE OF VALUATION, including shareholder reports, 10-Ks and 10-Qs if they are prepared. Parent Company Only and Consolidated.

Employee Stock Ownership Plan/Trust (If Applicable)

☐ ☐ 1. DATE OF VALUATION Financial Statement (unaudited) or most recent if DATE OF VALUATION Statement not yet prepared.

☐ ☐ 2. Accountant's Report for DATE OF VALUATION.

☐ ☐ 3. If ESOP is leveraged, name lender, amount, and terms of debt.

Other Financial Documents

☐ ☐ 1. Bank budget as of DATE OF VALUATION.

☐ ☐ 2. Holding company budget as of DATE OF VALUATION.

☐ ☐ 3. Any multiyear projection or business plan available for the bank and/or the holding company.

☐ ☐ 4. If you are a "public reporting company" with the SEC or the FDIC, copies of all documents filed with the SEC or FDIC during YEAR OF VALUATION.

☐ ☐ 5. Copies of any offering materials prepared in conjunction with any offering of equity or debt securities during YEAR or PRIOR YEAR OF VALUATION.

☐ ☐ 6. Directors' examination reports.

☐ ☐ 7. Letters from outside auditors.

Provided	N/A	
		Corporate Documents and Records

❑ ❑ 1. Summary shareholder list (for the entity being valued) showing names and number of shares owned and detailing:
  ▪ Directors and officers;
  ▪ Employee stock ownership plan; and
  ▪ All other 5 percent (or more) shareholders by name. If a family controls more than 5 percent even though no individual does, please note this.

❑ ❑ 2. If there is a controlling group of shareholders, please provide:
  ▪ The complete list of shareholders with their holdings;
  ▪ Copy of any Voting Trust Agreement between the controlling parties;
  ▪ Copy of any restrictive legends applicable to the institution's shares; and
  ▪ Copy of documentation regarding any hybrid equity securities at either the bank or holding company level, including:
    ▪ Stock options;
    ▪ Warrants (to purchase shares); and
    ▪ Other convertible securities (convertible debentures, convertible preferred stock, etc.).

❑ ❑ 3. Board of directors' minutes: Provide copies of bank and/or holding company minutes during YEAR OF VALUATION, or
excerpts pertaining to discussions of these topics:
  ▪ Merger with or acquisition by another banking institution;
  ▪ Purchase or sale of branch facilities;
  ▪ Purchase, sale, or creation of nonbank subsidiaries;
  ▪ Response to report of regulatory examination;
  ▪ Declaration or payment of dividends or establishment of dividend policy;
  ▪ Plans to raise capital in any form, including the refinancing of capital notes or holding company debt;
  ▪ Plans to renovate existing facilities or to build new facilities;
  ▪ Discussions of or approval of any off-balance sheet hedging activities;
  ▪ Discussions of nonroutine charges to the allowance for loan losses or provisions to the allowance for loan losses; and
  ▪ Business planning or financial projections for YEAR OF VALUATION and beyond.

❑ ❑ 4. ESOP Documentation:
  ▪ Copy of ESOP document provisions related to repurchase of employee shares specifying obligation to repurchase, terms or repurchase, and other material factors;
  ▪ Specify ESOPs repurchase obligation and terms of repurchase;
  ▪ If the holding company has a repurchase option or obligation related to ESOP shares, please specify;
  ▪ Copy of any ESOP study of its repurchase liability. If there is no study, please list known liquidity requirements for next three years from anticipated retirements or other commitments to repurchase shares;
  ▪ Current ESOP contribution policy or basis for determining annual contributions;
  ▪ Provide estimated ESOP contribution for YEAR OF VALUATION, VALYEAR+1 and VALYEAR+2; and
  ▪ Accounting treatment of leveraged ESOP if not noted in financial statements.

❑ ❑ 5. Documentation of transactions on known stock transactions during the last year(s) in this form:
  ▪ Date;
  ▪ Purchaser;
  ▪ Seller;
  ▪ Price/Director/Explanatory; and
  ▪ Shares Offered Comments.

(continues)

Provided N/A

Banking Facilities

❑ ❑ 1. List of all banking branch facilities, indicating for each:
- Branch name/location;
- Actual (or approximate) deposit and loan volumes;
- Whether full service or specific limited services;
- Number of (FTE) employees at branch;
- Whether facility-owned or leased (if lease, from whom on what terms?);
- Approximate square footage of the facility;
- Book value of facility on institution's books; and
- Approximate fair market value of the facility.

❑ ❑ 2. If the bank is holding-improved or unimproved real estate for future expansion (or which is otherwise not presently occupied), provide:
- Description;
- Date acquired and acquisition cost; and
- Estimated (or appraised) current fair market value.

Other Assets

❑ ❑ 1. Current list of equity securities (including convertible and preferred stocks) owned by the bank or holding company as of the DATE OF VALUATION, including:
- Name of security;
- Original (or current carrying) cost; and
- Current market value.

❑ ❑ 2. List of all mutual fund investments owned, including:
- Name of fund(s);
- Original cost(s); and
- Current carrying cost and the amount of any equity allowance related to the mutual funds.

❑ ❑ 3. Bond portfolio printout summary page(s) detailing book value, market value, weighted average rate, and weighted average maturity by each major category of the bond portfolio:
- U.S. Government and Agencies;
- Tax-exempt securities; and
- Other securities.

❑ ❑ 4. Summarize the bank's present investment portfolio positioning strategy in a paragraph or so.

❑ ❑ 5. Any additional assets that may be considered temporary (debt repossessions) or not directly related to the bank's normal course of business.

Data Processing Facilities

❑ ❑ 1. Description of the current data processing system in use by the bank and discussion of its adequacy for the current level of operations.

❑ ❑ 2. If the system is an in-house system, when did the bank go on it?

❑ ❑ 3. If using a data center, list its name and the date use began.

❑ ❑   Are there currently any plans for changing data centers or purchasing an in-house system? If so, please discuss briefly.

Nonbank Subsidiaries of the Bank or Bank Holding Company, Whether Controlled or Not

❑ ❑ 1. Name and description of the business of any operating nonbank subsidiaries.

❑ ❑ 2. Year-end financials for the subsidiaries if not in audited statements or in consolidating financial statements.

Provided	**N/A**	

Trust Department Activities

❑	❑	1. Brief description of trust activities, including services rendered, number of employees, assets under management, revenues for last three years.
❑	❑	2. Summarize future plans for this department.

Liquidity and Asset/Attainability Management

❑	❑	1. State the bank's Liquidity Policy (or operating practice) in a paragraph or so in terms of objectives, target ratios, or other terms you use to track and monitor liquidity.
❑	❑	2. GAP (Asset/Liability Management) Policy.
❑	❑	3. State the bank's GAP Policy in a paragraph or so.
❑	❑	4. Who are the management and board members of ALCO Committee (or equivalent)?
❑	❑	5. If available, provide a recent printout from your asset/liability system or planning model providing: ▪ Projected balance sheets and income statements over projection horizon GAP reports; and ▪ A brief statement of the bank's positioning relative to its objectives.

Loan Portfolio Information—Determining the Adequacy of the Allowance for Loan Losses (i.e., the loan loss reserve)

❑	❑	1. Description of the method used and the frequency of the determination.
❑	❑	2. If a written report is developed, please provide a copy (or a summary of results) for the most recent determination.
❑	❑	3. Description of the system or process of loan review in use at the bank.

Lending Policy and Practice

❑	❑	4. List the major types of loans routinely made by type and describe typical pricing and maturities for each type.
❑	❑	5. Summarize (or provide a copy of the Loan Policy) the bank's: ▪ Stated lending limit authorities "effective Lending Limits in Practice Policy" for out-of-territory loans. ▪ Number and dollar volume of loans outside the bank's CRA (Community Reinvestment Act) territory, including any loan participations purchased.
❑	❑	6. What is the bank's legal lending limit? What is the in-house lending limit?

Lending Concentrations

❑	❑	7. List all loans at the lending limit. If credits to related borrowers constitute a concentration of 50 percent of the lending limit or more, include the relationship totals.
❑	❑	8. Does the bank have any known industry concentrations or exposures in its loan portfolio? If so, discuss briefly.

Regulation and Regulatory Compliance

❑	❑	1. Dates of the two most recent regulatory examinations by appropriate category.

	BANK BY STATE AGENCY	BANK BY FDIC (OCC IF NAT'L BANK)	HOLDING COMPANY BY FEDERAL RESERVE
Most Recent	_____	_____	_____
Next Most Recent	_____	_____	_____

(continues)

Provided

N/A

Regulation and Regulatory Compliance (*continued*)

☐ ☐ 2. Is the bank and/or the holding company operating under a formal, written agreement with any regulatory body? If so, provide:
- Agency;
- Data and Type of Agreement (Memorandum of Understanding, Cease and Desist, Other);
- Basic reasons for its issuance;
- General description of its requirements; and
- State of the institution's compliance with the order.

Management and the Directorate

☐ ☐ 1. Management compensation: for the top five officers of the bank and holding company:
- Name/title;
- Annual compensation, including bonuses, for VALYEAR and FOLLOWINGYEAR; and
- Beneficial stock ownership in bank or bank holding company.

☐ ☐ 2. Senior management (key officers of the bank or holding company):
- Name/title/age/years of service with bank;
- Current operating responsibilities;
- Prior jobs with bank;
- Prior banking experience;
- Other relevant experience;
- If bank carries life insurance on key executives, provide coverage amounts and annual premiums; and
- If executive is working under an employment agreement, please summarize its terms.

☐ ☐ 3. Board of directors: Please summarize this information for the bank/holding company:
- For bank: name/board title/age/board tenure in years/occupation;
- For holding company: name/board title/age/board tenure in years/occupation (for significant overlaps between bank and holding company, provide entire list and indicate for each individual whether bank, holding company, or both);
- Please name and describe membership and functions of major board committees; and
- How are outside board members compensated?

Background and History

☐ ☐ 1. For the bank:
- Date of formation and name(s) of principal founder(s);
- Type of charter;
- If applicable, approximate dates of acquisitions of other banks or branches since formation;
- Name changes, if any, since formation;
- If there is a current control group, the date this group obtained control;
- Other significant historical events; and
- If a written history exists, provide a copy.

☐ ☐ 2. For the holding company:
- Date of formation and name(s) of principal founder(s);
- Description of process of gaining control of the bank; and
- Date control acquired.

Competition and the Local Economy

☐ ☐ 1. List major competitors (bank, thrift, or credit union). If a market share study exists, provide a copy of the most recent study.

☐ ☐ 2. Include background information available on the economy of city/county/region (e.g., from Chamber of Commerce and local university economics departments).

CHECKLIST 8.7: VALUATION INFORMATION REQUEST (VIR) EMINENT DOMAIN

Business Name	Date of Damages

This is a generalized information request. Some items may not pertain to your company, and some items may not be readily available to you. In such cases, indicate N/A or notify us if other arrangements can be made to obtain the data. Items already provided are indicated. If you have any questions on the development of this information, please call.

Provided / N/A

Financial Information

❑ ❑ 1. Financial statements for fiscal years ending FIVE YEARS (order of preference: audited, reviewed, compiled, and internal).

❑ ❑ 2. Financial projections for the DAMAGE year and the next three years.

❑ ❑ 3. Federal and State Corporate Income Tax Returns and supporting schedules for fiscal years ending FIVE YEARS.

Products and Markets

❑ ❑ 4. Major product services or product lines of the Company.

❑ ❑ 5. Top 10 customers of the Company, indicating sales and unit volume for each of the past three fiscal years.

❑ ❑ 6. Major competitors (full name, location, size, and estimated market share of each).

❑ ❑ 7. Trade association memberships and brochures of the Company.

Operations

❑ ❑ 8. In a paragraph or so, please complete this statement: "The Company is in the business of . . ."

❑ ❑ 9. List the top 10 suppliers.

❑ ❑ 10. Dividend policy, dividend history, and prospects for future dividends.

❑ ❑ 11. Copies of any appraisals of the stock of the Company made during the last three years.

Facilities

❑ ❑ 12. Location, age, and approximate size of each facility.

❑ ❑ 13. Ownership of each facility and other major fixed assets. If leased, include name of lessor and lease terms or agreements.

❑ ❑ 14. Real estate appraisal, which should include a fair market value of price per square foot.

❑ ❑ 15. Copies of appraisals of any Company-owned real property or personal property performed during the last three years.

Personnel

❑ ❑ 16. Current organizational chart.

❑ ❑ 17. Number of employees (distinguish between full-time and part-time).

❑ ❑ 18. Description of the management team, including current title, age, length of company service, and background.

❑ ❑ 19. Full names of the board of directors.

Provided

N/A

		Corporate Documents and Records
❑	❑	20. Corporate charter, articles of incorporation, and/or bylaws.
❑	❑	21. Minutes of board of directors and shareholders' meetings for the most recent three years.
❑	❑	22. Stock ledger.
❑	❑	23. All closing statements and purchase agreements related to all purchases of the Company's stock over the history of the Company.
❑	❑	24. All closing statements and purchase agreements related to all mergers or acquisitions by the Company up to the valuation date.

		Engineering Data
		Engineering report should include:
❑	❑	25. Actual square footage of the take;
❑	❑	26. Effect of the take on parking and maneuverability;
❑	❑	27. Actual square footage of the building loss due to the taking;
❑	❑	28. Suggestions of possible cures, if any; and
❑	❑	29. Cost associated to items lost on the property, such as sign, and so on.

CHECKLIST 8.8:   VALUATION INFORMATION REQUEST (VIR) GAS AND OIL RIGHTS

Business Name	Date of Damages

This is a generalized information request. Some items may not pertain to your company, and some items may not be readily available to you. In such cases, indicate N/A or notify us if other arrangements can be made to obtain the data. Items already provided are indicated. If you have any questions on the development of this information, please call.

Provided   N/A

Financial Information

☐ ☐ 1. Financial statements for fiscal years ending FIVE YEARS (order of preference: audited, reviewed, compiled, and internal).

☐ ☐ 2. Federal and State Corporate Income Tax Returns and supporting schedules for fiscal years ending FIVE YEARS.

☐ ☐ 3. Provide division orders or other documents showing the subject interests, property identification, and legal description for all producing properties.

☐ ☐ 4. All reserve studies related to the producing properties.

☐ ☐ 5. All remittance advice, canceled checks, statements from banks, and statements from entities controlling distributions related to the oil and gas rights.

☐ ☐ 6. Names, addresses, and phone numbers of operators and purchasers related to the producing properties.

☐ ☐ 7. Joint interest bills for the past 12 months.

Operations

☐ ☐ 8. Unit agreements.

☐ ☐ 9. Operating agreements.

☐ ☐ 10. Field descriptions including geologic data and well logs, core analyses or studies, pressure data, fluid analyses, drill stem tests, completion reports, gravity information, and other geologic information related to the producing properties.

☐ ☐ 11. Proposed drilling activities, timing related to the proposed drilling activities, estimated costs, and other activities proposed.

☐ ☐ 12. Gas contracts, gathering and transportation agreements, gas balancing and processing agreements.

☐ ☐ 13. Severance and ad valorem tax rates.

☐ ☐ 14. Gas BTU content, including shrinkage data.

☐ ☐ 15. Production histories.

☐ ☐ 16. Decline curves and projections.

☐ ☐ 17. Future oil contracts.

☐ ☐ 18. Posted field prices for oil, gas, condensate, or other minerals or metals.

☐ ☐ 19. Amounts of bonuses or delay rentals for nonproducing properties.

CHECKLIST 8.9:   VALUATION INFORMATION REQUEST (VIR) HIGH-TECH BUSINESS

Business Name	Date of Damages

This is a generalized information request. Some items may not pertain to your company, and some items may not be readily available to you. In such cases, indicate N/A or notify us if other arrangements can be made to obtain the data. Items already provided are indicated. If you have any questions on the development of this information, please call.

Provided	N/A		
			Financial Information
❏	❏	1.	Financial statements for fiscal years ending FIVE YEARS (order of preference: audited, reviewed, compiled, and internal).
❏	❏	2.	Interim financial statements to date as of DATE OF VALUATION and one year prior.
❏	❏	3.	Federal and State Corporate Income Tax Returns and supporting schedules for fiscal years ending FIVE YEARS.
❏	❏	4.	Financial projections for a minimum of five years. Projections should include balance sheets, income statements, cash flow statements, and identification of any adjustments of assets to fair market value. Assumptions supporting the projections must be provided.
❏	❏	5.	Summary of agings of current accounts receivables and payables.
			Products and Markets
❏	❏	6.	A complete market study. This market study must include potential users by market (geographic and service). The study should also include current and expected competition and current and expected market share.
❏	❏	7.	Analysis of actual or perceived competition. Should include discussion of alternative sources of information service or product that would be used if the business did not exist.
❏	❏	8.	Complete website statistical analysis.
❏	❏	9.	Copies of any relevant industry studies you have purchased, produced, or obtained.
❏	❏	10.	Description of all strategic alliances and/or partnerships.
❏	❏	11.	Description and a strength and weaknesses analysis of your information technology infrastructure (software, hardware, bandwidth, etc.).
❏	❏	12.	Copies of sales materials or other promotional literature.
❏	❏	13.	History of Company and major competitors.
			Operations
❏	❏	14.	List of all stock options and warrants, including owner, date granted, number of shares, option period, and exercise price.
❏	❏	15.	List of all venture funding, including investor, date of investment, number of shares, and type of shares (if preferred).
❏	❏	16.	Notification of any discussions held or planned to be held with potential investors, buyers, investment bankers, or underwriters.
❏	❏	17.	Copies of latest two versions of Company's business plan.
❏	❏	18.	Copies of all prior appraisals of the Company.
❏	❏	19.	List of five largest customers and their percentage of total sales (if applicable).
❏	❏	20.	List of five major suppliers, including amounts paid (if relevant).

(continues)

Provided / N/A

Facilities

❏	❏	21. Detailed real property information, including any recent appraisals.
❏	❏	22. Detailed fixed asset information, including brand, type, age, serial number, and condition of fixed assets (if available).
❏	❏	23. Addresses and descriptions of all facilities.

Personnel

❏	❏	24. Officers' compensation for last five years.
❏	❏	25. Detail of Company ownership and any recent transactions involving Company stock or stock options.

Corporate Documents and Records

❏	❏	26. Corporate charter, articles of incorporation, and/or bylaws.
❏	❏	27. Minutes of board of directors and shareholders' meetings for the most recent three years (may be reviewed by us on-site).
❏	❏	28. Summary of major covenants or agreements binding on the business (e.g., union contracts, capital leases, employment contracts, service contracts, product warranties, etc.).
❏	❏	29. Description of any pending litigation, including parties involved, date of filing, description and nature of the lawsuit or claim, current status, expected outcome, and financial impact.
❏	❏	30. List of all subsidiary companies and the percentage ownership in each.
❏	❏	31. Name of any "related" companies (common ownership, common shareholders, etc.) and briefly describe the relationship(s).
❏	❏	32. Stock ledger.
❏	❏	33. All closing statements and purchase agreements related to all purchases of the business's stock over the history of the business.
❏	❏	34. All closing statements and purchase agreements related to all mergers or acquisitions by the business up to the valuation date.
❏	❏	35. Copies of any appraisals of the stock of the business made during the last three years.
❏	❏	36. State(s) and year of incorporation or registration.
❏	❏	37. Form of ownership (C corporation, S corporation, general partnership, limited partnership, sole proprietorship).
❏	❏	38. List of the largest ownership interests in the business, including name of owner, percentage of shares held and position with business or inactive in business, total shares authorized, total shares issued, and total shares outstanding.
❏	❏	39. Description of any unusual stock features (i.e., voting or nonvoting, preferred or convertible, class A and class B).
❏	❏	40. Description of any restrictions on the sale or transfer of ownership interests (buy-sell agreement, lettered stock option to buy, stock options, etc.).
❏	❏	41. Description of familial or other relationships between owners.
❏	❏	42. Description of sales or transfers of any ownership interests in the business in the past five years, including how the price or value was determined.
❏	❏	43. Description of any bona fide offers to purchase the business during the past five years.
❏	❏	44. Analysis of adequacy of the current business insurance.
❏	❏	45. Description of any subsidiaries, joint ventures, or investments of a material nature in other companies.

CHECKLIST 8.10:   VALUATION INFORMATION REQUEST (VIR) PROFESSIONAL PRACTICE

Practice Name	Valuation Date

This is a generalized information request. Some items may not pertain to your company, and some items may not be readily available to you. In such cases, indicate N/A or notify us if other arrangements can be made to obtain the data. Items already provided are indicated. If you have any questions on the development of this information, please call.

Provided   N/A

		Financial Information
❏	❏	1. Financial statements for fiscal years ending FIVE YEARS (order of preference: audited, reviewed, compiled, and internal).
❏	❏	2. Interim financial statements as of DATE OF VALUATION and one year prior.
❏	❏	3. Financial projections for the current year and the next three years. Include any prepared budgets and/or business plans.
❏	❏	4. Federal and State Corporate Income Tax Returns and supporting schedules for fiscal years ending FIVE YEARS. Include State Intangible Personal Property Tax Returns.
❏	❏	5. Explanation of significant nonrecurring and/or nonoperating items appearing on the financial statements in any fiscal year if not detailed in footnotes.
❏	❏	6. Accounts payable aging schedule or summary at DATE OF VALUATION.
❏	❏	7. Accounts receivable aging schedule or summary at DATE OF VALUATION.
❏	❏	8. A listing of work-in-process, including fees earned but not billed.
❏	❏	9. The fee schedule in effect at the valuation date for each staff member, plus each average realization rate (percentage) for the last year.
❏	❏	10. Fixed asset and depreciation schedule at DATE OF VALUATION.
❏	❏	11. Amortization schedules of mortgages and notes payable; and terms of bank notes, credit lines, and/or ESOP debt agreement(s).
❏	❏	12. Current financial statements for the ESOP, profit sharing, pension, or other employee benefit trust.
❏	❏	13. Current level of over (under) funding for any defined benefit plan.
		Services and Markets
❏	❏	14. List the major services of the Practice and provide copies of marketing materials, including sales brochures, catalogs, or other descriptive sales materials.
❏	❏	15. Sales and profit contributions analysis by service category.
❏	❏	16. Unit volume analyses for existing services for the past five years.
❏	❏	17. Major services added in the last two years (or anticipated) and current expectations as to sales potential.
❏	❏	18. New services under development, with expectations as to potential.
❏	❏	19. List the top 10 customers of the Practice, indicating sales (or sales on which commissions were earned) and unit volumes for each of the past three fiscal years.
❏	❏	20. Major accounts gained (lost) in the last year, indicating actual sales in the current year and beyond.
❏	❏	21. Major competitors (full name, location, size, and estimate market share of each).
❏	❏	22. Trade association memberships.
❏	❏	23. Majority industry publications of interest to management.

Provided	N/A		

Operations

☐ ☐ 24. In a paragraph or so, complete this statement: "The Practice is in the business of . . ."

☐ ☐ 25. Briefly name and describe the operations of all major operating entities, whether divisions, subsidiaries, or departments.

☐ ☐ 26. List the top 10 suppliers (or all accounting for 5 percent or more of total purchases) and the level of purchases in each of the past two years (include total purchases by the Practice in each year).

☐ ☐ 27. Identify services on which the Practice is single-sourced or suppliers on which the Practice is otherwise dependent.

☐ ☐ 28. Dividend policy, dividend history, and prospect for future dividends.

☐ ☐ 29. Copy of any existing employee stock ownership plan (ESOP).

☐ ☐ 30. Copies of all other stock option plans or option agreements, or any other plan providing vested benefits in Practice stock. Also list number of options granted and to whom, and the stated exercise price(s) and expiration date(s).

☐ ☐ 31. For the ESOP, pension plan, and/or profit sharing plan: basis for Practice contributions (contribution policy), contributions in each of the past five years, and projection for future contributions.

☐ ☐ 32. The most recent projection of emerging ESOP repurchase liability. If no study has been done, list known ESOP liquidity requirements during the next three years (e.g., known retirements during periods).

☐ ☐ 33. Copies of any appraisals of the stock of the Practice made during the last three years.

Facilities

☐ ☐ 34. Location, age, and approximate size of each facility. Provide or estimate business volume by major facility.

☐ ☐ 35. Ownership of each facility and other major fixed assets. If leased, include name of lessor and lease terms or agreements. If owned by the Practice, include date purchased, purchase price, recent appraisals, insurance coverage, and book values.

☐ ☐ 36. If accelerated depreciation is used for financial statement purposes, provide estimated depreciation as if all assets were on a straight-line depreciation basis. If not readily available, please call so we can discuss how to obtain a reasonable estimate with minimal effort.

☐ ☐ 37. Copies of appraisals of any company-owned real property or personal property performed during the last three years.

Personnel

☐ ☐ 38. Current organization chart.

☐ ☐ 39. Number of employees (distinguish full-time and part-time) at year-end for the last six years, including current employee classifications, general wage scales, and approximate rate.

☐ ☐ 40. List all union relationships, including name of union, date of current agreement, workers and facilities covered.

☐ ☐ 41. Number of part-time and full-time Practice-employed sales persons, including compensation arrangements or schedules. If there are none, describe how sales are obtained and by whom.

☐ ☐ 42. Description of management team, including current title, age, length of Practice service, and background. Also, annual salary and bonus of each person for the current year and each of the last two years.

☐ ☐ 43. Full names of the board of directors. For outside members, provide occupation.

(continues)

Provided N/A

		Corporate Documents and Records
❑	❑	44. Corporate charter, articles of incorporation, bylaws, and/or partnership agreements.
❑	❑	45. Minutes of board of directors and shareholders' meetings for the most recent three years (may be reviewed by us on-site.)
❑	❑	46. Summary of major covenants or agreements binding on the Practice, for example, union contracts, capital leases, employment contracts, service contracts, product warranties, and so on.
❑	❑	47. Description of any pending litigation, including parties involved, date of filing, description and nature of the lawsuit or claim, current status, and expected outcome and financial impact.
❑	❑	48. List all subsidiary companies and the percentage ownership in each.
❑	❑	49. Name any "related" companies (common ownership, common shareholders, etc.) and briefly describe the relationship(s).
❑	❑	50. Stock ledger.
❑	❑	51. All closing statements and purchase agreements related to all purchases of the Practice's stock over the history of the Practice.
❑	❑	52. All closing statements and purchase agreements related to all mergers or acquisitions by the Practice up to the valuation date.

CHECKLIST 8.11: VALUATION INFORMATION REQUEST (VIR) MEDICAL PRACTICE

Practice Name	Valuation Date

This is a generalized information request. Some items may not pertain to your company, and some items may not be readily available to you. In such cases, indicate N/A or notify us if other arrangements can be made to obtain the data. Items already provided are indicated. If you have any questions on the development of this information, please call.

Provided / N/A

Financial Information

☐ ☐ 1. Financial statements for fiscal years ending FIVE YEARS (order of preference: audited, reviewed, compiled, and internal).

☐ ☐ 2. Interim financial statements for the month-end DATE OF VALUATION and one year prior.

☐ ☐ 3. Financial projections, if any, for the current year and the next three years. Include any prepared budgets and/or business plans.

☐ ☐ 4. Federal and State Corporate Income Tax Returns and supporting schedules for fiscal years ending FIVE YEARS.

☐ ☐ 5. Additional financial information:
a) Assets included in the financial records not related to the practice;
b) Description of the classes of corporate stock (if more than one);
c) List of ownership of stock at DATE OF VALUATION; and
d) Description of any recent transactions in stock. If none, please so indicate.

☐ ☐ 6. Copies of buy-sell or other restrictive agreements.

☐ ☐ 7. Copies of any prior real estate and business appraisals, if any.

☐ ☐ 8. Reconciliation of amounts distributed to the practice from an Independent Practice Association or similar entity, if applicable.

☐ ☐ 9. Copy of fee schedule with allowables from insurers.

☐ ☐ 10. Data from billing system for the current year and two years prior, by provider and for the entire practice (separate professional from ancillary components), including:
a) Most recent aged accounts receivable by payor class with credit balance amounts.
b) Annual patient encounter statistics (type [CPT code or similar description] by units of service, gross charge, and receipts.
c) Charges/receipts by payor class and self-pay.
d) wRVUs by provider.

Operations

☐ ☐ 11. Historical compensation (W-2, 1099, Schedule K) by provider.

☐ ☐ 12. A fixed asset schedule, including all furniture, fixtures, and equipment used in the office. This schedule should include the date of purchase, original cost, approximate condition, and the estimated remaining useful life.

☐ ☐ 13. Copies of profit sharing, pension, or 401-K plans.

☐ ☐ 14. List of inventory and whether it is valued LIFO, FIFO, or specific identification.

(continues)

Provided | N/A |

Other Documents and Records

☐ ☐ 15. Corporate charter, articles of incorporation, and/or bylaws.

☐ ☐ 16. Minutes of board of directors and shareholders' meetings for the most recent three years (may be reviewed by us on-site).

☐ ☐ 17. Summary of major covenants or agreements binding on the professional practice, such as capital leases, employment contracts, service contracts, and so on.

☐ ☐ 18. Description of any pending litigation, including parties involved, date of filing, description and nature of the lawsuit or claim, current status, and expected outcome and financial impact.

☐ ☐ 19. Name of any "related" companies or professional associations (common ownership, common shareholders, etc.) and the relationship(s). Include percentage of ownership in each.

☐ ☐ 20. Stock ledger.

☐ ☐ 21. Leases.

Facilities

☐ ☐ 22. Location, age, and approximate size of each facility. Please provide or estimate business volume by major facility.

☐ ☐ 23. Ownership of each facility and other major fixed assets. If leased, include name of lessor and lease terms or agreements. If owned by the Practice, include:
    a) Date purchased;
    b) Purchase price;
    c) Recent appraisals;
    d) Insurance coverage; and
    e) Book value.

☐ ☐ 24. If accelerated depreciation is used for financial statement purposes, please provide estimated depreciation as if all assets were on a straight-line depreciation basis.

Personnel

☐ ☐ 25. Current organization chart.

☐ ☐ 26. Number of employees (distinguish full-time and part-time) at year-end for the last six years, including current employee classifications, general wage scales, and approximate rate.

☐ ☐ 27. Description of the management team, including current title, age, length of Practice service, and background. Also, list the annual salary and bonus of each person for the current year and each of the last two years.

☐ ☐ 28. Full names of the board of directors. For outside members, please provide outside occupation.

☐ ☐ 29. Curriculum vitae for each of the providers.

CHECKLIST 8.12:   VALUATION INFORMATION REQUEST (VIR) CONSTRUCTION INDUSTRY

Business Name	Valuation Date

This is a generalized information request. Some items may not pertain to your company, and some items may not be readily available to you. In such cases, indicate N/A or notify us if other arrangements can be made to obtain the data. Items already provided are indicated. If you have any questions on the development of this information, please call.

Provided **N/A**

		Financial Information
❏	❏	1. Financial statements for fiscal years ending FIVE YEARS (order of preference: audited, reviewed, compiled, and internal).
❏	❏	2. Job schedule (listing of completed and in-process jobs) for fiscal years ending FIVE YEARS (order of preference: audited, reviewed, compiled, and internal).
❏	❏	3. Interim financial statements for the month-end DATE OF VALUATION and one year prior.
❏	❏	4. Interim job schedule (listing of completed and in process jobs) for the month-end DATE OF VALUATION and one year prior.
❏	❏	5. Financial projections, if any, for the current year and the next three years. Include any prepared budgets and/or business plans.
❏	❏	6. Federal and State Corporate Income Tax Returns and supporting schedules for fiscal years ending FIVE YEARS.
❏	❏	7. Explanation of significant nonrecurring and/or nonoperating items appearing on the financial statements in any fiscal year if not detailed in footnotes.
❏	❏	8. Accounts payable aging schedule or summary as of DATE OF VALUATION, including retentions payable.
❏	❏	9. Accounts receivable aging schedule or summary and management's general evaluation of quality and credit risk as of DATE OF VALUATION, including retentions receivable.
❏	❏	10. Restatement of inventories and cost of goods sold on a FIFO basis for each of the past five fiscal years if LIFO accounting is used for inventory reporting purposes.
❏	❏	11. Fixed asset and depreciation schedule as of DATE OF VALUATION.
❏	❏	12. Amortization schedules of mortgages and notes payable; and terms of bank notes, credit lines, and/or debt agreements as of DATE OF VALUATION.
❏	❏	13. Current financial statements for any ESOP, profit sharing, pension, or other employee benefit trust at DATE OF VALUATION.
❏	❏	14. Current level of over (under) funding for any defined benefit plan at DATE OF VALUATION.
❏	❏	15. Description of any compensation, salaries, dividends, or distributions received by persons not active in the operations of the business, including the year and respective compensation.
❏	❏	16. Estimated total revenue, gross profit, and net income for the current fiscal year.
❏	❏	17. Explanation of fluctuations, growth, or decline in revenue of the business during the past five years.
❏	❏	18. Explanation of expected failure of the business to meet this year's budget based on the year-to-date financial data, if applicable.
❏	❏	19. Description of any anticipated significant rate increases in the cost of labor or materials.

(continues)

Provided	N/A		

Financial Information (*continued*)

❑ ❑ 20. Estimate revenues, gross profits, and earnings before interest and tax (EBIT) for the next five years if revenue growth, gross margins, or net margins are expected to be significantly different as compared to the past five years.

❑ ❑ 21. Explanation of expected changes in the amount of capital expenditures during the next five years if expectations differ from those incurred during the past five years, including the anticipated new levels of capital expenditures.

❑ ❑ 22. Average borrowing rate for the business and financial ratios that must be maintained to comply with lenders' credit terms.

❑ ❑ 23. Description of any assets with stated net book value on the balance sheet that differ significantly from the fair market value that could be realized if the business were liquidated (i.e., appreciated real estate, obsolete inventory or equipment).

❑ ❑ 24. Description of any assets owned by the business that are not being used in the operations of the business (i.e., excess land, investments, excess cash, unused equipment, etc.).

Products and Markets

❑ ❑ 25. List of the major products, services, or product lines of the business and copies of marketing materials, including sales brochures, catalogs, or other descriptive sales materials.

❑ ❑ 26. Sales and profit contributions analysis by product, product line, service category, customer, subsidiary, and/or location (whichever is applicable).

❑ ❑ 27. Unit volume analyses for existing product lines for the past five years.

❑ ❑ 28. Description of major products or services added in the last two years (or anticipated) and current expectations as to sales potential.

❑ ❑ 29. Description of the features, if any, that distinguish the business's products or services from the competition.

❑ ❑ 30. Causes for the cost of products and services supplied to your business to fluctuate and list of alternative suppliers available at similar rates, if any.

❑ ❑ 31. Description of new products under development, with expectations as to potential.

❑ ❑ 32. List of the top 10 customers of the business, indicating sales (or sales on which commissions were earned) and unit volumes for each of the past three fiscal years if customers are consolidated.

❑ ❑ 33. Summary of major accounts gained (lost) in the last year, indicating actual sales in the current year and beyond.

❑ ❑ 34. List of major competitors (full name, location, size, and estimate market share of each).

❑ ❑ 35. List of trade association memberships and industry publications of interest to management.

❑ ❑ 36. Classification of the business's industry (SIC No. or NAICS No.).

❑ ❑ 37. Description of any significant business operations that have been discontinued in recent years or expected to be discontinued in the future (i.e., sale of facility or business line, closed-out product line, etc.), including date of discontinuation and impact on revenues and profits.

❑ ❑ 38. Description of any significant business operations that have been added in recent years or expected to be added in the near future (i.e., purchase of facility, business acquisition, introduction of new product line, etc.), including date of addition and financial impact.

❑ ❑ 39. List of the names of all principal suppliers accounting for over 10 percent of total purchases.

❑ ❑ 40. Summary of terms of any existing purchase agreements with principal suppliers.

❑ ❑ 41. Characteristics of customers (i.e., industries served, demographics).

Provided

N/A

		Products and Markets (*continued*)
❏	❏	42. Approximate number of customers that the business has and percentage that are repeat clientele.
❏	❏	43. Approximate time the average customer has been purchasing from the business.
❏	❏	44. Description of customers that account for over 10 percent of annual revenue or gross profit of the business.
❏	❏	45. Summary of any contractual agreements with customers and/or distributors.
❏	❏	46. Description of any contracts or agreements with customers, suppliers, or distributors that would be nontransferable if the business were sold.
❏	❏	47. Number of clients that would discontinue relations with the business if the business were sold, including reason(s) and the estimated impact on revenues.
❏	❏	48. Summary of factors that stimulate demand for the business's products or services.
❏	❏	49. Description of seasonal or cyclical factors, if any.
❏	❏	50. Reason for increases or decreases of major competitors during the past five years, including their respective market share.
❏	❏	51. Approximate percentage of the market the subject business holds.
❏	❏	52. Description of level of difficulty to enter into the market or industry by potential competitors.
❏	❏	53. Description of the differences of the subject business to its competitors, including price, quality, strengths, and weaknesses.
❏	❏	54. List any publicly held companies or subsidiaries known to operate in your industry.
❏	❏	55. Name, address, and phone number of contact at industry organization that assists with market data, if any.
		Operations
❏	❏	56. In a paragraph or so, complete this statement: "Our company is in the business of . . ."
❏	❏	57. Name and description of the operations of all major operating entities, whether divisions, subsidiaries, or departments.
❏	❏	58. List of the top 10 suppliers (or all accounting for 5 percent or more of total purchases) and the level of purchases in each of the past two years (include total purchases by the business in each year).
❏	❏	59. List of product(s) on which the business is single-sourced or suppliers on which the business is otherwise dependent.
❏	❏	60. Dividend policy, dividend history, and prospect for future dividends.
❏	❏	61. Copy of any existing ESOP.
❏	❏	62. Copies of all other stock option plans or option agreements, or any other plan providing vested benefits in business stock. Also list number of options granted and to whom, and the stated exercise price(s) and expiration date(s).
❏	❏	63. Basis for business contributions (contribution policy), contributions in each of the past five years, and projection for future contributions to the ESOP, pension plan, and/or profit sharing plan.
❏	❏	64. The most recent projection of emerging ESOP repurchase liability. If no study has been done, list known ESOP liquidity requirements during the next three years (e.g., known retirements during periods).
❏	❏	65. Copies of any appraisals of the stock of the business made during the last three years.
❏	❏	66. State(s) and year of incorporation or registration.
❏	❏	67. Form of ownership (C corporation, S corporation, general partnership, limited partnership, sole proprietorship).
❏	❏	68. List of the largest ownership interests in the business, including name of owner, percentage of shares held and position with business or inactive in business, total shares authorized, total shares issued, and total shares outstanding.

(*continues*)

Provided	N/A	
		Operations (*continued*)
❑	❑	69. Description of any unusual stock features (i.e., voting or nonvoting, preferred or convertible, class A and class B).
❑	❑	70. Description of any restrictions on the sale or transfer of ownership interests (buy-sell agreement, lettered stock option to buy, stock options, etc.).
❑	❑	71. Description of familial or other relationships between owners.
❑	❑	72. Description of sales or transfers of any ownership interests in the business in the past five years, including how the price or value was determined.
❑	❑	73. Description of any bona fide offers to purchase the business during the past five years.
❑	❑	74. Analysis of adequacy of the current business insurance.
❑	❑	75. Description of any subsidiaries, joint ventures, or investments of a material nature in other companies.
❑	❑	76. Description of any services performed for, or by, a related party or business, including services provided, dollar amounts, nonmonetary benefits, and if transactions are at market rates.
		Facilities
❑	❑	77. Location, age, and approximate size of each facility. Provide or estimate business volume by major facility.
❑	❑	78. Ownership of each facility and other major fixed assets. If leased, include name of lessor and lease terms or agreements. If owned by the business include: a) Date purchased; b) Purchase price; c) Recent appraisals; d) Insurance coverage; and e) Book values.
❑	❑	79. Estimated depreciation of all assets on a straight-line depreciation basis if accelerated depreciation is used for financial statement purposes.
❑	❑	80. Copies of any appraisals of real estate or personal property owned by the business.
❑	❑	81. Copies of any appraisals of any company-owned real property or personal property performed during the last three years.
❑	❑	82. Comparison of rates of leases to market rates if facilities are rented from a related party.
❑	❑	83. Description of the terms of your real estate lease, including date of expiration, anticipated lease rate changes, and whether it is renewable.
❑	❑	84. Estimate of the cost to relocate business operations, including lost profits from business interruption.
❑	❑	85. Percentage of total capacity (expressed as percentage of total revenue) of the current business operations.
❑	❑	86. Description of changes in total operating capacity during the past five years (i.e., physical expansion, technological improvement), including related expenditures.
❑	❑	87. Based on future expected growth, description of when additional facilities or expansion (if foreseeable) will be needed, including approximate cost.
❑	❑	88. List of current backlog, including the name of the job, the contract price, the estimated gross profit, and the estimated starting date.
		Personnel
❑	❑	89. Current organization chart.
❑	❑	90. Number of employees (distinguish full-time and part-time) at year-end for the last six years, including current employee classifications, general wage scales, and approximate rate.
❑	❑	91. List all union relationships, including name of union, date of current agreement, workers, and facilities covered.

Provided	N/A	

Personnel (*continued*)

❑	❑	92. Number of part-time and full-time business-employed salespersons, including compensation arrangements or schedules. If there are none, describe how sales are obtained and by whom.
❑	❑	93. Description of the management team, including current title, age, length of service, background, annual salary, and bonus for the current year and each of the last two years.
❑	❑	94. Full names of the board of directors, including occupation of outside members.
❑	❑	95. Summary of employee turnover (i.e., below average, average, or above average) compared to your industry.
❑	❑	96. Adequacy of supply of labor.
❑	❑	97. Summary of employee compensation (i.e., below average, average, or above average) compared to your industry.
❑	❑	98. Description of any significant staffing changes or increases anticipated during the next three to five years.
❑	❑	99. Description of terms of any contracts with personnel, such as noncompete agreements or employment contracts.
❑	❑	100. Description of significant adverse effect on the operating performance of the business due to the loss of a key employee or manager, including potential revenue losses.
❑	❑	101. Specify succession of management, if determined.
❑	❑	102. Description of staff members who would not be retained if your business were sold, including their respective current compensation and position with the business.

Corporate Documents and Records

❑	❑	103. Corporate charter, articles of incorporation, and/or bylaws.
❑	❑	104. Minutes of board of directors and shareholders' meetings for the most recent three years (may be reviewed by us on-site).
❑	❑	105. Summary of major covenants or agreements binding on the business (e.g., union contracts, capital leases, employment contracts, service contracts, product warranties, etc.).
❑	❑	106. Copy of current bonding contracts.
❑	❑	107. Description of any pending litigation, including parties involved, date of filing, description and nature of the lawsuit or claim, current status, expected outcome, and financial impact.
❑	❑	108. List of all subsidiary companies and the percentage ownership in each.
❑	❑	109. Name of any "related" companies (common ownership, common shareholders, etc.) and briefly describe the relationship(s).
❑	❑	110. Stock ledger.
❑	❑	111. All closing statements and purchase agreements related to all purchases of the business's stock over the history of the business.
❑	❑	112. All closing statements and purchase agreements related to all mergers or acquisitions by the business up to the valuation date.
❑	❑	113. Terms of any offers to purchase the business.

CHECKLIST 8.13:   MANAGEMENT INTERVIEW—OPERATIONS

Exact Business Name	Date of Valuation
Address	Phone
Analyst/Interviewer	Date of Interview

The objective of this management interview is to provide us with operational information that will aid in the valuation of your business. We will keep the information confidential. Describe the following to the best of your ability. If necessary, use a separate sheet of paper, with reference to each item number. If some items are not applicable, please indicate N/A. Items already provided are indicated.

Provided N/A

Interviewee(s)

❏ ❏ 1.   Name   Title

_____   _____

_____   _____

_____   _____

Purpose and Objective of the Valuation

❏ ❏ 2. The activity or transaction giving rise to the valuation.

Other Information Regarding the Transaction

❏ ❏ 3. Number of shares being valued (each class).
❏ ❏ 4. Total number of shares issued (each class).
❏ ❏ 5. Total number of shares outstanding (each class).
❏ ❏ 6. Date of the valuation.
❏ ❏ 7. State of incorporation.
❏ ❏ 8. Standard of value.

Corporate Information

❏ ❏ 9. Name, address, and telephone number of the business attorney.
❏ ❏ 10. Name, address, and telephone number of the business accountant or bookkeeper.

Description of the Business

❏ ❏ 11. Type of business.
❏ ❏ 12. Products/services sold.
❏ ❏ 13. Type of customers/clients.
❏ ❏ 14. Location of sales/services.
❏ ❏ 15. Business code (see tax return).
❏ ❏ 16. SIC number or NAICS number.
❏ ❏ 17. Type of industry(ies).
❏ ❏ 18. Important industry trends.
❏ ❏ 19. Date business started.
❏ ❏ 20. Fiscal year-end date.
❏ ❏ 21. Factors you consider most important to your business's success.

Provided	N/A	

History of the Business

☐ ☐ 22. From founding to the present, history including people, date, places, new products, markets, and physical facilities.

Ownership

☐ ☐ 23. Shareholder list as of the date of valuation.

☐ ☐ 24. Transactions in the common stock and basis for price (parties, dates, shares, and prices).

☐ ☐ 25. Offers to purchase the company, if any. Discuss price, dates, terms, and current status of negotiations.

☐ ☐ 26. Prior appraisals.

Management

☐ ☐ 27. Current organizational chart.

☐ ☐ 28. List key management personnel with title, length of service, age, and annual compensation.

☐ ☐ 29. Key management positions open at this time.

☐ ☐ 30. Plans for succession if key-person dependency exists.

☐ ☐ 31. Adverse impact on business if sudden loss or withdrawal of any key employee.

☐ ☐ 32. Amount and description of key-person life insurance policy, if any.

Products and Services

☐ ☐ 33. Business mix.

☐ ☐ 34. Changes in business mix.

☐ ☐ 35. New products/services.

☐ ☐ 36. Development procedure(s) of new products/services.

☐ ☐ 37. Expected performance of new products/services.

☐ ☐ 38. Percent of output manufactured by company.

☐ ☐ 39. Percentage of manufactured products for resale.

☐ ☐ 40. Proportion of sales that are replacement parts.

☐ ☐ 41. Note any important differences in profit margins by product line.

Markets and the Economy

☐ ☐ 42. Market area.

☐ ☐ 43. Determination of market area by market segment, geography, or customer type.

☐ ☐ 44. Important characteristics of the relevant economic base (obtain information from local Chamber of Commerce if needed).

☐ ☐ 45. Business sensitivity to economic cycles or seasonal influences.

☐ ☐ 46. Industry(ies) of market concentration.

☐ ☐ 47. Approximate percentage of foreign sales, and, if any, total dollar amount of foreign sales.

☐ ☐ 48. Difference in profit margins of foreign sales to domestic sales, if any.

☐ ☐ 49. New product lines or services under consideration.

Customers

☐ ☐ 50. Major customers and the annual sales to each.

☐ ☐ 51. Length of relationships and customer turnover.

☐ ☐ 52. Company dependency, if any, on small group of large customers or large group of small customers.

(continues)

Provided	N/A		
			Marketing Strategy
❑	❑	53.	Sales and marketing strategy.
❑	❑	54.	Sales procedures.
❑	❑	55.	Sales personnel.
❑	❑	56.	Basis of sales personnel compensation.
❑	❑	57.	Risks of obsolescence or replacement by new or similar products.
			Operations
❑	❑	58.	Corporate organization structure (divisions, departments, etc.).
❑	❑	59.	Flow of operations that produce the product or service.
			Production
❑	❑	60.	Operating leverage of business (high or low level).
❑	❑	61.	Relationship of variable costs and fixed costs to total revenue.
❑	❑	62.	Difficulty obtaining liability insurance, if any.
❑	❑	63.	Insurance rates.
❑	❑	64.	OSHA or EPS concerns in the work environment, if any, including the prospective cost of compliance.
❑	❑	65.	Concerns over environmental hazards due to location or previous uses of land or facility.
❑	❑	66.	Dependency in the production process on patents, licenses, or other contracts not controlled by the company.
❑	❑	67.	Major suppliers and for what production inputs.
❑	❑	68.	Raw material suppliers that are manufacturers.
❑	❑	69.	Raw material suppliers that are wholesalers.
❑	❑	70.	Dependency for critical components of the product or service on any one supplier.
❑	❑	71.	Name of union, if any.
❑	❑	72.	Status of union contract or future organizing activities.
❑	❑	73.	Number of past union strikes.
❑	❑	74.	Number of full- and part-time employees.
❑	❑	75.	Number of employees by division or department.
❑	❑	76.	General experience, skill, and compensation levels of employees.
			Real Property
❑	❑	77.	List real estate and equipment used by the company, including name of owner, affiliated parties (if leased), and market terms (if leased).
❑	❑	78.	Size, age, condition, and capacity of the facilities.
❑	❑	79.	Adequacy of facilities or plans for future expansion.
❑	❑	80.	Plant/office facilities including:

    a) Owners

    b) Real estate taxes

    c) Land:
- Acreage
- Cost
- Assessed value
- Fair market value, if known

    d) Buildings:
- Type of construction
- Age and condition
- Location on the property
- Assessed value

Provided

N/A

			Real Property (*continued*)

- Fair market value, if known
- Fire insurance amount
- Square feet

e) Machinery and equipment:
- Description
- Age and condition
- Efficiency utilization (older equipment or state of the art)
- Future plant, machinery, and equipment requirements, including estimated repairs

❑ ❑ 81. Current value of the real estate and equipment.
❑ ❑ 82. Appraisals of real estate and equipment, or estimates.

		Description of the Capital Structure

❑ ❑ 83. Classes of securities.
❑ ❑ 84. Common stock restrictions (such as a buy-sell agreement or charter restrictions), if any.
❑ ❑ 85. Preferred stock terms of issue and protective covenants.
❑ ❑ 86. Subordinated debt terms of issue and protective covenants.
❑ ❑ 87. Outstanding stock options or warrants.
❑ ❑ 88. Obtain and attach copies of the option agreement.

		Other

❑ ❑ 89. Dividend policy and dividend history.
❑ ❑ 90. Anticipated future dividend payments.
❑ ❑ 91. Pending litigation and potential impact on the company.
❑ ❑ 92. Existing buy-sell or other restrictive agreements.
❑ ❑ 93. Prenuptial agreement, if any.
❑ ❑ 94. Profit-sharing, ESOP, or other retirement plans.
❑ ❑ 95. Copy of the ESOP plan, if not already provided.
❑ ❑ 96. Copies of provisions related to shareholder liquidity in the plan.
❑ ❑ 97. Company's regulators (e.g., public service commissions, bank regulators).
❑ ❑ 98. Copies of regulatory orders, if any.
❑ ❑ 99. General outlook (if not covered elsewhere).
❑ ❑ 100. Other pertinent information about the business.

CHECKLIST 8.14:   MANAGEMENT INTERVIEW—FINANCIAL REVIEW

Exact Business Name	Date of Valuation
Address	Phone
Analyst/Interviewer	Date of Interview

The objective of this management interview is to provide us with financial information that will aid us in the valuation of your business. We will keep the information confidential. Describe the following to the best of your ability. If some items are not applicable, please indicate N/A. Items already provided are indicated.

Remember that the objective of the interview is not only to identify changes in numbers but also to ascertain the reasons for the changes.

Provided   N/A

Interviewee(s)

❑ ❑   1.   Name   Title

         _____   _____

         _____   _____

         _____   _____

Financial Statement Review

❑ ❑   2.   Quality of the financial statements

❑ ❑   3.   Reason(s) for qualifications of audited and qualified statements, if applicable

❑ ❑   4.   Consistency of accounting principles of company-prepared interim statements with accountant-prepared statements

Balance Sheet Review

❑ ❑   5.   Approximate total asset book value

❑ ❑   6.   Approximate net book value

❑ ❑   7.   Cash

❑ ❑   8.   Minimum level of cash required to operate the company

❑ ❑   9.   Accounts receivable:
- Normal terms of sale
- Comparison of collection period to industry norms and history
- History of bad debts
- Receivables concentration by customer

❑ ❑   10.   Inventory:
- Accounting method used to calculate inventories
- Trend in level of inventories and turnover rate
- Obsolete inventory and the amount paid for it

❑ ❑   11.   Other current assets:
- List of current assets
- Current assets not related to the business, if any

Provided	N/A	

Balance Sheet Review (*continued*)

❑ ❑ 12. Fixed assets:
- Major fixed assets
- Depreciation calculations for book and tax purposes
- Capital budget for the coming years
- Types of fixed assets needed in the future
- List of excess assets

❑ ❑ 13. Notes receivable:
- Names and terms (if due from officers and affiliates, comparison of terms to market rates)

❑ ❑ 14. Other assets:
- Long-term

❑ ❑ 15. Notes payable:
- Names and terms of vendors

❑ ❑ 16. Accounts payable:
- General terms of purchase of goods and services
- Trend in payables and turnover ratios

❑ ❑ 17. Taxes payable and deferred taxes

❑ ❑ 18. Other accrued expenses

❑ ❑ 19. Long-term debt:
- Names and terms (if secured, state asset[s] used as security)

❑ ❑ 20. Mortgage notes payable:
- Terms and collateral

❑ ❑ 21 Any contingent liabilities

Income Statement

❑ ❑ 22. Approximate annual sales volume

❑ ❑ 23. Sales:
- Reason for changes in sales over the past five years
- Attribution of growth in sales:
- Unit volume
- Inflation
- Comparison of growth rate in sales to other items on the income statement
- Projections for the current year and beyond
- Basis for projections

❑ ❑ 24. Costs of goods sold:
- Key factors that affect cost of goods sold
- Changes in accounting procedures, if any

❑ ❑ 25. Gross profit margin (GPM):
- Changes in GPM for the last five years (price increases, cost increases, inventory write-downs, etc.)

❑ ❑ 26. General and administrative expenses:
- Major expense items of the company
- Fluctuations in expenses over the last five years
- Nonrecurring expenses included in the totals

(*continues*)

Provided

N/A

		Income Statement (*continued*)

❑ ❑ 27. Other income/expense:
- Sources

❑ ❑ 28. Taxes:
- Federal tax rate
- State tax rate

❑ ❑ 29. Hidden or intangible assets, such as:
- Patents
- Favorable leases
- Favorable financing arrangements
- Number of recurring, stable customers
- Employment contracts
- Copyrights
- Long-term customers' contracts
- Trademark
- Unique research and development
- Highly trained staff in place
- Undervalued securities or other investments

❑ ❑ 30. Key liabilities
- Commitments for new buildings or machinery
- Long-term loans outstanding and terms

CHECKLIST 8.15: MANAGEMENT INTERVIEW—INSURANCE AGENCY

Exact Agency Name	Date of Valuation
Address	Phone
Analyst/Interviewer	Date of Interview

The objective of this management interview is to provide us with operational information that will aid us in the valuation of your business. We will keep the information confidential. Describe the following to the best of your ability. If necessary, use a separate sheet of paper, with reference to each item number. If some items are not applicable, please indicate N/A. Items already provided are indicated.

Provided   N/A

Interviewee(s)

❏ ❏ 1. Name   Title

     _____   _____

     _____   _____

     _____   _____

History of the Business

❏ ❏ 2. Brief but complete description of the start-up of business.

❏ ❏ 3. Date business started.

❏ ❏ 4. Purchases of other businesses during the development of the agency.

Corporate Information

❏ ❏ 5. Name, address, and telephone number of the business accountant or bookkeeper.

Owners

❏ ❏ 6. List all owners by class of stock and percentage owned.

❏ ❏ 7. Job history and experience (i.e., curriculum vitae) of the owners.

❏ ❏ 8. Ages and health of the owners.

❏ ❏ 9. Recent transactions in the common stock of the company.

❏ ❏ 10. Ownership and management perquisites.

Personnel

❏ ❏ 11. List all personnel with title, length of service, age, and annual compensation.

❏ ❏ 12. Are there any part-time employees?

❏ ❏ 13. Describe licenses and designations of key personnel, including the year earned.

❏ ❏ 14. Would losing a key employee affect the business drastically?

❏ ❏ 15. Provide copies of all noncompete agreements, if any.

Real Property

❏ ❏ 16. Describe the office facilities.

❏ ❏ 17. Is owned or leased? Provide a copy of the lease, if applicable.

Furniture and Equipment

❏ ❏ 18. Describe the furniture and equipment.

❏ ❏ 19. Is owned or leased? Provide a copy of the lease(s), if applicable.

❏ ❏ 20. For all owned furniture and equipment, please provide a fixed asset schedule.

(continues)

Provided	N/A	
		Insurance Carriers
☐	☐	21. List any electronic data processing terminals owned by insurance carriers that are used in the agency.
☐	☐	22. Provide copies of all insurance carrier contracts.
☐	☐	23. Have any new carrier contracts been applied for?
☐	☐	24. List all carriers that have terminated contracts, the dates terminated, and the amounts and types of coverage formerly provided in the last full year of representation.
☐	☐	25. Provide the amount of the limit to settle claims, if any.
		Book of Business
☐	☐	26. Describe the amounts of direct billed and agency billed.
☐	☐	27. Describe the amounts of property/casualty, life, and health premiums.
☐	☐	28. Describe the amounts of commercial and personal lines premiums.
		Policy Holders
☐	☐	29. If available, please attach a list of all policyholders by product line, the original years of coverage, and if applicable, the years of termination.
☐	☐	30. List the five largest policyholders, the amounts of premium, and descriptions of coverage, including the original issue date.
☐	☐	31. Provide the amount of written premium and commissions earned by carrier.
☐	☐	32. Provide the amount of contingency commissions, the applicable carrier, and the year earned.
		Financial Statements
☐	☐	33. Provide complete financial statements of the business for the last five years.
☐	☐	34. Provide corporate tax returns for the last five years.
☐	☐	35. Provide all production reports for the last five years (or all years available).
☐	☐	36. Provide all photocopies of any buy-sell or other restrictive agreements.
☐	☐	37. Describe any hidden assets or liabilities. These would be items or benefit (or liability) to the agency that may not have been fully reflected in the financial statements. They would include such things as long-term policyholder contracts, lawsuits, or undervalued securities.
☐	☐	38. Have there been any extraordinary or highly unusual downturns or upturns to the business?
☐	☐	39. Have there been any unusual or nonrecurring or credits not evident on the income statements?
☐	☐	40. List any nonoperating assets that are included on recent balance sheets. These would include assets not necessary in the day-to-day operations of the business.
		Other
☐	☐	41. General outlook (if not covered elsewhere).
☐	☐	42. Is there anything else we should know about the business that we have not already discussed?

CHECKLIST 8.18: MANAGEMENT INTERVIEW—PROFESSIONAL PRACTICE

Exact Practice Name	Date of Valuation
Address	Phone
Analyst/Interviewer	Date of Interview

The objective of this management interview is to provide us with operational information that will aid us in the valuation of your practice. We will keep the information confidential. Describe the following to the best of your ability. If necessary, use a separate sheet of paper, with reference to each item number. If some items are not applicable, please indicate N/A. Items already provided are indicated.

Provided   N/A

Interviewee(s)

☐ ☐   1.   **Name**   **Title**

_____   _____

_____   _____

_____   _____

Purpose and Objective of the Valuation

☐ ☐   2. The activity or transaction giving rise to the valuation.

Partners

☐ ☐   3. List key personnel with title, and approximate annual compensation (with bonuses listed separately).

☐ ☐   4. Provide an abbreviated curriculum vitae of each partner, including age, education, board certification, and unusual experience.

☐ ☐   5. Would the health of all partners be considered excellent? If not, describe any limitations due to health.

☐ ☐   6. Describe life insurance in which the firm is the beneficiary.

☐ ☐   7. Describe a typical week for the average partner, including the percentage of time spent in the following areas:
a) Directly billable
b) Administrative
c) Promotion
d) Civic affairs

Practice

☐ ☐   8. If not correct above, what is the exact name of the Practice?

☐ ☐   9. When was the Practice established? Provide a brief history of the development of the Practice, including past partners, important dates, previous locations, and so on.

☐ ☐   10. Provide a current organizational chart. Describe the management team, including current title, age, length of service, and background. Also, include the annual salary and bonus of each person for the current year and the last two years.

☐ ☐   11. Attach a list of all personnel (other than partners and the management team), stating the title/function and compensation of each.

☐ ☐   12. List the board of directors by name and title. For outside members, please provide occupation.

(continues)

Provided | **N/A**

Practice (*continued*)

☐ ☐ 13. Describe the growth trends and revenue and operating capacity (billable hours).

☐ ☐ 14. Are any changes in services offered being considered?

☐ ☐ 15. Is the firm responsive to seasonal fluctuations? Please explain.

☐ ☐ 16. How have services been marketed or advertised?

Facilities

☐ ☐ 17. Describe any land owned, including:
   a) Acreage
   b) Original cost
   c) Approximate fair market value

☐ ☐ 18. Describe any building owned, including:
   a) Age and condition
   b) Original cost
   c) Approximate fair market value
   d) Fire insurance amount
   e) Square feet

☐ ☐ 19. Furniture, fixtures, and equipment (FF&E). Because the FF&E schedule has been requested in our valuation information request, there will be no need to duplicate the listing here. What is requested is a discussion of the future plans for significant purchases of FF&E.

☐ ☐ 20. Library:
   a) Description by major service and/or groups of works
   b) Original cost
   c) Replacement cost
   d) Unique volumes, if any

☐ ☐ 21. Please describe anything else that should be known about the practice for valuation purposes. Any information that will add to (or detract from) the reputation of the practice or the individual practitioners will have a similar effect on the valuation.

CHECKLIST 8.17: MANAGEMENT INTERVIEW—MEDICAL PRACTICE

Exact Practice Name:	Date:
Address:	Phone:
Interviewer:	

The objective of this management interview is to provide us with operational information that will aid us in the valuation of your business. We will keep the information confidential. Describe the following information to the best of your ability on a separate sheet of paper, with reference to each item number. If some items are not applicable, please indicate N/A.

1. Interviewee(s)

Name	Title
a)	
b)	
c)	
d)	

2. Description of the Business

a) Full name of the practice

b) Date the practice was established

c) Discuss the history of the practice, from founding to present, including past physicians, important dates, past locations, and so on.

3. Name, Address, and Telephone Number of the Practice's Attorney(s)

4. Name, Address, and Telephone Number of the Practice's Accountant(s)

5. Physicians

a) For all doctors, provide

    1) Name

    2) Age

    3) Education background

    4) Special license requirements

    5) Board certification

    6) Number of years of experience

    7) Articles written

    8) Lectures delivered

(continues)

9) General health (excellent, good, or poor)

10) Expectations of retirement in the near term, if any

b) Describe life insurance in which the practice is the beneficiary

c) Describe the typical work week for each doctor, including

1) Average number of patients per day

2) Nature of treatment

3) Average time per patient/treatment

4) Hours worked per day

5) Time spent in

   i) Office visits/treatments

   ii) Surgery—hospital

   iii) Surgery—in office

   iv) Administration

   v) Promotion

   vi) Civic affairs

6. Personnel

a) Provide a current organizational chart

b) Provide a list of employees, other than physicians, at year-end for last year, including current employee classifications, general wage scales, and approximate rate (distinguish full-time and part-time)

c) List management personnel with title, length of service (LOS), age, and annual compensation (including bonuses) for the current year and past two years

Name	Title	LOS	Age	Compensation
1)				
2)				
3)				
4)				
5)				

d) List board of directors by name and title, including occupation for outside members

e) Does the practice use physician extenders? What type of oversight is provided to the extenders?

7. The Practice

a) Type of marketing

1) Professional referral

2) Patient referral

3) Direct mail

4) Yellow pages

5) Other

b) Provide list of competition

1) Specialized

2) General

3) Mini-hospitals

c) Discuss growth trends, revenue, operating capacity, and equity

1) Past

2) Projected

3) Limiting factors

    4) New products/services being considered

    5) Any recent sales of stock (or interests) or offers to buy (or sell)

    6) Any comparable sales of similar practices

8. Property and Equipment

a) Describe your office facilities

    1) Square feet

    2) Number of examining rooms

    3) Number of operating rooms

    4) Number of X-ray rooms

    5) If owned, provide

        i) Age and condition

        ii) Assessed value

        iii) Fair market value, if known

    6) If leased, amount of monthly payment

b) Discuss specialized equipment

    1) If owned, provide

        i) Age and condition

        ii) Assessed value

        iii) Fair market value, if known

    2) If leased, provide amount of monthly payment

c) List and discuss company-owned vehicles

d) Describe the library

    1) Original cost

    2) Replacement cost

    3) Unique volumes

9. General Outlook (if not covered elsewhere)

_____

_____

_____

10. Other Pertinent Information about the Practice

_____

_____

_____

CHECKLIST 8.18: MANAGEMENT INTERVIEW—CONSTRUCTION INDUSTRY

Exact Business Name	Date of Valuation
Address	Phone
Analyst/Interviewer	Date of Interview

The objective of this management interview is to provide us with operational information that will aid us in the valuation of your business. We will keep the information confidential. Describe the following to the best of your ability. If necessary, use a separate sheet of paper, with reference to each item number. If some items are not applicable, please indicate N/A. Items already provided are indicated.

Provided **N/A**

Interviewee(s)

❑ ❑   1.   <u>Name</u>   <u>Title</u>

_____   _____

_____   _____

_____   _____

Purpose and Objective of the Valuation

❑ ❑   2. The activity or transaction giving rise to the valuation.

Other Information Regarding the Transaction

❑ ❑   3. Number of shares being valued (each class).

❑ ❑   4. Total number of shares issued (each class).

❑ ❑   5. Total number of shares outstanding (each class).

❑ ❑   6. Date of the valuation.

❑ ❑   7. State of incorporation.

❑ ❑   8. Standard of value.

Corporate Information

❑ ❑   9. Name, address, and telephone number of the business attorney.

❑ ❑   10. Name, address, and telephone number of the business accountant or bookkeeper.

Description of the Business

❑ ❑   11. Type of business
a) General Contractor
b) Subcontractor

❑ ❑   12. Products/services sold.

❑ ❑   13. Type of customers/clients.

❑ ❑   14. Location of sales/services.

❑ ❑   15. Business code (see tax return).

❑ ❑   16. SIC number or NAICS number.

❑ ❑   17. Type of industry(ies).

❑ ❑   18. Important industry trends.

❑ ❑   19. Date business started.

❑ ❑   20. Fiscal year-end date.

❑ ❑   21. Factors you consider most important to the success of the business.

Provided	N/A	
		History of the Business
❑	❑	22. From founding to the present, history including people, dates, places, new products, markets, and physical facilities.
		Ownership
❑	❑	23. Shareholder list as of the date of valuation.
❑	❑	24. Transactions in the common stock and basis for price (parties, dates, shares, and prices).
❑	❑	25. Offers to purchase the company, if any. Discuss price, dates, terms, and current status of negotiations.
❑	❑	26. Prior appraisals.
		Management
❑	❑	27. Current organizational chart.
❑	❑	28. List key management personnel with title, length of service, age, and annual compensation.
❑	❑	29. Key management positions open at this time.
❑	❑	30. Plans for succession if key-person dependency exists.
❑	❑	31. Adverse impact on business if sudden loss or withdrawal of any key employee.
❑	❑	32. Effectiveness of job cost estimators.
❑	❑	33. Amount and description of key-person life insurance policy, if any.
		Products and Services
❑	❑	34. Business mix.
❑	❑	35. Changes in business mix.
❑	❑	36. New products/services.
❑	❑	37. Development procedure(s) of new products/services.
❑	❑	38. Expected performance of new products/services.
❑	❑	39. Note any important differences in profit margins by product line.
		Markets and the Economy
❑	❑	40. Market area.
❑	❑	41. Determination of market area by market segment, geography, or customer type.
❑	❑	42. Important characteristics of the relevant economic base (obtain information of local chamber of commerce if needed).
❑	❑	43. Business sensitivity to economic cycles or seasonal influences.
❑	❑	44. Industry(ies) of market concentration.
❑	❑	45. Approximate percentage of foreign sales, and, if any, total dollar amount of foreign sales.
❑	❑	46. Difference in profit margins of foreign sales to domestic sales, if any.
❑	❑	47. New product lines or services under consideration.
		Customers
❑	❑	48. Major customers and the annual sales to each.
❑	❑	49. Length of relationships and customer turnover.
❑	❑	50. Company dependency, if any, on small group of large customers or large group of small customers.
❑	❑	51. Company dependency on bid contracts versus no-bid contracts.

(continues)

Provided	N/A	

Bonding

❑	❑	52. Surety agent.
❑	❑	53. Length of time they have provided bonding credit.
❑	❑	54. Amount of bonding credit extended.
❑	❑	55. Manner in which the amount of bonding credit is computed.
❑	❑	56. Multiple used by the Surety to compute bonding credit.

Marketing Strategy

❑	❑	57. Sales and marketing strategy.
❑	❑	58. Sales procedures.
❑	❑	59. Sales personnel.
❑	❑	60. Basis of sales personnel compensation.
❑	❑	61. Risks of obsolescence or replacement by new or similar products.

Operations

❑	❑	62. Corporate organization structure (divisions, departments, etc.).
❑	❑	63. Flow of operations that produce the product or service.

Production

❑	❑	64. Operating leverage of business (high or low level).
❑	❑	65. Relationship of variable costs and fixed costs to total revenue.
❑	❑	66. Difficulty obtaining liability insurance, if any.
❑	❑	67. Insurance rates.
❑	❑	68. OSHA or EPS concerns in the work environment, if any, including the prospective cost of compliance.
❑	❑	69. Concerns over environmental hazards due to location or previous uses of land or facility.
❑	❑	70. Dependency in the production process on patents, licenses, or other contracts not controlled by the company.
❑	❑	71. Major suppliers and for what production inputs.
❑	❑	72. Raw material suppliers that are manufacturers.
❑	❑	73. Raw material suppliers that are wholesalers.
❑	❑	74. Dependency for critical components of the product or service on any one supplier.
❑	❑	75. Name of union, if any.
❑	❑	76. Status of union contract or future organizing activities.
❑	❑	77. Number of past union strikes.
❑	❑	78. Number of full- and part-time employees.
❑	❑	79. Number of employees by division or department.
❑	❑	80. General experience, skill, and compensation levels of employees.

Real Property

❑	❑	81. List real estate and equipment used by the company, including name of owner, affiliated parties (if leased), and market terms (if leased).
❑	❑	82. Size, age, condition, and capacity of the facilities.
❑	❑	83. Adequacy of facilities or plans for future expansion.

Provided	N/A	

Real Property (*continued*)

☐ ☐ 84. Plant/office facilities, including:
    a) Owners
    b) Real estate taxes
    c) Land
        ▪ Acreage
        ▪ Cost
        ▪ Assessed value
        ▪ Fair market value, if known
    d) Buildings
        ▪ Type of construction
        ▪ Age condition
        ▪ Location on the property
        ▪ Assessed value
        ▪ Fair market value, if known
        ▪ Fire insurance amount
        ▪ Square feet
    e) Machinery and equipment
        ▪ Description
        ▪ Age and condition
        ▪ Efficiency utilization (older equipment or state of the art)
        ▪ Future plant, machinery, and equipment requirements, including estimated repairs

☐ ☐ 85. Current value of the real estate and equipment.

☐ ☐ 86. Appraisals of real estate and equipment, or estimates.

Description of the Capital Structure

☐ ☐ 87. Classes of securities.

☐ ☐ 88. Common stock restrictions (such as a buy-sell agreement or charter restrictions), if any.

☐ ☐ 89. Preferred stock terms of issue and protective covenants.

☐ ☐ 90. Subordinated debt terms of issue and protective covenants.

☐ ☐ 91. Outstanding stock options or warrants.

☐ ☐ 92. Obtain and attach copies of the option agreement.

Other

☐ ☐ 93. Dividend policy and dividend history.

☐ ☐ 94. Anticipated future dividend payments.

☐ ☐ 95. Pending litigation and potential impact on the company.

☐ ☐ 96. Existing buy-sell or other restrictive agreements.

☐ ☐ 97. Prenuptial agreement, if any.

☐ ☐ 98. Profit sharing, ESOP, or other retirement plans.

☐ ☐ 99. Copy of the ESOP plan, if not already provided.

☐ ☐ 100. Copies of provisions related to shareholder liquidity in the plan.

☐ ☐ 101. Company's regulators (e.g., public service commissions, bank regulators).

☐ ☐ 102. Copies of regulatory orders, if any.

☐ ☐ 103. General outlook (if not covered elsewhere).

☐ ☐ 104. Other pertinent information about the business.

(*continues*)

Provided   N/A

Financial Statement Review

❑ ❑ 105. Quality of the financial statements.

❑ ❑ 106. Reason(s) for qualifications of audited and qualified statements, if applicable.

❑ ❑ 107. Consistency of accounting principles of company-prepared interim statements with accountant-prepared statements.

❑ ❑ 108. Method of accounting for long-term contracts.

Balance Sheet Review

❑ ❑ 109. Approximate total asset book value.

❑ ❑ 110. Approximate net book value.

❑ ❑ 111. Cash.

❑ ❑ 112. Minimum level of cash required to operate the company.

❑ ❑ 113. Minimum level of cash required to satisfy bonding requirements.

❑ ❑ 114. Marketable securities and other investments and normal terms of sale.

❑ ❑ 115. Accounts receivable
    a) Normal terms of sale
    b) Comparison of collection period to industry norms and history
    c) History of bad debts
    d) Receivables concentration by customer
    e) Typical retention percentage

❑ ❑ 116. Costs and estimated earnings in excess of billings (underbillings) and management's billing policy on uncompleted jobs.

❑ ❑ 117. Inventory
    a) Accounting method used to calculate inventories
    b) Trend in level of inventories and turnover rate
    c) Obsolete inventory and the amount paid for it

❑ ❑ 118. Other current assets
    a) List of current assets
    b) Current assets not related to the business, if any

❑ ❑ 119. Fixed assets
    a) Major fixed assets
    b) Depreciation calculations for book and tax purposes
    c) Capital budget for the coming years
    d) Types of fixed assets needed in the future
    e) List of excess assets

❑ ❑ 120. Notes receivable, including names and terms (if due from officers and affiliates, comparison of terms to market rates).

❑ ❑ 121. Other assets (describe and identify whether short-term or long-term).

❑ ❑ 122. Notes payable, including names and terms of vendors.

❑ ❑ 123. Accounts payable
    a) General terms of purchase of goods and services
    b) Trend in payables and turnover ratios
    c) Typical retentions percentage

❑ ❑ 124. Billings in excess of costs and estimated earnings (overbillings).

❑ ❑ 125. Taxes payable and deferred taxes.

❑ ❑ 126. Other accrued expenses.

❑ ❑ 127. Long-term debt, including names and terms (if secured, state asset(s) used as security).

❑ ❑ 128. Mortgage notes payable, including terms and collateral.

❑ ❑ 129. Any contingent liabilities.

Provided	N/A	
		Income Statement
❑	❑	130. Approximate annual sales volume.
❑	❑	131. Sales
		a) Reason for changes in sales over the past five years
		b) Attribution of growth in sales
		i. unit volume
		ii. inflation
		c) Comparison of growth rate in sales to other items on the income statement
		d) Projections for the current year and beyond
		e) Amount of bonding credit compared to projections
		f) Basis for projections
❑	❑	132. Costs of goods sold
		a) Key factors that affect cost of goods sold
		b) Changes in accounting procedures, if any
❑	❑	133. Gross profit margin (GPM), including changes in GPM for the last five years (price increases, cost increases, inventory write-downs, etc.).
❑	❑	134. General and administrative expenses
		a) Major expense items of the company
		b) Fluctuations in expenses over the last five years
		c) Nonrecurring expenses included in the totals
❑	❑	135. Other income/expense and sources.
❑	❑	136. Taxes
		a) Federal tax rate
		b) State tax rate
❑	❑	137. Hidden or intangible assets, such as:
		a) Patents
		b) Favorable leases
		c) Favorable financing arrangements
		d) Number of recurring, stable customers
		e) Employment contracts
		f) Copyrights
		g) Long-term customers' contracts
		h) Trademark
		i) Unique research and development
		j) Highly trained staff in place
		k) Undervalued securities or other investments
❑	❑	138. Key liabilities
		a) Commitments for new buildings or machinery
		b) Long-term loans outstanding and terms
		Schedules of Completed and Uncompleted Contracts (Job Schedule)
❑	❑	139. Approximate annual volume of contracts.
❑	❑	140. Comparison of gross profit margins of completed contracts with the same contract on the prior year's uncompleted jobs.
❑	❑	141. Comparison of gross profit margins on uncompleted contracts with completed contracts and other uncompleted.

CHECKLIST 8.19: MANAGEMENT INTERVIEW—LAW PRACTICE

Exact Business Name	Date
Address	Phone
Analyst/Interviewer	

The objective of this management interview is to provide us with operational information that will aid us in the valuation of your business. We will keep the information confidential. Describe the following to the best of your ability on a separate sheet of paper, with reference to each item number. If some items are not applicable, please indicate N/A.

1. Interviewee(s)

	Name	Title
a)	_____	_____
b)	_____	_____
c)	_____	_____
d)	_____	_____

2. Attorneys

a) List key personnel with title, and approximate annual compensation (with bonuses listed separately)

	Name	Title	Compensation	Bonus
1)	_____	_____	_____	_____
2)	_____	_____	_____	_____
3)	_____	_____	_____	_____
4)	_____	_____	_____	_____
5)	_____	_____	_____	_____
6)	_____	_____	_____	_____
7)	_____	_____	_____	_____
8)	_____	_____	_____	_____
9)	_____	_____	_____	_____
10)	_____	_____	_____	_____

b) Provide an abbreviated curriculum vitae of each attorney, including age, education, board certification, and unusual experience

c) Describe any limitations of each attorney due to health

d) Describe life insurance in which the firm is the beneficiary

e) Describe a typical week for the average partner, including the percentage of time spent in the following areas:

     1) Directly billable

     2) Administrative

     3) Promotion

     4) Civic affairs

3. The Firm

a) Provide a brief history of the development of the firm, including date firm was established, past partners, important dates, previous locations, and so on.

b) Provide a current organizational chart. Describe the management team, including current title, age, length of service, background, the annual salary, and bonus of each person for the current year and the last two years.

c) Attach a list of all personnel (other than attorneys and the management team), stating the title/function and compensation of each.

d) List board of directors by name and title, including occupation for outside members.

e) Describe the growth trends, revenue, and operating capacity (billable hours).

f) Describe changes in legal services offered that are being considered.

g) Describe firm responsiveness to seasonal fluctuations. (For instance, does the firm have a disproportionate estate practice susceptible to northern residents?)

h) Previous and future marketing and advertising plans.

i) Please describe the office facilities, including:

   1) Any land owned

      i) Acreage

      ii) Original cost

      iii) Approximate fair market value

   2) Buildings owned

      i) Age and condition

      ii) Original cost

      iii) Approximate fair market value

      iv) Fire insurance amount

      v) Square feet

   3) Furniture, fixtures, and equipment (FF&E). (Because the FF&E schedule has been requested in our valuation information request, there will be no need to duplicate the listing here. What is requested is a discussion of the future plans for significant purchases of FF&E.)

   4) Library

      i) Description by major service and/or groups of works

      ii) Original cost

      iii) Replacement cost

      iv) Unique volumes, if any

4. Other Pertinent Information about the Firm

Any information that will add to (or detract from) the reputation of the firm or the individual practitioners and would have a similar effect on the valuation.

CHECKLIST 8.20: MANAGEMENT INTERVIEW—ACCOUNTING PRACTICE

Exact Business Name	Date
Address	Phone
Analyst/Interviewer	

The objective of this management interview is to provide us with operational information that will aid us in the valuation of your business. We will keep the information confidential. Describe the following to the best of your ability on a separate sheet of paper, with reference to each item number. If some items are not applicable, please indicate N/A.

1. Interviewee(s)

	Name	Title
a)	_____	_____
b)	_____	_____
c)	_____	_____

2. Accountants

a. List key personnel with title, and approximate annual compensation (with bonuses listed separately)

	Name	Title	Compensation	Bonus
1)	_____	_____	_____	_____
2)	_____	_____	_____	_____
3)	_____	_____	_____	_____
4)	_____	_____	_____	_____
5)	_____	_____	_____	_____

b) Abbreviated curriculum vitae of each accountant, including age, education, specialty certification, and unusual experience

c) Accountant limitations due to health, if any

d) Life insurance in which the practice is the beneficiary

e) Typical week for the average partner, including the percentage of time spent in the following areas:

   1) Directly billable

   2) Administrative

   3) Promotion

   4) Civic affairs

3. The Practice

a) If not correct above, exact name of the practice

b) Date practice established

c) Brief history of the development of the practice, including past partners, important dates, previous locations, and so on

3. The Practice (*continued*)

d) Current organizational chart

e) List the management team, including current title, age, length of service, background, annual salary, and bonus of each person for the current year and the last two years

f) List all personnel (other than accountants and the management team), stating the title/function and compensation of each

g) List board of directors by name and title, including occupation for outside members

h) Growth trends, revenue, and operating capacity (billable hours) by service line, for example, audit, tax

    i) Changes in accounting services being considered

j) Practice sensitivity to seasonal fluctuations (e.g., does the practice have a disproportionate tax practice)

k) Sales and marketing strategy

l) Office facilities, including:

    1. Any land owned

      i) Acreage

      ii) Original cost

      iii) Approximate fair market value

    2. Buildings owned

      i) Age and condition

      ii) Original cost

      iii) Approximate fair market value

      iv) Fire insurance amount

      v) Square feet

    3. Furniture, fixtures, and equipment (FF&E). (Because the FF&E schedule has been requested in our valuation information request, there will be no need to duplicate the listing here. What is requested is a discussion of the future plans for significant purchases of FF&E.)

    4. Library

      i) Description by major service and/or groups of works

      ii) Original cost

      iii) Replacement cost

      iv) Unique volumes, if any

4. Other Pertinent Information about the Practice

Any information that will add to (or detract from) the reputation of the practice or the individual practitioners and would have a similar effect on the valuation.

CHECKLIST 8.21:   VALUATION INFORMATION REQUEST (VIR)
COPYRIGHTS

Business Name	Valuation Date

This is a generalized information request. Some items may not pertain to your company, and some items may not be readily available to you. In such cases, indicate N/A or notify us if other arrangements can be made to obtain the data. Items already provided are indicated. If you have any questions on the development of this information, please call.

Provided
N/A

Copyrights

❑ ❑ 1. Provide a list of all copyrighted registrations.

❑ ❑ 2. Provide a list of works (articles, books, paintings, etc.).

❑ ❑ 3. Identify copyright names that are associated with products and/or services (such as software or report templates).

❑ ❑ 4. Identify historical sale of products and/or services employing the works for the last five years.

❑ ❑ 5. Provide projection of products and/or services that will employ the works for the next five years.

❑ ❑ 6. Are you licensing in or out any copyrighted works? If yes, provide details.

CHECKLIST 8.22:   VALUATION INFORMATION REQUEST (VIR) CUSTOMER RELATIONSHIPS

Business Name	Valuation Date

This is a generalized information request. Some items may not pertain to your company, and some items may not be readily available to you. In such cases, indicate N/A or notify us if other arrangements can be made to obtain the data. Items already provided are indicated. If you have any questions on the development of this information, please call.

Provided
N/A

Customer Relationships

☐ ☐   1. Provide customer sales history for the last five years for the top 10 customers.

☐ ☐   2. Provide complete customer history for the last five years (this would be for lifing).

☐ ☐   3. Provide financial data representing annual costs for the last five years associated with developing/soliciting new customers.

☐ ☐   4. Provide schedule of new customers gained in each of the last five years with sales.

☐ ☐   5. For the last five years, how many customers in a given year failed to purchase in the following year? Provide those customers' sales for the prior year.

CHECKLIST 8.23: VALUATION INFORMATION REQUEST (VIR) IN-PROCESS RESEARCH AND DEVELOPMENT

Business Name	Valuation Date

This is a generalized information request to assist in preparing an analysis of In-process Research and Development (IPR&D) for fair value accounting under ASC 805, *Business Combinations*, based on guidance from the AICPA *Accounting & Valuation Guide: Assets Acquired to Be Used in Research and Development Activities.*

Some items may not pertain to your company, and some items may not be readily available to you. In such cases, indicate N/A or notify us if other arrangements can be made to obtain the data. Items already provided are indicated. If you have any questions on the development of this information, please call.

Provided   N/A

		In-Process Research and Development (IPRD) Assets
❑	❑	1. Describe the IPR&D.
❑	❑	2. Describe competitive advantages and disadvantages of the IPR&D.
❑	❑	3. Describe the industry trends and competitive pressures that may affect the useful life of the IPR&D.
❑	❑	4. Describe whether each IPR&D project has substance—the acquired company has performed R&D activities that constitute more than insignificant efforts that meet the definition of R&D under FASB ASC 730-10 and result in the creation of value.
❑	❑	5. Describe whether each IPR&D is incomplete and identify the remaining risks.
❑	❑	6. In support of questions 4 and 5, describe each of the following aspects of the IPR&D at the valuation date:

    ■ Phase of development of the related IPR&D project;

    ■ Nature of the activities and costs necessary to further develop the related IPR&D;

    ■ The risks associated with the further development of the related IPR&D project;

    ■ The amount and timing of benefits expected to be derived in the future from the developed asset(s);

    ■ Whether there is an intent to manage costs for the developed asset(s) separately or on a combined basis in areas such as strategy, manufacturing, advertising, selling, and so on; and

    ■ Whether the asset, whether an incomplete IPR&D project or when ultimately completed, would be transferred by itself or with other separately identifiable assets.

❑	❑	7. If available, please provide cost records documenting development of the IPR&D:

    ■ Person-hours to develop;

    ■ Various technical levels of persons working on the assignment;

    ■ Pay scales for individuals at each technical review; and

    ■ Information to determine overhead rate.

❑	❑	8. In the absence of cost records, estimate effort to create the IPR&D:

    ■ Who would work on the assignment (employees and consultants);

    ■ Pay rates for individuals in above; and

    ■ Information to determine overhead rate.

❑	❑	9. What is the probability of completion of each of the IPR&D projects?
❑	❑	10. What are the post-completion maintenance research and development costs?

Provided	N/A	
		In-Process Research and Development (IPR&D) Assets (*continued*)
❏	❏	11. Will the IPR&D result in cost savings to manufacturing? If so, what are the projected savings by year?
❏	❏	12. Will the IPR&D result in a premium to the pricing of goods or services? If so, what is the projected premium by year?
❏	❏	13. Are there multiple future decision points related to the costs and benefits of the IPR&D for which probabilities of contingent outcomes may be estimated?
❏	❏	14. Provide projections of products and/or services that will employ the in-process research and development for the next five years:
		▪ Project revenues, including licensing income for the life-span of the IPR&D;
		▪ Project direct expenses associated with producing revenue including the costs to complete the IPR&D; and
		▪ Obtain or develop indirect expenses (i.e., overhead).
❏	❏	15. Does the company currently license in or license out technology? If so, please provide copies of related contracts and historical royalty payments and related product revenues.

CHECKLIST 8.24:   VALUATION INFORMATION REQUEST (VIR) KNOW-HOW

Business Name	Valuation Date

This is a generalized information request. Some items may not pertain to your company, and some items may not be readily available to you. In such cases, indicate N/A or notify us if other arrangements can be made to obtain the data. Items already provided are indicated. If you have any questions on the development of this information, please call.

Provided N/A

		Know-How
❑	❑	1. Describe know-how, including competitive advantages and disadvantages.
❑	❑	2. Describe industry trends and competitive pressures that may affect the useful life of the know-how.
❑	❑	3. In light of 1 and 2, what is the estimated useful life of the know-how?
❑	❑	4. What products or services employ the know-how?
❑	❑	5. If available, provide historical cost records documenting development of the know-how: a) Person hours to develop b) Various technical levels of persons working on the assignment c) Pay scales for individuals in 5b d) Information to determine overhead rate
❑	❑	6. In the absence of historical cost records, estimate corporate effort to re-create the know-how if it were to be developed from scratch: a) Who would work on the assignment (employees and consultants) b) Pay rates for individuals in 6a c) Information to determine overhead rate
❑	❑	7. Identify historical sale of revenues for products and/or services employing know-how for the last five years.
❑	❑	8. Know-how associated with products and/or services: a) Provide projection of products and/or services that employ the know-how for the next five years b) Project direct expenses associated with producing revenue in 8a c) Obtain or develop indirect expenses (i.e., overhead)
❑	❑	9. Are you licensing in or out any know-how? If yes, provide details.

CHECKLIST 8.25: VALUATION INFORMATION REQUEST (VIR) PATENTS

Business Name	Valuation Date

This is a generalized information request. Some items may not pertain to your company, and some items may not be readily available to you. In such cases, indicate N/A or notify us if other arrangements can be made to obtain the data. Items already provided are indicated. If you have any questions on the development of this information, please call.

Provided **N/A**

Patent

❑ ❑ 1. Provide a summary of patents held by the Company.

❑ ❑ 2. Provide copies of patent applications and patent abstracts.

❑ ❑ 3. Distinguish which patents have commercial applications (i.e., are producing or are reasonably forecast to produce revenue in the future).

❑ ❑ 4. If available, provide historical cost records documenting development of the patent(s):
a) Person hours to develop
b) Various technical levels of persons working on the assignment
c) Pay scales for individuals in 4b
d) Information to determine overhead rate

❑ ❑ 5. Identify patents and associated products that now have or are expected to have commercial viability.
a) Prepare forecast or projection of revenues related to patent over the life of the patent
b) Project direct expenses associated with producing revenue in 5a

❑ ❑ 6. Comment on the possibility of extending patent protection beyond statutory life of patent.

❑ ❑ 7. Are you licensing in or out any patents? If yes, provide details.

CHECKLIST 8.26:   VALUATION INFORMATION REQUEST (VIR) SOFTWARE

Business Name	Valuation Date

This is a generalized information request. Some items may not pertain to your company, and some items may not be readily available to you. In such cases, indicate N/A or notify us if other arrangements can be made to obtain the data. Items already provided are indicated. If you have any questions on the development of this information, please call.

Provided   **N/A**

Software

❑ ❑ 1. Describe the function of the software.

❑ ❑ 2. If available, provide historical cost records documenting development of the software:
    a) Person hours to develop
    b) Various technical levels of persons working on the assignment
    c) Pay scales for individuals in 2b
    d) Information to determine overhead rate

❑ ❑ 3. In the absence of historical cost records, estimate effort to re-create the software if it were to be developed from scratch:
    a) Who would work on the assignment (employees and consultants)
    b) Pay rates for individuals in 3a
    c) Information to determine overhead rate

❑ ❑ 4. What was the expected useful life at inception and at valuation date. Obtain support for estimate:
    a) When was software actually placed in use
    b) Describe internal development that may extend life
    c) Describe internal development of replacement software that might shorten life
    d) Describe external factors that may affect life

❑ ❑ 5. Obtain historical revenues applicable to software.

❑ ❑ 6. Provide projection of revenues applicable to the software for the next five years:
    a) Project revenues, including licensing income for life-span of software
    b) Project direct expenses associated with producing revenue in 6a
    c) Obtain or develop indirect expenses (i.e., overhead)

CHECKLIST 8.27: VALUATION INFORMATION REQUEST (VIR) PROPRIETARY PROCESS/PRODUCTS TECHNOLOGY

Business Name	Valuation Date

This is a generalized information request. Some items may not pertain to your company, and some items may not be readily available to you. In such cases, indicate N/A or notify us if other arrangements can be made to obtain the data. Items already provided are indicated. If you have any questions on the development of this information, please call.

Provided **N/A**

Proprietary Processes/Products Technology

❑ ❑ 1. Describe the proprietary process/product technology.

❑ ❑ 2. Describe competitive advantages and disadvantages of the proprietary process/product technology.

❑ ❑ 3. Describe industry trends and competitive pressures that may affect the useful life of the proprietary process/product technology.

❑ ❑ 4. In light of 2 and 3, what is the estimated useful life of the proprietary process/product technology support?

❑ ❑ 5. If available, please provide historical cost records documenting development of the process/product technology:
a) Person hours to develop
b) Various technical levels of persons working on the assignment
c) Pay scales for individuals in 5b
d) Information to determine overhead rate

❑ ❑ 6. In the absence of historical cost records, estimate effort to re-create the process/product technology if it were to be developed from scratch:
a) Who would work on the assignment (employees and consultants)
b) Pay rates for individuals in 6a
c) Information to determine overhead rate

❑ ❑ 7. Identify historical sale of products and/or services employing process/product technology for the last five years.

❑ ❑ 8. What products or services employ the proprietary process/product technology?

❑ ❑ 9. Provide projection of products and/or services that employ the process/product technology for the next five years:
a) Project revenues, including licensing income for the life-span of process/product technology
b) Project direct expenses associated with producing revenue in 9a
c) Obtain or develop indirect expenses (i.e., overhead)

❑ ❑ 10. Are you licensing in or out any technology? If yes, provide details.

CHECKLIST 8.28: VALUATION INFORMATION REQUEST (VIR) TRADEMARK/TRADE NAME

Business Name	Valuation Date

This is a generalized information request. Some items may not pertain to your company, and some items may not be readily available to you. In such cases, indicate N/A or notify us if other arrangements can be made to obtain the data. Items already provided are indicated. If you have any questions on the development of this information, please call.

Provided / N/A

Trademark/Trade Name

☐ ☐ 1. Provide a list of all trademark/trade name registrations.

☐ ☐ 2. Provide a list of trademark/trade names that are not registered.

☐ ☐ 3. Identify trademarks/trade names that are associated with products and/or services.

☐ ☐ 4. Identify historical sale of products and/or services employing trademarks/trade names for the last five years.

☐ ☐ 5. Provide projection of products and/or services that employ the trademarks/trade names for the next five years.

☐ ☐ 6. Is the company licensing in or out any trademarks/trade names? If yes, provide details.

CHECKLIST 8.29: PROCEDURES FOR THE VALUATION OF INTANGIBLE ASSETS

Business Name	Valuation Date

The definition of intangible asset should include current and noncurrent assets (excluding financial instruments) that lack physical substance. An intangible asset acquired in a business combination shall be recognized as an asset apart from goodwill if that asset arises from contractual or other legal rights. If an intangible asset does not arise from contractual or other legal rights, it shall be recognized as an asset apart from goodwill only if it is separable, that is, it is capable of being separated or divided from the acquired enterprise and sold, transferred, licensed, rented, or exchanged (regardless of whether there is an intent to do so). For GAAP purposes, an intangible asset that cannot be sold, transferred, licensed, rented, or exchanged individually is considered separable if it can be sold, transferred, licensed, rented, or exchanged with a related contract, asset, or liability. However, the value of an assembled workforce of at-will employees acquired in a business combination shall be included in the amount recorded as goodwill regardless of whether it meets the criteria for recognition apart from goodwill.

The purpose of this checklist is to guide the analyst in the valuation of intangible assets. For each item, the analyst should indicate completion, or check the item N/A.

Completed   N/A

Valuation

☐ ☐ 1. Determine the standard of value:
    a) Fair market value
    b) Fair value
    c) Investment value
    d) Intrinsic value or fundamental value
    e) Other: _____

☐ ☐ 2. State the purpose of the valuation:

☐ ☐ 3. Determine the premise of value:
    a) Value in use, as part of a going concern (This premise contemplates the contributory value to an income producing enterprise of the intangible asset as part of a mass assemblage of tangible and intangible assets.)
    b) Value in place, as part of an assemblage of assets (This premise contemplates that the intangible asset is fully functional, is part of an assemblage of assets that is ready for use, but is not currently engaged in the production of income.)
    c) Value in exchange, in an orderly disposition (This premise contemplates that the intangible asset will be sold in its current condition, with normal exposure to its appropriate secondary market, but without the contributory value of any associated tangible or intangible assets.)
    d) Value in exchange, in a forced liquidation (This premise contemplates that the intangible asset is sold piecemeal, in an auction environment, with an artificially abbreviated exposure to its secondary market.)

Intangible Asset Description

☐ ☐ 4. Is the intangible asset subject to specific identification or a recognizable description?

☐ ☐ 5. Categorize the intangible asset as:
    a) Marketing related
    b) Customer related
    c) Artistic related
    d) Contract related
    e) Technology related

(continues)

Completed	N/A	

Intangible Asset Description (*continued*)

☐	☐	6. Determine and list the intangible assets eligible for appraisal.
☐	☐	7. Describe fully the intangible asset identified. Attach necessary contracts, drawings, patents, listings, and so on to fully identify the intangible asset.

History of the Asset

☐	☐	8. Describe the legal existence and protection associated with the intangible asset.
☐	☐	9. Is the transferability of the ownership restricted? Explain.
☐	☐	10. Describe the susceptibility of the asset being destroyed.
☐	☐	11. Describe the inception of the intangible asset (attach a list providing start dates for all customer or client lists).
☐	☐	12. To what degree is the revenue associated with these intangible assets due to the day-to-day efforts of the owner? Explain.
☐	☐	13. Provide isolated financial results directly related to the asset, such as: a) Historical cost to create the asset b) Annual cost to maintain the asset c) Specific cash flow related to the asset
☐	☐	14. Provide a description of the history of the asset, including year(s) created.
☐	☐	15. Provide all contracts or agreements.
☐	☐	16. Provide all strategic, marketing, and business plans related to the asset.

Industry and Market

☐	☐	17. Provide all market or industry surveys or studies related to the asset.
☐	☐	18. Describe the competitive environment related to the asset.
☐	☐	19. Describe the general economic environment related to the asset.

Financial Information

☐	☐	20. Describe the specific industry environment related to the asset.
☐	☐	21. Provide all previous valuation reports related to the asset.
☐	☐	22. Provide all financial projections, including unit sales.
☐	☐	23. Provide all budgets/forecasts.
☐	☐	24. Determine associated cost of capital related directly to the asset.

Life Cycle

☐	☐	25. At what stage in its life cycle is the asset?
☐	☐	26. Please describe the product life cycle.

Valuation Approaches

☐	☐	27. Determine valuation approach: a) **Cost approach:** The cost approach is based on the principle of substitution. A prudent investor would not pay more for an intangible asset than it would cost to replace that intangible asset with a ready-made comparable substitute. Some intangible assets likely to be valued using the cost approach include computer software, automated databases, technical drawings, and documentation,

Completed

N/A

Valuation Approaches (*continued*)

blueprints and engineering drawings, laboratory notebooks, technical libraries, chemical formulations, food and other product recipes, and so on.

b) **Market approach:** The market approach compares the subject intangible asset with similar or comparable intangible assets that have been sold or listed for sale in the appropriate primary or secondary market. Correlations must be extrapolated.

c) **Income approach:** The income approach measures future economic benefits, discounted to a present value. Different measures of economic income may be relevant to the various income approach methodologies. Given the different measures of economic income that may be used in the income approach, an essential element in the application of this valuation approach is to ensure that the discount rate or the capitalization rate used is derived on a basis consistent with the measure of economic income used.

Cost Approach

☐ ☐ 28. Determine the appropriate cost method:

a) Reproduction cost (The cost at current prices to construct an exact duplicate or replica of the subject intangible asset. This duplicate would be created using the same materials, standards, design, layout, and quality of workmanship used to create the original intangible asset.)

b) Replacement cost (The cost to create at current prices an asset having equal utility to the intangible asset. Replacement cost uses modern methods and standards, state of the art design and layout, and the highest available quality of workmanship.)

☐ ☐ 29. Determine the appropriate adjustment for obsolescence:

a) Physical deterioration (The reduction from cost due to physical wear and tear resulting from continued use.)

b) Functional obsolescence (The reduction due to the inability to perform the function or yield the periodic utility for which the asset was originally designed.)

c) Technological obsolescence (The reduction due to improvements in technology that make an asset less than an ideal replacement for itself, generally resulting in improvements in design or engineering technology and resulting in greater standardized measure of utility production.)

d) Economic obsolescence (The reduction due to the effects, events, or conditions that are not controlled by, and thus external to, the current use or condition of the subject asset.)

☐ ☐ 30. Determine the number of employees involved in creating the intangible asset.

☐ ☐ 31. Categorize the employees by salary level.

☐ ☐ 32. Capture the associated employer cost related to each hour of salary level.

☐ ☐ 33. Determine the number of hours per employee salary level used to develop the asset.

☐ ☐ 34. Extend the number of hours per salary level by the salary and associated employer cost for an estimate of reproduction costs new.

☐ ☐ 35. Adjust reproduction cost new for associated deterioration or obsolescence.

☐ ☐ 36. Compare net result of reproduction cost with replacement cost new.

☐ ☐ 37. Complete the cost approach analysis.

(*continues*)

Completed	N/A	

		Market Approach
❑	❑	38. Determine the market served by the guideline or comparable asset.
❑	❑	39. Complete a primary and secondary market search for similar guideline assets, including an analysis of available public data specific to royalty rates and intellectual property transactions.
❑	❑	40. Determine the historical return on the investment earned by the subject intangible asset.
❑	❑	41. Determine the income-generating capacity of the subject intangible asset.
❑	❑	42. Determine the expected prospective return on the investment earned by the guideline asset.
❑	❑	43. Determine the expected prospective return by the subject intangible asset.
❑	❑	44. Determine the historical age and expected remaining useful life of the guideline or comparable intangible asset.
❑	❑	45. Determine the historical age and the remaining useful life of the subject intangible asset.
❑	❑	46. Analyze the terms of the sale of the guideline or the comparable intangible asset, including: a) The time of the sale b) The price paid c) The payout terms d) Other related terms (including special seller financing and earn-out agreement, noncompete agreement, and so on)
❑	❑	47. Determine the degree of adjustment necessary to the guideline or comparable intangible asset related to: a) Physical deterioration b) Functional obsolescence c) Technological obsolescence d) Economic obsolescence
❑	❑	48. Determine the degree of adjustment necessary to the subject intangible asset related to: a) Physical deterioration b) Functional obsolescence c) Technological obsolescence d) Economic obsolescence
❑	❑	49. Complete extrapolation of market approach correlation.

		Income Approach
❑	❑	50. Determine the economic income related to the identified intangible asset for the following: a) Net income before tax b) Net income after tax c) Net operating income d) Gross rental income e) Gross royalty or license income (actual or hypothetical if a relief from royalties method is employed, in which case should include an analysis of available public data specific to royalty rates and intellectual property transactions) f) Gross or operating cash flow g) Net or free cash flow

Completed

N/A

Income Approach (*continued*)

☐ ☐ 51. Determine the direct cost associated with maintaining the identified intangible asset. These costs should include cost of operating the asset, storing the asset (facilities), and managing a return from the asset (staff expenses). Pay particular attention to any anticipated unusual costs (such as renewing a patent).

☐ ☐ 52. Determine specific cash flow to the intangible asset by taking an economic return on contributory assets that are part of the initial cash flow stream. Contributory assets include:
a) Working capital
b) Fixed assets
c) Other intangible assets

☐ ☐ 53. Determine an appropriate discount rate reflecting a fair return on the investment by considering:
a) The opportunity cost of capital
b) The term period of the investment (including consideration of the expected remaining life of the subject intangible asset)
c) The systematic risk of the investment
d) The unsystematic risk of the investment
e) The time value of money
f) Growth (used for computing terminal value)

☐ ☐ 54. Obtain the necessary data to complete the actuarial retirement rate methodology, including:
a) Inception dates for all active files
b) Inception dates and retirement dates for all inactive files comprising the subject intangible asset (five-year history desirable)

☐ ☐ 55. In absence of hard data for No. 54, obtain management's representations as to:
a) Average age of all active files
b) Average remaining life of all active files
c) Estimate number of visits per file

☐ ☐ 56. Complete the actuarial retirement rate methodology by:
a) Observing the data
b) Determine the curve fitting using appropriate statistical tools (S-curve, O-curve, L-curve, R-curve)

☐ ☐ 57. Match the actuarial retirement rate curve with the actual data.

☐ ☐ 58. Determine the probable life curve.

☐ ☐ 59. Determine the remaining useful life and survivorship percentages.

☐ ☐ 60. Apply the survivorship percentages to the discounted cash flow.

☐ ☐ 61. Complete income approach methodology.

Relief from Royalties Method

☐ ☐ 62. How is the licensed product unique? What are the competitive advantages of the licensed product, including the scope and remaining life of any patents related to the products?

☐ ☐ 63. Analyze the markets in which the licensee will sell the licensed products, including:
a) Market size
b) Growth rates
c) Extent of competition
d) Recent developments

(*continues*)

Completed	N/A	
		Relief from Royalties Method (*continued*)
❑	❑	64. Determine the degree of complexity in the sale of the licensed product.
❑	❑	65. Determine the extent of customization in customer-specific applications. (Note: Royalty rates are generally inversely related to the level of complexity and licensee customization.)
❑	❑	66. Determine the size of the licensed territory, including any restrictions or exclusivity. (Note: Exclusivity is directly correlated to higher royalty rates.)
❑	❑	67. Determine the length of the initial license term and provisions for renewal. (Note: Royalty rates will increase if the provisions for renewal are favorable for licensing.)
❑	❑	68. What are the provisions for termination? (Note: The conditions for unilateral license termination generally protect the licensor from a material breach committed by the licensee. These terms should be identified.)
❑	❑	69. Does a minimum royalty rate exist?
❑	❑	70. Analyze the licensee's ability to assign the license to a third party, either directly or indirectly (e.g., through the purchase of stock ownership).
❑	❑	71. What is the licensor's presence within its own markets?
❑	❑	72. What is the licensor's financial viability?
❑	❑	73. What is the licensor's size and market share?
❑	❑	74. What is the licensor's depth of senior management and stability?
❑	❑	75. What is the licensor's depth of technical knowledge?
❑	❑	76. What is the licensor's business plan related to the licensed products, including R&D funding and market analysis?
❑	❑	77. To what extent and timeliness does the licensor offer to support the licensee, including: a) Technical product advice b) Assisting the licensee with sales c) Assisting the licensee with marketing efforts in the defined territory
❑	❑	78. Determine the licensee's available profit percentage available for the royalty (25%? 50%?) dependent on the following: a) Available profitability as compared with the industry b) The nature of the long-term competitive advantage of the product c) The degree the license terms are favorable to the licensee d) The degree of support and market share offered by the licensor e) The degree of any noncash value offered by the licensee to the licensor f) The degree the licensee is required to purchase certain components used in the manufacturing of licensed products from the licensor (mandatory supply arrangement) g) The degree of foreign exchange risk borne by either the licensee or the licensor (the risk of future devaluation)

CHECKLIST 8.30:   ROYALTY FACTORS

Exact Business Name	Date of Valuation

The objective of this checklist is to provide the analyst with a list of those items generally needed for the valuation of royalty rates. The analyst should initial as each item is obtained. Items not needed may be marked N/A.

Obtained   **N/A**

❑ ❑   1. The royalties received by the patentee for the licensing of the patent in suit, proving or tending to prove an established royalty.

❑ ❑   2. The rates paid by the licensee for the use of other patents comparable to the patent in suit.

❑ ❑   3. The nature and scope of the license, as exclusive or nonexclusive; or as restricted or nonrestricted in terms of territory or with respect to whom the manufactured product may be sold.

❑ ❑   4. The licensor's established policy and marketing program to maintain their patent monopoly by not licensing others to use the invention or by granting licenses under special conditions designed to preserve that monopoly.

❑ ❑   5. The commercial relationship between the licensor and licensee, such as whether they are competitors in the same territory in the same line of business or whether they are inventor and promoter.

❑ ❑   6. The effect of selling the patented specialty in promoting sales of other products of the licensee; the existing value of the invention to the licensor as a generator of sales of their nonpatented items; and the extent of such derivative or convoyed sales.

❑ ❑   7. The duration of the patent and the term of the license.

❑ ❑   8. The established profitability of the product made under the patent; its commercial success; and its current popularity.

❑ ❑   9. The utility and advantages of the patent property over the old modes or devices, if any, that had been used for working out similar results.

❑ ❑   10. The nature of the patented invention; the character of the commercial embodiment of it as owned and produced by the licensor; and the benefits to those who have used the invention.

❑ ❑   11. The extent to which the infringer has made use of the invention; and any evidence probative of the value of that use.

❑ ❑   12. The portion of the profit or of the selling price that may be customary in the particular business or in comparable businesses to allow for the use of the invention or analogous inventions.

❑ ❑   13. The portion of the realizable profit that should be credited to the invention as distinguished from nonpatented elements, the manufacturing process, business risks, or significant features or improvements added by the infringer.[1]

❑ ❑   14. The opinion testimony of qualified experts.

(continues)

Obtained   N/A

☐   ☐   15. The amount that a licensor (such as the patentee) and licensee (such as the infringer) would have agreed on (at the time the infringement began) if both had been reasonably and voluntarily trying to reach an agreement; that is, the amount that a prudent licensee—who desired, as a business proposition, to obtain a license to manufacture and sell a particular article embodying the patented invention—would have been willing to pay as a royalty and yet be able to make a reasonable profit and which amount would have been acceptable by a prudent patentee who was willing to grant a license.[2]

[1] Business appraisers may wish to compare *Georgia-Pacific* (318 Federal Supplement 1116 (1970)) Factor 13 to traditional excess-earnings approaches.

[2] Compare to business appraisal concept of "fair market value."

CHECKLIST 8.31:   MANAGEMENT INTERVIEW—PATENT VALUATION

Exact Business Name	Date of Valuation
Address	Phone
Analyst/Interviewer	Date of Interview

The objective of this management interview is to provide us with operational information that will aid us in the valuation of your business. We will keep the information confidential. Describe the following to the best of your ability. If necessary, use a separate sheet of paper, with reference to each item number. If some items are not applicable, please indicate N/A. Items already provided are indicated.

Provided   N/A

Interviewee(s)

☐ ☐   1.   Name   Title

Purpose and Objective of the Valuation

☐ ☐   2. The activity or transaction giving rise to the valuation.

Patent

☐ ☐   3. List of patents to be valued, including copy of complete application.

☐ ☐   4. Provide descriptions of the products and processes encompassed by the patents.

☐ ☐   5. Describe how the patent will be used in a product(s)?

☐ ☐   6. Describe the firm's R&D facilities.

☐ ☐   7. Identify the portion of time spent on R&D by each member of the group.

☐ ☐   8. What has company done to exploit the patent and what are the results?

☐ ☐   9. Describe the marketplace for the patent, including potential uses, current uses, size of market, and so on.

☐ ☐   10. If there are competing patents, what market share does each of the patents have?

☐ ☐   11. Have there been any market studies performed related to the patent?

☐ ☐   12. How will the lack of additional registrations affect the size of the marketplace for the products and the market penetration in other parts of the world?

☐ ☐   13. How defendable is the patent?

☐ ☐   14. Why was it not registered in additional countries?

☐ ☐   15. Has there been any actual, threatened, or potential litigation involving the patent?

☐ ☐   16. What's the estimated time until the patent becomes technically obsolete?

☐ ☐   17. What alternatives (real or perceived) are there for the patents for potential users?

☐ ☐   18. How does the patent benefit the user?

(continues)

Provided	N/A	
		Patent (*continued*)
☐	☐	19. What is the cost to upgrade technology for necessary enhancements to keep it competitive?
☐	☐	20. What are the untapped uses of the patent?
☐	☐	21. Has the patent ever been offered (or planned to be) for license? If so, on what terms?
☐	☐	22. Has the patent ever been (or planned to be) offered for sale? If so, at what price?
☐	☐	23. Has the patent ever been valued by internal or external parties?
☐	☐	24. If the company is gifting the patent, why does the company want to get rid of the patent? Why was it developed if it isn't necessary?
☐	☐	25. If applicable, why do you believe the tax benefit of a charitable donation is more valuable to the company than exploiting the patent?

CHECKLIST 8.32:   MANAGEMENT INTERVIEW—REASONABLE COMPENSATION

Exact Business Name	Date of Valuation
Address	Phone
Analyst/Interviewer	Date of Interview

The objective of this management interview is to provide us with information that will aid us in the analysis of reasonable compensation. We will keep the information confidential. Describe the following to the best of your ability. If necessary, use a separate sheet of paper, with reference to each item number. If some items are not applicable, please indicate N/A. Items already provided are indicated.

Provided   N/A

Interviewee(s)

☐ ☐   1.   Name   Title

Description of Duties of Professional

☐ ☐   1. Discuss the impact of the professional on the company's financial performance.

☐ ☐   2. Provide the qualifications—training, education, licensing, and experience—of the professional.

☐ ☐   3. How many hours does the professional work? How many are typically required for these duties?

☐ ☐   4. What are the travel requirements of the position?

☐ ☐   5. What unique technical, marketing, or innovation skills are required by this position that would be difficult to replace, if any?

☐ ☐   6. Provide the fringe benefits and reimbursed expenses of this position.

☐ ☐   7. What duties, responsibilities, and aspects of the business are handled by this professional?[1]

☐ ☐   8. What are the roles/titles used by the company to describe this position?[1]

☐ ☐   9. What are the achievements and successes of the professional in the position?

☐ ☐   10. What have been the struggles and failures of the professional in the position?

☐ ☐   11. Does the professional have relationships with customers, prospective customers, regulators, referral sources, suppliers, lenders, and employees? What is the nature and "stickiness" of these relationships?

☐ ☐   12. Does the company's reputation rely on the professional's reputation?

☐ ☐   13. Does a compensation committee or unrelated group (board of directors) set compensation?

☐ ☐   14. How is compensation or bonuses of nonowner employees determined?

☐ ☐   15. Who are the highest paid nonrelated employees and what are their duties?

(continues)

Provided	N/A	
		Description of Duties of Professional (*continued*)
❑	❑	16. On what formula or measurement is the owner's/family member's compensation based?
❑	❑	17. Has the professional been under-compensated in previous years? Was the intent of the company to make up for the lower compensation to the individual in the future?
❑	❑	18. When is the compensation received by the professional?
❑	❑	19. How many people would be hired to replace the professional? a) What would the roles/titles/duties be of these individuals? b) What would be the fair compensation for such individuals?
❑	❑	20. Has the professional provided guarantees of debt on behalf of the company?
❑	❑	21. Does the professional have duties, hobbies, activities, obligations, and so on outside of work that occupy a significant amount of time?
❑	❑	22. Is there anything else I should know regarding the compensation or characteristics of the professional or company that would be relevant to setting compensation?
		Other Information Requested
❑	❑	23. Employment contracts, noncompete agreements, buy-sells, or other agreements between individuals and the company.
❑	❑	24. Owners' compensation history.
❑	❑	25. History of distributions taken.

[1] Be careful of titles. The title used by one business might not be the same as that used by another. Many owners perform multiple duties that would typically be described by various job titles. In some cases, multiple titles/positions may be analyzed for one individual. When one person has multiple titles, it may be appropriate to determine pay for the highest position and then increase it by some reasonable allowance.

CHECKLIST 8.33: REASONABLE COMPENSATION: ADDITIONAL DISCUSSION QUESTIONS

Company

1. How long has the business been established?
2. Is the company's current financial condition favorable?
3. Are financial ratios favorable in terms of sales, income, assets, and so on?
4. Are sales and profits stable or growing?
5. How do current economic conditions affect the company?
6. Does the company prosper in poor economic or industry conditions?
7. Does the corporation have a history of paying (at least some) dividends?

Economy and Industry

8. Are economic conditions in the industry favorable?
9. Is the industry highly competitive?

Policies

10. Does the company have a (written) salary policy as to all employees?
11. Does the company offer a pension plan or profit-sharing plan to employees? If not, higher compensation may be given as an alternative.
12. Does the company have a documented compensation policy that has been followed?
13. Are there similarities to how compensation or bonuses of other nonowner employees are determined?
14. How does the level of fringe benefits compare to those offered at other companies or to other individuals?
15. Was the individual reimbursed for business expenses that the individual paid personally?

Comparisons

16. Are data available for individuals performing comparable duties at the subject company or a competitor/comparable company?
17. Is the comparison being made to companies in the same or similar geographic area?
18. Are compensation levels reasonable in comparison to what individuals of similar businesses receive?
19. How does compensation compare to salaries paid with the individual's gross and net?
20. How does compensation compare to distributions to officers and retained earnings?
21. How does compensation compare to compensation of nonowner employees within the company?
22. Does the company consistently pay above-market rates for other employees? If so, an above-market rate may be appropriate for an owner.
23. How does the company compare in terms of size, specialization, and complexity of the business?
24. How do hours worked compare to previous years and other individuals in the same company and comparable companies?
25. Are the quality and/or quantity of services provided by the individual clearly exceptional compared to others?

Compensation

26. What is the individual's salary history?
27. How consistent has the individual's compensation been over time?
28. Was the employee underpaid in earlier years? Was it documented?
29. Is the greater part of compensation in the form of salary rather than bonuses?
30. When is compensation received—throughout the year, end of year to zero out income, or other timing?
31. Would an independent investor have approved the compensation?

Skills, Duties, and Responsibilities

32. What are the employee's qualifications?
33. What training, education, licensing, and experience are truly required?
34. Does the individual have a high level of education or specialized training?
35. Does the individual have much experience in the industry?
36. Is the individual a mentor?
37. Does the individual have excellent decision-making and strategic planning skills?

(continues)

Skills, Duties, and Responsibilities (*continued*)

38. Does the individual perform the duties of several positions (CFO, marketing director, personnel)?
39. Does the individual perform marketing and business-development duties?
40. Does the individual have good leadership skills?
41. Does the individual manage other employees?
42. Is the individual the company's face to the outside world?
43. Does the individual work long hours and have heavy workloads?
44. Does the individual handle diverse aspects of the business?
45. Have all duties of the individual been captured?
46. Does the individual operate with relatively low levels of staff support?
47. Does the job title of the individual compare to the job description?

Individual

48. Would the business flounder without the individual?
49. Does the individual possess unique technical, marketing, or innovation skills that would be difficult to replace?
50. Has the individual made identifiable contributions to the success of the company?
51. Does the individual's personality affect performance?
52. Does the individual guarantee the employer's debt?
53. What is the individual's degree of control of the business?
54. Does the individual have a length of service that demonstrates loyalty and commitment?
55. Would the individual be difficult to replace with someone having comparable experience and skills?

CHECKLIST 8.34:   REVENUE RULING 59-60: VALUATION CHECKLIST

Revenue Ruling 59-60 contains a wealth of information. This checklist presents the ruling in an easy-to-follow format.

The primary information concerning discounts and premiums is highlighted by an asterisk (*).

1a. Purpose

- ❑ Estate tax
- ❑ Gift tax
- ❑ Income tax (as amplified by Revenue Ruling 65-192)

1b. Type of Subject Entity/Assets

- ❑ *Value of closely held corporations
- ❑ *Value of thinly traded stock
- ❑ *Value of other business entities such as partnerships, proprietorships, and so on (as amplified by Revenue Ruling 65-192)

2. Background Definitions

Date of Valuation
- ❑ Date of death
- ❑ Alternate date (six months after date of death)

Definition of Fair Market Value
- ❑ "The price at which the property would change hands between a willing buyer and a willing seller when the former is not under any compulsion to buy and the latter is not under any compulsion to sell, both parties having reasonable knowledge of relevant facts."
- ❑ "The hypothetical buyer and seller are assumed to be able, as well as willing, to trade and to be well informed about the property and concerning the market for such property."

3. Approach to Valuation

- ❑ Facts and circumstances
- ❑ No general formula applicable
- ❑ Wide difference of opinion as to fair market value
- ❑ Valuation is not an exact science.
- ❑ Sound valuation:
  - ❑ Relevant facts
  - ❑ Common sense
  - ❑ Informed judgment
  - ❑ Reasonableness
- ❑ Future outlook:
  - ❑ Value varies as general economic conditions change.
  - ❑ Optimism versus pessimism
  - ❑ Uncertainty as to the stability or continuity of future income
  - ❑ Risk of loss of earnings and value
  - ❑ Highly speculative value to very uncertain future prospects
  - ❑ Valuation is a prophecy as to the future.
- ❑ Use of guideline public companies

4. Factors to Consider

Nature of the Business and History of the Enterprise from Inception
- ❑ Past stability or instability
- ❑ Growth or lack of growth
- ❑ *Diversity or lack of diversity of its operations

(continues)

4. Factors to Consider (*continued*)

- ☐ *Degree of risk in the business
- ☐ Study of gross and net income
- ☐ *Dividend history
- ☐ Nature of the business
- ☐ Products or services
- ☐ Operating and investment assets
- ☐ *Capital structure
- ☐ Plant facilities
- ☐ Sales records
- ☐ *Management
- ☐ Due regard for recent significant changes
- ☐ Discount events of the past that are unlikely to recur in the future
- ☐ Value has a close relation to future expectancy.
- ☐ Recent events are of greatest help in predicting the future.

Economic Outlook in General and Condition and Outlook of the Specific Industry in Particular
- ☐ Current and prospective economic conditions
- ☐ National economy
- ☐ Industry or industries
- ☐ More or less successful than its competitors; stable with competitors
- ☐ Ability of industry to compete with other industries
- ☐ Prospective competition
- ☐ Price trends in the markets for commodities and securities
- ☐ *Possible effects of a key person or thin management/lack of succession
- ☐ Effect of the loss of the manager on the future expectancy of the business
- ☐ *Key person life insurance could be partially offsetting.

Book Value of the Stock and the Financial Condition of the Business
- ☐ Two historical fiscal year-end balance sheets
- ☐ Balance sheet as of the end of the month preceding the valuation date
- ☐ *Liquid position (ratio of current assets to current liabilities)
- ☐ Gross and net book value of principal classes of fixed assets
- ☐ Working capital
- ☐ Long-term indebtedness
- ☐ *Capital structure
- ☐ Net worth
- ☐ *Revalued nonoperating assets (i.e., investments in securities and real estate) on the basis of their market price
- ☐ Generally, nonoperating assets command lower rates of return.
- ☐ Acquisitions of production facilities or subsidiaries
- ☐ Improvements in financial position
- ☐ *Recapitalizations
- ☐ *Changes in capital structure
- ☐ *Classes of stock
- ☐ *Examine charter or certificate of incorporation for rights and privileges of the various stock issues, including:
  - ☐ Voting powers
  - ☐ Preference as to dividends
  - ☐ Preference as to assets in the event of liquidation

The Earning Capacity of the Company
- ☐ Preferably five or more years of detailed profit and loss statements
- ☐ Gross income by principal items
- ☐ Deductions from gross income:
  - ☐ Operating expenses
  - ☐ Interest and other expense on each item of long-term debt
  - ☐ Depreciation and depletion
  - ☐ *Officers' salaries in total if reasonable and in detail if they appear excessive
  - ☐ Contributions based on nature of business and its community position
  - ☐ Taxes

4. Factors to Consider (*continued*)

- ❏ *Net income available for dividends
- ❏ *Rates and amounts of dividends paid on each class of stock
- ❏ Remaining amount carried to surplus
- ❏ Adjustments to, and reconciliation with, surplus as stated on the balance sheet
- ❏ Separate recurrent from nonrecurrent items of income and expense
- ❏ *Distinguish between operating income and investment income.
- ❏ Ascertain whether or not any line of business is operating consistently at a loss and might be abandoned with benefit to the company.
- ❏ *Note percentage of earnings retained for business expansion when considering dividend-paying capacity.
- ❏ Secure all information concerning past income that will be helpful in predicting the future (potential future income is a major factor in many valuations).
- ❏ Prior earnings records are usually the most reliable guide as to future earnings expectancy.
- ❏ The use of arbitrary 5- or 10-year averages without regard to current trends or future prospects will not produce a realistic valuation.
- ❏ If a record of progressively increasing or decreasing net income is found, consider according greater weight to the most recent years' profits in estimating earning power.
- ❏ Look at margins and percentages of sales to assess risk:
  - ❏ Consumption of raw materials and supplies for manufacturers, processors, and fabricators
  - ❏ Cost of purchased merchandise for merchants
  - ❏ Utility services
  - ❏ Insurance
  - ❏ Taxes
  - ❏ Depreciation and depletion
  - ❏ Interest

Dividend-Paying Capacity
- ❏ *Primary consideration to dividend-paying capacity rather than dividends actually paid
- ❏ *Recognition of the necessity of retaining a reasonable portion of profits to meet competition
- ❏ *When valuing a controlling interest, the dividend factor is not a material element because the payment of such dividends is discretionary with the controlling stockholders.
- ❏ *The individual or group in control can substitute salaries and bonuses for dividends, thus reducing net income and understating the dividend-paying capacity of the company.
- ❏ *Dividends are a less reliable factor for valuation than dividend-paying capacity.

Whether the Enterprise Has Goodwill or Other Intangible Value
- ❏ Goodwill is based on earning capacity.
- ❏ Goodwill value is based on the excess of net earnings over and above a fair return on the net tangible assets.
- ❏ Factors to consider to support intangible value:
  - ❏ Prestige and renown of the business
  - ❏ Trade or brand name
  - ❏ Record of success over a prolonged period in a particular locality
- ❏ Sometimes it may not be possible to make a separate valuation of tangible and intangible assets.
- ❏ Intangible value can be measured by the amount that the value of the tangible assets exceeds the net book value of such assets.

Sales of the Stock and the Size of the Block of Stock to Be Valued
- ❏ Prior sales should be arm's length.
- ❏ Forced or distressed sales do not reflect fair market value.
- ❏ Isolated sales in small amounts may not control as a measure of value.
- ❏ *Blockage is not an issue because the stock is not publicly traded.
- ❏ *Size of the block of stock is a relevant factor.
- ❏ *A minority interest in an unlisted corporation's stock is more difficult to sell than a similar block of listed stock.
- ❏ *Control of a corporation, either actual or in effect, may justify a higher value for a specific block of stock because it is an added element of value.

(*continues*)

4. Factors to Consider (*continued*)

Market Price of Stocks of Corporations Engaged in the Same or a Similar Line of Business Having Their Stocks Actively Traded in a Free and Open Market, Either on an Exchange or Over-the-Counter

- ❏ *Must be evidence of an active free public market for the stock as of the valuation date to be used as a comparable company
- ❏ Use only comparable companies.
- ❏ The lines of business should be the same or similar.
- ❏ A comparable with one or more issues of preferred stock, bonds, or debentures in addition to its common stock should not be considered to be directly comparable to one having only common stock outstanding.
- ❏ A comparable with a declining business and decreasing markets is not comparable to one with a record of current progress and market expansion.

5. Weight to Be Accorded Various Factors

- ❏ Certain factors carry more weight than others because of the nature of the company's business.
- ❏ Earnings may be the most important criterion of value in some cases, whereas asset value will receive primary consideration in others.
- ❏ Give primary consideration to earnings when valuing stocks of companies that sell products or services to the public.
- ❏ Give greatest weight to the assets underlying the security to be valued for investment or holding-type companies.
- ❏ Closely held investment or real estate holding company:
  - ❏ Value is closely related to the value of the assets underlying the stock.
  - ❏ The appraiser should determine the fair market values of the assets of the company.
  - ❏ *Operating expenses of such a company and the cost of liquidating it, if any, merit consideration.
  - ❏ The market values of the assets give due weight to potential earnings and dividends of the particular items of property underlying the stock, capitalized at rates deemed proper by the investing public at the valuation date.
  - ❏ Adjusted net worth should be accorded greater weight in valuing the stock of a closely held investment or real estate holding company, whether or not it is family owned, than any of the other customary yardsticks of appraisal, such as earnings and dividend-paying capacity.

6. Capitalization Rates

- ❏ Capitalize the average or current results at some appropriate rate.
- ❏ One of the most difficult problems in valuation
- ❏ No ready or simple solution will become apparent by a cursory check of the rates of return and dividend yields in terms of the selling price of corporate shares listed on the major exchanges.
- ❏ Wide variations will be found even for companies in the same industry.
- ❏ The ratio will fluctuate from year to year depending on economic conditions.
- ❏ No standard tables of capitalization rates applicable to closely held corporations can be formulated.
- ❏ *Important factors to consider:
  - ❏ Nature of the business
  - ❏ Risk
  - ❏ Stability or irregularity of earnings

7. Average of Factors

- ❏ Valuations cannot be made on the basis of a prescribed formula.
- ❏ There is no means whereby the various applicable factors in a particular case can be assigned mathematical weights to derive the fair market value.
- ❏ No useful purpose is served by taking an average of several factors (e.g., book value, capitalized earnings, and capitalized dividends) and basing the valuation on the result.
- ❏ Such a process excludes active consideration of other pertinent factors, and the end result cannot be supported by a realistic application of the significant facts in the case except by mere chance.

8. Restrictive Agreements

- ❑ *Where shares of stock were acquired by a decedent subject to an option reserved by the issuing corporation to repurchase at a certain price, the option price usually is accepted as the fair market value for estate tax purposes.
- ❑ *The option price is not determinative of fair market value for gift tax purposes.
- ❑ *Where the option or buy and sell agreement is the result of voluntary action by the stockholders and is binding during the life as well as at the death of the stockholders, such agreement may or may not, depending on the circumstances of each case, fix the value for estate tax purposes.
- ❑ *Such restrictive agreements are a factor to be considered, along with other relevant factors, in determining fair market value.
- ❑ *Where the stockholder is free to dispose of their shares during life and the option is to become effective only on their death, the fair market value is not limited to the option price.
- ❑ *Determine whether the agreement represents a bona fide business arrangement or is a device to pass the decedent's shares for less than an adequate and full consideration in money or money's worth:
  - ❑ Relationship of the parties
  - ❑ Relative number of shares held by the decedent
  - ❑ Other material facts

CHECKLIST 8.35: REVENUE RULING 77-287: VALUATION CHECKLIST

Revenue Ruling 77-287 deals with the valuation of "restricted securities." These types of securities are also referred to as unregistered securities, investment letter stock, control stock, and private placement stock. A thorough understanding of this revenue ruling will also assist in determining discounts for lack of marketability (DLOM) in closely held companies.

1. Purpose

- ❑ Amplifies Revenue Ruling 59-60
- ❑ Valuation of securities that cannot be resold because they are restricted from resale pursuant to federal securities laws

2. Nature of the Problem

- ❑ Valuation of stock that has not been registered for public trading when the issuing company has stock of the same class that is actively traded in the securities markets
- ❑ Determine the difference between the fair market value of the registered actively traded shares versus the unregistered shares of the same company.
- ❑ For estate and gift tax as well as when unregistered shares are issued in exchange for assets or the stock of an acquired company

3. Background and Definitions

- ❑ Restricted securities cannot lawfully be distributed to the general public until a registration statement relating to the corporation underlying the securities has been filed and has become effective under the rules of the SEC and federal securities laws.
- ❑ *Restricted securities:* Defined in Rule 144 as "securities acquired directly or indirectly from the issuer thereof, or from an affiliate of such issuer, in a transaction or chain of transactions not involving any public offering."
- ❑ *Unregistered securities:* Securities where a registration statement, providing full disclosure by the issuing corporation, has not been filed with the SEC pursuant to the Securities Act of 1933. The registration statement provides the prospective investor with a factual basis on which to make an investment decision.
- ❑ *Investment letter stock:* Also called *letter stock.* Shares of stock issued without SEC registration. The stock is subject to resale and transfer restrictions set forth in a letter of agreement requested by the issuer and signed by the buyer. Such stock may be found in the hands of individual or institutional investors.
- ❑ *Control stock:* The stock is held by an officer, director, or other person close to corporate management. These people are subject to certain requirements pursuant to SEC rules on resale of shares they own in such corporations.
- ❑ *Private placement stock:* The stock has been placed with an institution or other investor who will presumably hold it for a long period and ultimately arrange to have the stock registered if it is to be offered to the general public. This stock may or may not be subject to a letter agreement. Private placements are exempted from the registration and prospectus provisions of the Securities Act of 1933.
- ❑ *Exempted securities:* Expressly excluded from the registration provisions of the Securities Act of 1933 and the distribution provisions of the Securities Exchange Act of 1934.
- ❑ *Exempted transactions:* Certain sales or distributions that do not involve a public offering and are excluded from the registration and prospectus provisions of the 1933 and 1934 Acts. Issuers do not have to go through the registration process.

4. Securities Industry Practice in Valuing Restricted Securities

- ❑ Investment company valuation practices:
  - ❑ Open-end investment companies must publish the valuation of their portfolios on a regular basis.
  - ❑ Many own restricted and unrestricted securities of the same companies

4. Securities Industry Practice in Valuing Restricted Securities (*continued*)

❑ Valuation methods:
  ❑ Market price of unrestricted publicly traded stock less a constant percentage discount based on purchase discount
  ❑ Market price of unrestricted publicly traded stock less a constant percentage discount different from purchase discount
  ❑ Market price of unrestricted publicly traded stock less a discount amortized over a fixed period
  ❑ Market price of the unrestricted publicly traded stock
  ❑ Cost of the restricted stock until it is registered
❑ The SEC stated that there are no automatic formulas.
❑ The SEC has determined that it is the responsibility of the board of directors of the particular investment company to determine the "fair value" of each issue of restricted securities in good faith.

Institutional Investors Study
❑ The SEC undertook an analysis of the purchases, sales, and holding of securities by financial institutions.
❑ Published in March 1971
❑ Includes an analysis of restricted securities
❑ Period of study is January 1, 1966, through June 30, 1969
❑ Characteristics of the restricted securities purchasers and issuers
❑ The size of transactions in both dollars and shares
❑ Marketability discounts on different trading markets
❑ Resale provisions
❑ The amount of discount allowed for restricted securities from the freely traded public price of the unrestricted securities was generally related to the following factors:

Earnings
  ❑ Earnings and sales have significant influence on the size of the discounts.
  ❑ Earnings patterns rather than sales patterns determine the degree of risk of an investment.

Sales
  ❑ The dollar amount of sales of the issuers' securities also has a major influence on the amount of discounts.
  ❑ Generally, companies with the lowest dollar amount of sales during the period accounted for most of the transactions involving the highest discounts while they accounted for the lowest number that involved the lowest discounts.

Trading Market
  ❑ Higher discounts for over-the-counter, followed by the American Stock Exchange, then the New York Stock Exchange

Resale Agreement Provisions
  ❑ The discount from market price provides the main incentive for a potential buyer to acquire restricted securities.
  ❑ Two factors are important in judging the opportunity cost of freezing funds in a restricted security:
    ❑ The risk that the underlying value of the stock will change in a way that, absent the restrictive provisions, would have prompted a sale
    ❑ The risk that the contemplated means of legally disposing the stock may not materialize
  ❑ Seller may be relieved of the expenses of registration and public distribution as well as the risk that the market will adversely change before the offering is completed.
  ❑ Buyer and seller bargaining strengths influence the discount.
  ❑ Most common provisions are:
    ❑ Option for "piggyback" rights to register restricted stock with the next registration statement, if any, filed by the issuer with the SEC
    ❑ Option to require registration at the seller's expense
    ❑ Option to require registration, but only at the buyer's own expense

(*continues*)

4. Securities Industry Practice in Valuing Restricted Securities (*continued*)

- ❏ Right to receive continuous disclosure of information about the issuer from the seller
- ❏ Right to select one or more directors of the issuer
- ❏ Option to purchase additional shares of the issuer's stock
- ❏ Provision giving the buyer the right to have a greater voice in operations of the issuer, if the issuer does not meet previously agreed-on operating standards
- ❏ Institutional buyers often obtain these rights from sellers of restricted stocks.
- ❏ The more rights a buyer can acquire, the lower the buyer's risk, thus the lower the buyer's discount.
- ❏ Small buyers may not be able to negotiate the large discounts or the rights and options that the volume buyers are able to negotiate.

Summary

- ❏ A variety of methods have been used by the securities industry to value restricted securities.
- ❏ The SEC rejects all automatic or mechanical solutions to the valuation of restricted securities.
- ❏ The SEC prefers to rely on good-faith valuations by the board of directors of each company.
- ❏ An SEC study found that restricted securities generally are issued at a discount from the market value of freely traded securities.

5. Facts and Circumstances Material to the Valuation of Restricted Securities

- ❏ Often a company's stock cannot be traded because of securities statutes, as in the case of investment letter restrictions.
- ❏ Stock may also be restricted from trading because of a corporate charter restriction or a trust-agreement restriction.
- ❏ The following documents and facts, when used in conjunction with those discussed in section IV of Revenue Ruling 59-60, are useful in the valuation of restricted securities:
  - ❏ Any declaration of trust agreement or any other agreements relating to the shares of restricted stock
  - ❏ Any documents showing any offers to buy or sell or indications of interest in buying or selling the restricted shares
  - ❏ Latest company prospectus
  - ❏ Three to five years of annual reports
  - ❏ Trading prices and trading volume and the related class of traded securities one month preceding the valuation date
  - ❏ The relationship of the parties to the agreements concerning the restricted stocks, such as whether they are members of the immediate family or whether they are officers or directors of the company
  - ❏ Whether the interest being valued represents a majority or minority ownership

6. Weighing Facts and Circumstances Material to Restricted Stock Valuation

- ❏ Depending on the circumstances of each case, certain factors may carry more weight than others.
- ❏ Earnings, net assets, and net sales must be given primary consideration.
- ❏ In some cases, one element may be more important than others.
- ❏ For manufacturing, producing, or distributing companies, primary weight must be accorded earnings and net sales.
- ❏ For investment or holding companies, primary weight must be given to the net assets.
- ❏ Careful review of resale provisions found in restricted agreements
- ❏ The two elements of time and expense should be reflected in a discount.
- ❏ The longer the buyer of the shares must wait to liquidate the shares, the greater the discount.
- ❏ If certain provisions make it necessary for the buyer to bear the expense of registration, the discount is greater.
- ❏ If the provisions of the restricted stock agreement make it possible for the buyer to "piggyback" shares of the next offering, the discount would be smaller.

6. Weighing Facts and Circumstances Material to Restricted Stock Valuation (*continued*)

❑ The relative negotiating strengths of the buyer and seller of restricted stock
❑ A tight money situation may cause a buyer to have more negotiating strength.
❑ In some cases, the relative strengths may tend to cancel each other.
❑ The market experience of freely tradable securities of the same class as restricted securities is also significant.
❑ Whether the shares are privately held or publicly traded
❑ Securities traded on a public market generally are worth more to investors than those not traded on a public market.
❑ The type of public market in which the unrestricted securities are traded can be given consideration.

CHECKLIST 8.36:   REVENUE RULING 93-12: VALUATION CHECKLIST

The IRS revoked Revenue Ruling 81-253, which applied family attribution to determine control when valuing minority interests in closely held companies. After Revenue Ruling 81-253 was issued, the IRS lost a majority of the court cases concerning family attribution.

Revenue Ruling 93-12 states that a minority discount on stock transferred to a family member will not be challenged solely because the transferred interest, when aggregated with interests held by other family members, but will be a part of a controlling interest. This ruling arose from a gift tax case.

1. Issue

❑   If a donor transfers shares in a corporation to each of the donor's children, is the factor of corporate control in the family to be considered in valuing each transferred interest?

2. Facts

❑   Taxpayer owned all the shares of stock of a corporation.
❑   Taxpayer made simultaneous gifts of 20 percent blocks of stock to each of five children.

3. Law and Analysis

❑   The value of the property at the date of the gift shall be considered the amount of the gift.
❑   The value of the property is the price at which the property would change hands between a willing buyer and a willing seller, neither being under any compulsion to buy or to sell, and both having reasonable knowledge of relevant facts.
❑   Fair market value on the date of the gift
❑   Among the factors to be considered is the degree of control of the business being represented by the block of stock to be valued.
❑   Revenue Ruling 81-253, 1981-1 C.B. 187 holds that, ordinarily, no minority shareholder discount is allowed with respect to transfers of shares of stock between family members if, based on a composite of the family members' interests at the time of the transfer, control (either majority voting control or de facto control through family relationships) of the corporation exists in the family unit.
❑   Revenue Ruling 81-253 states that the Internal Revenue Service will not follow the decision in the 1981 case *Estate of Bright v. United States.*
❑   In *Bright*, the court allowed a 27.5 percent interest to be valued as a minority interest, even though the shares were to be held by the decedent's surviving spouse.
❑   *Propstra v. United States* (1982), *Estate of Andrews v. Commissioner* (1982), and *Estate of Lee v. Commissioner* (1978). These cases held that the corporations' shares owned by other family members cannot be attributed to an individual family member for determining whether the individual family member's share should be valued as a controlling interest of the corporation.
❑   The IRS has concluded, in the case of a corporation with a single class of stock, notwithstanding the family relationship of the donor, the donee, and other shareholders, the shares of other family members will not be aggregated with the transferred shares to determine whether the transferred shares should be valued as part of a controlling interest.
❑   The five 20 percent interests that were gifted should be valued without regard to the family relationship of the parties.

4. Holding

❑   If a donor transfers shares in a corporation to each of the donor's children, the factor of corporate control in the family is not considered in valuing each transferred interest.
❑   The IRS will follow *Bright, Propstra, Andrews*, and *Lee* in not assuming that all voting power held by family members may be aggregated as part of a controlling interest.
❑   A minority discount will not be disallowed solely because a transferred interest, when aggregated with interests held by family members, will be part of a controlling interest.
❑   This will be the case whether the donor held 100 percent or some lesser percentage of the stock immediately before the gift.

5. Effect on Other Documents

❑ Revenue Ruling 81-253 is revoked.

CHECKLIST 8.37: WORK PROGRAM

Subject Entity	Purpose of Valuation/Calculation	Valuation Date
Analyst/Date Completed	Principal/Date Reviewed	Estimated Due Date

The purpose of this Work Program is to provide guidance to the analyst throughout the engagement in completing the project. As the analyst completes each major section of the engagement, that portion of the assignment should be forwarded to the principal for review. *Persons responsible for each function are noted in each section following.*

Completed / Date

Planning—Principal

☐ ☐ 1. Review and accept the engagement letter.

☐ ☐ 2. Determine appropriate checklists (SSVS or other) to use to ensure that engagement is in compliance with applicable standard(s).

☐ ☐ 3. Identify critical valuation/calculation issues in consultation with principal.

☐ ☐ 4. Determine the file organization and sections.

☐ ☐ 5. Request information from client (submit VIR).

☐ ☐ 6. Establish target dates for key elements of the assignment, including the target report release date.

☐ ☐ 7. Identify/set up report template.

☐ ☐ 8. Identify/set up exhibit template(s).

Data Received—Principal and/or Analyst

☐ ☐ 9. Determine if the appropriate data have been received.

☐ ☐ 10. Review inventory; update information request.

☐ ☐ 11. Update inventory.

Financial Statement Analysis—Analyst

☐ ☐ 12. Spread/enter financial information.

☐ ☐ 13. Determine relevant SIC/NAICS code and industry data.

☐ ☐ 14. Verify accuracy of financial input.

☐ ☐ 15. Perform and document financial analysis, including rationale for judgment areas.

☐ ☐ 16. Perform and document management interview (Principal responsibility).

Market Research—Analyst

☐ ☐ 17. Research economic and industry outlooks.

☐ ☐ 18. Search for guideline companies and or external transactions.

☐ ☐ 19. Determine and document acceptance of guideline companies.

☐ ☐ 20. Gather information on guideline companies and/or external transactions.

Completed	Date	

Guideline Public Companies—Analyst

❑	❑	21. Spread/enter guideline public company financial information.
❑	❑	22. Verify accuracy of input.
❑	❑	23. Analyze financial ratios and determine final pricing ratios.
❑	❑	24. Finalize value conclusion/calculation.

Guideline Company Transactions—Analyst

❑	❑	25. Spread/enter guideline transaction information.
❑	❑	26. Verify accuracy of input.
❑	❑	27. Analyze financial ratios and determine final pricing ratios.
❑	❑	28. Finalize value conclusion/calculation.

Asset-Based Approach—Analyst

❑	❑	29. Determine assets and liabilities to be restated.
❑	❑	30. Obtain appraisals performed by other appraisers.
❑	❑	31. Obtain client representations, and so on.
❑	❑	32. Verify accuracy of input.
❑	❑	33. Finalize value conclusion/calculation.

Income Approach—Analyst

❑	❑	34. Develop the discount rate and/or capitalization rate; document rationale.
❑	❑	35. Normalize the financial statements, if appropriate.
❑	❑	36. Develop ongoing earnings base and/or projections; document rationale.
❑	❑	37. Verify accuracy of input.
❑	❑	38. Finalize value conclusion/calculation.
❑	❑	39. Control premium, discount for lack of marketability, discount rate, and so on.
❑	❑	40. Value indicator and weight of each.
❑	❑	41. Determine final value conclusion/calculation.

Allocation of Intangible Assets—See Separate Work Program for Intangibles
Report Narrative—Analyst and Principal

❑	❑	42. Prepare Draft Report.
❑	❑	43. Complete **Review Report and Math.**
❑	❑	44. Complete final review of report after draft changes are processed.
❑	❑	45. Initial Gold Sheet in appropriate areas.

CHECKLIST 8.38: SSVS VS SECTION 100 COMPLIANCE CHECKLIST—VALUATION ENGAGEMENT

To Be Used in Conjunction with SSVS Compliance Flowchart

Business Name	Subject Interest	Valuation Date
Valuation Purpose	Standard of Value	Premise of Value
Analyst (sign and date)	Manager (sign and date)	Principal (sign and date)

This checklist assists the valuation analyst so that:

1. Their work is in compliance with the American Institute of Certified Public Accountants' (AICPA) Statement on Standards for Valuation Services VS Section 100 (SSVS). This checklist must be used in conjunction with the SSVS Compliance Flowchart and SSVS in order to provide more confidence that SSVS requirements are met.

2. The working papers support the valuation conclusion(s) or calculation(s).

All "No" or "N/A" answers should be individually explained in the space provided on the last page of this checklist.

Yes   No   N/A   ¶SSVS

INTRODUCTION AND SCOPE

			Scope
❑	❑	❑	¶.01, .04.	Does the assignment cause the valuation analyst (analyst) to estimate the value of a business, business ownership interest, security, or intangible asset (subject interest) by applying valuation approaches/methods while using professional judgment in applying those approaches/methods? (This question applies whether the assignment is a valuation engagement or an analysis that is part of a larger engagement.)
❑	❑	❑	¶.03.	Has the analyst considered the applicable government regulations and other professional standards applicable to the engagement?

			Exceptions from SSVS
❑	❑	❑	¶.05.	Valuation estimate is part of an attest engagement (as defined by the "Independence Rule" of the AICPA Code of Professional Conduct), such as an audit, review, or compilation of financial statements.
❑	❑	❑	¶.06.	Value of subject interest was provided by client or third party and valuation approaches/methods are not applied by the analyst.
❑	❑	❑	¶.07.	This is an internal use assignment between employer and employee not in public accounting practice, as defined in the AICPA Code of Professional Conduct (ET Sec. 0.400.42).
❑	❑	❑	¶.08.	This engagement is to exclusively determine economic damages (e.g., lost profits), but not to estimate value.
❑	❑	❑	¶.09.	The valuation estimate is a result of a mechanical computation (i.e., valuation approaches/methods and professional judgment are not used).
❑	❑	❑	¶.09.	It's not practical or not reasonable to obtain or use relevant information (i.e., can't apply valuation approaches and methods).

Yes	No	N/A	SSVS

Jurisdictional Exception

☐ ☐ ☐   ¶.10. Jurisdictional Exception*—SSVS differs from published governmental, judicial, or accounting authority, or such authority specifies valuation development procedures or valuation reporting procedures.

       * Comply with relevant standard(s) for that portion(s) of the engagement; SSVS applies to remaining section(s).

OVERALL ENGAGEMENT CONSIDERATIONS

Professional Competency (AICPA Code of Professional Conduct E.T. Sec. 1.300.101 and 2.300.001)

☐ ☐ ☐   ¶.11. Analyst or analyst's firm can reasonably expect to provide services with professional competence that involve special knowledge and skill so that analyst can identify, gather, and analyze data; consider/apply appropriate approaches/methods; use professional judgment to estimate value.

       ¶.12. Did the analyst consider:

☐ ☐ ☐   a) The subject entity and its industry

☐ ☐ ☐   b) Subject interest

☐ ☐ ☐   c) Valuation date

       d) Scope of valuation engagement:

☐ ☐ ☐   i) Purpose of valuation engagement

☐ ☐ ☐   ii) Assumptions and limiting conditions (¶.18)

☐ ☐ ☐   iii) Standards of value and premise of value

☐ ☐ ☐   iv) Type of report to be issued; intended use and users of the report; restrictions on the use of the report (¶.48)

☐ ☐ ☐   e) If governmental regulations or other professional standards apply to subject interest or engagement

Assess Nature and Risk of Valuation Services and Client Expectations

       ¶.13. Did the analyst consider:

☐ ☐ ☐   a) Proposed terms of the engagement

☐ ☐ ☐   b) Identity of client

☐ ☐ ☐   c) Nature and ownership rights in the subject interest; control characteristics; degree of marketability

☐ ☐ ☐   d) Procedural requirements and the extent, if any, to which procedures will be limited by either the client, or circumstances beyond the client's or the analyst's control

☐ ☐ ☐   e) The use and limitations of the report and the conclusion of value

☐ ☐ ☐   f) Any obligation to update the valuation

Objectivity and Conflict of Interest

☐ ☐ ☐   ¶.14. Was the analyst objective and did they understand the obligation to be impartial, intellectually honest, disinterested, and free from conflicts of interest?

☐ ☐ ☐   ▪ Did the analyst disclose any potential conflict of interest and obtain consent as required under AICPA "Conflicts of Interest" Interpretation E.T. Sec. 1.110.010 and 2.110.010?

Independence and Valuation

☐ ☐ ☐   ¶.15. Did the analyst meet the requirements included in the interpretations of the "Non Attest Services" subtopic (E. T. Sec. 1.295) under the "Independence Rule" (E. T. Sec. 1.200.001) if valuation services are performed for a client for which an attest engagement is also performed by the valuation analyst/firm?

(continues)

Yes	No	N/A	SSVS	
				Establish an Understanding with the Client
❑	❑	❑		¶.16. Is the understanding with the client documented either in writing or, if oral, in the analyst's file or working papers?
❑	❑	❑		▪ If applicable, did the analyst modify the understanding if a modification is encountered?
				¶.17. At a minimum, obtain an understanding between the valuation analyst and the client regarding:
❑	❑	❑		▪ Nature, purpose and objective of the engagement
❑	❑	❑		▪ Client's responsibilities
❑	❑	❑		▪ Valuation analyst's responsibilities
❑	❑	❑		▪ Applicable assumptions and limiting conditions (¶.18)
❑	❑	❑		▪ Type of report
❑	❑	❑		▪ Standard of value
				Assumptions and Limiting Conditions
❑	❑	❑		¶.18. Did the analyst disclose the assumptions and limiting conditions in the valuation report as provided in SSVS Appendix A?
				Scope Restrictions and Limiting Conditions
❑	❑	❑		¶.19. Did the analyst discuss any restrictions or limitations on the scope of the analyst's work or data available to the analyst known at the time?
				Work of Specialist(s)
❑	❑	❑		¶.20. Did the analyst note in the assumptions and limiting conditions the level of responsibility, if any, assumed by the analyst for the work of the third-party specialist(s)?
❑	❑	❑		▪ Did the analyst consider the option of including the report of the third-party specialist in their valuation report?

DEVELOPMENT—VALUATION ENGAGEMENT

Yes	No	N/A	SSVS	
				Determine Type of Engagement: Valuation or Calculation
❑	❑	❑		¶.21. Establish with the client whether the engagement is a valuation or calculation engagement.
❑	❑	❑		¶.21a. Was the analyst free to apply the valuation approaches and methods they deem appropriate in the circumstances?
				Hypothetical Conditions
❑	❑	❑		¶.22. Did the analyst use any hypothetical conditions?
❑	❑	❑		▪ If so, did the analyst indicate the purpose for including the hypothetical condition(s) and discuss these conditions in the report?
				Conducting a Valuation Engagement: Obtaining and Analyzing Information
❑	❑	❑		¶.23. In performing the valuation engagement, did the analyst:
❑	❑	❑		▪ Analyze the subject interest
❑	❑	❑		▪ Consider and apply appropriate valuation approaches and methods
❑	❑	❑		▪ Prepare and maintain appropriate documentation
❑	❑	❑		¶.24. Did the analyst choose their own sequence for the requirements and guidance in the standards?
				¶.25. Did the analyst consider the analysis of the subject interest, including, at a minimum:

Yes	No	N/A	SSVS¶	
				Conducting a Valuation Engagement: Obtaining and Analyzing Information (*continued*)
❏	❏	❏		■ Nature of the subject interest
❏	❏	❏		■ Scope of the valuation engagement
❏	❏	❏		■ Valuation date
❏	❏	❏		■ Intended use of the valuation
❏	❏	❏		■ Applicable standard of value
❏	❏	❏		■ Applicable premise of value
❏	❏	❏		■ Assumptions and limiting conditions
❏	❏	❏		■ Applicable governmental regulations or other professional standards
❏	❏	❏	¶.26.	Did the analyst consider the financial and nonfinancial information, including the type, availability, and significance of such information?
			¶.27.	Did the analyst, as available and applicable, obtain sufficient nonfinancial information to understand the subject entity, including its:
❏	❏	❏		■ Nature, background, and history
❏	❏	❏		■ Facilities
❏	❏	❏		■ Organizational structure
❏	❏	❏		■ Management team
❏	❏	❏		■ Classes of equity ownership interests and rights attached thereto
❏	❏	❏		■ Products and/or services
❏	❏	❏		■ Economic environment
❏	❏	❏		■ Geographical markets
❏	❏	❏		■ Industry markets
❏	❏	❏		■ Key customers and suppliers
❏	❏	❏		■ Competition
❏	❏	❏		■ Business risks
❏	❏	❏		■ Strategy and future plans
❏	❏	❏		■ Governmental or regulatory environment
			¶.28.	Did analyst obtain, where applicable and available, sufficient ownership information to:
❏	❏	❏		■ Determine type of ownership interest being valued and whether the interest exhibits control characteristics
❏	❏	❏		■ Analyze different ownership interests of other owners and assess potential effect on value of subject interest
❏	❏	❏		■ Understand classes and rights attached to the company's equity
❏	❏	❏		■ Understand rights included in, or excluded from, each intangible asset
❏	❏	❏		■ Understand other matters that may affect the value of the subject interest, such as:
❏	❏	❏		■ For a business, business interest, or security: relevant agreements such as shareholder agreements, partnership agreements, operating agreements, voting trust agreements, buy-sell agreements, loan covenants, restrictions, and any other contractual obligations or restrictions affecting the owners and the subject interest.
❏	❏	❏		■ For an intangible asset: legal rights, licensing and sublicensing agreements, nondisclosure agreements, developmental rights, commercialization or exploitation rights, and other contractual obligations.

(continues)

Yes	No	N/A	[SSVS]	
				Conducting a Valuation Engagement: Obtaining and Analyzing Information (*continued*)
			¶.29.	Did the analyst obtain, where appropriate and available, financial information on the subject interest such as:
❑	❑	❑		▪ Historical annual/interim financial statements; key ratios, statistics
❑	❑	❑		▪ Prospective financial information (e.g., budgets, forecasts, projections)
❑	❑	❑		▪ Comparative summaries of financial statements or information for a relevant period
❑	❑	❑		▪ Comparative common size financial statements/information of the entity and for the industry for an appropriate/relevant number of years
❑	❑	❑		▪ Income tax returns for an appropriate/relevant number of years
❑	❑	❑		▪ Owner compensation, including benefits and personal expenses
❑	❑	❑		▪ Key person or officers' life insurance
				▪ Management's response to inquiry regarding:
❑	❑	❑		▪ Advantageous or disadvantageous contracts
❑	❑	❑		▪ Contingent or off-balance-sheet assets or liabilities
❑	❑	❑		▪ Information on prior sales of company stock
❑	❑	❑	¶.30.	Did analyst read and evaluate the information to determine that it is reasonable for the purposes of the engagement?
				Conducting a Valuation Engagement: Valuation Approaches and Methods
❑	❑	❑	¶.31.	Did the analyst consider the three most common valuation approaches (i.e., income, asset/cost, and market)?
❑	❑	❑	¶.32.	Did the analyst use the valuation approaches and methods that are appropriate for the valuation engagement?
			¶.33a.	Did the analyst use the capitalization of benefits method (income approach); if so, consider:
❑	❑	❑		▪ Normalization adjustments
❑	❑	❑		▪ Nonrecurring revenue and expense items
❑	❑	❑		▪ Taxes
❑	❑	❑		▪ Capital structure and financing costs
❑	❑	❑		▪ Appropriate capital investments
❑	❑	❑		▪ Noncash items
❑	❑	❑		▪ Qualitative judgments for risks used to compute discount and capitalization rates
❑	❑	❑		▪ Expected changes (growth or decline) in future benefits
			¶.33b.	Did the analyst use the discounted future benefits method (income approach); and, if so, consider:
❑	❑	❑		▪ Normalization adjustments
❑	❑	❑		▪ Nonrecurring revenue and expense items
❑	❑	❑		▪ Taxes
❑	❑	❑		▪ Capital structure and financing costs
❑	❑	❑		▪ Appropriate capital investments
❑	❑	❑		▪ Noncash items
❑	❑	❑		▪ Qualitative judgments for risks used to compute discount and capitalization rates
❑	❑	❑		▪ Expected changes (growth or decline) in future benefits
❑	❑	❑		▪ Forecast/projection assumptions
❑	❑	❑		▪ Forecast/projected earnings or cash flows
❑	❑	❑		▪ Terminal value

Yes	No	N/A	¶SSVS	
				Conducting a Valuation Engagement: Valuation Approaches and Methods (*continued*)
			¶.33c.	For an intangible asset, did the analyst also consider, when relevant:
❑	❑	❑		▪ Remaining useful life
❑	❑	❑		▪ Current and anticipated future use of intangible asset
❑	❑	❑		▪ Rights attributable to the intangible asset
❑	❑	❑		▪ Position of intangible asset in its life cycle
❑	❑	❑		▪ Appropriate discount rate for the intangible asset
❑	❑	❑		▪ Appropriate capital or contributory asset charge, if any
❑	❑	❑		▪ Research and development or marketing expense needed to support the intangible asset in its existing state
❑	❑	❑		▪ Allocation of income (e.g., incremental, residual, or profit split income) to intangible asset
❑	❑	❑		▪ Whether any tax amortization benefit would be included
❑	❑	❑		▪ Discounted multiyear excess earnings
❑	❑	❑		▪ Market royalties
❑	❑	❑		▪ Relief from royalty
			¶.34.	Did the analyst use the Adjusted Net Asset Method (asset/cost approach) and consider, as appropriate, the following information related to the premise of value:
❑	❑	❑		▪ Identification of the assets and liabilities
❑	❑	❑		▪ Value of assets and liabilities (individually or in the aggregate)
❑	❑	❑		▪ Liquidation costs (if applicable)
			¶.35.	Did the analyst use the cost approach to value intangible assets and consider:
❑	❑	❑		▪ Type of cost to use (e.g., reproduction or replacement cost)
❑	❑	❑		▪ Appropriate depreciation/obsolescence, where applicable
❑	❑	❑		▪ Remaining useful life, where applicable
❑	❑	❑	¶.36.	Did the analyst consider the market approach to value a business, business ownership interest, or security?
❑	❑	❑		▪ Guideline public company method
❑	❑	❑		▪ Guideline company transactions method
❑	❑	❑		▪ Guideline sales of interest in the subject entity
			¶.36.	Did the analyst use the market approach to value intangible assets?
❑	❑	❑		▪ Comparable uncontrolled transactions method (uses arm's-length sales or licenses of guideline intangible assets)
❑	❑	❑		▪ Comparable profit margin method (compare profit margin earned by the subject entity that owns or operates the intangible asset to profit margins earned by guideline companies)
❑	❑	❑		▪ Relief from royalty method (the royalty rate, often expressed as a percentage of revenue, the subject entity would be obligated to pay to hypothetical third-party licensor for use of intangible asset)
❑	❑	❑		▪ When valuing intangible assets and using a method that relies on guideline intangible assets, consider the remaining useful life of the subject intangible asset and those of the guideline intangible assets, if available
			¶.37.	In determining valuation pricing multiples or metrics when using the market approach, did the analyst consider:
❑	❑	❑		▪ Qualitative and quantitative comparisons
❑	❑	❑		▪ Arm's-length transactions and prices
❑	❑	❑		▪ Dates and relevance of the market data
❑	❑	❑	¶.38.	Did analyst set forth in the report the rationale and support for valuation methods used?

(*continues*)

Yes	No	N/A	¶SSVS¶	

Conducting a Valuation Engagement: Obtaining and Analyzing Information (*continued*)

☐ ☐ ☐   **¶.39.** Did the analyst use a rule of thumb (technically not a valuation method) to estimate the value of the subject interest?

☐ ☐ ☐   ▪ As is typical, did the analyst use a rule of thumb as a reasonableness check against other methods and not use it as the only method?

Conducting a Valuation Engagement: Valuation Adjustments

  ¶.40. Did the analyst appropriately consider the following adjustments to a pre-adjustment value, when valuing a business, business ownership interest, or security:

☐ ☐ ☐   ▪ Discount for lack of marketability or liquidity

☐ ☐ ☐   ▪ Discount for lack of control

☐ ☐ ☐   ▪ If the analyst valued an intangible asset, was an adjustment for obsolescence considered?

  ¶.41. When valuing a controlling ownership interest under the income approach, did the analyst properly consider and separately value and add to or delete from the value of the operating entity the:

☐ ☐ ☐   ▪ Value of any nonoperating assets

☐ ☐ ☐   ▪ Value of any nonoperating liabilities

☐ ☐ ☐   ▪ Value of any excess or deficient operating assets

    ▪ When valuing a noncontrolling ownership interest under the income approach, did the analyst properly consider whether the following should be separately valued depending on an assessment of the influence exercisable by the noncontrolling interest, the:

☐ ☐ ☐   ▪ Value of any nonoperating assets

☐ ☐ ☐   ▪ Value of any nonoperating liabilities

☐ ☐ ☐   ▪ Value of any excess or deficient operating assets

☐ ☐ ☐   ▪ When using the asset-based or cost approach, did the analyst understand that it may not be necessary to separately consider and add back or delete from the value any nonoperating assets, nonoperating liabilities, or excess or deficient operating assets?

Conducting a Valuation Engagement: Conclusion of Value

  ¶.42. In arriving at conclusion of value, did the analyst:

☐ ☐ ☐   ▪ Correlate and reconcile results obtained under different approaches and methods used

☐ ☐ ☐   ▪ Assess the reliability of results under different approaches and methods using the information gathered during the valuation engagement

☐ ☐ ☐   ▪ Determine, based on *a* and *b*, whether the conclusion of value should reflect the results of one valuation approach and method or reflect a combination of results of more than one valuation approach and method

Conducting a Valuation Engagement: Subsequent Events

  ¶.43. Did the analyst consider:

☐ ☐ ☐   ▪ The valuation date is the specific date at which the analyst estimates the value of the subject interest and concludes on their estimate of value

☐ ☐ ☐   ▪ Only circumstances existing at the valuation date and events occurring up to the valuation date

Yes	No	N/A	SSVS	
				Conducting a Valuation Engagement: Subsequent Events (*continued*)
❑	❑	❑		■ That subsequent events are indicative of conditions that were not known or knowable at the valuation date, including conditions that arose subsequent to the valuation date
❑	❑	❑		■ That the valuation would not be updated to reflect those events or conditions
❑	❑	❑		■ That the valuation report would typically not include a discussion of those events or conditions because a valuation is performed as of a point in time—the valuation date—and the events described in this subparagraph (¶.43), occurring subsequent to that date, are not relevant to the value determined as of that date
❑	❑	❑		■ That in situations in which a valuation is meaningful to the intended user beyond the valuation date, the events may be of such nature and significance as to warrant disclosure (at the option of the valuation analyst) in a separate section of the report in order to keep users informed (¶.52*p*, 71*r*, and 74)
❑	❑	❑		■ That such disclosure should clearly indicate that information regarding the events is provided for informational purposes only and does not affect the determination of value as of the specified valuation date
				Documentation
				¶.44. Did the analyst prepare and retain appropriate records (based on analyst's professional judgment) to document the information obtained and analyzed, procedures performed, valuation approaches/methods considered and used, and the conclusion of value, such as:
❑	❑	❑		■ Information gathered and analyzed to obtain an understanding of matters that may affect the value of the subject interest (¶.25–¶.30)
❑	❑	❑		■ Assumptions and limiting conditions (¶.18)
❑	❑	❑		■ Any scope restriction or scope limitation on the analyst's work or data available (¶.19)
❑	❑	❑		■ Basis for using any valuation assumption during valuation engagement
❑	❑	❑		■ Valuation approaches and methods considered
❑	❑	❑		■ Valuation approaches and methods used, including rationale and support for their use
❑	❑	❑		■ If applicable, information on subsequent events considered by the analyst (¶.43)
❑	❑	❑		■ If rule of thumb(s) was/were used, the source of data, and how the rule was applied (¶.39)
❑	❑	❑		■ Other engagement documentation considered relevant by the analyst
❑	❑	❑		¶.45. Did the analyst retain (or intends to retain) documentation for a sufficient time to meet the needs of the applicable legal, regulatory, or other professional requirements for records retention?
❑	❑	❑		¶.46. Did analyst consider obtaining written representations from management regarding information provided to analyst?

(*continues*)

Explanation of "No" or "N/A" Answers	
¶. No.	Explanation
_____	_____
_____	_____
_____	_____
_____	_____
_____	_____
_____	_____
_____	_____
_____	_____
_____	_____

CHECKLIST 8.39: SSVS VS SECTION 100 COMPLIANCE CHECKLIST—DETAILED REPORT (VALUATION ENGAGEMENT)

To Be Used in Conjunction with SSVS Compliance Flowchart

Business Name	Subject Interest	Valuation Date
Valuation Purpose	Standard of Value	Premise of Value
Analyst (sign and date)	Manager (sign and date)	Principal (sign and date)

This checklist assists the valuation analyst so that:

1. Their work is in compliance with the American Institute of Certified Public Accountants' (AICPA) Statement on Standards for Valuation Services VS Section 100 (SSVS). This checklist must be used in conjunction with the SSVS Compliance Flowchart and SSVS in order to provide more confidence that SSVS requirements are met.

2. The working papers support the valuation conclusion(s) or calculation(s).

All "No" or "N/A" answers should be individually explained in the space provided on the last page of this checklist.

Yes	No	N/A	SSVS ¶	REPORTING GUIDELINES
				The Valuation Report
❑	❑	❑	¶.47.	Does the analyst understand that a valuation report is a written or oral communication to the client containing the conclusion of value or the calculation of value of the subject interest?
❑	❑	❑	¶.48.	Does the analyst understand that there are three types of written reports that an analyst may use to communicate the results of an engagement to estimate value: for a valuation engagement, a detailed report or a summary report; and for a calculation engagement, a calculation report (*each of these reports has a separate checklist; please refer to that checklist for additional requirements*)?
❑	❑	❑	¶.48a.	Does the analyst understand that a detailed report may be used only to communicate the results of a valuation engagement (conclusion of value); it should not be used to communicate the results of a calculation engagement (calculated value; ¶.51)?
❑	❑	❑	■	Does the analyst understand that, for a valuation engagement, the determination of whether to prepare a detailed report or a summary report is based on the level of reporting detail agreed to by the analyst and the client?
❑	❑	❑	¶.49.	Did the analyst indicate in the valuation report the restrictions on the use of the report (which may include restrictions on the users of the report, the uses of the report by such users, or both)?

(continues)

Yes	No	N/A	SSVS ¶	
				Reporting Exemption
❑	❑	❑		¶.50. Does the SSVS reporting exemption for certain controversy proceedings apply to the engagement?
❑	❑	❑		▪ Does the analyst understand that:
❑	❑	❑		▪ A valuation performed for a matter before a court, an arbitrator, a mediator, or other facilitator, or a matter in a governmental or administrative proceeding is exempt from SSVS reporting provisions
❑	❑	❑		▪ That the reporting exemption applies whether the matter proceeds to trial or settles
❑	❑	❑		▪ That the exemption applies only to the SSVS reporting provisions and that the developmental provisions of SSVS still apply
				Detailed Report: Valuation Engagement
❑	❑	❑		¶.51. Does the analyst understand that a detailed report is structured to provide sufficient information to permit intended users to understand the data, reasoning, and analyses underlying the analyst's conclusion of value? A detailed report should include, as applicable, the following sections titled using wording similar in content to that shown following:
❑	❑	❑		▪ Letter of transmittal
❑	❑	❑		▪ Table of contents
❑	❑	❑		▪ Introduction (see ¶.52)
❑	❑	❑		▪ Sources of information (see ¶.53)
❑	❑	❑		▪ Analysis of the subject entity and related nonfinancial information (see ¶.57)
❑	❑	❑		▪ Financial statement/information analysis (see ¶.58)
❑	❑	❑		▪ Valuation approaches and methods considered (see ¶.60–¶.62)
❑	❑	❑		▪ Valuation approaches and methods used
❑	❑	❑		▪ Valuation adjustments (see ¶.63)
❑	❑	❑		▪ Nonoperating assets, nonoperating liabilities, and excess or deficient operating assets, if any (see ¶.64)
❑	❑	❑		▪ Representation of the valuation analyst (see ¶.65)
❑	❑	❑		▪ Reconciliation of estimates and conclusion of value (see ¶.68)
❑	❑	❑		▪ Qualifications of the valuation analyst (see ¶.67)
❑	❑	❑		▪ Appendices and exhibits
❑	❑	❑		▪ Does the analyst understand that the previously listed report sections and detailed information within the sections described in ¶.52– ¶.77 may be positioned in the body of the report or elsewhere in the report at the discretion of the valuation analyst?
❑	❑	❑		¶.52. Does the report include an introduction that provides an overall description of the valuation engagement and contains sufficient information to enable the intended user(s) to understand the nature and scope of the valuation engagement, as well as the work performed, and may include, among other things, the following information (Note: If items following are not included in the introduction, they should be included elsewhere in the report):
❑	❑	❑		a) Identity of the client
❑	❑	❑		b) Purpose and intended use of the valuation
❑	❑	❑		c) Intended users of the valuation

Yes	No	N/A	SSVS ¶	
				Detailed Report: Valuation Engagement (*continued*)
❑	❑	❑		d) Identity of the subject entity
❑	❑	❑		e) Description of the subject interest
❑	❑	❑		f) Ownership control characteristics and degree of marketability of the business interest
❑	❑	❑		g) Valuation date
❑	❑	❑		h) Report date
❑	❑	❑		i) Type of report issued (i.e., detailed report)
❑	❑	❑		j) Applicable premise of value
❑	❑	❑		k) Applicable standard of value
❑	❑	❑		l) Assumptions and limiting conditions (could also be in an appendix) (¶.18)
❑	❑	❑		m) Restrictions or limitations in scope of work or data available for analysis (¶.19)
❑	❑	❑		n) Hypothetical conditions used in valuation engagement, including basis for their use (¶.22)
❑	❑	❑		o) Describe how any specialist's work was relied on, if any (¶.20)
❑	❑	❑		p) Disclose subsequent events in certain circumstances (¶.43)
❑	❑	❑		q) Any application of the jurisdictional exception (¶.10)
❑	❑	❑		r) Any additional information the analyst deems useful to enable the user(s) of the report to understand the work performed
❑	❑	❑	¶.53.	Does the report include a section(s) that identifies the relevant sources of information used in performing the valuation engagement, and may include the following:
❑	❑	❑		a) For a business, business interest, or security, a section stating whether and to what extent the subject entity's facilities were visited
❑	❑	❑		b) For an intangible asset, whether legal registration, contractual documentation, or other tangible evidence of the asset was inspected
❑	❑	❑		c) Names, positions, titles of persons interviewed and their relationships to the subject interest
❑	❑	❑		d) Financial statements and information (¶.54 and ¶.56)
❑	❑	❑		▪ For financial statements that were reported on (e.g., audit, review, compilation, or attest) by the analyst's firm, the report should disclose this fact and the type of report(s) issued.
❑	❑	❑		▪ For financial statements that were not reported on by the analyst's firm, the report should disclose this fact and state the analyst assumes no responsibility for the financial information.
❑	❑	❑		▪ For financial statements prepared by management and not audited, reviewed, compiled, or otherwise attested to by the analyst, identify the financial statements; state the analyst did not audit, review, compile, or attest under the AICPA's SSAEs; and the analyst assumes no responsibility for that information.
❑	❑	❑		e) Tax information (¶.55)
❑	❑	❑		▪ For tax returns used by the analyst to obtain any information used in the valuation analysis, identify the tax returns used and any existing relationship between the analyst and the tax preparer.
❑	❑	❑		▪ For tax returns used by the analyst to obtain any information in the valuation analysis, if the analyst or analyst's firm did not audit, review, compile, or attest under AICPA's SSAEs to any financial information derived from the tax returns used in the valuation analysis, the report should state this fact and that the analyst assumes no responsibility for that information.

(continues)

Yes	No	N/A	SSVS ¶	
				Detailed Report: Valuation Engagement (*continued*)
❑	❑	❑		f) Industry data
❑	❑	❑		g) Market data
❑	❑	❑		h) Economic data
❑	❑	❑		i) Other empirical information
❑	❑	❑		j) Relevant documents and other sources of information provided by or related to the entity
				Analysis of the Subject Entity and Related Nonfinancial and Financial Information
❑	❑	❑	¶.57.	Description of the relevant nonfinancial information used in the analysis (¶.27)
❑	❑	❑	¶.58.	Description of the relevant financial information used in the analysis (¶.29). Description may include:
❑	❑	❑		▪ Rationale underlying any normalization or control adjustment to financial information
❑	❑	❑		▪ Comparison of current performance with historical performance
❑	❑	❑		▪ Comparison of performance with industry trends and norms, where available
				Detailed Report—Valuation Approaches and Methods Used
❑	❑	❑	¶.59.	Valuation approaches/methods considered (¶.31)
❑	❑	❑	¶.60.	Did the analyst identify valuation methods used under each approach and the rationale for their use?
❑	❑	❑	¶.61a.	If the income approach was used, identify:
❑	❑	❑		▪ Composition of representative benefit stream
❑	❑	❑		▪ Method(s) used and summary of most relevant risk factors considered in selecting appropriate discount rate, capitalization rate, or both
❑	❑	❑		▪ Other factors (see ¶.33)
❑	❑	❑	¶.61b.	If the asset-based approach was used, describe any adjustments made by the analyst to balance sheet data.
❑	❑	❑	¶.61b.	If the cost approach was used, describe:
❑	❑	❑		▪ Type of cost used
❑	❑	❑		▪ How this cost was estimated
❑	❑	❑		▪ If applicable, forms of and costs associated with depreciation and obsolescence used under the approach and how those costs were estimated
❑	❑	❑	¶.61c.	If the market approach was used, describe:
				For the guideline public company method:
❑	❑	❑		▪ Selected guideline companies and process used in their selection
❑	❑	❑		▪ Pricing multiples used, how they were used, rational for selection, and any adjustments
				For the guideline company transactions method:
❑	❑	❑		▪ Sales transactions used, how they were used, and rationale for selection
❑	❑	❑		▪ Pricing multiples used, how they were used, and rationale for selection
❑	❑	❑		▪ If multiples were adjusted, rationale for the adjustments
				For guideline sales of interests in subject entity method:
❑	❑	❑		▪ The sales transactions used and how they were used
❑	❑	❑		▪ Rationale for determining that these sales were representative of arm's-length transactions
❑	❑	❑	¶.62.	If rule of thumb was used, in combination with other methods, did analyst disclose source of data and how rule was applied?

Yes	No	N/A	SSVS ¶	
				Detailed Report—Valuation Adjustments
❏	❏	❏	¶.63.	If the analyst made valuation adjustments:
❏	❏	❏		a) Identify each valuation adjustment considered and determined applicable (e.g., DLOM, DLOC)
❏	❏	❏		b) Describe the rationale for using the adjustment; factors considered in selecting amount/percentage used
❏	❏	❏		c) Describe the pre-adjustment value to which the adjustment was applied (¶.40)
				Detailed Report—Nonoperating and Excess Operating Assets
❏	❏	❏	¶.64.	For a business, business interest, or security, did valuation report identify any related nonoperating asset and/or liabilities, or excess/deficient operating assets and/or liabilities, and their effect on the valuation?
				Detailed Report—Analyst Representation and Qualifications; Client Responsibilities
❏	❏	❏	¶.65.	Does the report include the analyst(s) representation that summarizes factors guiding the work, such as the following examples:
❏	❏	❏		a) Analyses, opinions, and conclusion of value are personal to the analyst and are subject to the specified assumptions and limiting conditions (see ¶.18).
❏	❏	❏		b) Economic and industry data obtained from sources believed to be reliable; the analyst has not performed corroborating procedures to substantiate data.
❏	❏	❏		c) Valuation engagement was performed in accordance with AICPA SSVS.
❏	❏	❏		d) The parties the valuation report is intended for and restricted to; report should not be used by anyone other than identified parties.
❏	❏	❏		e) State whether the analyst's compensation is either fee-based or contingent on the outcome of the valuation.
❏	❏	❏		f) Identify any outside specialist; state the level of responsibility, if any, assumed by the analyst.
❏	❏	❏		g) The analyst has no obligation to update report or opinion of value for information that comes to their attention after the date of the report.
❏	❏	❏		h) Person(s) assuming responsibility for valuation signed the representation in their own name(s); no firm signature; names of those providing significant professional assistance are listed.
❏	❏	❏	¶.67.	Does report contain information regarding qualifications of the analyst?
				Detailed Report—Conclusion of Value
❏	❏	❏	¶.68.	In addition to a discussion of the rationale underlying the conclusion of value, this section should include the following or similar statements:
❏	❏	❏		a) The fact that a valuation engagement was performed, identifying the subject interest and valuation date
❏	❏	❏		b) Analysis performed solely for the purpose stated in report; resulting estimate of value should not be used for any other purpose
❏	❏	❏		c) Valuation engagement was conducted in accordance with AICPA SSVS
❏	❏	❏		d) A statement that the estimate of value resulting from a valuation engagement is expressed as a conclusion of value
❏	❏	❏		e) Explain scope of work or data available for the analyses, including any restrictions or limitations
❏	❏	❏		f) A statement describing the conclusion of value, either single amount or a range
❏	❏	❏		g) The conclusion of value subject to the assumptions and limiting conditions (¶.18) and to the analyst's representation (see ¶.65)

(continues)

Yes	No	N/A	¶ SSVS	
				Detailed Report—Conclusion of Value (*continued*)
❑	❑	❑		h) The report is signed in the name of the analyst or analyst's firm
❑	❑	❑		i) The date of valuation report is included
❑	❑	❑		j) The analyst has no obligation to update report or conclusion of value for information that comes to their attention after the date of the report
❑	❑	❑	¶.69.	Did the analyst consider using the example report language for reporting on a valuation engagement?
❑	❑	❑	¶.70.	Did the analyst use appendices and exhibits, including assumptions and limiting conditions and the analyst's representation?

Explanation of "No" or "N/A" Answers

¶ No.	Explanation
_____	_____
_____	_____
_____	_____
_____	_____
_____	_____
_____	_____
_____	_____
_____	_____
_____	_____
_____	_____
_____	_____
_____	_____

CHECKLIST 8.40: REVIEW CHECKLIST—EMINENT DOMAIN

Business Name	Valuation Date

This work program checklist has been developed for the purpose of providing a convenient method of establishing that the necessary procedures have been completed, thus ensuring the working papers adequately support valuation conclusions in an Eminent Domain valuation. The reviewer should check in the appropriate space following to indicate completion of the various phases of review.

Completed   N/A

Analysis

❑ ❑ 1. Check that the scope of our work has been unrestricted.

❑ ❑ 2. Obtain and review information gathered during the initial stages of this engagement, including a copy of the right-of-way map and any related memos or notes.

3. Coordinate an initial meeting with the business owner and perform the following procedures:

❑ ❑   a) Verify the history of the business and determine its qualifications for business damages. (The business, not necessarily the same owner, has been at that location for a minimum of four years as of the date of taking; there is a partial taking of property that affects the business on the remainder; the business has been damaged as a result of the take of property, with due consideration given to any limitation on access to and from the business.)

❑ ❑   b) As determined necessary, coordinate efforts with other experts, including:
- Real estate appraisers
- Engineers
- Customer surveys
- Marketing/site research
- Other

❑ ❑   c) Discuss the taking with the business owner and determine the general effect to the business. Prepare a memo.

❑ ❑   d) Obtain a general understanding of the business, its history, and ownership in detail.

❑ ❑   e) Determine the future plans the owner has for the business and document in detail.

❑ ❑   f) Obtain copies of the required financial information (usually this would include the prior five years' tax returns and financial statements, building leases, and current financial information since the latest year-end).

❑ ❑   g) Obtain necessary operational information required.

❑ ❑ 4. Immediately after meeting with the business owner, follow up with a letter summarizing the meeting.

❑ ❑ 5. If appropriate, initiate engagement letter for signature.

❑ ❑ 6. On receipt of financial information, submit it with proper instructions to the financial analyst for input.

❑ ❑ 7. Analyze output of financial data and calculate projections based on historical information. The resultant projections should represent the expected revenues and expenses for the business in the foreseeable future, adjusted for nonrecurring items, owner salaries, use of facilities, and equipment.

8. Review and verify the material consistency with reports submitted by other experts including:

(continues)

Completed	N/A	

Analysis (*continued*)

☐ ☐   a) Real estate appraisers

☐ ☐   b) Engineers

☐ ☐   c) Customer surveys

☐ ☐   d) Marketing/site research

☐ ☐   e) Other

☐ ☐   9. Using the financial projections and any other information obtained, including the operational data if applicable, determine the preliminary effect of the taking on the business. This analysis should include any possible reductions in revenues (and gross profits), savings from reduced expenses, required increases in expenses, and other costs to mitigate damages.

☐ ☐ 10. If it does appear economically feasible to continue in operation at the present location, consider a relocation of the business. This analysis would usually include an understanding of the customer base, the competitive nature of the business, the market rent situation, and any other pertinent factors.

☐ ☐ 11. In conjunction with the previous steps, calculate the value of the business.

     12. Conclude business damages as limited to the lesser of:

☐ ☐   a) Actual damage

☐ ☐   b) Relocation

☐ ☐   c) Value of the business

Reporting

☐ ☐ 13. Prepare a thorough list of the assumptions and information sources used.

☐ ☐ 14. Prepare a draft of the business damage report.

☐ ☐ 15. Review the report draft, and make any necessary changes.

☐ ☐ 16. Make arrangements to have the business owner and other pertinent parties review the report draft.

☐ ☐ 17. Incorporate agreed-on changes from all reviewers into final report and produce a final draft of the report.

Administrative Items

☐ ☐ 18. Review the final report and make sure all initials are obtained on a report control sheet.

☐ ☐ 19. Coordinate with Time and Billing personnel to ensure a detailed printout will be available of total time. Have a standard detailed billing prepared.

☐ ☐ 20. If necessary, prepare a representation letter and have it signed by the business owner.

☐ ☐ 21. Deliver appropriate copies of report and billing.

☐ ☐ 22. Review work paper file to make sure all work papers are properly prepared and support the final report.

CHECKLIST 8.41: NON-APPRAISER'S GUIDE TO REVIEWING BUSINESS VALUATION REPORTS

Check if the following items are reflected in the report.

Yes	No	
		Are the Following Clearly Stated?
❑	❑	1. Specific definition of what is being appraised[1]
❑	❑	2. Purpose of appraisal[1]
❑	❑	3. Date of valuation[1]
❑	❑	4. Date of report preparation[1]
❑	❑	5. Standard of value, including reference to statutes if a statutory standard is applicable[1]
		Are the Following Adequately Described to Give You a Basic Knowledge of
❑	❑	6. Form of ownership (corporate, partnership, etc.)[2]
❑	❑	7. History of the company[1]
❑	❑	8. Major assets, both tangible and intangible (goodwill, patents, etc.)[1]
❑	❑	9. Products or services[1]
❑	❑	10. Markets or customers[1]
❑	❑	11. Competition[1]
❑	❑	12. Management[2]
❑	❑	13. Who owns the company
❑	❑	14. How the company is capitalized
❑	❑	15. Outlook for the economy, industry, and company[1]
❑	❑	16. Past transactional evidence of value (sale of stock, etc.)[1]
❑	❑	17. Sensitivity to seasonal or cyclical factors[2]
❑	❑	18. State of incorporation
❑	❑	19. Sources of information[2]
		Financial Analysis[1]
❑	❑	20. Is there a discussion of the firm's financial statements?[2]
❑	❑	21. Are there exhibits summarizing balance sheets and income statements for a sufficient period of time?[2]
❑	❑	22. Are any adjustments made to the financial statements as explained?[2]
❑	❑	23. Are company financial statements compared to those of its industry?[2]
❑	❑	24. If discounted future earnings or cash flows are used, are the appropriate statements summarized and key assumptions included?[2]
		Valuation Methodology and Report
❑	❑	25. Are the methods used identified and the reasons for their selection discussed?[1]
❑	❑	26. Are the steps followed in the application of the method(s) understandable and do they lead you to the value conclusion?[1]
❑	❑	27. When applicable, are sales of similar businesses or capital stock of publicly traded similar businesses used for comparison?[3]
❑	❑	28. Does the report explain how any discounts, capitalization rates, or valuation multiples were determined or used?[2]
❑	❑	29. Is the terminology used in the report defined so that it is understandable?
❑	❑	30. Does the report identify the appraisers and have the appraisers signed the report?[1]
❑	❑	31. Does the report contain the statement of certification signed by the appraiser?[1]

(continues)

Yes No

Does the Appraiser's Statement of Qualifications Present Relevant Qualifications for This Appraisal?

❏   ❏   32. Education

❏   ❏   33. Technical training

❏   ❏   34. Professional designations

❏   ❏   35. Professional appraisal organization memberships and activities

❏   ❏   36. Type and years of experience

❏   ❏   37. Does the report contain a statement of confidentiality?[2]

Does the Report Contain a Statement of Assumptions and Limiting Conditions,[1] Regarding

❏   ❏   38. Conflicts of interest[2]

❏   ❏   39. Reliance on data and information supplied by others without verification[2]

❏   ❏   40. The valuation only being valid for the valuation date and stated purpose[2]

❏   ❏   41. Does the report, in your opinion, cover all the material factors that affect the value of the business?[2]

❏   ❏   42. Is the value conclusion reasonable, as a result of all the factors presented in the report?

1. Specifically mentioned in the Appraisal Foundation's Uniform Standards of Professional Appraisal Practice, the American Society of Appraisers' Business Valuation Standards AICPA SSVS VS Section 100.
2. Specifically mentioned only by American Society of Appraisers.
3. Specifically mentioned only by the Appraisal Foundation.

CHECKLIST 8.42:   AUDITOR REVIEW OF VALUATION FOR FINANCIAL REPORTING

Business Name	Valuation Date
Reviewer	Valuation Type

Each item on this checklist is to be reviewed progressively by the responsible auditor and by category as the valuer completes the engagement. Scheduling this progressive review of the valuation engagement will eliminate surprises at the end of the engagement, which could cause a delay in issuing the audit. This checklist does not replace the valuation audit program, but is intended to facilitate communication between the valuers and the auditors concerning key valuation issues as the valuation progresses. When completed, this review checklist will ensure the auditor has completed critical steps in the audit program.

Completed

Are the Following Clearly Stated?

☐   1. Does the valuer have specialized training in business valuation and intangible assets?

☐   2. Does the valuer hold the appropriate professional designations in business valuation, for example, CPA/ABV, ASA, CBA, CVA?

☐   3. Can the valuer adequately discuss the appropriate accounting guidance for the engagement?

☐   4. Does the valuer have adequate experience in valuing intangible assets?

☐   5. Does the valuer meet the qualifications for a valuation specialist per AU Section 336 and SSVS VS Section 100?

Industry and Company Risks

☐   6. Does the valuer understand your perception of the industry's business and financial risks applicable to the company?

☐   7. Does the valuer understand your perception of the company's business and financial risks?

☐   8. If the valuer is not familiar with the industry's business and financial risks, did they adequately communicate how they would obtain sufficient relevant knowledge about the industry's business and financial risks?

Company Projections

☐   9. Did the valuer perform a mathematical check of the company projections?

☐ 10. If so, did they find any mathematical errors?

☐ 11. Can the valuer adequately explain how they tested the underlying assumptions?

☐ 12. Does the valuer have a list of the assumptions that required additional analysis or support?

☐ 13. Does the valuer's risk analysis of the underlying assumptions correspond with your analysis of the underlying assumptions?

☐ 14. If not, can you reconcile the differences?

Guideline Companies Selected

☐ 15. Can the valuer adequately explain the process used in selecting the guideline companies?

☐ 16. Does the valuer have a list of considered but excluded companies?

☐ 17. Are all the guideline companies in the same industry?

☐ 18. If not, can the valuer explain why the guideline companies have the same investment risk characteristics as the subject company?

☐ 19. Do you agree that the guideline companies selected appear appropriate?

(continues)

Completed

Discount Rate Development

❑ 20. Did the valuer use the capital asset pricing model?

❑ 21. Did the valuer use the build-up method as a fundamental analysis?

❑ 22. Did the valuer use the weighted average cost capital?

❑ 23. If so, does the equity portion match either the capital asset pricing model or the build-up method?

❑ 24. If so, can the valuer justify the selection of the interest rate used?

❑ 25. If so, is the tax rate used in determining the after-tax interest rate appropriate for the subject company?

❑ 26. If so, can the valuer justify the weighting between the equity and the debt portions of the weighted average cost capital model?

❑ 27. Does the valuer have supporting documentation for the input items in the various discount rate development models?

Economic Adjustments

❑ 28. Has the company or valuer identified all the appropriate nonrecurring economic events or costs?

❑ 29. Can the valuer justify any other economic adjustments made to the income statements?

❑ 30. If using an adjusted balance sheet method, did the valuer provide appropriate documentation for the economic adjustments made to the balance sheet?

Allocation of Income to Identifiable Intangible Assets

❑ 31. Has the valuer made a list of identifiable intangible assets applicable to the subject company?

❑ 32. Does the schedule of income allocation have appropriate supporting documentation?

❑ 33. Does the schedule of income allocation reconcile to total company income?

❑ 34. Are there any reasons to disagree with the income allocation schedule?

❑ 35. If so, have these issues been discussed with the valuer?

Royalty Rates

❑ 36. Does the valuer have a list of royalty rates applicable to each identifiable intangible asset?

❑ 37. Were the royalty rates derived from a royalty rate survey?

❑ 38. If so, did the valuer present any analysis related to the quality or the survey?

❑ 39. Did the value use a rule of thumb in determining the royalty rate?

❑ 40. Were the royalty rates derived from a study of actual licensing transactions?

❑ 41. Can the valuer adequately explain the selection process used in determining the guideline licensing transaction?

❑ 42. Can the valuer explain any adjustments to the guideline royalty rate transactions?

CHECKLIST 8.43:   FAIR VALUE MEASUREMENT CHECKLIST

Target Name	
Acquirer Name	
Acquisition Date	
Type of Deal—Equity or Asset	
Consideration	
Purpose—Financial Reporting or Tax Reporting or Both	

This is a generalized outline intended to guide the analyst through the developmental processes required of ASC 805, Business Combinations. Some items may not pertain to the subject transaction or the subject company. The analyst using this checklist may note such items with N/A. Checklist items should be cross-referenced to the source document whether in electronic or printed form. Obtain sufficient relevant data to afford a reasonable basis for conclusions or recommendations in relation to each process.

Provided / N/A

I. Subject Company (Target)

**Determine the balance sheet account subject to fair value determination.
Distinguish between the Unit of Account and Unit of Valuation.**

☐ ☐   A. Determine highest and best use
☐ ☐   1. Physically possible
☐ ☐   2. Legally permissible
☐ ☐   3. Financially feasible
☐ ☐   4. Determine valuation premise
☐ ☐   a) Most advantageous of
                ■ In-use
                ■ Maximum value while used in combination with other assets
                ■ Aggregated
                ■ In exchange
                ■ Maximum value on a standalone basis
                ■ May be aggregated or disaggregated
☐ ☐   b) Determination is based on valuation premise likely selected by market participants.
☐ ☐   B. Consideration for valuing assets:
☐ ☐   1. The fair value should exclude assumptions relating to the specific buyer's (yours) unique synergies unless such synergies would be included by market participants in determining fair value
☐ ☐   C. Consideration for valuing liabilities:
☐ ☐   1. Nonperformance risk <u>must be considered</u>
☐ ☐   2. Nonperformance risk must be the <u>same before and after</u> the assumed transfer
☐ ☐   3. Nonperformance risk is the <u>risk of not fulfilling</u> the obligation
☐ ☐   4. Nonperformance risk <u>includes</u> the reporting unit's <u>credit risk</u>

(continues)

Provided N/A

II. Market Basis for Fair Value—Principal Market

Determine the principal market for the asset or liability.

☐	☐	A. Start with NAICS code, Chicago Board of Exchange, public market, or other (state)
☐	☐	1. May or may not be direct competitors
☐	☐	2. May be outside industry of NAICS code
☐	☐	B. Define principal market
☐	☐	1. Data must be observable
☐	☐	2. Based on greatest volume of transaction activity (frequency)
☐	☐	3. Based on highest level of transaction activity (size or severity)
☐	☐	C. If a principal market cannot be clearly defined based on frequency and size of transaction activity, then:
☐	☐	1. Determine which of the markets is most advantageous based on achieving
☐	☐	a) Highest price for an asset
		b) Lowest price for a liability
☐	☐	D. If a principal or most advantageous market is not the one being used by the reporting entity, then:
☐	☐	1. Determine why
☐	☐	a) Location
☐	☐	b) Difference in unit of accounting
☐	☐	c) Difference in quality or specific attributes of asset being measured and assets being exchanged on the principal market
☐	☐	E. Select the principal market
☐	☐	1. May be different for each
		■ Asset
		■ Liability
☐	☐	2. Would include an array of buyers and sellers in the most advantageous market for the subject asset or liability

III. Market Basis for Fair Value—Market Participant

Determine the market participant for the subject asset or liability.

☐	☐	A. Must be independent of reporting unit
☐	☐	B. Must be knowledgeable (would have all relevant information, including obtaining information through customary due diligence) or capable to gain knowledge
☐	☐	C. Must have ability to transact
☐	☐	D. Must be willing to transact (motivated but not compelled)
☐	☐	E. Data must be observable
☐	☐	1. Full transactions must be observable
☐	☐	a) At subject asset or liability level
☐	☐	b) In public domain
☐	☐	2. Failing full transactions
☐	☐	a) Component inputs must be observable
☐	☐	b) Inputs comprise and supersede subject entity's own assumptions
☐	☐	F. Select the market participants
☐	☐	1. For each subject asset
☐	☐	a) If available, observe synergies within market participants

Providedd	N/A	
		III. Market Basis for Fair Value—Market Participant (*continued*)
❏	❏	2. For each subject liability
❏	❏	a) Define nonperformance risk within market participants
❏	❏	■ Specifically include reporting unit's credit risk
		IV. Determine Fair Value
		Determine fair value for the subject asset or liability.
❏	❏	A. Identify measurement date
❏	❏	B. Determine if pricing data are observable
❏	❏	1. If yes, determine if full pricing data are for identical or similar assets or liabilities
❏	❏	a) If identical (or similar) assets
❏	❏	■ Select the most reasonable price most appropriate to apply to subject
❏	❏	■ State reason for selection
		■ Point estimate most identical to subject
		■ Mean or median most representative of subject
❏	❏	■ Verify
		■ Subject company-specific synergies are excluded
		■ Transaction costs are excluded
		■ Transportation costs may be included
		■ Blockage adjustments are excluded
		■ Restricted stock adjustments (related to the restriction) may be included if the restriction would transfer to the market participant
		■ Mean or median most representative of subject
❏	❏	■ Render opinion of fair value
❏	❏	b) If identical (or similar) liabilities
❏	❏	■ Identify price(s) paid to transfer the liability
❏	❏	■ Select the most reasonable price most appropriate to apply to subject
❏	❏	■ State reason for selection
		■ Point estimate most identical to subject
		■ Mean or median most representative of subject
❏	❏	■ Verify
		■ Subject company-specific synergies are excluded
		■ Transaction costs are excluded
		■ Blockage adjustments are excluded
		■ Nonperformance risk is included
		■ Must include reporting unit's own credit risk
❏	❏	■ Render opinion of fair value
❏	❏	2. If no, determine if input data (assumptions) are for identical or similar assets or liabilities to subject asset or liability
❏	❏	a) Identify the methodology applicable
❏	❏	■ Determine the reporting unit's methodology input components
❏	❏	■ Identify the inputs available from market participants
❏	❏	■ Apply market participant inputs to reporting unit selected methodology
❏	❏	■ Determine whether tax amortization benefits should be included in fair value calculation
❏	❏	■ Determine market participant risk/uncertainty premium if cash flow or income approach is used

(*continues*)

Provided / N/A

IV. Determine Fair Value (*continued*)

❑ ❑ ▪ Verify
- Subject company-specific synergies are excluded
- Transaction costs are excluded
- Transportation costs may be included
- Blockage adjustments are excluded
- Restricted stock adjustments (related to the restriction) may be included if the restriction would transfer to the market participant

❑ ❑ ▪ Render opinion of fair value

❑ ❑ C. Adjust fair value opinion based on subsequent events

V. Determine Disclosure Level

Select hierarchy level that applies to subject asset or liability (based on the lowest level of inputs that are significant to the measurement).

❑ ❑ A. Level 1 (observable)
❑ ❑   1. Market participants are defined
❑ ❑   2. Market is observable
❑ ❑   a) Quoted prices
❑ ❑   b) Identical to subject assets or liabilities
❑ ❑   c) Market is active
❑ ❑   d) Market is accessible at measurement date
❑ ❑ B. Level 2 (observable)
❑ ❑   1. Market participants defined
❑ ❑   2. Market is observable
❑ ❑ C. Level 3 (unobservable)
❑ ❑   1. Principal market not able to be defined
❑ ❑   2. Market participants not able to be defined
❑ ❑   3. Pricing data are not observable
❑ ❑   4. Component input data are not observable
❑ ❑   5. Component input data are not able to be corroborated
❑ ❑   6. Must use reasonable inputs based on
❑ ❑   ▪ Assumptions market participants would use
❑ ❑   ▪ Market participant assumptions must preclude specific assumptions of reporting unit

About the Website

This book includes a companion website, which can be found at www.wiley.com\go\Hitchner5ewb. Enter password: valuation.

The website includes the exhibits and forms found in Chapter 7 and the checklists found in Chapter 8.

Index